THE

MOOHUMMUDAN LAW OF SALE,

ACCORDING TO THE HUNEEFEEA CODE

THE

MOOHUMMUDAN LAW OF SALE,

ACCORDING TO THE HUNEEFEEA CODE:

FROM

THE FUTAWA ALUMGEEREE,

A Digest of the whole Law,

PREPARED BY COMMAND OF

THE EMPEROR AURUNGZEBE ALUMGEER.

SELECTED AND TRANSLATED,
from the Original Arabic,

BY
NEIL B. E. BAILLIE

GYAN

Published by

Gyan Publishing House
5, Ansari Road
Daryaganj, New Delhi-110002
Phone: 011-47034999, 9811692060
E-mail: books@gyanbooks.com

Distribution Network
gyanbooks.com
India, USA, Canada, UK, Australia, France

ISBN: 978-81-212-8124-9 (PB)
First Published, 1850

2nd Impression 2023

Printed at: Gyan Press, Delhi.

THE MOOHUMMUDAN LAW OF SALE, ACCORDING TO THE HUNEEFEEA CODE
Translator: NEIL B. E. BAILLIE

THE

MOOHUMMUDAN LAW OF SALE,

ACCORDING TO THE HUNEEFEEA CODE.

THE

MOOHUMMUDAN LAW OF SALE,

ACCORDING TO THE HUNEEFEEA CODE:

FROM

THE FUTAWA ALUMGEEREE,

A Digest of the whole Law,

PREPARED BY COMMAND OF

THE EMPEROR AURUNGZEBE ALUMGEER.

SELECTED AND TRANSLATED,

From the Original Arabic,

WITH

AN INTRODUCTION AND EXPLANATORY NOTES,

BY

NEIL B. E. BAILLIE,

AUTHOR OF "THE MOOHUMMUDAN LAW OF INHERITANCE."

LONDON:

SMITH, ELDER AND CO., 65, CORNHILL.

1850.

PRELIMINARY REMARKS.

THE *Futawa Alumgeeree* is received in India as an acknowledged authority on Mussulman Law, and has become celebrated in Arabia and other Moohummudan countries. At Mecca it is known as the *Futawa-i-Hind*, or Indian Expositions. It was compiled in India by eminent lawyers assembled for the purpose by the Emperor Aurungzebe Alumgeer, from different parts of his dominions, and placed under the superintendence of Sheikh Nizam. It was commenced in the eleventh year* of the emperor's reign; about which time, as related by Mr. Elphinstone,† he discontinued the regular annals of the empire, "and so effectually put a stop to all record of his transactions, that from the eleventh year of his reign, the course of events can only be traced through the means of letters on business, and of notes taken clandestinely by private individuals." This remarkable change in the emperor's conduct is mentioned by the English historian only as one of a series of measures which he has characterized as a "long course of bigotry and impolicy;" but it is honorably connected by native writers with the preparation of the work in question. It was, they say, when Meerza Kazim, the author of the *Alumgeernameh*, had finished and presented to his majesty the history of the first ten years of his reign, that it occurred to

* About A. D. 1670.

† History of India, vol. ii. p. 492.

the king that historical works, from their popularity, require not the patronage of princes and the great; that the foundation of good government is justice, which depends on a knowledge of the ordinances of the law; but that the precedents from which such knowledge might be gathered were widely dispersed and difficult to be found; while many were unnecessarily repeated, others omitted, and decisions of less weight not sufficiently distinguished from those of full authority. For these reasons, it seemed proper to his majesty to discontinue the allowance to Meerza Kazim, and to compile a new *Futawa*, which should be arranged in the most approved manner, and contain the most authoritative decisions of law on every case which had been decided, without repetition or omission. Several years and a large sum of money were spent in its preparation, but it was at length completed, and styled after its illustrious projector, the *Futawa Alumgeeree.* *

The word *futawa* is the plural form of *futwa*, a term in common use in Moohummudan countries, to signify an exposition of law by a public officer called the *mooftee*, on a case submitted to him by the *kazee*, or judge. The offices of *kazee* and *mooftee* are usually quite distinct, though the *kazee* ought to be well acquainted with the law, as well as competent, from his experience of human affairs, to apply it, when duly expounded, to the various cases that come before him. The *Futawa Alumgeeree* is composed of extracts in Arabic from several collections of *futawa* of older date, and also from other legal treatises of a more abstract character, by writers of the Huneefeea sect. To each extract is appended the name of the original work from whence it was taken, and the whole are so arranged as to form a complete digest of Moohummudan law. It is a common affectation

* Remarks by the *Kazee-ool-Koozzat* of the *Sudder Nizamut Adawlut*, referred to in Mr. Harrington's *Elementary Analysis of the Laws and Regulations enacted by the Governor-General in Council, at Fort William, in Bengal*, vol. i. p. 243.

of lawyers to deliver their opinions in an oracular form, without the reasons on which they are founded; and in this respect Mussulman lawyers do not differ from their legal brethren in other countries. But in the *Futawa Alumgeeree* the cases are so well arranged, and so judiciously interspersed with the more abstract parts of the work, as in general to carry their own reasons to the mind. It is only when the ground of an exposition is an express text of the *Kooran*, or a traditional saying of the Prophet, that it cannot be discovered by a moderate exercise of thought, or that its omission is calculated to embarrass the reader. And in these cases the omissions may be readily supplied by a reference to parallel passages in other works, such as the *Hidayah*, and its various commentaries. With such occasional aid, the *Futawa Alumgeeree* may be adapted to the purpose of an elementary treatise on Mussulman law. As an useful repertory from which the judge may obtain authoritative precedents for his guidance, its value has never been disputed. It is briefly noticed by Sir William Jones * as a work that would greatly facilitate the preparation of a digest of the *Mussulman Laws of Inheritance and Contract.* It does not appear to what extent he contemplated making use of its contents, for the only digest of Mussulman Law which he seems to have undertaken was one of the Imameea code, or law according to the tenets of the twelve Imáms, which was made by learned natives employed at his suggestion, and placed under his superintendence, by the supreme government of Bengal. An eminent Orientalist † was afterwards employed to translate this digest into the English language; but one volume out of four, which the translation was expected to extend to, was all that he accomplished. And the translation was not resumed, probably, because the Imameea code is not recognised

---

* *Letter to Earl Cornwallis, Governor-General of India.*

† Captain, afterwards Lieut.-Colonel John Baillie, and late a Member of the Court of Directors for the affairs of the East India Company.

by the courts of justice in India, except in matters of inheritance, when both the parties to a suit are Shias, or followers of the twelve Imams. It seems, also, from the translator's remarks, that the original digest is imperfect, and would require considerable additions to render it complete.

The Moohummudans of India are chiefly Soonnees of the Huneefeea sect, though there are many Shias among them. Indeed, the lower orders of Soonnees have adopted so many of the superstitious notions and observances of the Shias, that they are Soonnees in little more than in name. They are, however, very tenacious of the name; and the Moohummudan sovereigns of India having been Soonnees of the Huneefeea sect, the Huneefeea code was accordingly the general law of the country while it remained under the sway of the Moohummudans.

The Moohummudan law may be divided into two parts, as it relates to spiritual or to temporal matters. The former comprehends the rites and ceremonies of religion; the latter, what is usually comprised under the heads of civil, criminal, and international law. Both parts of the law are obligatory on Moohummudans, even when living under a foreign dominion; but it is only the temporal law which has ever been imposed by them on persons of a different religion.

The temporal law of the Moohummudans, according to the Huneefeea code, was for six centuries the general law of the countries which now form the British territories in India. In its application to the Hindoo inhabitants, some allowance was probably made for their peculiar institutions in matters connected with their religion, such as marriage, adoption, and inheritance. But there is no reason to suppose that in matters of contract and the ordinary dealings of men with each other, the Moohummudan law was not applied to them, in the same way as it is applied in other Moohummudan countries to *Zimmees*, or non-*Mooslim* subjects. Indeed, it does not appear that the Hindoos ever had any law of sale of their own sufficiently well defined to be applicable to the actual business of life, except in the earliest stages of society when positive law is scarcely distinguishable from moral precepts. All that now remains of a Hindoo law of sale, or at least all of it that has been translated into the English language, are a few scattered fragments, some of which bear a resemblance to parts of the Moohummudan law; and if they were not borrowed from that law, serve to indicate that it was suited to the condition of Hindoo society. I allude, in particular, to the doctrine of options or powers of cancellation in sale, which is found in both the Hindoo and Moohummudan laws, but is stated very vaguely in the former, and without the qualifications and restrictions which, under the latter, render it compatible with the ordinary conditions of a contract of sale. Sir William Jones has adverted to the meagreness of the Hindoo law of contract, and in the digest compiled under his superintendence, and translated by Mr. Colebrooke, all that is to be found on the important subject of sale are two chapters; one on "Sale without Ownership," and the other on "Rescission of Purchase and Sale," arranged under heads widely separated from, and quite unconnected with, each other.

It is probable, therefore, that if the Hindoos ever had a more perfect law of sale of their own, it fell into desuetude during their subjection to the Moohummudans, and that any attempt now to revive it would be futile. During that period, the dealings of the Hindoos, even among themselves, must have been regulated by the general law of the country, which was the Moohummudan. Long use would have familiarized them with its maxims, and from being constantly referred to or implied in their ordinary transactions, it would at length become, in a manner, a part of their customs or usage. Accordingly, we now find the Hindoos asserting their claim to rights which though originally derived from the Moohummudan law, are insisted on as the usage of the country. I may mention the right of *Shoefaa*, or pre-emption, and the conditional sale, or mortgage, called *Bye-bil-wufa*, as two instances of rights originating in the Moohummudan law, which have been sanctioned and confirmed by decisions of the courts of justice, or regulations of the supreme government, as parts of the general usage of the country, to which all its inhabitants—Hindoo and Mussulman—are alike entitled.

It is only in cases where an appeal is made to the Moohummudan law as the usage of the country, that it can now be applied to the cases of Hindoos in civil matters, by the courts of justice in the British territories in India. It is possible, however, that it may still be referred to by the Hindoos themselves in their ordinary dealings, and it is most probably the source from whence have been derived their principal notions of right and liability connected with particular contracts. If such be the case, the Moohummudan law must afford to the judge the readiest means of ascertaining the meaning of even Hindoo parties to a contract, where it has not been sufficiently expressed, or cannot be implied from the circumstances of the case.

In the view last mentioned, the Moohummudan law must always be of great importance in the decisions of suits where the parties are Moohummudans. It has ceased to be positive law, even for them, in the courts of justice of the East India Company, except in matters which have relation to religion, marriage, or inheritance. It is, nevertheless, observed by themselves in their dealings with each other, and affords the surest standard for equitably determining their disputes. It is accordingly administered by the Company's judges, as a rule of justice, equity, and good conscience, in almost all the cases to which it is applicable, when both the parties are Moohummudans.*

---

* In the *Principles and Precedents of Moohummudan Law*, by the late Sir W. H. Macnaghten, Bart., the decided cases which have been selected as precedents are arranged under the following heads: — In-

The judges of her Majesty's Supreme Courts of Judicature at the three presidencies of Calcutta, Madras, and Bombay, are expressly enjoined by Acts of Parliament to administer Moohummudan law in all cases where both the parties to a suit are Moohummudans, and the matter relates to their successions, contracts, and dealings.

It thus appears, that to all persons connected with the administration of justice in India, it is of some importance that they should have the means of being acquainted with the Moohummudan Law of Sale.

There is another point of view in which the Moohummudan law of Sale is of some importance. In a mixed population like that of India, there must, to some extent, be separate laws for determining the private rights of each great section of the people. It may be difficult to define exactly the limits within which such separate laws ought to be confined; but in general there can be little community or collision of interest, in questions of marriage or inheritance, among persons who differ so widely in religion, manners, and institutions, as the Hindoos, Moohummudans, and Christians. Accordingly, the two former classes have been secured in the enjoyment of their own particular laws, in all matters relating to religion, marriage, or inheritance, by positive regulations of the Indian Government. And when such questions have arisen in the courts of justice of the East India Company among Christians, they have been usually determined according to English law when the parties were British subjects, or by special custom when they were Armenians. It has been found in practice, both in the suits of Hindoos and of Moohummudans, that in questions regarding marriage and inheritance, other questions frequently arise on collateral points of law. This is particularly the case in the suits of Moohummudans; and points

---

heritance—Sale—Pre-emption—Gifts—Wills—Marriage, Dower, Divorce and Parentage — Guardians and Minority — Slavery — Endowments — Debts and Securities—Claims and Judicial matters.

relating to the law of sale are thus frequently involved in questions of inheritance, as scarcely a suit relating to inheritance occurs in which there is not either a real or fictitious deed of *Heba-bil-ivuz*, or gift for a consideration, which is treated in the law as in every respect a sale. The contract of sale, however, is the most common ground on which the different classes of the community meet together, and some general rules of law must necessarily, at no great distance of time, be adopted for regulating their dealings with each other. The people of England are perhaps* entitled, after the example of the Moohummudans and other conquerors, to impose their own law on the other classes of the community, in all matters where the different classes come in contact, and each cannot be indulged in a separate law of its own consistently with the rights of the others. But it becomes a wise and generous nation, and is conformable to the practice of England, in other countries acquired by conquest or by treaty, to respect the laws which have been long established in the acquired territory. This has been done in Canada, some of the West India settlements, the Cape of Good Hope, and the Mauritius; but in none of them could the people appeal to a law so long established as the Moohummudan law has been established in India. It is true that the Moohummudan law has for some time ceased to be positive law for the largest part of the population; but there is reason to believe, as already mentioned, that it still continues to influence to some extent the transactions of the Hindoos even

---

* In the *Firman* or Grant, by the Emperor Shah Alum to the East India Company, of the Province of Ghazeepore, &c., dated 29th December 1764, it was expressly stipulated that they "were to use their best endeavours in deciding causes and settling matters agreeably to the rules of Moohummud and the law of the empire;" and in the *Perwanneh* for the twenty-four Pergunnahs by the Nuwab Jaffier Ally Khan, there was a similar stipulation that the Company "should be careful to govern according to established custom without any gradual deviation."

among themselves. With regard to the Moohummudans, it may be said that their dealings are almost entirely regulated by it; and they are by no means an insignificant part of the population. It has been estimated* that they amount to about one-seventh of the whole, or ten millions of people, on a low computation of the entire population. Ten millions of persons spread over the country, but regulating their dealings by a well ascertained law of their own, which they believe to be of divine origin, and binding on their consciences, form an element which cannot be wisely, or perhaps safely, disregarded in the formation of a law for the whole community. Such a law, however alien to their habits, might not at first meet with any active opposition from them; but, when passed, it might be neglected. The Moohummudans would probably still continue to regulate their dealings without reference to it, according to notions of right and liability derived from their own law; and occasions full of embarrassment might consequently arise in the administration of justice. It is an admitted principle of jurisprudence, that contracts are to be construed according to the intention of the parties, except when opposed to the policy of the law of the country. Recourse is had, however, to that law as the best interpreter of intention when not sufficiently expressed, because its general provisions are presumed to be in the view of parties when they enter into a contract. This supposition could hardly be made by a judge of the Company's courts, when construing a contract between Moohummudans, and a question of some difficulty might arise,—whether such a contract, when ambiguous, should be equitably construed according to the general law of the land, or the particular law of the parties, by which alone perhaps it could be interpreted in harmony with their intentions so far as expressed. Good policy seems to suggest, that, whatever the new law may be, it

* *Geographical, Statistical, and Historical Description of Hindoostan;* by Walter Hamilton. Introduction, p. 28.

should be accommodated to so much of the Moohummudan law as is likely to be retained by so large a section of the people as the rule of their dealings, provided that it be not unsuited to the condition of the remainder of the population, or calculated to retard the advance of society in India, under the new impulse which has been given to it by its connection with England. Sufficient reason has already been shown why the Moohummudan law should not be considered unsuited to the condition of the Hindoos. But the other point is open to some doubt. The Moohummudan law of sale contains restrictions, which may be considered restraints on the free spirit of commerce. Some of these are derived directly from the Moohummudan religion, but the greater part, though founded on injunctions of the Prophet, were imposed for the purpose of removing uncertainty in sale, and preventing the disputes which might thence arise. Of the former class of restriction, is the prohibition of interest on loans of every kind. This restriction pervades and complicates the whole law, and is by many Moohummudans considered to be of doubtful obligation in the altered circumstances in which they are now placed, as under a foreign dominion in India. It is true that it is observed by the more scrupulous among them; but there is no reason to suppose that the other restrictions, which are of a more subtle character, are observed to any considerable extent by the bulk of Moohummudans in their ordinary dealings. That they have been felt to be burdensome in all ages, is evident from the curious doctrine of *Heela* or legal devices, which has been superinduced on the law for the purpose of evading in many cases its strict letter. The whole of the restrictions of both kinds might therefore be abolished, as, practically, they have been abolished in India; and if this were done, the Moohummudan law of sale would not only be well suited to the present condition of Indian society, but sufficiently accommodated to its progress. In some respects, it seems to be better adapted to the people of India than unmixed English law. Thus, *caveat emptor* is a leading principle of the latter, while the Moohummudan law is characterized by an anxious attention to the interests of the purchaser. It implies a warranty for title, and against defects in all cases, unless expressly waived; and, further, allows the purchaser an option of cancelling his bargain whenever he has purchased a thing that he has not seen. In these respects, as already observed, it corresponds with what remains of the old Hindoo law.

These remarks may not be considered impertinent, as introductory to a treatise on the Moohummudan Law of Sale. The importance of the Moohummudan law might further be demonstrated by showing its intimate connection with the judicial system of the East India Company. Much of the procedure in the Company's courts of justice has been derived from it; and through this means, and also through the subordinate officers and pleaders of the courts — who with a very few exceptions are Moohummudans, or Hindoos trained to the same methods, and have derived any knowledge of jurisprudence they possess from that source—it exercises a powerful though unseen influence on the administration of justice, even by English judges. But enough, it is hoped, has been said for the present to meet the objection of *cui bono*, if it should be raised, to the publication in the English language of a work on the Moohummudan law.

The only work on the Mohummudan Law of Sale, accessible to the English reader, is the translation of the *Hidayah*, by Mr. Charles Hamilton, in which the subject is imperfectly treated, and is not well arranged. The *Hidayah* is a work of very high authority, but is ill adapted for communicating a knowledge of the law to beginners. In its original language, the Arabic, its form is that of a commentary on a very brief text, both of which are said to have been the works of the same author, named *Sheikh Boorhan-ood-deen-Alee.** In the com-

* Mr. Harrington's *Analysis*, vol. i. p. 237. But the *text* of the *Hidayah* corresponds generally with the *Koodooree;* and from this circumstance,

ment, the author pours out a profusion of learning, in which principles of law and illustrations are heaped together without regard to arrangement; the most important principles being frequently thrown into a parenthesis, and occurring in parts of the work where they could least be expected. These defects are aggravated in the English translation, which was made from an intermediate version in Persian, and has mixed up text and comment together, with interpolations of the Persian translators, and blended the whole without any distinction, into a continued treatise. In the *Futawa Alumgeeree*, the subject of sale is given with great detail and apparent completeness, and seems to be on the whole well arranged. But many of the cases, though useful as authorities, are redundant for the purpose of illustration. They admit, however, in most instances, of being retrenched, without impairing the meaning or usefulness of the context; for the extracts in juxtaposition are frequently derived from different authors, and are not otherwise connected with each other, than by the common subjects to which they relate.

The following treatise is a selection from two books of the *Futawa Alumgeeree*, that comprise the whole subject of sale. The rule adopted in making the selections, was to retain everything of the nature of a general proposition, but to reject particular cases, except when they were considered to involve or illustrate some principle or maxim of law. The division and arrangement of the original into chapters and sections has been strictly observed, except in a few instances, which have been mentioned in the notes.* The extracts have

---

and a similar correspondence between it and the text of the *Jowhurrut-oon-Nuyyerah*, I was led to infer (*Advertisement to Treatise on the Moohummudan Law of Inheritance*) that the *Koodooree* was really the original text of the *Hidayah*. The late Major-General Sir Archibald Galloway, K.C.B., whose opinion on a question of Moohummudan law is entitled to great respect, had previously come to the same conclusion, though I was not then aware of it.

* There is also a slight transposition of Chapter XVII., which is XIV. in the original.

also, with some exceptions, been taken consecutively, though often at considerable intervals, and the originals of them may be found under the proper heads, without much trouble, by any one competent to make the search. It was, therefore, thought unnecessary to load the pages at every line, as would have been required, with references to the names of the original works, or the page of the printed edition of the *Futawa Alumgeeree*,* where the extracts from them are inserted. Beyond the running margins and explanatory notes, there is nothing in the body of the work that the translator can consider his own, though he has found it necessary in some instances to fuse the extracts into each other, so as to preserve the character of a continued treatise. He has not, however, carried this license very far. He is sensible that the transitions may therefore be thought abrupt, and that, besides asperities of style, and the frequent recurrence of the same modes of expression, passages occasionally occur in the text which are somewhat obscure. For defects of style, he hopes that his anxiety to adhere as closely as possible to a literal translation of the original, will be received as some apology. Some degree of obscurity is, perhaps, inseparable from the nature of the work; but he trusts that it will disappear before the reader, as he becomes better acquainted with the principles of the law. A more readable book might, perhaps, have been made, by recasting the materials into a different form; but it would not have had the same authority. And the translator preferred adopting a course which, though it calls for the exercise of more thought on the part of the reader, may yet, it is hoped, enable him to refer to the work with some confidence, as a faithful transcript of writings of high authority on the Moohummudan law.

Explanatory notes have been subjoined to the text whenever they appeared to be necessary; but as the explanation

* Published at Calcutta under the authority of the Committee of Public Instruction, in 6 large 4to. volumes: 1828.

in some instances would have exceeded the length of an ordinary note, it has been deemed advisable to throw a good deal of it into the form of a general introduction, which the reader may find it of some advantage to peruse before he proceeds to the work itself, recollecting, however, that it is no part of the original work, and has no pretension to any authority. The matter of the notes, as well as of the introduction, has been derived in a great degree from the *Hidayah*, and two of its commentaries, the *Kifayah* and *Inayah*. When the *Hidayah* has been referred to, the original and translation have usually been cited, the latter, as Hamilton's *Hedaya*, the word being so spelled in the title of the translation, while the original is cited as the *Hidayah*, according to the spelling in the English title-page of the printed edition. Wherever the translation of the *Hidayah* has appeared to differ from the original Arabic, the discrepancy has been remarked in a note. In some instances, the difference may be ascribed to alterations by the Persian translators. In others, perhaps, to errors in the Arabic manuscript, from which their version was made. And if some remain that must be ascribed to mistakes of the English translator, they are not numerous for a work of such magnitude, and detract little from its value, while some allowance for them is due to the "material disadvantages under which he laboured, in not having completed his arduous and laudable undertaking in India."* The assistance of learned natives, which is so easily procurable in that country, renders the task of translating a work on Moohummudan law one of comparative facility; and Mr. Hamilton's translation of the *Hidayah* seems to have been at least commenced in India, and probably with the aid of the Persian translators. The compiler of the following treatise has had no such assistance, for it has been prepared entirely in England; and he hopes that this circumstance will be considered as affording some extenuation of the errors which, notwithstanding his utmost

* Mr. Harrington's *Analysis*, vol. i. p. 241.

care, it may be found to contain. These errors may either be of judgment in making his selections, or of translation in rendering them into the English language. The latter, he trusts, will not be found to be many nor of much importance; for he has compared his selections with the original extracts several times, and the language of the original is in general very perspicuous. In this respect, he has had some advantage over Mr. Hamilton, the original language of the *Hidayah* being not unfrequently obscure. The compiler has more anxiety in regard to the errors of judgment with which he may be chargeable. He has had before him the necessity of confining the work within as moderate limits as possible, and though it is probably no more than a third of the original, some persons may be of opinion that it is still too voluminous for English readers. In other instances, it may be thought that he has erred in the other extreme, by rejecting too much until, occasionally, there is very little left in a section to correspond to its title. These two sources of error the reader ought to keep distinctly in his view, when he endeavours to form any opinion of the original *Digest.* As a specimen of that work, as it came from the hands of Sheikh Nizam and his co-labourers, the reader is referred to the extracts under the head of *Bye-al-wufa,* in Chapter XX. of the First Book, which, for a special reason, are given at length, with the names of the original works from whence they were taken. The *Kifayah* and the *Inayah,* the two commentaries on the *Hidayah* above referred to, are both in Arabic, and have not, so far as the compiler of this work is aware, been translated into any other language, though the originals have been published at Calcutta, under the authority of the Committee of Public Instruction. The former is printed with the Arabic *Hidayah,* which is given on the upper part of the page, and the comment underneath, and the combined work has been referred to under the double or single name, as the reference is to both text and comment, or to one or the other of them.

It remains for the compiler of the following treatise to mention, that though he has had no assistance in making or translating his selections from the *Futawa Alumgeeree*, and is alone responsible for the errors which it may contain, he has been indebted for many valuable suggestions and advice in the preparation of his work for the press, to J. F. Leith, Esq. of the Middle Temple, Barrister-at-Law, and late of the Calcutta Bar, to whom he takes this opportunity of expressing his acknowledgments.

He has still a grateful duty to perform, in rendering his thanks to the Court of Directors for the affairs of the East India Company, who, in terms personally gratifying to him, have been pleased to authorize the publication of the following treatise at the public expense. To the Chairman, Deputy-Chairman, and other Members of that Court, therefore, he begs respectfully, though without the formality of a regular Dedication, to inscribe his work.

SYNOPSIS OF CONTENTS.

INTRODUCTION.

BOOK I.

SALES IN GENERAL.

CHAPTER I.

SALE DEFINED.—HOW CONSTITUTED, CONDITIONS, LEGAL EFFECT, AND DIFFERENT KINDS OF SALE.

CHAPTER II.

FORM OF THE CONTRACT.

SECTION I.—Of what relates to the act of contracting.

PAGE

SECTION II.—Of taking possession under an inchoate bargain.

SECTION III.—Of distinguishing the thing sold from the price, and of acts of ownership with regard to either, before taking possession.

CHAPTER III.

OF WANT OF CORRESPONDENCE BETWEEN THE PROPOSAL AND ACCEPTANCE.

CHAPTER IV.

OF DELIVERY AND POSSESSION.

SECTION I.—Of retaining the thing sold as security for the price.

SECTION II.—Of surrender of the thing sold, and what is, and is not possession.

PAGE

Section II.—Of what is included in a sale of lands and orchards.

Section III.—Of what is included in the sale of moveables.

CHAPTER VI.

OF OPTION BY STIPULATION.

Section I.—Of valid and invalid options.

Section II.—Effect of an option by stipulation on the right of property.

CHAPTER VII.

OPTION OF INSPECTION.

SECTION II.—Of what prevents, and of what does not prevent, a return on account of defect, and for what defects compensation may, and for what it may not, be claimed.

SECTION III.—Of suits regarding defects and the production of evidence.

SECTION IV.—Of a release from defects and security for them.

SECTION V.—Of compounding defects.

CHAPTER IX.

OF LAWFUL AND UNLAWFUL SALES.

CHAPTER X.

OF CONDITIONS THAT VITIATE, AND SUCH AS DO NOT VITIATE, A CONTRACT OF SALE.

CHAPTER XI.

OF THE EFFECT OF UNLAWFUL SALES.

CHAPTER XII.

OF THE EFFECT OF DEPENDENT SALES, AND OF SALES BY ONE OF TWO COPARTNERS.

CHAPTER XIII.

OF *IKALUT*, OR THE DISSOLUTION OF SALES.

CHAPTER XIV.

OF A RIGHT IN A THIRD PARTY TO THE THING SOLD.

CHAPTER XV.

OF ADDITION TO THE PRICE AND ABATEMENT AND DISCHARGE FROM IT.

CHAPTER XVI.

OF SALE BY A FATHER, EXECUTOR, OR JUDGE OF A MINOR'S PROPERTY, AND PURCHASERS BY THEM FOR HIM.

CHAPTER XVII.

OF *MORABUHUT*, *TOWLEEUT*, AND *WUZEEUT* SALES.

CHAPTER XVIII.

OF *SULUM*.

Section I. — Definition, Constitution, Conditions, and Legal Effect of *Sulum*.

Section II.—Of things with regard to which *Sulum* is or is not lawful.

Section III.—Of possession of the capital stock and the goods advanced for.

Section IV.—Of disputes between the contracting parties as to matters of fact.

PAGE

SECTION V.—Of *Ikalut* composition and the option of defect in *Sulum* sales.

SECTION VI.—Of agency in *Sulum*.

CHAPTER XIX.

OF *KURZ*, OR LENDING AND BORROWING FOR CONSUMPTION, AND *ISTISNAA*, OR MAKING TO ORDER.

CHAPTER XX.

OF ABOMINABLE SALES AND UNLAWFUL GAINS.

SECTION.—Of *Ihtikar*, or hoarding.

BOOK II.

OF SURF.

CHAPTER I.

DEFINITION, CONSTITUTION, EFFECT, AND CONDITIONS OF *SURF*.

CHAPTER II.

OF THE RULES OF THE CONTRACT WITH REFERENCE TO THE THINGS CONTRACTED FOR.

SECTION I.—Of the sale of gold and silver.

SECTION II.—Of the sale of ornamented swords, and similar articles, in which gold or silver is connected with other substances; and of the sale of things, the weight of which is found to be more or less than was stipulated for.

CHAPTER III.

RULES WITH REGARD TO DISPOSING OF THE THINGS EXCHANGED, AFTER THE CONTRACT OF *SURF*.

CHAPTER IV.

OF THE CONTRACT AS IT IS AFFECTED BY THE CONDITION OF THE CONTRACTING PARTIES.

INTRODUCTION.

SALE, in its ordinary acceptation, is a transfer of property in consideration of a price in money. The word has a more comprehensive meaning in the Moohummudan law, and is applied to every exchange of property for property with mutual consent. It, therefore, includes barter as well as sale, and also loan, when the articles lent are intended to be consumed, and replaced to the lender by a similar quantity of the same kind. This transaction, which is truly an exchange of property for property, is termed *kurz* in the Moohummudan law, and is treated of at some length in the first book of the following treatise. Page 1.

Between barter and sale there is no essential distinction in most systems of law, and the joint subject may in general be considerably simplified by being treated of solely as a sale. A course has been adopted in the Moohummudan law, which obliges the reader to fix his attention on both sides of the contract. This may at first appear to him to be an unnecessary complication of the subject; but when he becomes acquainted with the definition of price, and the rules for the prohibition of excess in the exchange of a large class of commodities, which apply to every form of the contract, he will probably be of opinion that to treat of the subject in any other way would be attended with at least equal difficulties.

The first point which seems to require his attention, is the meaning of the word "property," as it occurs in the definition of sale. The original term (*mal*) which has been thus translated, is defined by Moohummudan lawyers to be "that which can be taken possession of and secured." This definition seems to imply that it is tangible or corporeal, and THINGS or substances are accord- Note, p. 51

ingly the proper subjects of sale. Mere rights are not Note, p. 51. *mal*, and cannot therefore be lawfully sold apart from the corporeal things with which they may happen to be connected. Of such rights one of the most important is the right of a creditor to exact payment of a debt, which is Note, p. 5. not a proper subject of sale. In other words, debts cannot, by the Moohummudan law, any more than by the common laws of England and Scotland, be lawfully sold.

Things are commonly divided into moveable and immoveable, the latter comprehending land and things permanently attached to it. But the distinction is not of much importance in the Moohummudan law, as the transfer of land is in nowise distinguished from that of other kinds of property.

A more important division of things is that into *mislee* and *keemee*. The former are things which, when they happen to perish, are to be replaced by an equal quantity of something similar to them; and the latter are things which, in the same circumstances, are to be replaced by their value. These two classes have been aptly styled similars and dissimilars by Mr. Hamilton, in his translation of the *Hidayah*. Similars are things which Note † p. 7. are usually sold or exchanged by weight, or by measurement of capacity, that is by dry or liquid measure, and dissimilars are things which are not sold or exchanged in either of these ways. Articles which are nearly alike, and are commonly sold or exchanged by number or tale, are classed with the first division of things, and may be termed similars of tale; while articles which differ materially from each other, yet are still usually sold or exchanged by number, belong to the second division, and may be called dissimilars of tale. *Dirhems* and *deenars*, the only coined money known to the old Arabs, are included among similars of weight.

Similars of weight and capacity are distinguished in the Moohummudan law from all other descriptions of property in a very remarkable way. When one article of weight is sold or exchanged for another article of weight, or one of measure is sold or exchanged for another of measure, the delivery of both must be immediate from hand to hand, and any delay of delivery in one of them is unlawful and prohibited. Where, again, the articles exchanged are also of the same kind, as when wheat is sold for wheat, or silver for silver, there must not only be reciprocal and immediate delivery of both before the separation of the parties, but also absolute equality of weight or measure, according as the articles are weighable or measurable, and any excess on either side is also unlawful and prohibited. These two prohibitions constitute in brief the doctrine of *reba* or usury, which is a marked characteristic of the Moohummudan law of sale, and they are worthy of the reader's careful recollection, as he will meet with them very early in his progress, and find that they pervade the whole subject, and are constantly requiring his attention. The word *reba* properly signifies excess, and there are no terms in the Moohummudan law which correspond to the words interest and usury, in the sense attached to them in the English language; but it was expressly prohibited by Moohummud to his followers to derive any advantage from loans, and that particular kind of advantage which is called by us interest, and consists in the receiving back from the borrower a larger quantity than was actually lent to him, was effectually prevented by the two rules above mentioned. These, like some other principles of Moohummudan law, are applied with a rigour and minuteness that may to us seem incommensurate with their importance, but are easily accounted for when we know that they are believed to be of divine origin.

Note, ‡ p. 291.

Similars of weight and capacity have a common feature of resemblance, which distinguishes them in their own nature from other commodities, and marks with further peculiarity their treatment in the Moohummudan law. They are aggregates of minute parts, which are either exactly alike, or so nearly resemble each other, that the difference between them may be safely disregarded. For this reason they are usually dealt with in bulk, regard being had only to the whole of a stipulated quantity, and not to the individual parts of which it is composed. When sold in this manner, they are said to be indeterminate. They may, however, be rendered specific in several ways. Actual delivery, or production with distinct reference at the time of contract, seems to be sufficient for that purpose in all cases. But something short of this would suffice for all similars but money. Thus, flour or any kind of grain may be rendered specific by being enclosed in a sack; or oil, or any liquid, by being put into casks or jars; and though the vessels are not actually produced at the time of contract, their contents may be sufficiently particularized by description of the vessels and their locality. Money is not susceptible of being thus particularized, and *dirhems* and *deenars* are frequently referred to in the following pages as things which cannot be rendered specific by description, or specification as it is more literally termed. Hence money is said to be always indeterminate. Other similars, including similars of tale, are sometimes specific and sometimes indeterminate. Dissimilars, including those of tale, are always specific.

When similars are sold indeterminately, the purchaser has no right to any specific portion of them until it be separated from a general mass, and marked or identified as the subject of the contract. From the moment of offer till actual delivery, he has nothing to rely upon but the seller's obligation, which may therefore be considered the direct subject of the contract. Similars taken indeterminately are accordingly termed *deyn*, or obligations, in the Moohummudan law. When taken specifically, they are classed with dissimilars, under the general name of *ayn*. The literal meaning of this term is "substance or thing"; but when opposed to *deyn*, it means something determinate or specific. The subjects of traffic may thus be divided into two classes,—specific and indeterminate,—or if we substitute for the latter the word obligation, and omit the word specific as unnecessary when not opposed to indeterminate, these classes may, according to the view of Moohummudan
Page 7. lawyers, be described as THINGS and OBLIGATIONS.

There is some degree of presumption in using a word in

any other than its ordinary acceptation; and it is not without hesitation that I have ventured to employ the word obligation to signify indeterminate things. My reasons for doing so are these; first, it expresses the exact meaning of the Arabic word *deyn*, and yet distinguishes this use of it from another sense, in which it is also employed in the Moohummudan law; second, it preserves consistency in the law. Thus, it will be found hereafter that the effect of sale is said to be to induce a right in the buyer to the thing sold, and in the seller to the price, and that this effect follows the contract immediately before reciprocal possession by the contracting parties. Now, it is obvious that this is impossible with regard to things that are indeterminate, if the things themselves are considered the subject of the contract, and a case is mentioned in the following work, where it is expressly Page 33. stated, that there is no transfer of property to the purchaser, when similars of weight or capacity are sold without being distinctly specified, until actual possession take place. The difficulty disappears, if we consider not the thing itself but the obligation to render it to be the subject of contract; for a right to the obligation passes immediately to the purchaser, and the seller may be compelled to perform it. If we now revert to the division of things into similars and dissimilars—money, which it has been remarked is always indeterminate, is therefore an obligation; dissimilars, which are always specific, are never obligations; and other similars, except money, being sometimes specific and sometimes indeterminate, are at one time obligations, and at another time things or substances.

Before proceeding farther, it is necessary to advert more particularly to the other sense in which the word *deyn* is frequently employed in the Moohummudan law. It means strictly, obligation, as already observed; but the obligation may be either that of the contracting party himself, or of another. In the former sense, *deyn* is not only a proper subject of traffic, but forms the sole subject of one important kind of sale hereafter to be noticed. But when *deyn* is used to signify the obligation of another than the contracting party, it is not a proper subject of traffic, and, as already observed, cannot be lawfully sold. In the following pages, *deyn* has been always translated by the word *debt* when it signifies the obligation of a third party, and generally by the word *obligation* when it signifies the engagement of the contracting party himself, though when the things represented by the obligation are more prominently brought forward, it has sometimes been found necessary to substitute the expression, *indeterminate things*.

Though barter and sale for a price are confounded under one general name in the Moohummudan law, it is sometimes necessary to consider one of the things exchanged as more strictly the subject of sale or thing sold, and the other the price. In this view the former is termed *mabeea*, and the latter *thumun*. *Thumun*, or price, is defined to be *deyn fee zimmah*, or, literally, an obligation in responsibility. From which, unless the expression is a mere pleonasm, it would appear that the word *deyn* is sometimes used abstractly, and in a sense distinct from the idea of liability. That idea, however, is necessary to constitute price; for though cloth, when properly described, may, by reason of its divisibility and the similarity of its parts, be sometimes
Page 20. assumed to perform the function of price in a contract of sale, it is only when it is not immediately delivered, but is to remain for some time on the responsibility of the contracting party, that it can be adopted for that purpose.

It is a general principle of the Moohummudan Law of
Note, p. 259 Sale, founded on a declaration of the Prophet, that credit cannot be opposed to credit, that is, that both the things exchanged cannot be allowed to remain on the responsibility of the parties. Hence, it is only with regard to one of them that any stipulation for delay in its delivery is lawful. Price, from its definition above given, admits of being left on responsibility, and accordingly a stipulation for delay in the payment of the price is quite lawful and valid. It follows that a stipulation for delay in the delivery of the thing sold should not be lawful. And this is the case, with the exception of one particular kind of sale hereafter to be noticed, in which the thing sold is always

indeterminate, and the price is paid in advance. It may, therefore, be said of all specific things when the subject of sale, that a stipulation for delay in their delivery is illegal, and would invalidate a sale. The object of this rule may have been to prevent any change of the thing sold before delivery, and the disputes which might in consequence arise between the parties. But if they were allowed to select whichever they pleased of the articles exchanged to stand for the price, and the other for the thing sold, without any regard to their qualities, the object of the last-mentioned rule, whatever it may have been, might be defeated. This seems to have led to another arrangement of things into different classes according to their capacities for supporting the functions of price or of the thing sold in a contract of sale. The first class comprehends *dirhems* and *deenars*, which are always price. The second class comprises the whole division of dissimilars (with the single exception of cloth), which are always the thing sold, or subject of sale in a contract. The third class comprises, 1st, all similars of capacity; 2nd, all similars of weight, except *dirhems* and *deenars*; and 3rd, all similars of tale. The whole of this class is capable of supporting both functions, and are sometimes the thing sold, and sometimes the price. The fourth class comprises cloth, and the copper coin called *fooloos*.

Page 208.

Page 19.

Sale implies a reciprocal vesting of the price in the seller, and of the thing sold in the purchaser. This, as already remarked, is called its legal effect; and sale may be divided into different stages or degrees of completeness, according as this effect is immediate, suspended, invalid, or obligatory. Thus, sale must first of all be duly constituted or contracted. After that, there may still be some bar to its operation, which occasions a suspension of its effect. This generally arises from a defect of power in the seller, who may not be fully competent to act for himself, or may have insufficient authority, or no authority whatever, over the subject of sale. In this class of sales, the effect is dependent on the assent or ratification of some other person than the party actually contracting, and they are fully treated of in Chapter XII. of the first Book. But whether the effect of a sale be immediate or suspended, there may be some taint of illegality in the mode of constituting it, or in its subject, or there may be other circumstances connected with it, which render it invalid. The causes of illegality are many and various, and form the subject of Chapter IX. of the first Book, while the effect of Illegal Sales is fully treated of in the eleventh chapter of the same Book But even though a sale should be unimpeachable on the previous grounds, that is, though it should be duly constituted, operative or immediate in its effect, and free from any ground of illegality, still it may not be absolutely binding on the parties. This brings us to another remarkable peculiarity of the Moohummudan law, viz., the doctrine of option, or right of cancellation. The Prophet himself recommended one of his followers to reserve a *locus penitentiæ,* or option for three days in all his purchases. This has led to the option by stipulation, which may be reserved by either of the parties, and forms the subject of Chapter VI. in the first Book. But besides this, the purchaser has an option without any stipulation, with regard to things which he has purchased without seeing, and also on account of defects in the thing sold. These options form the subjects of the two next chapters in the same Book. The greatest of all defects is a want of title or right in the seller, and the purchaser's right of cancellation on that account is treated of in Chapter XIV. The two last options to the purchaser constitute a complete warranty of title and against all defects on the part of the seller, in which respect the Moohummudan more nearly resembles the Scotch than the English Law of Sale.

There are many different kinds of sale. Twenty or more have been enumerated in the *Nihayah,* of which eight are mentioned and explained in the following Treatise. Four of these, which have reference to the thing sold, may require some notice in this place. The first,
Page 7. called *Mookaizut,* is described as a sale of things for things, and corresponds nearly with barter; but the word thing (*ayn*) is here opposed to obligations, and *Mookaizut* is therefore properly an exchange of specific for specific

things. So that if the goods exchanged were on both sides, or on either side indeterminate, the transaction would not, I think, be a *mookaizut,* though still barter. The second sale is called *surf,* and is defined to be an exchange of Page 7.
obligations for obligations. The usual objects of this contract are *dirhems* and *deenars,* which being obligations, the definition is generally correct. But an exchange of money for bullion, or bullion for bullion, is also a *surf,* and every sale of an obligation for an obligation is not a *surf,* so that the definition is redundant as well as defective. It is essential to the legality of this kind of sale, that both the things exchanged should be delivered and taken possession of before the separation of the parties, and that when they are of the same kind, as silver for silver, or gold for gold, they should also be exactly equal by weight. These rules are necessary for the avoidance of *reba* or usury, as already explained, and the whole of *surf,* which is treated of at a length quite disproportionate to its importance, and forms the sole subject of the second book, may be considered as a continued illustration of the doctrine of *reba.* The third kind of sale is *sulum.* It has been already observed that there can be no lawful stipulation for a postponement of the delivery of the thing sold except under one particular form of sale. The form alluded to is *sulum.* This word means, literally, an advance; and in a *sulum* sale the price is immediately advanced for goods to be delivered at a future fixed time. It is only things of the class of similars that can be sold in this way, and as they must necessarily be indeterminate, the proper subject of sale is an obligation; while, on the other hand, as the price must be actually paid or delivered at the time of the contract before the separation of the parties, and must, therefore, even in the case of its being money, be produced, and in consequence be particularized or specific, a *sulum* sale is strictly and properly the sale of an obligation for a thing, as defined in the first chapter. Until actual Page 7.
payment or delivery of the price, however, it retains its character of an obligation, and for this reason the price and the goods are both termed debts, and are adduced in the Page 5.

same chapter as examples of the principle that the sale of a debt, that is of the money or goods which a person is under engagement to pay or deliver, before possession, is invalid. The last of the sales referred to is the ordinary exchange of goods for money, which being an obligation, the trans-
Page 7. action is defined to be the sale of things for obligations.

There is another transaction which comes within the definition of sale, and has been already noticed, but may be further adverted to in this place. It is that which is called *Kurz* in the Arabic, and loan in the English language. The borrower acquires an absolute right of property in the things lent, and comes under an engagement to return an equal quantity of things of the same kind. The transaction is therefore necessarily limited to similars, whether of weight, capacity, or tale, and the things lent and repaid being of the same kind, the two rules already mentioned for the prevention of *reba* or usury must be strictly observed. Hence, it follows that any stipulation on the part of the borrower for delay or forbearance by the lender, or any stipulation by the lender for interest to be paid by the borrower are alike unlawful.

Notwithstanding the stringency of the rules for preventing usury, or the taking any interest on the loan of money, methods were found for evading them, and still keeping within the letter of the law. It had always been considered lawful to take a pledge to secure the repayment of a debt. Pledges were ordinarily of moveable property, and when given as security for a debt, and the pledge happened to perish in the hands of the pawnee, the debt was held to be released to the extent of the value of the pledge. Land, though scarcely liable to this incident,
Page 293. was sometimes made the subject of pledge, and devices were adopted for enabling the lender to derive some advantage from its possession while in the state of pledge. But the moderate advantage to be derived in this way does not seem to have contented the money-lenders, who in all ages and countries have been of a grasping dis-
Page 301. position; and the expedient of a sale with a condition for redemption was adopted, which very closely resembles

an English mortgage. In the latter, the condition is usually expressed in one of two ways, viz., either that the sale shall become void, or that the lender shall resell to the seller, on payment of principal and interest at an assigned term. The first of these forms would be inconsistent with the nature of sale under the Moohummudan law, but a sale with a covenant by the lender to re-convey to the seller on repayment of the loan, seems to have been in use probably long before the form was adopted in Europe. It is probable that a term was fixed within which the repayment should be made. If repayment were made at the assigned term, the lender was obliged to re-convey; but if not, the property would remain his own, and the difference between its value and the price or sum lent might have been made an ample compensation for the loss of interest. This form of sale which was called *Bye-al-wufa*, seems to have been strictly legal according to the most approved authorities, though held to be what the law calls abominable, as a device for obtaining what it prohibits.

Page 302.

In constituting sale, there is no material difference between the Moohummudan and other systems of law. The offer and acceptance which are expressed or implied in all cases, must be so connected as to obviate any doubt of the one being intended to apply to the other. For this purpose, the Moohummudan law requires that both shall be interchanged at the same meeting of the parties, and that no other business shall be suffered to intervene between an offer and its acceptance. A very slight interruption is sufficient to break the continuity of a negotiation, and to terminate the meeting in a technical sense, though the parties should still remain in personal communication. An acceptance after the interruption of an offer made before it, would be insufficient to constitute a sale. This has led to distinctions of the meeting which may appear unnecessarily minute to a reader unacquainted with the manners of Eastern countries, where the people are often very dilatory in their bargains, interspersing them with conversation on indifferent topics. It is only when

Page 13.

a meeting has reference to the act of contracting that its meaning is thus liable to be restricted; for when the word occurs in other parts of the law, as, for instance, when it
Page 313. is said of a *surf* contract that the things exchanged must be taken possession of at the meeting, the whole period that the parties may remain together is to be understood. As personal communication may be inconvenient in some cases, and impossible in others, the integrity of the meeting
Page 14. is held to be sufficiently preserved, when a party who receives an offer by message or letter declares his acceptance of it, on receiving the communication and apprehending its contents.

When a sale is lawfully contracted, the property in the things exchanged passes immediately from and to the parties respectively. In a legal sale, delivery and possession are not necessary for this purpose. Until possession is taken, however, the purchaser is not liable for accidental loss, and the seller has a lien for the price on the thing sold. Delivery by one party is in general tantamount to possession taken by the other. It is, therefore, sometimes of great importance to ascertain when there is a sufficient delivery; and many cases, real or imaginary, on the subject, are inserted in the *Futawa Alumgeeree*, some of which have been transferred to the following work, and will be found in the fourth chapter, section second, of the first book. It sometimes happens that a person purchases a thing of which he is already in possession, and it then becomes important to determine in what cases his previous possession is convertible into a possession under the purchase. Unless so converted, it would be held that there is no delivery under the sale, and the seller would of course retain his lien and remain liable for accidental loss. Some cases on this curious point, and the principles by which they are governed, will be found in Book I. chapter iv. section iv.

Though possession is not necessary to complete the transfer of property under a legal sale, the case is different where the contract is illegal; for here property does not pass till possession is taken. The sale, however, though so far effectual, is still invalid, and liable to be set aside by a judge, at the instance of either of the parties, without any reference to the fact of the person complaining being able to come before him with what in legal phraseology is termed clean hands. A Moohummudan judge is obliged by his law to interfere, for the sake of the law itself, or, as it is more solemnly termed, for the right of God, which it is the duty of the judge to vindicate, though by so doing he may afford assistance to a party who personally may have no just claim to his interference.

The foregoing remarks comprise all that appears to me to be necessary as introductory to the Law of Sale; but frequent allusion is made in the following pages to the authorities of the Moohummudan law, and a few observations on that subject seem also to be necessary in this place.

The Moohummudan law is derived from the following sources:—1st, the *Koorân*, which is believed to be a direct revelation from heaven; 2nd, the *Soonnut*, or sayings and doings of Moohummud, who is revered as the apostle of God, and the seal or completion of prophecy; 3rd, the concurrent opinions or decisions of the *Sahabah* or companions of the prophet; and 4th, *Kiyas* or analogical reasoning, when nothing can be found in any of the preceding authorities expressly applicable to a particular case. "The fundamental grounds of disquisition (*ijtihad*)," says the author of the *Mookhtusur-ood-Doowul*, "are four: the "scripture (*kitâb*); the traditionary law (*soonnut*); the "concurrence of the prophet's companions (*jimaa*); and "analogy or analogical reasoning (*kiyas*); for when any "legal question arose respecting what was lawful or un"lawful, a regular investigation took place in the following "manner:—first, they searched the book of Almighty "God (the *koorân*), and if any clear text were found in it "such was adhered to. But, if not, they sought for a "precept or example of the prophet, and abided by it, if "applicable, as decisive. If none such were discovered, "they inquired for a concurrent opinion of the *sahabah*, "who, being directed in the right way, are not open to

" the suspicion of misleading; and, therefore, if their senti- " ments could be ascertained on the point in question, " they were deemed conclusive. If not, an ultimate resort " was had to analogy and reason; the variety of contingent " events being infinite, whereas the texts of the law are finite. " It thus appears certain that the exercise of reason may " be proper and necessary in legal disquisition. Imam " Daood, of Isfahan, however, entirely rejected the exer- " cise of reason; while, on the contrary, Aboo Huneefa " was so much inclined to it that he frequently preferred " it in manifest cases to traditions of single authority; but " Malik, Shafei, and Ibn-i-Humbul had seldom recourse to " analogical reasoning, whether manifest or recondite, when " they could apply either a positive rule or a tradition. " This gave rise to their different opinions and judgments; " which are recorded in books that treat of their dis- " putations; yet neither infidelity nor error is to be " charged against them on this account."*

The followers of the four leaders last mentioned constitute the orthodox sects of the Moohummudans. The sovereigns of India having been followers of Aboo Huneefa, the *Huneefeea Muzhib* (way), or code as it may be termed, was alone recognised in that country during the long period of the Moohummudan dominion. Aboo Huneefa, the leader of the sect, was born at Koofah, A. H. 80, and died at Baghdad, A.H. 150, in prison, into which, it is said, he was cast by the *Khuleefah* Al Munsoor, for refusing the office of *kazee* or judge of which he conscientiously deemed himself to be unworthy.† With Aboo Huneefa, the names of his two principal disciples, Aboo Yoosuf and Moohummud, are constantly associated in the following treatise and other works on the *Huneefeea* code. Aboo Yoosuf was born at Koofah, A. H. 113, and, after finishing his studies under Aboo Huneefa, was appointed *Kazee* of Baghdad by the *Khuleefah* Hadee. He

---

* Mr. Harrington's *Analysis of the Laws and Regulations of the Indian Government.*—Vol. i. p. 221.

† It does not appear that he left any work on jurisprudence.

was afterwards, in the reign of Haroon-oor-Rusheed, made *Kazee-ool-Koozzat* or chief judge, and retained that high station which is said to have been first instituted for him until his death, A. H. 182.* Moohummud was born at Wasit, in Arabian Irak, A. H. 132. He was a fellow pupil with Aboo Yoosuf under Aboo Huneefa, and on the death of the latter, continued his studies under the former. He is also said to have received instructions from Malik. He was appointed by Haroon-oor-Rusheed to administer justice in Persian Irak, and died at Ry, the former capital of that province, A. H. 179.†

It has been remarked by Sir William Jones, in his preface to the *Sirajiyyah*, "that although Aboo Huneefa "be the acknowledged head of the prevailing sect, and has "given his name to it, yet so great veneration is shown to "Aboo Yoosuf and the Lawyer Moohummud, that when "they both differed from their master, the Moohummudan "judge is at liberty to adopt either of the two decisions "which may seem to him to be more consonant to reason "and founded on the better authority." And Mr. Harrington observes, in his analysis of the laws and regulations of the Indian Government, that "this remark corresponds "with the received opinions of present lawyers, and is "sanctioned for the most part, by a passage from the "*Hamadeea*," which he quotes. "It appears, however," he adds, "that the ancient jurists held the authority of "Aboo Huneefa to be absolute, although both his dis-

* The only work he seems to have left was one on the *Duties of the Kazee*; but he is said to have furnished Moohummud with notes (*Amalee*) for a considerable part of his compositions, particularly the *Jama-i-Sugheer*.

† Moohummud was the author of several works on the Moohummudan law. Five of these, viz., the *Jama-i-Sugheer*, *Jama-i-Kubeer*, *Mubsoot*, *Zeeadut*, and *Siyur*, are well known, and frequently quoted separately, or together under the general designation of the *Zahir Rewayut*.

These particulars of the three Huneefeea doctors are derived from Mr. Harrington's *Analysis* before referred to, and the introductory discourse to the translation of the *Hidayah*.

"ciples might differ from him. This is stated without "reservation in a chapter 'On the Order of Authorities to "be observed in Practice,' forming part of the book entitled, "*On the Duties of the Kazee* in the *Futawa Alumgeeree*." The passage which he alludes to is inserted hereafter; but it appears to me to refer to a case where each of the three doctors entertained an opinion of his own different from the others, and to be not inconsistent with the remark of Sir William Jones, who evidently supposes that the disciples concur in one opinion in opposition to their master. There is, however, another passage in the first chapter of the same book, in which it is stated that the *futwa* or approved exposition is absolutely in accordance with the opinion of the *Imam*, that is Aboo Huneefa, then of Aboo Yoosuf, then of Moohummud, then of Zoofr, then of Husn-bin-Ziyad;* and that though it has been said that when the *Imam* is on one side and his two companions (Aboo Yoosuf and Moohummud) on the other, the *mooftee* is at liberty to adopt either of the decisions, yet it is only when the *mooftee* is a scientific jurist that this is true. Notwithstanding these authorities, there can hardly be said to be any fixed rule on the subject. Aboo Yoosuf and Moohummud are referred to by writers on the Moohummudan law as the *sahibein* or two companions, and are, perhaps, entitled to be considered in some degree as independent authorities, rather than the disciples of Aboo Huneefa in any inferior sense. Instances occur in the following pages where each of the three is said to have entertained a different opinion, yet the *futwa* or approved exposition is in accordance with that of one of the disciples.

Aboo Huneefa, as already remarked, was distinguished from the other orthodox leaders by his addition to reasoning in legal disquisitions; but his own decisions and those of his two companions or disciples, Aboo Yoosuf and Moohummud, have very much restrained the exercise of private judgment in their followers. And the accumu-

---

* The last two were also distinguished contemporaries and scholars of Aboo Huneefa.

lation of precedents since their time has tended still further to circumscribe the discretion of a modern Moohummudan judge. The respective limits of reason and of authority are well laid down in several works; extracts from which are inserted in the *Futawa Alumgeeree*, in the book already referred to, "On the Order of Authorities to be observed in Practice;" and I subjoin an abridged translation of some of these extracts for the information of the reader. It is necessary, however, to premise, for his better understanding of them,—1st, that the *Koorân*, having been communicated by Moohummud to his followers at different times and in separate portions, some of its texts are inconsistent with, or even contradictory of, others, and that in these cases the text of earlier is held to be abrogated by that of later revelation; 2nd, that the *Soonnut* were not committed to writing till after the Prophet's death, when all his companions and their contemporaries and successors were also dead, and that of the various reports or accounts of the precepts and examples of the prophet that have been handed down by tradition, many are spurious, and others of different degrees of authenticity. A person who possesses a comprehensive and discriminating knowledge of all that may be drawn from these two sources relative to legal rules and ordinances as distinguished from moral precepts, and of the different intrepretations of the *Koorân*, and gradations and comments of the traditions, with a right understanding or power of just reasoning, and experience in human affairs and usages, is called a *moojtuhid* or jurist, and his science is termed *ijtihad* or jurisprudence. The extracts above referred to are as follows:—

* It is incumbent on a judge to give judgment according to the book of God, to know what parts of it are in force, and what have been abrogated; and among the former, to distinguish between what is positive, and what

---

* Translations of these extracts are given in Mr. Harrington's *Analysis*, before referred to (p. 225), of which I have availed myself, changing the phraseology, however, where it did not seem to me to be sufficiently close to the original.

is doubtful and susceptible of different interpretations. If nothing be found in the book of God, judgment must be given according to what has been handed down from the prophet. And it is incumbent on the judge to discriminate between such reports as are received and such as have been exploded, and where reports differ, to take that which is most probable. He must also be acquainted with those that have obtained successive, notorious, or only single verification, and with the degrees and qualities of the reporters, some of whom were remarkable for their knowledge of law and justice, as the orthodox *Khuleefahs** and the *Abdoollahs*,† and others for their long fellowship with the prophet, and the excellence of their memories. Among reporters, preference is to be given to those who were remarkable for their knowledge of law and justice over those who were not so distinguished, and to those who had long fellowship with the prophet over those who had no such privilege. If a case arise to which none of the traditions of the prophet are applicable, the judge is to determine it according to the concurrent opinions of the *Sahabah* or companions, which are an obligatory rule of conduct. If the point be one on which the companions were divided between two opinions, let him compare their respective arguments, and give the preference to one of the opinions (supposing him to be a *moojtuhid*); but he is not at liberty to differ from both and adopt a third; for, notwithstanding their difference, they must have agreed on excluding every other than the two views in question. When the companions were agreed upon a point, with regard to which one of the *Tabieen* (their immediate successors) was of a different opinion, if the dissentient was not their contemporary, his opposition is not to be taken into account, and a judgment given in conformity with his opinion against the concurrent voice

---

* The four first successors of Moohummud.

† Viz., Abdoollah Ibn-i-Omar, Abdoollah Ibn-i-Abbas, and Abdoollah Ibn-i-Musood, three of the more learned of the companions.

of the companions would be void; but if he were their contemporary, and opposed them in expositions of the law, and they gave sanction to his disquisitions, as in the instances of Shureeh and Shabee, their concurrence is rendered inconclusive by reason of this difference.*

If the matter be one on which no opinion of the companions has come down, but all the *Tabieen* (their immediate successors) concurred in regard to it, the judge is to decide in accordance with their opinion. Should there be a difference of opinion among the *Tabieen,* he is to adopt that which he thinks best. If, however, none of these be applicable, and the judge be a *moojtuhid,* he is to decide according to his own judgment; but if he be not a *Moojtuhid,* he should take the opinion of the *Mooftee,* taking care not to decide without knowledge, being never ashamed to ask advice, and observing two rules,—one of which is, that when our three masters, Aboo Huneefa, Aboo Yoosuf, and Moohummud, have agreed upon any point, he is not at liberty to differ from them; and the other, that when they are of different opinions, that of Aboo Huneefa is to be preferred, according to Abdoollah bin al Mobaruk, because he was one of the *Tabieen,* and opposed them in opinions."†

If no report be found of any opinion of Aboo Huneefa and his companions, but one be found of subsequent lawyers, the judge is to abide by their judgment; but if there should be any difference in opinion among them, he ought to select the opinion of some one of them. If none, however, be forthcoming, he may exercise his own judgment when he is conversant with the reasons or principles of the law, and has consulted persons of legal knowledge on the point. If the lawyers of the time concur in a particular doctrine, and the *kazee* differing from them passes a contrary judgment, because he thinks it right, some hold his so doing to be legal, provided there were any antecedent difference of

---

* Extracted from the *Moheet.*

† Extracted from the *Moheet-oos-Surukhsee.*

opinion among the learned upon the point, whilst others deem it illegal notwithstanding such difference; but all agree upon the illegality of the opposite judgment, supposing no antecedent difference to have been entertained on the subject.*

When there is neither express law (*nuss*) nor concurrence of opinions for the guidance of the *kazee*, if he be a jurist, and have carefully formed an opinion for himself, he should act according to it though the opinions of other jurists may differ from his own, and he cannot lawfully adopt their opinion; for that which upon due deliberation appears to him to be right and just is accepted as such in the sight of God. If he experience any difficulty with regard to the bearing or effect of the circumstances in any case, he should diligently apply his own mind to the difficulty, and act accordingly; but it would be more proper first to consult other persons of legal experience. If they should differ as to the bearing of the facts, he should, after due deliberation, adopt that view which appears to be right. And even though they should concur in an opinion different from his, he is still to act on his own till he is convinced that it is ill founded; and to give judgment accordingly, but not precipitately, nor until he has duly weighed and examined the whole matter. When he has done so, he should be under no apprehension in acting on his own judgment, carefully guarding, however, against conjecture, as a judgment on mere conjecture will not stand good as between him and his God! What has been here said supposes the *kazee* to be a *moojtuhid*, or jurist, competent, from his talents and learning, to undertake legal disquisitions. If he be not a person so qualified, but possesses a knowledge of the opinions of our masters, and a recollection of the points and cases determined by the eminent lawyers of our persuasion, let him give judgment according to the opinion in which he confides and believes to be right. Should he have no

* From the *Tatar Khaneeut.*

sufficient recollection of their opinions, let him act upon expositions of the law by *mooftees* of our persuasion, or if there be only one such *mooftee* in the city, his single exposition may be acted upon without fear of imputed deficiency. *

It only remains to say a few words regarding the procedure in Moohummudan courts of law, to which frequent allusion is made in the following pages. The parties appear in person before the judge, and the plaintiff states his case verbally. It is necessary that he should indicate the subject of his demand in terms sufficiently clear and explicit to make it known, and also assign the grounds on which he rests his claim. If his statement be sufficient on these points, his suit is pronounced to be worthy of a hearing, and he is entitled to a direct answer from the defendant, in the affirmative or negative. If the defendant when called upon by the judge deny the demand, the plaintiff is required to produce his evidence. If his answer be that he has none, he is then told that he is entitled to the oath of the defendant. If the defendant decline to answer *yea* or *nay* to the plaintiff's demand, his silence is taken for a denial, so as to entitle the plaintiff to produce his evidence. If the defendant acknowledge the demand, or refuse when called upon to swear that he is not liable, or if his liability be established by the plaintiff's evidence, judgment is given against him accordingly. It is an universal rule that no one can be required to prove a negative, and as the plaintiff is usually in the position of the person who affirms, and the defendant of one who denies, the *onus probandi* is generally on the former, and the presumption is in favour of the latter, whose word and oath are accordingly said to be preferred or entitled to the preference. It requires some skill, however, to distinguish who it is that maintains the negative in a suit, as reality, and not appearances, are to be considered. Thus, when the trustee of a deposit says, "I have returned it," his word and oath are entitled to preference, because,

* From the *Bidayah*.

though he affirms the return, he denies his responsibility. It is, therefore, usual in treatises on the Moohummudan law to mention under the different heads, the party whose assertion is entitled to credit in the event of disputes regarding matters of fact; and the reader will meet with many instances of it in the following pages.

THE

MOOHUMMUDAN LAW OF SALE.

THE

MOOHUMMUDAN LAW OF SALE.

BOOK I.

SALES IN GENERAL.

CHAPTER I.

Sale defined — How constituted — Conditions, Legal Effect, and Different Kinds of Sale.

SALE is the exchange of property * for property, with mutual consent; and it is constituted by proposal and acceptance, or by reciprocal delivery. **Definition. How constituted.**

The conditions of a contract of sale are of four kinds, viz., conditions which are necessary to constitute it; to give it operation; to render it valid; to make it obligatory. **Conditions**

The conditions which are necessary to constitute a sale, and may be called essential, relate, in the first place, to the contracting parties. And with regard to them, it is required,— **of constitution**

1. That they shall be of sound understanding and discernment. This condition does not exclude sale by a **that relate to the contracting parties;**

---

* Arab. *mal.*

minor,* or an insane person,† when capable of understanding its nature and effects; by either of whom, in such circumstances, a sale may therefore be contracted.

2. That there shall be more than one party to the contract; and there is no contract where the same person acts both as the buyer and seller. From the operation of this rule, the following parties are excepted: 1st, A father, his executor,‡ and a judge, when either selling their own property to a minor, or purchasing a minor's property from him. With regard to the executor, however, it is necessary that the sale or purchase by him be evidently for the minor's benefit, to bring the transaction within this exception. 2nd, A messenger between both the parties. 3rd, A slave purchasing himself from his master, under his master's authority.

to the contract itself;

Essential conditions relate, in the second place, to the contract itself; in which the acceptance must be made to correspond with the proposal, by the purchaser accepting the thing proposed, and for the consideration proposed by the seller. If there be any variance in these respects, there is no contract; except only in cases where, the proposal being on the part of the purchaser, the seller accepts for less than the price offered, or the proposal being on the part of the seller, the purchaser accepts for more than the price mentioned, and the increase is accepted by the seller at the meeting.

to both the things exchanged;

Thirdly, It is essential to the constitution of sale that each of the things exchanged be property (*mal*); and there is no contract where either of them does not fall within this description.§

---

* Arab. *subee*, a youth under puberty. Puberty is majority in the Moohummudan law.

† Arab. *mâtooh*. A lunatic with lucid intervals.

‡ The executor of a father's will is guardian to his minor children. See chapter xvi.

§ The only things to which the term *mal* is inapplicable are carrion—that is, an animal that has died a natural death, or has been improperly slaughtered—and blood. Neither of which, it is supposed,

Fourthly, It is required that the thing sold,* as distinguished from the price, be in existence at the time of sale; and there is no contract where it is either non-existent or in danger of extinction, as the future offspring of a *fœtus* in the womb, or the *fœtus* itself; 2nd, That the thing sold be appropriated in itself, and not merely an appendage of other property, and that the seller, when he professes to sell on his own account, have a right of property in what he sells. Hence, there can be no contract of sale with regard to natural grass before it is cut, though growing on the land of the seller;† nor of anything which does not actually belong to him at the time of the sale, though he should afterwards acquire it, except only the goods advanced for under a *sulum* contract, and usurped property, the sale of which is rendered legal by the usurper subsequently making compensation to the lawful proprietor. 3rd, That the thing sold be property having value in law,‡ and be susceptible of delivery, either immediately or at some future time.

to the thing sold in particular;

Fifthly, It is further essential to the constitution of sale, in the opinion of all our doctors, that each of the contracting parties shall hear what is said by the other; and if the purchaser say "I have bought," and the seller does not hear him, there is no contract. But if other persons pre-

---

any people having a revealed religion can account to be property.—*Hidayah and Kifayah*, vol. iii. p. 88.

* Arab. *mabeea*. Sometimes this term is applied to both the things exchanged, but it is commonly restricted to one of them, the other being denominated the price. Rules for distinguishing the *mabeea* from the price are given in chapter ii. § 3.

† Because natural grass is considered to be the common property of all mankind. See chap. ix. § 2.

‡ Arab. *shura*, the distinctive appellation of the Moohummudan law. Value (*keemut*) is established in a thing by legal permission to make use of it. The quality of being property (*maleeut*) is dependent on the opinion of men in general, or some of them.—*Kifayah*, vol. iii. p. 88. Wine and pork, therefore, being accounted property by Christians, are *mal*, but have no *keemut*, because they are forbidden to Mussulmans.

sent at the meeting* should state that they heard the words of the buyer, the denial of the seller is not to be credited in a court of justice, unless he happens to be deaf.

to the place of meeting.

The sixth and last condition essential to the constitution of sale, is unity of the place of meeting;* insomuch that both the proposal and the acceptance must be expressed at the same place, and if there be any variance in this respect, there is no contract.

Conditions necessary to render a sale operative.

The conditions which are necessary to give operation to a sale are, first, A right of property in both the articles exchanged; and, second, That none but the seller have any right in the thing sold. The existence of any such right prevents the sale from being operative until the impediment is removed; as, for instance, when a thing is sold which has been already pledged or let to hire.

Conditions of validity. General.

Conditions necessary to the validity of sale are either general or special. General conditions of validity, which apply alike to all kinds of sale, are the following:—

First, All conditions essential to the constitution of sale are also conditions of its validity. But the converse of the proposition is not true; for invalid sales are held by us to be constituted and become operative when followed by possession.

Secondly, It is required to the validity of a sale that it be not limited in respect of time; and if so limited it is invalid.†

Thirdly, That both the thing sold and the price be so known and determined as to prevent disputes between the parties; and any ignorance that may tend to produce contention between them is sufficient to invalidate the sale; as in the sale of a single goat undefined from a particular flock, or of anything at a price to be fixed by another person.

Fourthly, It is required that there be some use in the

---

* Arab. *mujlis*,—literally, *place of sitting*.

† As, for instance, a sale for a year.

transaction; and a sale in which there is no use is invalid, as the sale of *dirhems** for *dirhems* equal in weight and quality.

Fifthly, It is necessary to the validity of all sales that they be free from vitiating or invalidating conditions, which are of various kinds, and will be explained at some length hereafter. They may be described generally in this place, as conditions that are not in harmony with the contract, or within the usual scope of such transactions among men, or conditions that are dependent on events that are either altogether fortuitous, or the time of the occurrence of which cannot be predicated with any degree of certainty.

The special conditions of validity, which are applicable only to particular kinds of sale, are the following:— Special.

First, In sales on credit, it is required that the term of payment be known; and if it be unknown the sale is invalid.

Secondly, In the resale of a purchased moveable, and in the sale of a debt,† previous possession by the seller is necessary. Hence the sale of a debt before possession of it is invalid;‡ as, for instance, the goods for which an advance has been made in a *sulum*, sale; and the advance itself,§ even after the sale has been dissolved,—that is, the seller of the goods, who is entitled to the advance, cannot sell it until he has obtained possession of it, and the purchaser of the goods, who if the sale be dissolved

---

* Silver coins so called.

† Arab. *deyn.* For an explanation of this term see the Introduction. It here evidently means the money or goods which a person is under engagement to pay or deliver.

‡ The important principle that a debt cannot be lawfully sold, is implied in several places in the *Hidayah*, and is expressly, though incidentally, stated in the book on Composition, as a reason for a particular composition among heirs being void, in these terms,—"for that would be the transfer of a debt to another person than the debtor."—Vol. iii. p. 614; *Translation*, vol. iii. p. 208.

§ Arab. *ras ool mal,*—literally, *capital stock.*

is entitled to a restoration of the advance, cannot sell it until he has resumed possession of it. Hence, also, a sale in consideration of a debt due by another party than the seller is invalid, contrary to the case of a sale where the consideration is the seller's own debt.

Thirdly, When the articles exchanged are of the class with regard to which *reba* or usury is prohibited,* absolute similarity between them is required, together with the absence of everything that can lead to a suspicion of usury.

Fourthly, In *surf* sales—when the articles exchanged are the precious metals—mutual possession by the parties before their separation is necessary to the validity of the transaction.

Fifthly, In *morâbŭhŭt, towleeŭt,* and *wuzeeŭt* sales,† it is necessary that the price previously given by the seller be made known to the buyer.

Conditions necessary to render a sale obligatory. The only condition that is further necessary, in addition to the preceding, to render a sale obligatory on the parties, is freedom from the four known or other options.‡

Legal effect of Sale. The legal effect of sale is to establish a right of property in the buyer to the thing sold, and in the seller to the price, when the sale is absolute; and when it is dependent, the establishment of these rights respectively on the sale being duly allowed.

Different kinds of Sale. Sale considered abstractly is of four kinds; operative,§ dependent, unlawful,‖ and void. An operative sale is that

---

* Fully explained in chapter ix. § 6.

† These are explained a little further on.

‡ Options are powers of cancellation, and are fully treated of in chapters vi. vii. and viii.

§ Arab. *nafiz*,—literally, *penetrating*, *passing*.

‖ Arab. *fasid*,—literally, *vicious*, or *vitiated*, and frequently opposed to *saheeh*, valid; hence it has been rendered *invalid* by Mr. Hamilton, in his translation of the *Hidayah*. But it is also used synonymously with *ghyr jaiz*, unlawful; and I prefer the latter word, as indicating the particular vice or taint existing in this kind of sale. It is invalid because unlawful. It should be observed, that the which takes effect immediately. A dependent sale is that which takes effect when allowed by the person on whose consent the contract is suspended. An unlawful sale is that which takes effect when followed by possession of the thing sold. And a void sale is that which can never take effect.

Sale, considered with reference to the thing sold, is also of four kinds. 1st, Sale of things for things,* which is called *mookaizut;* 2nd, Sale of obligations for obligations,† which is called *surf;*‡ 3rd, Sale of obligations for things, which is called *sulum;* and, lastly, the converse of this, or sale of things for obligations, which is the ordinary kind of sale.§

Again, viewed with reference to the price, sale is also of four kinds. 1st, *Moosâwŭmŭt,* or sale for a price mutually agreed upon; 2nd, *Moorâbŭhŭt,* which is a second sale of a thing for a greater price than that originally paid for it by the seller; 3rd, *Towleeŭt,* or such a sale at the exact original price; and, 4th, *Wuzeeŭt,* which is a second sale for a price less than that originally paid for the article sold.

---

terms *vitiated, invalid, unlawful,* are used indiscriminately in the following pages, as the corresponding expressions are in the original Arabic. In the *Principles and Precedents of Moohummudan Law,* p. 42, prin. 7, the sales referred to are termed *imperfect,* and their legal defect is said to be cured by Seizin; but this may be too general. See chapter xi.

* Arab. *ayn,*—literally, *essence,* or *substance,* but frequently used in law to signify something specific or distinctly particularized, as opposed to things that are undeterminate.

† Arab. *deyn.* See Introduction. The word is here applicable to money, grain, liquids, &c., and generally all commodities estimated by weight or measure of capacity, and taken undeterminately.

‡ This definition of *surf* is hardly correct; for neither is every sale of an obligation for an obligation a *surf* (see *post,* chap. ix. § 1), nor are all the things exchanged always obligations, that is, undeterminate; for an exchange of the precious metals, though the articles be specific, is a *surf.* See book ii. chap. ii. § 1.

§ Or a sale of goods for money.

CHAPTER II.

FORM OF THE CONTRACT.

SECTION I.

Of what relates to the Act of Contracting.

Sale is contracted by words, in the past or present tense.

SALE is contracted by any words in the past or present tense, which import the transfer and acceptance of property,* whether the words be in the Persian or the Arabic language, or the like. It is contracted by words in the past tense without intention, as if by the mere force of the expressions. But if the aorist tense be employed, intention is necessary.† Thus, if the seller should say, "I sell," or "bestow," or "give you this slave for a thousand *dirhems*," and the purchaser answer, "I buy" or "take him from you," both parties intending a declaration *de presenti*, or if the language of one of the parties be in the past tense, and that of the other in the aorist with an intention *de presenti*, sale is contracted; but without such intention there is no contract. When the aorist is restricted to the present time, as "I sell you now," there is no necessity for intention; but when restricted to the future by the particles *soof* or *seen*, or the imperative mood is employed, there is no contract, unless, as regards the

---

* Arab. *tumleek* and *tumullook*, second and third increased conjugations from *milk*, property or possessions.

† The aorist tense in the Arabic language is employed to express present and future time, though susceptible of restriction to either by the employment of certain particles, but without these it is ambiguous: the words "I sell," &c., in the text, meaning either "I do sell," or "I will sell."

imperative, when it demonstrates a present intention, as if the seller should say, "Take this for so much," and the purchaser answer, "I have taken it." Indeed, it would seem that when the imperative mood is employed, a triple *formula* is necessary according to the best opinions; as if the seller should say, "Buy of me," and the purchaser answer, "I have bought," there is no contract until the seller reply, "I have sold;" or if the purchaser say, "Sell to me," and the seller answer, "I have sold," there is no contract until the purchaser reply, "I have bought." By general agreement the interrogative form is insufficient to constitute sale. Thus, if the purchaser say, "Do you," or "will you sell to me this thing for so much?" or "Have you sold it to me for so much?" and the seller answer, "I have sold it," there is no contract until the addition of the buyer, "I have bought it."

Interrogative form is insufficient.

Any particular form of expression does not appear to be necessary to constitute sale. Thus, if one of the parties should say, "I have given you this slave for a thousand,"* or "This slave is sold to you in consideration of your debt," and the other should accept; or if one should say, "I have purchased your slave for a thousand *dirhems*," and the other should answer, "I have done," or "Well," or "Produce the price;" or one should say, "I have bought him for so much," and the other should answer, "He is yours," or "The slave is yours;" or one should say, "I have sold you such a thing for so much," and the other answer, "I have taken it;" or one should say, "I have exchanged my horse for your horse," and the other, "I have

A particular form of expression not necessary.

---

* The legal sufficiency of the word "*give*," to constitute sale, has given rise to the *heba bil ivuz* (or gift for a consideration), so common in India among the members of the same family. When property is held in an undivided share, as a half or a fourth, it cannot be made the subject of ordinary donation, because not susceptible of delivery, and the form of a *heba bil ivuz* is adopted, which, being in reality a sale, does not require possession to complete the transfer of the property. See *Principles and Precedents of Moohummudan Law*, p. 219.

done likewise;" in all these cases there is a valid contract of sale.

Sale with a gift of the price. If the seller should say, "I have sold you this slave for a thousand *dirhems*, and made you a present of the price," and the other party should answer, "I have bought him," there is no valid contract. But if, after sale for a price and acceptance by the purchaser, the seller should then release him from the price, or make him a present of it, or bestow it on him in charity, the contract remains valid. And though the seller be silent as to price, if the transaction be accompanied by possession of the thing sold, a transfer of property takes place according to both the disciples, the purchaser being liable for its value. If, however, the seller were actually to say, "I have sold it without a price," there is no transfer of property, though it were accompanied by possession.

Miscellaneous cases. A person says to another, "Go away with this merchandise, look at it to-day, and if you are satisfied with it, it is yours for a thousand *dirhems*;" or "If you are satisfied with it to-day, it is yours for a thousand *dirhems*," and the person addressed goes away with the merchandise; a proposal in such terms is considered equivalent to a sale with a condition of option to the purchaser, and the transaction is quite lawful. This is a favourable construction of the law, which has been adopted by our three sages.

If a person having purchased a piece of cloth by an unlawful contract, should meet the seller next day, and say to him, "Did you not sell to me this cloth of yours for a thousand *dirhems?*" and he should answer, "Yes," and the first thereupon reply, "And I took it," the transaction is void by reason of the first sale, which, though defective, is still subsisting, and must be abandoned before the second can be lawful. But when a man sells a slave for a thousand dirhems, saying to the purchaser, "If you don't bring the price to-day there is no sale between us," and the purchaser fails to do so, but meeting the seller next day, says to him, "Did you not sell to me this slave of yours for a thousand dirhems?" and he answering, "Yes," the purchaser then adds, "And I took him," there is a present purchase, to which the first (having been dissolved) is no bar. So also if he had said, "Unless you bring me the price within a year there is no sale between us;" for here there is no valid transaction, the time being longer than the allowed period of option.

When a person says to another, "If you pay me so many *dirhems* for this cloth, I have sold it to you," and the other pays the money at the meeting, this constitutes a valid sale on a favourable construction.

Consent implied from the silence of the party addressed.

If a person say to another, "I have sold you this my slave for so much," and the purchaser take possession saying nothing, sale is contracted; or if one should say, "I have bought provisions from you for a thousand *dirhems*," and then proceed to bestow them in charity on poor persons, doing so at the meeting, the sale is complete, though the seller has said nothing to indicate his assent. The case would be different, however, if the purchaser were to dispose of the provisions in the like manner after the separation of the parties, by reason of the intervening obstacle. So also if one should say, "I have sold this cloth for a thousand," and the other immediately cut it up into a *kamees* or shirt before separation, the sale is complete.

From his answering indirectly.

Should a person say, "I have sold you this my slave for a thousand *dirhems*," and the other answer, "He is free," the answer, according to one authority, is equivalent to acceptance, and the slave obtains his freedom; but according to another, the answer is not an acceptance, and the slave is not freed; whereas if the answer were, "Then he is free," there seems to be no doubt that emancipation would take place, and the purchaser be liable for the thousand *dirhems*. In a case where one said to another, "Sell me your slave for a thousand *dirhems*," and the other answered, "I have sold him," the first subjoining, "He is free," it is related that Aboo Huneefa considered the reply to be equivalent to taking possession, and the slave to be free; but that Moohummud was of the contrary opinion.

From his conduct.

Eating, or riding, or putting on the subject of sale, after the seller has said, "I have sold," is tantamount to consent. Hence, if a person should say to another, "All this provision is for the *dirhem* you owe me," and then eat up the provision, this amounts to a sale.

In a bargain for a piece of cloth, the seller says, "I will sell it for fifteen," and the purchaser, "I will take it only for ten;" but he goes away with it nevertheless, the seller saying nothing. In such circumstances, the price is fifteen if the cloth were at the time of bargaining in the hands of the purchaser; but if it were in the hands of the seller, and the purchaser took it from him, the seller not objecting, the price is ten. So also, if it were in the hands of the purchaser, and he should return it to the seller on his saying, "I will not sell it for less than fifteen," but again take it back and go away with it, the seller yielding it up and saying nothing, ten is still to be considered the price.

Option of acceptance during the meeting.

When one of the parties to a contract of sale has made his proposal, the other is at liberty to accept or reject it during the meeting, and this is called the option of acceptance; but it does not descend to heirs. It continues till the termination of the meeting;* the life of the proposer being, however, a condition of its subsistence; so that, if he die before acceptance, the proposal is of none effect. It is also void on either of the parties rising from the meeting before acceptance; or if, without rising, one of them should betake himself to any other business than the matter in hand, the proposal is void. But if a person, standing at the time of the proposal, should sit down and then accept, the sale is valid. So also if, having a cup of water in his hand, he should drink it off, or eat a morsel,

* Arab. *Mujlis*, literally, *place of sitting*. The following saying of the Prophet on the subject is recorded in the *Mishcat-ul-Musabih*, Translation, vol. ii. p. 10:—"The seller and the buyer have a mutual option as long as they are at the place of selling, and have not separated from each other. When they have separated and got up from the place of bargaining (or one of them), the option is done away." "And it is not right for the seller and buyer to separate from each other in a hurry."

and then accept, the sale is perfectly good. But taking a regular meal puts an end to the meeting; and if both or one of the parties should go to sleep, laid down or reclining, it is accounted a separation; but if they fall asleep sitting, the meeting continues. If they should both faint and revive, and then acceptance take place, it is lawful according to Aboo Huneefa: but according to Moohummud, if the faint should continue for any length of time, the meeting is at an end. A person says to another, "I give you this for so much," and the purchaser makes no answer until the seller address a third party on some necessary occasion: in such circumstances there is no sale. But if a person addressed were engaged in a religious duty, and after its performance should declare his acceptance, it is lawful; and even if he should add a *rookaa*, or genuflexion, over and above what duty requires, still the acceptance would be lawful. But if the purchaser, being in the house, should go out and then say, "I have bought," there is no contract.

What constitutes a meeting.

It is not lawful for one of the parties to a contract of sale to call out to the other from a distance or the other side of a wall; but if a person in the house should say to another on the roof, "I have sold it to you for so much," and the other answer, "I have bought," the transaction is valid, provided the parties be within sight of each other, and the distance be not such as to make any confusion or doubt in their words.

If the parties engaged in a bargain of sale are walking together, or riding either both on the same animal or separately, and the person addressed should give his answer in immediate connection with the proposal of his fellow, the contract is complete; but a short interval between them would invalidate the sale, though the parties were together on the same saddle. An answer after a step or two, however, would still be lawful if they are walking together. But if they were both standing at the time of the proposal, and should then move on, or one of them should proceed after the proposal and before acceptance, the proposal would be void. When parties are bargaining together in a boat which is in motion, an interval of silence between the proposal and acceptance does not prevent the contract, the boat being considered the same as a house.

Proposal and acceptance made simultaneously.

When a seller says, "I have sold," and a purchaser, "I have bought," and both expressions are uttered at the same time, it would seem that sale is duly contracted.

Acceptance must in all cases be declared before any change takes place in the thing sold.

It is necessary in all cases that the acceptance be declared before any change has taken place in the subject of sale. Thus, if one should sell grape-juice, which before acceptance becomes vinegar, or a female slave who before acceptance gives birth to a child, the sale is unlawful.

Proposer may retract before acceptance. Condition.

The proposer is at liberty to retract before acceptance by the other party; but it is necessary that the other party should hear the retraction. If, therefore, the seller should say, "I have sold you this slave for so much," and then add, "I have retracted," and the purchaser, without hearing the retraction, should say, "I have bought," sale is contracted. If the retraction and acceptance are uttered simultaneously, the sale is not complete; but if the retraction be after the acceptance, it is too late.

Sale completed by proposal and acceptance.

When proposal and acceptance duly take place, the sale is binding on both parties, neither having any option except on account of defect or want of inspection. No permission is required on the part of the seller to complete the contract, nor can the purchaser withdraw from it by saying, "I am unwilling."

Sale by letter or message.

A letter or message may be substituted for verbal and personal communication in the contract of sale, the place of receipt of the letter and delivery of the message being accounted the meeting. The form of the letter is as follows: after the usual compliments, "I have sold you my slave such an one for so much;" and if upon receipt and perusal of the letter, and understanding its contents, the person addressed should declare his acceptance at the meeting, the sale is valid. The form of the message is as follows:—"Go to such an one, and tell him that such an one has sold his slave such an one to you for so much;"

May be accepted verbally,

and if, on the messenger going and delivering the message, acceptance be declared at the meeting, it is valid. But if one were to say, "I have sold this to such a person now absent for so much," and the person referred to should accept on receiving the intelligence, this would be no valid sale. If, however, acceptance were made on his behalf by any person present at the meeting, the sale would be good, subject to his approval; and where authority is actually given by the seller to a messenger, information may be lawfully conveyed by another than the person indicated.

A person writes to another, "I have bought your slave," and the other writes in answer, "I have sold him,"— sale is effected; but if one should write to another, "Sell to me for so much," and the person addressed should write, "I have sold," there would be no sale until the purchaser say, "I have bought."

or by letter.

Offer by letter or message may be retracted before acceptance.

An offer sent by letter or message may be retracted before its receipt and acceptance, and the retraction is valid, whether known to the party addressed or not; so that, if acceptance be declared after an offer has been actually retracted, the sale is not completed.

Sale by reciprocal delivery.

Sale may also be contracted by reciprocally giving and taking the things exchanged, without the intervention of speech; and this sale is called *taatee*,* or reciprocal delivery. It makes no difference whether the things sold be of great or trivial value. Delivery on both sides is made a condition by many of our doctors. But by the more correct opinion possession on one side is enough, according to an express text of Moohummud, "that *taatee* sale is established by possession of one of the things exchanged," which may be either the price or the thing sold. But this implies an explanation of the price, when the article is one the price of which is unknown. With regard to bread and meat, the price of which is matter of notoriety, an explanation of the price is not necessary.

---

* Fourth increased conjugation from the root *ata*—giving, and denoting reciprocal action of the radical sense.

Cases. A person having purchased a load (of something) from another for eight *dirhems*, says to him, "Bring me another load for the same price and cast it there," the seller accordingly brings another load and casts it in the place indicated; this is a sale, and he is entitled to demand other eight *dirhems*. Again, a person says to a dealer in meat, "How do you sell your meat?" he answers, "Three *rutls** the *dirhem*;" and the other replying, "I have taken from you, weigh me so much," the dealer refuses, and he is at liberty to do so; and even though he should weigh it, either party may retract till possession is taken by the purchaser. But after he has taken possession, or the seller has put the meat into his basket by his desire, the sale is complete, and he must pay the price. A person delivers five *deenars*† to a dealer in wheat, with the intention of purchasing from him, and, saying, "How do you sell it?" he answers, "A hundred for the deenar;" whereupon the purchaser remains silent, but presently after demands the wheat; the seller says, "I will deliver it to-morrow;" and nothing further takes place between them as to the sale. The purchaser comes next day for his wheat, but the price has risen; the seller cannot, however, refuse, but must deliver at the price of the previous day.

Necessary conditions. Mutual delivery, to constitute sale, must be based on a transaction which is not in itself void or defective; otherwise there is no contract. Thus a person to whom a debt is due by another demands payment, and the debtor brings a certain known quantity of barley, saying "Take it at the rate of the city." If there be a fixed rate in the city, known to both the parties, the sale is completed; but if the rate be uncertain, or unknown to the parties, there is no sale.

Miscellaneous transactions. There are some miscellaneous transactions which may be reduced to sale by mutual delivery, of which the following may be adduced as examples:—1st, The surrender by a purchaser of a thing which he has purchased to one who

* The *rutl* is about a pound avoirdupois. † Gold coins so called.

demands it under a claim of preëmption, when there is, in fact, no such right in the case. 2nd, The surrender by an agent to his principal of an article which he had purchased for himself. 3rd, A person with whom a slave girl was placed for safe custody produces another to the owner, saying, "This is your slave girl;" the owner knows that she is not so; but the other swearing to the fact, he takes the slave so brought. In such circumstances, he may lawfully enjoy her, and she is capable of becoming his *oom-i-wulud*,* being, in fact, his property by right of the sale by *taatee*.

SECTION II.

Of taking Possession under an Inchoate bargain.

The cases that occur under this head relate chiefly to responsibility in the event of loss; and the following may suffice to illustrate the principles by which it is regulated:—

Effect of wilful destruction by purchaser after mention of price.

1. Two persons bargaining for a piece of cloth, the seller says, "It is yours for twenty *dirhems*," and the purchaser says, "Nay, but for ten;" the purchaser takes away the cloth, but the seller is not content to let him have it for ten. This is no sale, except in so far that if the purchaser should destroy the piece of cloth, he is liable for the twenty *dirhems*, though up to the time of its destruction he is at liberty to return it. Aboo Huneefa and Aboo Yoosuf, who gave this decision, said that, according to analogy, the purchaser should be made liable for the value of the cloth, but that they had abandoned analogy in the case, from regard to prevailing custom.

* Literally, mother of a child. A slave is so called who has borne a child to her master, which he acknowledges as his own. She can no longer be sold, and is entitled to her freedom at his death. Her subsequent children also are his without acknowledgment, unless expressly repudiated by him. The constructive sale here has a further important effect; for it saves the parties from the severe punishment to which they would have been otherwise liable by the Moohummudan law for criminal intercourse.

Effect of accidental loss in purchaser's hands after mention of a price.

2nd, When a person takes a piece of cloth after mutual haggling about the price, which has been mentioned but not positively fixed, and the cloth happens to perish in his hands, he is liable for its value: so, also, if his heirs after his death should destroy it, liability for its value is incurred.

3rd, A person takes a piece of cloth, saying, "I will take it away, and if I am satisfied with it, I will purchase it." He takes it away, and the cloth perishes in his hands; but he is nowise liable on account of it. If, however, he should say, "If I am satisfied with it, I will take it for ten *dirhems*," he would be responsible for its value.

4th, A person says, "This cloth is for twenty *dirhems*," and the purchaser says, "I will take it for ten," and goes away with it, and it perishes in his hands, he is liable for the value. But if the seller should say, "I will not abate any part of the twenty," the purchaser's liability, in the event of loss, would extend to that amount.

Effect of accidental loss when a thing is delivered for inspection.

5th, A person says, "This cloth is yours for ten," and the purchaser answers, "Give it to me that I may look at it," or "show it to another," and it perishes in his hands, he is liable for nothing, according to Aboo Huneefa; that is, it perishes as a trust in his hands. But if he should say, "Give it to me, and if I am satisfied with it I will take it," he would be liable for the price. The difference in these cases is, that, in the first place there is no sale, while, in the last, the delivery to the purchaser, with a view to his taking the thing, if satisfied with it, would be accounted a sale without any request on his part, and with such request, the case is of course stronger.

When so delivered, after mention of the price.

6th, A man comes to a dealer in glass, and says, "Let me look at this flask;" the dealer shows it to him, and says, "Take it up:" he does so, and the flask falls from his hands and is broken; yet he is in nowise liable, because he took it up with the permission of the dealer, and without any mention of price. But if he had commenced with asking the price of the flask, and on the dealer's saying, "So much," he had then laid hold of it with his permission, and it had fallen from his hands and broken, he would have been liable for the value; and if he took it without the permission of the owner, he would be liable, whether the price were mentioned or not.

7th, Two persons are bargaining about a cup or bowl, and the intending purchaser says, "Show me your cup that I may look at it;" the owner puts it into his hands, and it falls from them on other cups belonging to the same dealer, and is not only broken, but the other cups are broken also. In such a case, according to Moohummud, he is not liable for the first cup, for it was entrusted to him; but he is liable for all the others, because he broke them without any permission on the part of their owner.

Section III.

Of distinguishing the thing Sold from the Price, and of Acts of Ownership with regard to either before taking Possession.

According to Koodooree, what is particularized in a contract of sale is the thing sold, and what is not particularized is the price,* unless the word sale be distinctly applied to it. Things are of three kinds; some being always price, others always the thing sold, and others sometimes price, and sometimes the thing sold. The first class comprises *dirhems* and *deenars*,† which are always price, whether opposed to

General rule.

---

* Arab. *Thumun*.

† These appear to have been the only coins current among the old Arabs, and are emphatically called *nukdein*, or two monies. The *dirhem* was of silver, and equal to $6\frac{4}{11}$ annas in Indian money, or about $9\frac{1}{2}d.$ (*Galloway on the Law and Constitution of India*, p. 11), which seems to have been the value of the Attic drachma. Its legal weight, as fixed by the Khuleef Omar, was $\frac{7}{10}$ths of a *mithkal*, being a mean between three kinds of *dirhems* current in his time.—*Kifayah*, vol. i. p. 507. The deenar was of gold, and its weight a *mithkal*. The *mithkal* contained twenty *kerat*, and each *kerat* five *shueer*, or grains of barley. So that the *dirhem* was in weight fourteen *kerat* or seventy grains of barley, and the *deenar* twenty *kerat* or one hundred grains (*Fut. Alum.* vol. i. p. 251). In value, the *deenar* was legally equivalent to ten *dirhems*.—The *dirhem* and *deenar* are still used as weights in Egypt, the former being divided into sixteen *kerat*,

things similar to themselves, or to other things, or associated with the particle *ba* (with) or not.* The second class comprises things which are neither similars,† nor approximates of tale,‡ and are always the thing sold. From these, however, cloth must be excepted, when described and made deliverable at a future time, in order to represent price; for if one should purchase a slave for cloth, described, and which he binds himself to deliver at a future time, the sale is lawful, and is not annulled by the separation of the parties before the delivery of the slave. But if no term be assigned for the delivery of the cloth the sale is unlawful. It is to be observed, of all things of the second class, that the sale of them is not lawful except when they are specific.

The third class, which is sometimes price and sometimes the subject of sale, comprises all things that are estimated by weight or measurement of capacity, and all approximates of tale. When opposed to prices, they are to be considered the subjects of sale or things sold. When opposed to things that are similar to themselves, whether they be similars of weight, capacity, or tale, and the articles on both sides are specific, the sale is lawful, and both the articles are the subjects of sale or things sold. If one of them be specific, and the other undeterminate, being referred to only by description, and the article that is specific be made the thing sold and the other the price, the transaction is also lawful, but it is necessary that possession should be taken of the latter before the separation of the parties. While, if the article that is

---

and the *deenar* or *mithkal* into twenty-four *kerat*, each of three grains of barley, called *habbeh*, and fully equal in commerce to an English grain.—*Lane's Modern Egyptians*, vol. ii. Appendix.

* It is here added in the authority cited in the *Futawa Alumgeeree*, that *fooloos* are also prices, and like *dirhems* are not rendered specific by description, but this is only the opinion of Moohummud.

† Things estimated by weight or measurement of capacity.

‡ Things usually sold by number, the unities of which are nearly alike. These will in general be styled *similars of tale*.

specific be made the price, and that which is undeterminate the subject of sale, the transaction is altogether unlawful, even though possession were taken of the latter before the parties separate; for the seller is disposing of what he has not, which can be lawfully done only by way of *sulum*. If both the articles be undeterminate, the sale is unlawful for the same reason.* It is to be observed, that association with the particle *ba* (with) is the sign of price, and non-association with this particle an indication of the thing sold.

Fourth class.

• To the three classes before-mentioned, a fourth has been added by the author of the Kifayah,† to comprise things that, in their own nature, are goods or merchandise, but become the representatives of price when generally adopted or accepted as such. These things, so long as they pass current, are considered to be prices; but when they cease to be current, they revert to their original state of goods or merchandise. To this class may be referred the copper coin called *fooloos*, which, according to Aboo Huneefa and Aboo Yoosuf, can be rendered determinate by specification,‡ and are not therefore to be classed with *dirhems* and *deenars*, though generally employed as money.

A purchased moveable cannot be lawfully sold before possession.

The price and thing sold being duly distinguished from each other, it may now be stated with regard to the latter, that when moveable, it cannot be lawfully sold by the purchaser until he has first taken possession of it.§ This, however, is not peculiar to things acquired by purchase; for hire, when specific and conditioned to be promptly delivered, cannot be sold before possession. And the law is the same with regard to the consideration for compound-

* That is, when both of them are made the subjects of sale; for otherwise the sale would be lawful.—See chapter ix. § 1.

† Vol. iii. p. 239. ‡ See Hamilton's *Hedaya*, vol. ii. p. 495.

§ The reasons assigned for this are an express prohibition of the Prophet, and the chance of cancellation to which the first sale is exposed by the loss of its subject before delivery. If the purchaser, therefore, were to sell it before possession, he might be selling a thing which would never be his.—*Hidayah and Kifayah*, vol. iii. pp. 152-3.

ing a debt, which, when specific, cannot be sold previous to possession. Whereas, a woman's *muhr* or dower, and the consideration given by her for *khoola* or her release from marriage, and the consideration for compounding intentional homicide, may, when specific, be lawfully sold before possession. What cannot be lawfully sold before possession, cannot be let to hire before it. A female slave may be given in marriage by the purchaser before possession. And when the subject of sale is given away, or bestowed in charity, or lent, or pledged by the purchaser, before possession, though the transaction was accounted unlawful by Aboo Yoosuf, it was held to be lawful by Moohummud, whose opinion has been approved.* This, however, implies that the acts referred to are in favour of a stranger; for a pledge to the seller himself, would be invalid; and a gift to him, if accepted, would cancel the sale; if not accepted, the gift would be void, and the sale remain as before, unaffected by it. A sale to the seller, before possession, would be unlawful because it is so generally.

If the purchaser of a slave say, before taking possession, to the seller, "Emancipate him," and the seller does so, the emancipation is lawful as from the seller himself, but the sale is cancelled. And if the slave were a female, and the purchaser should before possession, say to the seller, "Sell or enjoy her;" or if the subject of sale were provisions, and the purchaser should say, "Eat them;" and in either case, the seller were to do as directed, the sale would be cancelled; but if he refrained from exercising the power given to him, it would remain good.

---

* Moohummud makes a distinction between acts that require possession to complete them, and such as do not, and states generally that the former when exercised by a purchaser before possession are lawful, and the latter unlawful. Thus, if a person purchase a particular thing, and before possession make a gift of it to another, as possession is necessary to complete the gift, the donation is valid as mentioned in the text, for though the thing should perish before delivery, and the sale be cancelled thereby, the gift would also fall to the ground from the impossibility of making delivery.

It is to be observed that, if a person acquire a moveable thing by will or inheritance, he may lawfully sell it before taking possession.

Moveables acquired by will or inheritance.

If a person purchase a house or land, and before taking possession give it to any other person than the seller, the gift is universally considered to be lawful; and a sale of it in such circumstances was also lawful in the opinion of Aboo Huneefa and Aboo Yoosuf, though it was rejected by Moohummud.* But they were all agreed that, to let it to hire before possession, whether to the seller or to any other person, was unlawful.

Gift or sale of land or houses before seizin is lawful.

An exercise of ownership over prices before possession and over obligations by accepting substitutes for them, is lawful according to us, except in cases of *surf* and *sulum.* An exercise of ownership over the subject of a *kurz* or loan for consumption, before possession, is not lawful according to *Tahavee*; but the Koodooree says this is an error; and, according to the valid opinion, it is lawful.

Acts of ownership over prices and obligations before possession.

---

* Moohummud insists on the absolute terms of the Prophet's prohibition, while Aboo Huneefa and Aboo Yoosuf maintain that the prohibition was founded on the other reason assigned in the note on page 21.

CHAPTER III.

OF WANT OF CORRESPONDENCE BETWEEN THE PROPOSAL AND ACCEPTANCE.

Acceptance in part.

WHEN a seller has made a proposal of sale with regard to two or three articles, and the purchaser is desirous of accepting it only as to one of them, he cannot do so if there be but one contract;* but where contracts are distinct and several, he may. And the rule is the same as regards the seller, when the proposal proceeds in the first instance from the purchaser. It is, therefore, of importance to determine when there is unity, and when there is severalty of contract. And, first, with regard to unity.—

Unity of contract.

When there is one sale, one purchase, one price in gross, one seller, and one purchaser, there can be but one contract on any construction. So, also, though the price be apportioned to the different parts of the thing sold, yet if the other elements mentioned preserve their unity, as if the seller should say, "I have sold you those ten pieces of cloth, each piece for ten dirhems," there is still but one contract. And in like manner, though there should be two sellers, or two purchasers, still—if the price be stated in gross, by the seller's saying to two persons, "I have sold this to you both for so much," and the purchasers answering, "We have bought this from you for so much,"—there would be but one contract. Again, as to severalty;

Severalty of contract.

if the things above-mentioned be kept separate, as, for

* Arab. *sufkut*, literally the act of *striking hands* in concluding a bargain.

instance, by an apportionment of the price to the parts of the thing sold, and a repetition of the sale or purchase, and there be two sellers and two purchasers, or one of the former or two of the latter, or *vice versa;* in such circumstances there would be separate contracts. So, also, if the price be apportioned, and the sale and purchase repeated, though there should be but one seller and one purchaser, as if the seller were to say to a person, "I have sold you these pieces of cloth; this I have sold you for ten, that I have sold you for five;" or the purchaser should say, "I have purchased from you these pieces of cloth; this I have purchased for ten, and that I have purchased for five,"—here, in like manner, there would be separate contracts by general agreement.

When a purchase may be cleared in part, and when not.

When a person has purchased two or more different things, or only one thing, and paid down a part of the price, intending to take a part of the things sold, he cannot do so if there was only one contract; but he may if there were separate contracts. Thus, when a person purchased from another ten pieces of Jewish cloth, at ten *dirhems* for each piece, and paid down ten *dirhems* as the price of one piece in particular, intending to take it, he was not allowed to do so, because there was but one contract. So, also, if the seller should release the purchaser from the price of one piece of cloth in particular, or should sell him one of them in particular on credit for a month, the purchaser would not be entitled to take possession of the piece so particularized; and even if the purchase were on condition that all the pieces but one should be on credit, the purchaser could not take any of them before paying the amount immediately payable. Further, if the price were a hundred *dirhems,* and ninety *dirhems* being previously due from the seller to the purchaser, it were agreed that they should be set off against the price, still he could not take possession of any of the pieces without paying down the remaining ten.

Clearance by one of two purchasers.

Two persons purchase a slave for a thousand *dirhems,* and one of them then absents himself, but the other is present; he has no title, however, to take possession of the slave until he pay the whole price. If he does so, and takes possession of the slave, he is not to be considered a volunteer in the transaction; and his partner, when he appears, has no right to participation in the slave until payment of his share of the price. If the slave should die in the meantime, he dies as a trust (*amanut*),* the person who took possession of him being entitled to claim a share of the price from the absent co-purchaser. In all the above cases, the rules would be reversed if there had been more than one contract.

---

* That is, the possessor is not liable on account of the loss.

CHAPTER IV.

OF DELIVERY AND POSSESSION.

SECTION I.

Of retaining the thing sold as security for the Price.

THE seller is entitled to keep possession of the thing sold as security for the price, when immediately payable; but if the sale were on credit, he has no right of retention, either before or after the expiration of the term for payment. If the sale be partly on credit and partly for ready money, he may retain the thing sold, as security for so much of the price as is presently payable; and if any part of it, however small, remain due, his right to retain the whole of the thing sold continues unabated. On the other hand, the purchaser cannot be called upon for payment of the price until the production of the thing sold, though it were in another city at the time of sale, and its production be attended with considerable trouble. When the price has been paid, and the thing sold has been delivered, or when it is delivered without payment of the price, or the purchaser takes possession of it with the permission of the seller, either expressed or implied (as, for instance, in his sight without his prevention), the seller cannot resume possession of it for the purpose of his lien. But he is at liberty to do so if possession were taken without his permission.

Seller's right of retention, until payment of the price, or possession with his permission.

The seller's right of retention does not abate by the purchaser's giving a pledge or a surety for the price; but it does abate by the seller's giving up the thing sold to the purchaser, though only by way of loan or deposit. And

When the right abates.

if the sale were originally on credit, but the purchaser should fail to take possession of the thing sold until the expiration of the term for payment, he is still at liberty to do so without payment, and the seller cannot prevent him. If the sale were originally for ready money, but the seller should subsequently agree to a postponement of the price, he loses his right of retention.

By manumission.

If a person purchase a slave, and, before taking possession, manumit him, or make him a *moodubbur,** the seller is not at liberty to retain the slave, even though the purchaser be poor; and the manumission takes effect. Nor is the slave bound to perform emancipatory labour for his value, for the benefit of the seller. If, however, the purchaser should, before possession of the slave, make him a *mookatib,*† or let him to hire, or give him in pledge, the seller may apply to the judge to have these different acts set aside; and if they are not cancelled before payment of the price, the *kitabut* is valid, but the lease and the pledge are void.

When the purchaser has paid or is released from the whole price, the seller's right of retention is at an end.

Seller may resume possession when taken without his permission.

A person purchases a door, and taking possession of it without permission of the seller, he nails it with iron nails, or he purchases a piece of cloth and dyes it, or a piece of land and erects a building or plants trees upon it; the seller may, notwithstanding, resume and retain possession of the subject of sale, and may remove the nails, or take up the plants, if it can be done without injury; but if the door or cloth should happen to perish in the hands of the seller, he would be liable for the value of the nails or the dye. If the subject of sale be a female slave, and the purchaser carnally enjoys her, and she becomes pregnant in consequence, and gives birth to a child, the seller can no longer retain her on account of his lien for the price, though

---

* From *tudbeer*—a gratuitous declaration of freedom to a slave by his master, to take effect at the latter's death.

* From *kitabut*—a contract of emancipation for a ransom entered into by a slave with his master.

he is at liberty to do so if she does not become pregnant, nor give birth to a child.

If a slave should say to his master, "I have bought myself from you for so much," and the master should say, "I have sold you," he cannot retain him for payment of the price; and, in like manner, if a stranger should commission the slave to buy himself from his master on the stranger's account, and the slave should inform his master and make the purchase, the seller cannot retain him on account of the price.

Exception in the case of a slave to seller's right of retention.

SECTION II.

Of Surrender of the thing sold, and what is and is not Possession.

In a sale of goods for money, the purchaser is first called upon to deliver the price; but, in a sale of goods for goods, or price for price, the delivery on both sides should be simultaneous.

Purchaser first called on for payment.

To surrender the thing sold, is to vacate it for the purchaser in such a manner that he may take possession of it without any one restraining him; and to surrender the price, is the like. With regard to all things but money,* it is requisite that the seller should say, "I have vacated between you and the thing sold, take possession of it." And in every case of surrender, a separation of the thing sold from any intermixture with the rights of third parties is implied. In legal sales, vacating is equivalent to actual possession, according to all our doctors; and though there are two reports with regard to unlawful sales, yet, according to the more authentic, vacating is equivalent to possession in them also.

Surrender defined.

Equivalent to possession.

Vacating in the house of the seller is valid, according to Moohummud, though Aboo Yoosuf was of the contrary opinion; and, therefore, when a person sold vinegar in a cask in his own house, and vacated it for the purchaser, who put his seal upon it and then left it in the seller's

Delivery in the seller's house sufficient.

---

* Arab. *ujnas*, plural of *jins*, goods, moveables, any estate not in money.—*Richardson's Dict.*

house, where it subsequently perished, it was held to have perished as the property of the purchaser, according to the opinion of Moohummud, which is approved and adopted. And where articles of capacity or weight are sold in the house of the seller, by measure in the former case, or by weight in the latter, the seller vacating them in the usual manner and giving up the key, this is accounted possession on the part of the purchaser, though he should fail to measure or weigh them for himself.* But giving up the key without the words, "I have vacated," &c., would not be sufficient.

Delivery of a house.

Taking possession of the key of a house is generally seizin of the house itself; and when a person sold a house, delivering the key to the purchaser, who took it but did not go to the house, he was held to be seized. But delivery and possession of the key without the words, "I have vacated between you and the house," would not be seizin. And if the house be out of sight, and the seller should say, "I have delivered it to you," and the purchaser should reply, "I have taken possession," this would not be seizin, unless the house were so near that the purchaser could lock the door. Hence, if a house be sold to a person in another city, and only verbally delivered, the purchaser may refuse to surrender the price.

Delivery must be after sale.

A person says to another, "I have sold you this merchandise and have delivered it to you," and the other replies, "I have accepted;" this is not a sufficient surrender until delivery take place after the sale.

Possession of a slave.

When a person having purchased a male or female slave, says to the slave, "Come or walk with me," and the slave makes a step, this is accounted possession. So also, if he were to send the slave on any necessary occasion.

Purchaser liable in case of loss

A person having purchased a slave in the house of the seller, the seller said to him, "I have vacated for you,"

---

* This alludes to a tradition of the Prophet, who is said to have forbidden the sale of any kind of grain (*tuam*) until it be measured both by the buyer and the seller; but this tradition is explained as not applicable to the case.—*Hamilton's Hedaya*, vol. ii. pp. 482-3.

but the purchaser refused to take possession, and the slave died; his loss was held to fall on the purchaser. So also, if one should buy a piece of cloth, and being directed by the seller to take possession, should neglect to do so until the cloth is usurped by a third party, here, if at the time of direction the purchaser could have taken possession of the cloth by merely stretching his hand to it without standing up, the delivery is valid and complete, but otherwise, not.

if he refuse or neglect to take possession.

In the sale of a house, if there should happen, at the time of delivery to the buyer, to be anything in it belonging to the seller, though of small value, the surrender is not valid until the things be removed. But, if the seller should permit the purchaser to take possession of the house and the things in it, the delivery would be valid; the seller's property left in the house being then in the nature of a deposit with the purchaser. In like manner, if land in which there is seed sown belonging to the seller, be sold and delivered to the purchaser, the delivery is not valid.

Separation from other property of the seller, necessary to the validity of delivery.

If two persons be riding on a beast the property of one of them, who sells it to the other, the purchaser does not become possessed of it: and the rule is the same with regard to a house in which the seller and purchaser are both at the time of sale. Even if the seller were a father residing in his own house, and the purchaser his minor son living with him in family, there could be no seizin on the part of the son until the removal of the father from the house. Hence, if the house should fall to ruin while the father still resides in it, it perishes as his property.* In like manner, if a father should sell to his minor son a quilted waistcoat, or a turban, or a ring, which he is wear-

Also entire divestiture of the seller.

* It appears from this and subsequent cases that the thing sold is at the seller's risk until delivery, contrary to the maxim of the civil law, "*periculum rei venditæ nondum traditæ est emptoris.* The principle of the Moohummudan law has been already adverted to in the note on page 21, and is thus more distinctly stated in the *Kifayah*, vol. iii. p. 183. "When the thing sold perishes before delivery, sale is cancelled, and the thing reverts to its former state as the property of the seller."

ing at the time, there is no possession on the part of the son, until a complete divestiture of the articles by the father. So also, of a beast which the father is riding at the time of sale to his minor son, there is no possession on the part of the latter until the father dismount.

Miscellaneous cases.

If a mare be in a stable of which the door is locked, so that she cannot get out, and if she be sold and vacated in the usual expressions to the purchaser, who then opens the door, whereupon the mare overpowers him and runs away, the purchaser is liable for the price, whether he can catch her or not; but if the door were opened by another person than the purchaser, or by the wind, it is then to be considered whether, if the purchaser had entered the stable, he could have seized her or not; and if he could, the delivery was sufficient, otherwise it was not. If the mare be in the hands of the seller, who is holding her, and says to the purchaser, "Take the mare," and he also lays hold of her, so that she is in both their hands, and if the seller should then say, "I have vacated her to you, and hold her, not to prevent you, but only till you secure her more firmly," and the mare should in such circumstances escape from their hands, the loss would fall on the purchaser. The case would be different if the seller alone had his hand on the mare, for, in such circumstances, if she should escape, though the purchaser could have seized and held her firmly, the loss would fall on the seller.

One of our doctors being asked with regard to the case of a horse feeding in a pasture, and the property of two persons, one of whom sold his share to the other, saying, "Go and take it," but before the purchaser went the horse died, answered, "That the loss should fall upon them both." And a case has occurred in our own times, which has given rise to a difference of opinion. A person purchased a cow feeding in a pasture, and the seller said to him, "Go and take possession of it." Some of our doctors decided that, if the cow were within sight of the eye, so that she could be distinctly pointed out, the delivery was sufficient, and otherwise not. But this decision is erroneous, and it would be more correct to say, that, if the cow were so near to the parties that the purchaser could have taken possession of her if he pleased, the delivery would have been sufficient.

Articles of weight or capacity, when specified, are sufficiently delivered by being weighed or measured in a vessel of the purchaser;

When oil distinctly specified is purchased, and weighed in a bottle furnished by the purchaser for the purpose, and in his presence, he becomes thereupon possessed of it, though the transaction should take place in the shop or house of the seller; and even, it is said—and the opinion is quite correct—though the purchaser were absent at the time of weighing the oil. And the rule is the same with regard to all other commodities estimated by weight or measurement of capacity, when weighed or measured in vessels furnished by the purchaser. But if the oil be not distinctly specified, there is no delivery, or even transfer of property to the purchaser, whether the weighing take place in his presence or not, and he cannot lawfully exercise the rights of ownership over it; but if he should afterwards take actual possession of the oil, his rights as a purchaser duly possessed would take effect, insomuch that if the oil should perish, the loss would be his by general agreement. According to some, however, he could not lawfully proceed to dispose of the oil until he repeat the process of weighing, but this opinion has not been adopted.*

or in one borrowed by him from the seller.

It is stated in the Koodooree, that when a person purchases wheat distinctly specified, and borrows a sack from the seller, telling him to measure the wheat in it, and he does so, then, if the sack also be distinctly specified, the purchaser becomes possessed of the wheat immediately on its being measured by the seller; but if the sack be not specific,—as if the purchaser should say, "Lend me a sack," and the seller should do so, and measure the wheat in it,—then it is only when the measurement takes place in the presence of the purchaser that he becomes possessed; and, according to Moohummud, his presence is equally necessary in both cases.

Case of oil sent by the purchaser's order.

When a person purchases oil, and delivers a bottle to the oilman, saying, "Send the bottle to my house," and

* See *ante* note, page 30.

he does so, and the bottle is broken by the way, then, if the purchaser had said, "Send it by the hand of my servant," and the oilman did so, the loss would fall on the purchaser; but if he had said, "Send it by the hand of your own servant," and the oilman did so, the loss would fall upon the seller, the servant in each case being the representative of his master. If the purchaser should say, "Send to my son," and the seller should hire a person to carry it to the son, this would not amount to possession on the part of the purchaser, and the seller would be liable for the hire. If, however, the purchaser should direct that a person be hired for the purpose, the possession of the person so hired is the possession of the purchaser, if he admit the hiring and delivery to the messenger; and if he deny these facts, his word is to be received.

Case of a cow perishing before delivery.

A person having purchased a cow says to the seller, "Drive her to your house, that I may follow you to your house, and then drive her to my own house," and the cow dies in the hands of the seller, she perishes as his property; and if he should allege an actual surrender or delivery of the cow, the word of the purchaser is to be received with his oath. And even when a person purchased a sick beast in the stable of the seller, saying, "Let it remain here for the night, and if it should die it will die as mine," still, on the beast dying, it was held to have died as the property of the seller, and not as that of the purchaser.

Of a female slave injured in the hands of a middleman.

A person sold a female slave, and placed her with a middleman, to whom the purchaser was to pay her price; she was injured while with the middleman, and the loss was held to be the seller's. And even when the purchaser of a piece of cloth, for which he did not immediately pay the price, said to the seller, "I will not trust you, place the cloth with such a person, and let it remain with him until I pay you the price," and the seller did so, and the cloth perished, still the loss was held to fall on the seller, because the person with whom it was placed held it on his account for payment of the price, and his possession was therefore the same as that of the seller.

If the seller should deliver the thing sold to a person in the family of the purchaser, he does not thereby become possessed of it; so that if the article should perish the sale is cancelled. **Delivery to a person in purchaser's family not sufficient.**

If a part of the price be paid, and the purchaser should say to the seller, "I have left the thing in pledge with you for the remainder," or "I have left it in deposit with you," this is no delivery.

If the purchaser should consume, or destroy, or only blemish the thing sold while in the hands of the seller, that is equivalent to taking possession of it; and if the seller should do so by his desire, the result would be the same. In like manner, where the subject of sale is a slave, and the seller emancipates him, or makes him a *moodubbur*,* or, when a female, declares her to be the mother of a child to him, all these acts when done by the purchaser, or by the seller at his desire, are equivalent to the purchaser taking possession of the slave. **Destruction of, or injury to, the thing sold by the purchaser equivalent to possession.**

If the purchaser direct the seller to take possession for him, and he does so, this is not possession by the purchaser; but if he desire the seller of wheat to grind it, and he does so, or of a slave to order the slave to do something for him, and the order is given and executed, the purchaser becomes possessed in either case. And if the purchaser of a slave desire the seller to make a gift of him to such an one, and it is done with delivery, the gift is lawful, and the purchaser becomes possessed. So, also, if he desire him to let the slave to hire (whether to a particular person or not), and it is done, the tenant becomes possessed for the purchaser in the first place, and then for himself. **Possession by the seller at purchaser's desire not sufficient.**

If the seller be directed by the purchaser to do something to the thing sold that does not induce any injury to it, as to clean or wash it, for hire or without hire, and he does so, this does not amount to possession on the part of the purchaser; but he is liable for the hire, if the work was directed to be done for hire, and if the work be such **Acts done by the seller at the purchaser's desire, when equivalent to possession.**

---

* See explanation, *ante* page 28, note.

as to injure the subject of sale, the purchaser becomes thereupon possessed of it. So, also, if the seller of a slave be hired by the purchaser to instruct him, or to shave his head, or cut his nails or whiskers, that does not amount to possession by the purchaser, unless the slave is injured in the operation; but the purchaser is liable for the hire.

Case of a female slave given in marriage by a purchaser.

If the purchaser of a slave girl should give her in marriage, that, by a favourable construction, does not amount to taking possession of her, until her husband has connubial intercourse with her, which, according to all our doctors, is equivalent to possession by the purchaser; and it has also been said, that if the husband should kiss or touch her, that also should be accounted possession by the purchaser. But it would seem that if the slave die before actual intercourse with her husband, there is no possession on the part of the purchaser, and her loss would fall on the seller; the sale itself being cancelled.

SECTION III.

Of taking Possession without permission of the Seller.

Possession may be resumed by seller when taken without his permission.

If a purchaser take possession of the thing sold without payment of the price or permission of the seller, the latter may require its restitution; but a mere vacating of it by the purchaser is not sufficient to reinstate the seller in possession; on the contrary, actual seizin of it is necessary for that purpose. And if the purchaser should have exercised any act of ownership over it, that admits of being undone, as if he had sold, or pledged, or let it to hire, or bestowed it in alms, the act is liable to cancellation; but if it does not admit of cancellation, as manumission, *tudbeer** or *isteelad*,† the seller cannot insist on his right of restitution.

Exceptions.

Where the price is paid in coin which the seller finds to

---

* See *ante* note, page 28.

† Literally claiming a child, that is declaring its mother an *oom-i-wulud*.—See note, page 17.

Seller may refuse delivery, and in general resume possession when the price is paid in base coin.

be base,* or bad,† or the property of a third party, either in whole or in part, he may refuse to deliver the thing sold. If the purchaser has already taken possession without his consent, he may cancel the possession, and any act of ownership over the thing sold that admits of cancellation. But, if he consented to the purchaser taking possession, then a distinction is to be made between cases where the coin is only base and where it is bad, or absolutely false, as lead or tin, or the property of a third party who seizes it. In the first case, the seller cannot reclaim possession of the thing sold, though he should return the coin; in the other cases, he may insist on restitution from the purchaser himself, but he cannot undo any act by which he may have disposed of the thing sold, whether it admit of cancellation or not.

When the thing sold may be followed in the hands of third parties.

The following case is given by Moohummud in the *Jama:*—A person purchases a slave girl for a thousand *dirhems*, and, without paying the price or having the permission of the seller, takes possession of her and sells her for a hundred *deenars* to another party. Mutual delivery of the slave girl and the *deenars* taking place, the first purchaser then withdraws, and the original seller appears to reclaim possession of the slave from the second purchaser. In these circumstances, if the second purchaser should admit the facts to be as stated by the seller, the latter is entitled to restitution of the slave, and the second sale is cancelled by the restitution. But if the second purchaser should deny the facts, or declare that he does not know whether the statement be true or false, there is no room for litigation between the parties until the reappearance of the first purchaser. If he should appear and acknowledge the facts as alleged, that would be no verification of them against the second purchaser, and if he should deny them, the original seller must be called upon for proof; and if he should prove his case in the presence of the first and

---

* Arab. *zooyoof.* † *Sitook.* The former, I believe to be coin in which the silver preponderates over the alloy, the latter, coin in which it is only equal to, or less than, the alloy.—See *post*, chap. ix. § 1.

second purchaser, the judge is to restore the slave to the original seller and to cancel the second sale, unless the first purchaser pay down the price before the restoration takes place. If that be done, the slave is not to be restored to the original seller; but if the payment be not made till after he has retaken possession of the slave, she is to be delivered up to the first purchaser, and the second has no right over her.

Liability in case of loss. If the slave should die in the hands of the second purchaser, he is liable to the original seller for her value, which, when restored to him, comes into the place of the slave herself: so that if this value should perish in the hands of the original seller, both sales would thereupon be cancelled, and the second purchaser might have recourse to the first purchaser for the price that he paid him, in the same way as if the slave herself had died after her restoration to the hands of the original seller: and if the value should not perish in the hands of the original seller, and the first purchaser should pay down the price, he is entitled to take the value, and the second purchaser has no right over it, any more than he would have had over the slave herself in similar circumstances, his remedy being against the first purchaser for the price that he paid him.

SECTION IV.

Of previous Possessions that may serve for Possession under a Purchase.

General rule. When a sale takes place, and the thing sold is already in the possession of the purchaser, under a right which would make him responsible for its value* in the event of its loss, his possession serves for possession under the purchase, because the latter is a kind of possession which also induces such responsibility. And whenever two possessions are of the same kind, as if both be in the nature

* That is, its own value, as contradistinguished from the value of something else, or a price.

of an *amanut* or trust, or both infer responsibility, they may mutually represent each other; and when they are of different kinds, the responsible possession may represent that which is irresponsible. Hence, if a thing be in the hands of a person by usurpation, or under an unlawful sale, and he should purchase it from the proprietor by a valid contract, the first possession would serve for the second; and if the thing should perish before the purchases goes to his own house, and reaches, or is able to take possession of it, its loss would fall upon him; while, if the thing were in his possession as a loan, or in deposit, or pledge,* he would not become possessed of it as a purchaser, unless it were in his presence at the time of sale, or until he return to it and is in a condition to take possession of it anew; but if the purchaser should do some act with regard to the loan or deposit, which amounts to taking possession of it, and the seller should then desire to retain it as security for the price, he cannot do so; while, if he can take the thing from the house of the custodier before the purchaser, that is the custodier himself, has reached his hand to it, he is at liberty to do so; but if the subject of sale were in the presence of the parties at the time of the contract, the seller would have no right to retain it.

Case of a slave sold in his absence by a father to his minor son.

A person despatches a slave on some necessary occasion, and sells him, while he is away, to his minor son; the sale is lawful; but if the slave should die before his return, he would die as the property of the father; for the possession of the latter is still subsisting, and being that of a trustee, cannot serve for possession under the purchase. If the slave should return, and the father be able to take possession of him, such possession would be sufficient under the purchase, as the father is guardian of his son. But if

* Though these three are joined together in the illustration, it is only of the first two that the possession is a trust; for, of the last, the possession infers responsibility, that is, the pledge is at risk, though not for itself, but for the debt for which it is pledged, and which is extinguished by its loss.

the return were delayed till the son had attained his majority, possession by himself would then be necessary.

Case of repurchase after a dissolution of sale.

And if one should purchase a slave, and after paying down the price and taking possession of him, the parties to the contract should agree to dissolve it, and, subsequently to all this, while the slave is still in the hands of the purchaser, the latter should again purchase him by a second contract, the transaction would be lawful (though a sale to a stranger would be invalid), but the purchaser would not become possessed by the mere act of contract. So that if the slave should die before possession of him were taken afresh by the purchaser, he would die as under the first contract, and the dissolution and second contract would both be void. The reason of this is, that the subject of sale remaining in the hands of the purchaser after the dissolution was at his risk for something else than itself, namely the price, (being in its own nature an *amanut* or trust), and was therefore like a thing pledged; but possession of such a description is not susceptible of becoming possession under a purchase.

Similar case, after dissolution of a barter or exchange of two slaves.

If, again, a person should purchase or exchange a male for a female slave, and the parties, after mutual possession and removal by each to his own house of what he had purchased, should dissolve the sale, and one of them should then repurchase the slave still in his hands, the purchase would not only be lawful, as in the last case, but the purchaser would become possessed under it by the mere act of contract; so that if the slave should die before the purchaser could lay his hand on him anew, he would die as the purchaser's property under the second contract, and the dissolution of the former would not be void; because, in this case, each of the subjects of sale was, after dissolution, at the risk of its possessor for its own value. This supposes that both the slaves were alive at the time of the dissolution; but though it should not take place till one of them (the male, for instance) had died, the dissolution would still be valid. If, however, in such circumstances, the person in whose hands the female slave remains, should, before restitution, repurchase her from her seller (the slave not being in their presence at the time of contract), and she should happen to die after the second contract, but before the purchaser had renewed his possession of her, she would be held to die as under the first purchase, and the dissolution and second purchase would both be void; for the female slave, after the death of the male, was at the risk of the purchaser for something else than her own value, namely, the value of the male, and possession of such a kind cannot be substituted for possession by purchase. And if, while both the slaves were alive after dissolution, each of the parties to the contract should repurchase for money, the slave remaining in his hands unrestored, and both the slaves were then to die simultaneously, or one in succession to the other, the loss of each would fall on the purchasers respectively; because each of the subjects of sale would, in the circumstances, be at risk for its own value: and for the same reason it is, that if one of them were to die after the dissolution, but before repurchase, the holder would be liable for his value.

Similar case, after a purchase for money, subject to option.

When a slave girl is purchased for money, subject to an option of three days in favour of the purchaser, and after mutual possession of the slave and the price, the purchaser cancels the sale under his option, but makes a repurchase while the slave is still in his possession, such purchase is quite lawful (and in the same circumstances a purchase by a stranger from the seller, though before his repossession, would also be lawful); but if the slave should die before the purchaser could put his hand on her, the second purchase would be void, and she would be held to have died as under the first; for a thing sold under an option to the purchaser is, after cancellation of the sale by him, at his risk, not for its own value, but for the price. The case would be different if the option had been reserved to the seller, and all the other circumstances were the same; for the second purchase would then be valid, and if the slave should die, she would be held to die as under it. What has here been said with regard to a reserved or stipulated option, is equally true of cancellations under the other options for inspection, and on account of defect.

General principle with regard to re-seizin after cancellation of sale.

In the last case, it has been stated that a second sale to a stranger after cancellation of the first would be valid, though before repossession by the seller; while in a previous case it has been said, that such a sale would not be lawful after a dissolution of the first by agreement of the parties. The reason for this difference is, that the last case is a cancellation as regards men in general, but the previous case is a cancellation only as regards the parties themselves, being a new contract with respect to the rest of mankind; and it is a general rule that where a cancellation is of the first description, a new sale of a moveable to a stranger, as well as a resale to the purchaser, is lawful without repossession by the seller, the thing sold reverting, as it were, to its former condition by the mere fact of cancellation; but that where the cancellation is of the second description, repossession by the seller is an indispensable condition to the sale of a moveable to a stranger.

SECTION V.

Of intermixtures of things Sold, and Trespasses in regard to them before Possession.

Between the sale and possession by the purchaser, the things sold may happen to be mixed together by the seller, or a trespass or aggression of some kind may be made by him, or a stranger, or the purchaser himself, in regard to the subject of sale, and many cases have occurred, or have been imagined, to explain the relative rights and liabilities of the contracting parties in such circumstances. A few of these are all that it appears necessary to adduce in this place.

Mixture of equal quantities of wheat and barley;

1. A person purchases a *koor* * of wheat and a *koor* of barley, both distinctly specified; but, before he takes possession of them, the seller mixes them together; in such circumstances, according to Moohummud, a *koor* of the mixed product, and a *koor* of the original wheat, are

* A dry Babylonish measure of 7,100 lb.—(*Richardson's Dict.*)

each to be valued, and the price agreed upon for the latter to be divided in proportion to these two values, any loss that may appear in the value of the wheat being deducted from its price, but the barley taken at the price originally agreed upon. And the rule would be the same if a *rutl** of each of the oils of white and yellow jasmine were purchased and mixed together by the seller before delivery. But if a person should sell one *rutl* of oil of jasmine, and a hundred *rutls* of olive oil, and before delivery to the purchaser should mix them together, the sale would be void as to the first, and the purchaser be at liberty to take a hundred *rutls* of the olive oil, that is of the mixture, it being, however, entirely optional with him to do so, though the olive oil cannot be deteriorated by so slight an admixture with the other.

or of the oils of white and yellow jasmine.

Unequal quantities.

2. A person purchases a slave for a thousand *dirhems;* but before he takes possession of him the seller cuts off his hand, the purchaser is at liberty to take the slave at half the price,† or if he please he may abandon him altogether and cancel the sale; and if the seller should slay the slave before possession by the purchaser, the latter would be freed from all obligation on account of the price. If a stranger cut off the slave's hand, the purchaser is at liberty to allow the contract (being liable in that case for the full price), and to pursue the aggressor for half the slave's value; but if he obtain it, and it should exceed half the price agreed upon, he is bound to bestow the excess in charity; and if the purchaser elect to cancel the sale (which he is at liberty to do), the seller may in like manner sue the aggressor for half the slave's value, being equally bound to bestow the excess over half of the price, if there be any, in works of charity.

Case of trespass by the seller before possession by the purchaser.

---

* About 1 ℔.—varies in Egypt, according to Mr. Lane, from 1 ℔. 2 oz. 5⅗ dwt. to about 1 ℔. 2 oz. 8 dwt. Troy; or from 15 oz. 10 dr. 22 1/16 gr. to nearly 15 oz. 13 dr. Avoirdupois.—*Modern Egyptians*, vol. ii. p. 378.

† This is the amount of fine incurred for striking off the hand of a slave.—*Hamilton's Hedaya*, vol. iv. p. 408.

Effect of possession after trespass by the seller.

3. If the seller should cut off the slave's hand, and the purchaser then take possession with or without his permission, and the slave should afterwards die in consequence of the seller's aggression, an abatement of half the price takes place; but the purchaser is liable for the remainder. This effect of possession arises from its interposition between the aggression and its fatal result, by which it would seem that the connection between them is severed. Possession completes the right of the purchaser, and may therefore be considered the act which finally changes the right of property to him from the seller, and any change of property interposed between the aggression and its results would have the same effect.* Thus, if a person were to cut off the hand of a slave, and his master should afterwards sell him, and the slave should die, in consequence of the wound, in the hands of the purchaser, the aggressor would be no further responsible than for cutting off the hand. It may be observed that possession, held or retained by the seller on account of his lien for the price, is not a possession of any use in completing a right of property, and therefore, if interposed between the act of aggression and its fatal result, would not have the effect of disconnecting them. Thus, if the purchaser were the person who cut off the slave's hand, he would by that act become possessed of the whole slave; and though the seller should subsequently insist on retaining the slave in right of his lien for the price, and the slave should die in his hands, yet if the death were in consequence of the wound inflicted by the purchaser, he would be liable for the whole price. He would be so *à fortiori* if there were no refusal on the part of the seller to surrender the slave. And though the slave should die from some other cause, if there were no refusal of surrender by the seller, the purchaser would still remain liable for the full price. But if there were

* This effect of the change of property may perhaps be ascribed to a doubt as to the party who is entitled to claim compensation.—See *Hamilton's Hedaya*, vol. iv. p. 408, and subsequent pages.

such refusal by the seller, the purchaser's liability in that case would be limited to half the price of the slave.

4. A person purchases a slave, and before delivery the slave is murdered; in such circumstances, the purchaser is at liberty, according to Aboo Huneefa, to reject the sale, or to confirm it and sue the slayer for retaliation, while, if he elect to cancel the sale, the seller may sue for retaliation; but, according to Aboo Yoosuf, though the purchaser is at liberty to do so in the event of his adopting the sale, the seller (in case of his rejection) can only claim the value of the slave from the seller; while Moohummud, on a favourable construction of the law, considered that only the value and not retaliation, could be claimed in both cases. Trespass by a third party before seizin.

5. A person purchases two goats, and before delivery one of them butts the other with his horns, and it dies; the purchaser has the option of taking the survivor at a rateable share of the price, or of rejecting the sale altogether. So, also, if he should purchase an ass and barley, and the ass should eat the barley before delivery; for brutes being irresponsible for their actions, the loss in both cases is the same as if occasioned by the act of God. Aggression by one of two purchased animals on the other; But when a person purchases two slaves, and one of them slays the other before delivery, or a slave and provisions, and the slave eats the provisions before delivery, the purchaser must either take the survivor at the full price of the whole, or reject the sale. While, if one of the slaves should die a natural death, the purchaser would be at liberty to take the survivor at a rateable share of the whole price. or one of two slaves.

6. If a person should sell a slave in exchange for bread defined and specified, and before reciprocal delivery the slave should eat the bread, the seller is held to have received the price, being responsible for the act of the slave while in his possession. Case of a slave exchanged for bread; eating it. But if the subjects of sale were an ass and barley, and before reciprocal delivery the ass should eat the barley, the sale is cancelled, and the seller of the ass is not held to have received the price. Of an ass, exchanged for barley; eating it.

SECTION VI.

Of the trouble which is incumbent on the contracting parties in giving delivery of the thing Sold, and Price.

General rule as to the place of delivery.

It is a general principle of the contract of sale, that it requires delivery of the thing sold in the place where it may be at the time of contract, and that it does not require such delivery at the place of contract. This is the doctrine of all our sages. So that if a person should purchase wheat, he being in town at the time, and the wheat in the suburbs, delivery is to take place at the latter.

Wheat sold in the ear must be thrashed by the seller.

If wheat be purchased in the ear, it is incumbent on the seller to extract it, by spreading it on the ground, treading it out, and sifting or winnowing it, and the straw belongs to him. So, if wheat be purchased by measure, it is incumbent on the seller to measure and pour it into the vessel of the purchaser. It may also be observed, that when water is purchased from a water-carrier in a bag, he is in like manner bound to pour it out, regard being had in this case to prevailing usage.

Things of quantity, when sold by conjecture, to be taken up by the purchaser.

All things of quantity, such as dates, grapes, onions, and carrots or parsnips, when sold by conjecture, are to be cut and taken up by the purchaser, who becomes possessed of them as soon as they are vacated by the seller; and when measure or weight is made a condition, these processes are incumbent on the seller. If wheat be sold on board a boat, it is the purchaser's duty to remove it; so, also, if it be sold in a house, the seller being only bound to open the door.

Wages of measurer, weigher, and teller of goods, and weigher and assayer of coin, by whom to be paid.

The wages of the measurer, weigher, or teller of the things sold are to be paid by the seller, when he has sold on a condition of weight or measure. But the wages of the weigher of the price are to be paid by the purchaser, and those of the examiner or assayer also, according to the most approved opinion, and the decisions of modern times;* that is, when the assay is made before possession

* The point is left in doubt by the author of the *Hidayah* (see

by the seller of the price; but if the assay should be made after the seller has taken possession, it must be at his own expense.

When a person purchases a load of wood, the seller is bound by custom to carry it to his house; and with regard to all things sold on the backs of animals, it would seem that if the seller should refuse to take them to the purchaser's abode, he may be compelled to do so. So, also, with regard to wheat when so purchased; but if wheat in a heap be purchased on condition of its being carried to the purchaser's abode, the sale is vitiated.

Things on the backs of animals to be conveyed by the seller.

In the sale of a mansion, if the purchaser should require the seller to write a bill of sale,* and he should refuse, he cannot be compelled to do so. But if the purchaser should prepare a bill of sale at his own expense, and require the seller to execute it† in the presence of two witnesses, he may be ordered to do so, as the purchaser is entitled to have proof of the transaction. It is necessary, however, that the purchaser should bring two witnesses with him, whom the seller may call upon to bear testimony to the sale, that he may not be put to the trouble of going out for that purpose. Should the seller refuse, the matter may be referred to the judge, and on the seller's acknowledging the sale before him, he is to make a record or decree in the matter, and to attest it.

The seller is not required to write a bill of sale, but must execute one prepared by the purchaser.

Translation, vol. ii. p. 378), who gives two reports of Moohummud's opinion, one for the expense of assay falling on the seller, and the other for its falling on the purchaser. The *Kifayah*, vol. iii. p. 28, gives an additional authority for the latter opinion. And in the *Fut. Alum.* it is stated expressly that the *Zahir Rewayut* and *Futwa* are in its favour.

* Arab. *Sukk*, literally, *striking violently;* and hence its application to coining, in the term *Sicca* rupee. It also means the written and signed sentence of a judge, the writer of which is termed the *Sukkak*. The reader is referred to the *Inshae Hurkurn*, translated by Dr. Balfour, p. 163, *et seq.* for several examples, which are all in the form of declarations by the seller, made before a judge, as is still practised among Mussulmans in India, a native *Kazee* being appointed in most villages by Government for this and other purposes.

† Arab. *Ishhad*, literally, *call upon witnesses to attest it.*

Seller not bound to deliver previous title-deed.

In like manner, the seller cannot be called upon to deliver up the previous bill of sale; but he may be required to produce it, that a new bill of sale may be prepared after it as an examplar, to remain as proof with the purchaser, the old bill of sale being left with the seller for the like purpose. And if the seller should refuse to produce the previous bill of sale for such purpose, he may be compelled to do so.

CHAPTER V.

OF WHAT IS INCLUDED IN THE THING SOLD WITHOUT EXPRESS MENTION, AND WHAT IS NOT SO INCLUDED.

SECTION I.

Of what is included in the Sale of a Mansion, or the like.

ACCORDING to Moohummud, if a person should purchase a lodging (*munzil**) above which there is another lodging, the latter is not included in the sale, unless the first were sold with all its rights or advantages, or everything, small and great, belonging to it. But in the sale of a mansion (*dar*) the upper and lower stories are both included, without mention of all its rights, or the like; and in the purchase of an apartment (*beit*) the upper story is not included without positive mention, notwithstanding the general words "all its rights" be added. It is said, however, that these distinctions are founded on the usage of the people of Koofa, and that according to our usage the upper story is included in the sale, whichever of the above terms be employed, for all are used synonymously with *khanuh* in the Persian language, which signifies a house, and is applied to all dwellings, great or small, except the palace of the Sooltan, which is called a *sura*.

---

* Literally, *place of descending or alighting;* and hence applied to an inn or stage for travellers. According to the author of the *Kifayah*, vol. iii. p. 180, it comprehends several apartments (*beit*) with a covered area and kitchen, and is such as a man may reside in with his family. *Dar*, by the same authority, comprehends the two others (*beit* and *munzil*) with an open area, while *beit* is properly a sleeping place, or a single roofed-apartment with a vestibule.

Case of a porch to a house,

A covering or platform projecting over a road, and having one of its sides supported on the wall of a mansion, and the other on the wall of another mansion, or on pillars in the road, is not included, according to Aboo Huneefa, in the sale of the first mansion, unless all its rights be mentioned, and there be an entrance from it to the mansion; but, according to Aboo Yoosuf and Moohummud, the existence of such an entrance, without the general words, is sufficient to include the covering or platform in the sale of the mansion.

and of a way or stream of water in a mansion.

If a lodging, or apartment, or dwelling (*muskin*) in a mansion be sold, a way or stream of water* in the mansion is not included, without special mention, or the addition of the words, "with all its rights† and advantages."‡ Nor is a way included in the purchase of a mansion, without being specially mentioned, or the addition of the words, "with all its rights and advantages," or, "everything, great and small, belonging to it, or entering or issuing out of it."

Different kinds of ways.

Ways are of three kinds: first, a way leading to the public road; second, a way leading to an open street not a thoroughfare; and, third, a private way in a person's property. It is the private way that does not enter into a sale without being mentioned specially, or by virtue of general words, as "rights or advantages." But the other two kinds of way are included in a sale without any such special or general mention. In like manner, a right to a stream of water in private property, or to draw water from a well in private property, is not included in a sale without special mention, or by virtue of general words.

---

* The words in the original may either imply actual property in the way or stream, or only the right of using them. See *Hamilton's Hedaya*, vol. ii. p. 440.

† Arab. *hookook*, plural of *hukk*, which is defined by the author of the *Kifayah* (vol. iii. p. 23) to be something that follows the thing sold, and is necessary to it, and has no object or design except on account of it, as a *shirb*, or *right to water*, and *a way*.

‡ Arab. *moorafik*, which by the same authority are described as among appendages that are of use to the thing sold, like a privy, kitchen, or water-course.

When a way is not included in a sale, and there is no opening on the highway, the purchaser is entitled to cancel the sale, unless he were previously aware of the fact.

If there be no way, sale may be cancelled.

The sale of an upper story, when actually constructed, without the lower, is quite lawful; but if not constructed, the sale is unlawful.* The sale of a lower story is lawful, whether constructed or demolished. The roof of the latter belongs to the owner of it; but the purchaser of the upper has the right of resting upon it, and of erecting his dwelling upon it should it happen to be demolished.

The right to construct an upper story cannot be sold.

The sale of a mansion (*dar*),† without mention of its rights and advantages, or everything, great and small, belonging to it, includes all lodgings and apartments, upper and lower, kitchens, bakehouses, privies, stables, and wells, contained within its four boundaries; but the sale of a lodging or apartment in a mansion does not include any of these things, without express mention. An apartment (*beit*) is a building roofed in with a door; and the sale of it comprehends the walls, roof, and door.

What is comprehended in the sale of a mansion.

A villa (*kureeut*) is like a mansion (*dar*), and if in either of them there be a door, or wood, or bricks, or plaster laid up, these are not included in the sale, though the words "rights and advantages," or even "everything, great or small, in it or belonging to it," be added. And if there had been an old road to the mansion which the proprietor had shut up, making a new one to it, the latter only, and not the former, would be included in a sale of the mansion with all its rights.

Things laid up in a villa or mansion are not included in its sale.

If some specific apartments in a mansion be sold with all their rights or advantages, the seller cannot, without the consent of the purchaser, remove the principal door of the mansion.

---

* Because the right to be above is not property (*mal*); for *mal* is that which can be taken possession of and secured.—*Kifayah*, vol. iii. p. 103.

† From *dowr*, a circuit or circle, and defined by the *Hidayah* to be a place comprehended within an enclosure.—*Translation*, vol. ii. p. 502.

When a garden is included in the sale of a mansion.

A garden,* whether small or great, if within a mansion, is included in the sale of it; but if without the mansion, it is not included, though there should be a door from the mansion to it.

All buildings and fixtures included.

It is a general rule, that all buildings within a mansion, and all things fixed or attached to the buildings, are included in the sale of it, as accessories, without special mention; and that what is not so fixed or attached is not included in the sale, unless it be something that by custom a seller does not usually withhold from a purchaser.† On this principle, locks of the fixed kind are included in the sale of a mansion, and their keys follow them, on a favourable construction; but locks of the hanging kind, as padlocks, are not included (neither are their keys) in the sale of mansions, nor of shops or apartments, though the doors should happen to be locked. Stairs, when fixed, enter into the sale of a mansion or house, but otherwise they do not. A shed or covering erected on the top, and whether made of reeds or tiles, is also included in the sale of a mansion, but not in that of an apartment (*beit*) into which the upper story does not enter, as already mentioned. Ovens, when fixed, are included in the sale of a mansion, but otherwise not. But a millstone turned by a camel is not included, though the mansion were purchased with all its rights and advantages; contrary to the case of a water-wheel on an estate or villa, which is included in the purchase when sold with all rights. In like manner, all other wheels on an estate are included, except such as are worked by oxen. Steps or ladders made of wood, when fixed in the walls of a

---

* *Bostan*, a Persian word, *a garden for flowers or herbs.—Richardson's Dictionary.* In law it is defined to be "land enclosed with a wall, and containing different kinds of palms, grape vines, and other trees, with cultivated ground interspersed."—*Futawa Alumgeeree*, vol. ii. p. 339.

† The area or ground is properly to be considered the principal or original part of a mansion, and the buildings and fixtures to them are included in the sale of it only as accessories to the area, or ground to which they are permanently attached.—*Kifayah*, vol. iii. p. 21.

mansion, are included in the sale, but not so when they are moveable; and the rule is the same with regard to chains or lamps fixed with nails to the roof.

No part of price opposed to an accessory.

It is of importance to observe, that whenever a thing is included in a sale merely as an accessory, no part of the price is held to be opposed to it. Hence it has been said, that if the buildings of a mansion were to fall down before delivery, there would be no abatement from the price.

Doubt as to the ground on which a wall is erected being included in its sale.

When a person purchases a wall, the ground beneath it is included in the sale, according to some authorities, without being mentioned; but, according to others, this was only the opinion of Moohummud and Husn, while Aboo Yoosuf considered that it was not included.

When things found in the walls of a house belong to the seller, and when to the purchaser.

When a person purchases a house or shop, and on the walls falling down finds among them tin, or lead, or timbers, these belong to the purchaser if they formed part of the buildings, as, for instance, the beams or piles under the house, on which its walls may have been erected; but if they were laid up or deposited there, they remain the property of the seller.*

Miscellaneous cases.

In the sale of a shop, a shed or covering, such as is usual in bazaars, is included if advantages be mentioned, but otherwise not; and in the sale of a blacksmith's shop, his forge is included without any mention of advantages; but the forge is not included in the sale of a silversmith's shop though advantages should be mentioned; the reason of the difference being that the forge in the former case is fixed, and not so in the latter; and a blacksmith's bellows is not included in the sale of his shop. Nor are the pots and utensils of dyers, fullers, washermen, nor the jars of an oil-merchant, included in such sales, whether the shop be mentioned absolutely, or with its rights and advantages. So, also, with regard, in general, to the implements of a bath, though the pots or kettles for heating water are included in the sale without being specially

* With regard to mines and treasure found in the ground, see the following section.

mentioned, probably because they are built in, or fixed to the walls.

Section II.

Of what is included in a Sale of Lands and Orchards.†*

General rule.

In a sale of land, or an orchard, whatever is erected or planted on the soil for permanence, such as buildings, and trees or saplings, is included without special mention, or the addition of general words, such as "rights and advantages," or, "everything, small and great, belonging to it;" and there is no difference between fruit and other trees, or between great and small trees. But there seems to be some doubt with regard to firewood. According to one authority, trees of that description are on the same footing with other trees; while, according to another, the learned are of opinion that trees planted expressly to be cut down, such as trees for firewood, are not included, without special mention, in a sale of land. And sticks already dry, and in a condition to be cut, are not included, as they are in the nature of firewood laid up or stored.

Mines and minerals pass to the purchaser,

Mines and minerals are included in a sale of land. The products of mines are said to be of three kinds: first, such as are ductile in the fire, as gold, silver, lead, tin, copper; second, such as are fluid in their own nature, as naphtha or bitumen; and, third, such as fall under neither description, as quicklime, gypsum or plaster, and precious stones;‡ but all pass alike to the purchaser as constituent parts of the soil.§

---

* Arab. *arazee*, plural of *urz*, the earth, ground, soil (Richardson), and seems applicable to any land.

† *Kooroom*, plural of *kurm*. *Terra lapidibus purgata* (Freytag). In law it is defined to be "land inclosed with a wall, and containing different kinds of palms, grape vines, and other trees, so closely planted that the land between them cannot be sown or cultivated."—*Futawa Alumgeeree*, vol. ii. p. 339.

‡ *Futawa Alumgeeree*, vol. i. p. 259.

§ *Hamilton's Hedaya*, vol. i. p. 43; and see *Kifayah*, vol. i. p. 523.

Things laid up or stored on land, as gathered fruits, reaped harvests, firewood, or bricks, are not included in the sale of it, except by express condition; and the same rule is applicable to things deposited under the surface, such as concealed treasures, which do not pass to the purchaser. Growing crops and fruits are, by a favourable construction of law, excluded from a sale of land, unless expressly stipulated for, though the land should be sold "with all its rights and advantages," or "with everything, great or small, in it or of it, of its rights and advantages." But if the last part of the phrase were omitted, and the expression stood, "together with everything, great or small, in it or of it," all growing crops, such as corn, pot-herbs, and odoriferous plants, would be included in the sale.*

but not things laid up, or concealed treasures,

or growing crops or fruits.

Tombs within a piece of land are not included in the sale of it; but the sale is valid with regard to all of the land besides. And a place or station for casting the harvest is not considered to be among the rights and advantages of land, and therefore does not enter into a sale of it, together with all its rights and advantages.

Nor tombs.

In a sale of land, or an orchard, "with its rights and advantages," things are included which would not be included without the addition of these words, as a *shirb* or right to water for irrigation, or a water-course, or a private way.

Things comprehended in general words.

The leaves and flowers of the mulberry, myrtle, saffron, and rose trees, are considered in the same light as fruits, and the trees themselves like palm or other trees. Cotton is also like fruit, and does not enter into a sale of land, without special mention; and it has been said that the plant likewise is not included, and the opinion appears to be correct.

Leaves and flowers of certain trees not included.

Tamarask trees, and the trunks or stems of the sallow and willow, are included in a sale of land, but not the

Rule as to trees.

---

* There seems to be no limit to the meaning of the expression, "everything, great and small, in it and of it," when not restricted by the others.—*Inayah*, vol. iii. p. 22.

osiers* of the latter, whether they have arrived at a time for cutting or not. Deciduous plants, and generally everything which is not permanent (though approaching to it, as reeds, firewood, and dry grass), do not enter into a sale of land; while everything, on the other hand, that has a stem or trunk that is not cut down till it becomes a tree is included, without special mention, in the sale of the land on which it may be growing.

As to seed.

If a man should sow his land, and then sell it before the seed has sprung up, the seed is not included in the sale, because it is not an appendage of the land until it vegetates. And if it should have actually sprung up, but is yet of no separate value, it is included in the sale, according to the most authentic opinion. The proper distinction seems to be, that if the seed have rotted in the ground at the time of sale, it belongs to the purchaser, but otherwise it remains the property of the seller; and if the purchaser should water the seed that had not rotted in the ground at the time of his purchase, he is a mere volunteer, and the seed still remains the property of the seller.

Rule as to fruit, when expressly included.

When a person sells land in which there are palm and other trees, these are included in the sale, though not specified as already mentioned; and if the trees be in fruit at the time of the contract, and it be expressly stipulated that the fruit shall be comprised in the purchase, a part of the price is opposed to the fruit. Hence, if the land, the trees, and the fruit, were each of the value of five hundred, and the fruit should perish, either by an intervention of Providence † or an act of the seller, before delivery to the purchaser, the price would be subject to an abatement of one-third, and the purchaser have the option of taking the land and the trees at the remaining two-thirds of the price, or rejecting the contract. It is to be observed, that when the loss is occasioned by the act of the seller,

* *Kuwaim*, plural of *kaim*, literally, *standers* or *standing*.

† Arab. *afut sumaviyyut*, literally, *heavenly calamity*. The piety of a Moohummudan does not allow him, even in common parlance, to ascribe anything to accident.

as by his eating the fruit, its value is to be taken as it stood at the time it was eaten by him. If the fruit were not in existence at the time of the sale, but should appear before delivery to the purchaser, it is his property, and is considered an accession to both land and trees by Aboo Huneefa and Moohummud, but only to the trees by Aboo Yoosuf. To explain this difference of opinion, let us suppose that the values of the land, trees, and fruit, are each five hundred, and that the seller eats the fruit before delivery of the land; he must abate a third of the price according to both Aboo Huneefa and Moohummud, the purchaser taking the land and trees at the remaining two-thirds (without the alternative of rejecting the bargain according to Aboo Huneefa, but with such alternative according to Moohummud), while in the opinion of Aboo Yoosuf, only a fourth of the price is to be deducted, and the purchaser has the option of taking land and trees at the remaining three-fourths, or rejecting the bargain altogether. If the loss of the fruit were not occasioned by an act of the seller, but by an intervention of Providence, there would be no abatement from the price, nor would the purchaser have the option of rejecting the contract, according to all their opinions.

Rule as to palm trees without a right of water.

When a person has purchased land with palm trees which have no right of water, and he was not aware of the fact, he has the option of rescinding the contract.

Sale of trees. Rule as to their fruit.

If a person sell palm or other trees on which there is fruit at any stage of growth, whether it have any value or not, the fruit belongs to the seller, unless its inclusion in the purchase had been expressly stipulated for.*

May be sold with a condition for their removal.

If a person should purchase a tree on condition of extracting it, the transaction is lawful, and he may take it up by the roots. So, also, if he should purchase the tree on condition of cutting it down, the sale is lawful according to the better and more valid opinions, and he may cut

* For this there is also the authority of a saying of the Prophet. See *Mishcat-ul-Musabih*, translated by Captain White, vol. ii. p. 24.

it level with the surface of the earth, but he is not entitled to dig up its roots, unless by express condition.

Different ways in which trees may be purchased.

It is only in three ways that a tree can be purchased: first, it may be purchased for extraction, and without the ground on which it stands. In this case, the purchaser may be required to extract it, and he is entitled to do so with the roots, which are included in the sale, but he is not at liberty to dig the earth to the extreme termination of the roots, and only so far as is usual and customary in such cases. If it be expressly stipulated that the tree is to be cut level with the surface of the earth, or to cut it in any other way would be injurious to the seller, as, for instance, by its proximity to a wall or the like, the purchaser is obliged to cut it in that manner. When the tree has been cut level with the earth, or eradicated, and anything thereafter springs from its roots, it is the property of the seller; but if cut some way up the stem, the aftershoot belongs to the purchaser. Secondly, a tree may be purchased with the ground on which it stands, and in this case the purchaser cannot be called upon to remove it; and if he should do so, he is entitled to plant another in its site. Or, thirdly, a tree may be purchased unconditionally. In this case, the land on which it stands is not included in the sale according to Aboo Yoosuf, but according to Moohummud the land is included, and his opinion is approved and adopted. All are agreed that if a tree be purchased for cutting, the ground on which it stands is not included in the sale; but that if purchased to remain, the ground is included.

Rule as to the ground on which a tree stands when purchased with it.

It is to be observed, that whenever the ground under a tree is included in the sale of it, no more than corresponds to the size of the tree at the time of contract is included; that any subsequent increase in size may be restrained by the owner of the soil; and that land, as far as the roots and branches may extend, is by no means to be understood as comprehended in the sale.

Growing trees sold by conjecture as to

If a person should ask another to sell him the trees on his ground, and the parties concur in the appointment of intelligent persons to estimate the number of loads, and the persons appointed agree in estimating the number of loads to be twenty-five, whereupon the purchase is concluded for a known price; but on cutting the trees they are found to contain more than twenty-five loads, and the seller wishes to retain the excess from the purchaser, he is not at liberty to do so, but must allow him to take the whole.

the quantity of timber.

When a village is sold without specifying its boundaries, the houses and buildings are included without the cultivated land belonging to it; and if there should happen to be another village contiguous to it, and also the property of the seller, and this village be described as one of the boundaries of the village that is sold, then the lands of the village that is not sold are included in the lands of the sold village on the side to which they are contiguous; but if the boundary of the sold village were described to be the lands of the contiguous village, then the latter would not be included in the sale of the former.

Sale of a village.

SECTION III.

Of what is included in the Sale of Moveables.

When a person sells a slave, whether male or female, he is liable to the purchaser for so much clothes as are necessary to cover the loins of the slave. The clothes of a male or female slave are by usage included in a sale of the slave, without stipulation, unless the clothes are rich and expensive; but these, for want of usage, are not included, except by express stipulation, since usage is confined to the ordinary or working-apparel of the slave. The seller, however, is not restricted to the identical clothes which the slave may happen to have on at the time of the sale. Usage requires only clothes of the same description. Hence the clothes, not being specific, are not opposed to any part of the price; and if a third party should establish a right to part of them, the purchaser has no recourse on that account against the seller;

In the sale of a slave, his clothes are included.

nor, in like manner, when they appear to be blemished, can he insist on returning them. So also, on the other hand, if the slave should be returned for a defect, and his clothes have intermediately perished, the purchaser is entitled to a return of the whole price; but if the clothes are extant, they must be returned with the slave.

Jewels not included; The jewels which a female slave may have on are not included in her sale; but if delivered to her by the seller they are hers, and if he see them on her and make no demand of them, his silence is accounted acquiescence.

nor the property belonging to a slave. If a slave be sold who is possessed of some property, it is not included in the sale unless mentioned, but belongs to his master the seller; and if the slave be sold together with his property, and the property is not explained, the sale is invalid. The sale is in like manner invalid though the property be explained, if it consist in whole or in part of debts due to the slave.* If the property consist of specific things, not money, the sale is lawful; but if the property be money, and the price of the slave and his property be of the same kind,—as, for instance, if both be *dirhems,*—then it is only when the price exceeds the property that the sale is lawful; for if the price be less than the property, or only equal to it, the sale is unlawful. When the price of the slave and his property are of different kinds, as if one be *dirhems* and the other *deenars,* and possession of both is taken at the meeting of the parties, or possession is taken only of the slave's property, and part of the price is told down, the sale is lawful; but if the parties separate before such possession, the contract is void as to the slave's property.†

Bridle of a horse and halter of a camel included. The bridle of a horse, and the halter in the nose-ring of a camel, are included in the sale of these animals, because they cannot be held or restrained without them;

---

* Because the sale of debts is unlawful. See *ante*, page 5.

† For the reasons of these distinctions, the reader is referred to chapter ix. section 6, on Reba or Usury.

contrary to the case of an ass, but the rope tied to his neck is by usage included in the sale of the latter, unless a particular usage should happen to be against it.

The pack-saddle of an ass, and the saddle-cloth, are also, according to the most authentic opinions, included in his sale, whether the ass be saddled at the time of the contract or not. So, also, the panniers are included without being specially mentioned. **So also the pack-saddle, &c., of an ass.**

There is no distinct report in any of the books with regard to the saddle which may be on a horse at the time of his sale; but it would seem more proper that the saddle should not be included in the sale without special mention, unless the price be high, and the horse be such a one as is not usually sold without a saddle. **Doubt as to the saddle of a horse.**

The bridle and housings of cattle, or the rope tied to the horn of a cow, are not included in the sale of these animals, unless by some special usage or express stipulation. **Bridle and housings of cattle.**

A camel's colt, and the foal of a mare, or an ass, and calves, are included in the sale of their mothers, when taken with them to the place of sale, unless there be a usage to the contrary. **Young of animals.**

Our doctors are agreed that when a person has purchased a fish, and finds a pearl in its belly, if the pearl be contained in a shell it is the property of the purchaser; but if not in a shell, and the seller had caught the fish, the pearl must be returned to him, with whom it is to remain as a trove, and to be advertised, and bestowed in charity, in the manner prescribed for such things. **A pearl in the stomach of a fish.** As a general rule, everything not food for fishes, and found in the stomach of a fish, belongs to the seller, and what is food for fishes belongs to the purchaser. **General rule as to things so found,** Hence, if a fish be sold, and another fish be found in its stomach, the latter also is the property of the purchaser; and if ambergris be found in it, it is in like manner his property. If shell-fish be purchased, to eat the meat within them, and pearls be found in some of them within the meat, they belong to the purchaser.

and in the crops of birds.

The rule is the same with regard to a dunghill-fowl, and birds in general: anything found in their crops or maws which is their proper food belongs to the purchaser; but if the thing found be not the food of the bird, it belongs to the seller. Hence a pearl found in the crop of a dunghill fowl is his property.

CHAPTER VI.

OF OPTION BY STIPULATION.*

SECTION I.

Of valid and invalid options.

SALE is valid with a stipulation for an option to both or either of the contracting parties, or to a person who is a stranger to the contract. An option, is a power to cancel, not to confirm the contract. Hence, if the option be extinguished by expiration of its period, the contract is completed.

Option, what.

Some options are invalid by general agreement, as if the purchaser should say, "I have purchased on condition of an option," or "on condition that I shall have an option for days," or, "for ever." Others, again, are valid by general agreement, as if he should say, "on condition of an option for three days," or, "less than three days;" while, with regard to others, opinions differ, as if one should say, "on condition of an option for one or two months." Such an option would be lawful according to Aboo Yoosuf and Moohummud, but invalid according to Aboo Huneefa, the latter considering three days to be the extreme limit for options by stipulation, while the former held an option for a longer period to be equally

Option valid, if not stipulated for longer than for three days.

* Arab. *Khiyar-oos-shurt*. This option is founded upon a recommendation of the Prophet to *Haban*, who was liable to be imposed upon in his bargains.—*Hamilton's Hedaya*, vol. ii. p. 380. The words of the saying, as given in the original, are, "Haban, when you buy or sell, say, *No deceit, and I must have an option for three days.*"

lawful, provided a known period be mentioned. The Imam's opinion, however, is the more correct.* Yet if a person should stipulate for an option longer than three days, or even for ever, which would vitiate the contract, but should afterwards allow or confirm it within three days, we hold that in such case the contract is valid. Upon this point opinions differ as to the view taken by Aboo Huneefa of the contract in its inception. Some say that he considered the contract to be originally unlawful, but to be rendered valid by the extinction of the option before the fourth day; and this is the opinion of the people of Irak. While others maintain that he considered its legality to be in suspense, and that the contract did not become invalid until the expiration of some part of the fourth day. This is the opinion of the people of Khoorassan, and of the Imam Surukhsee, and others of the learned men of Mawara'oon Nuhr, and appears to be the most proper, though the Zahir Rewayut is said to accord with the former opinion. Where the period of option is undefined, but the person in whose favour it has been reserved renders it void after three days, Aboo Huneefa was of opinion that the contract remained invalid, though his disciples considered that it became lawful.

This option may be established in an unlawful sale.

An option by stipulation may be established in an unlawful as well as a lawful contract of sale. Thus, if a person should sell a slave for a thousand *dirhems* and a *rutl* of wine, with the reservation of an option to himself, and the purchaser should take possession of the slave, with the seller's permission, and then manumit him, the

---

* The Hidayah leaves this important point in doubt. Though in the translation (vol. ii. p. 380), the words occur, "but it must not be extended beyond that period," there is nothing to correspond with them in the printed edition of the original. According to Aboo Huneefa, the reservation of an option is repugnant to the nature of the contract, and can be justified only by the Prophet's permission, which he thinks must be strictly construed. The disciples, however, support it on the ground of expediency, as affording time for reconsideration, and another saying, reported by Ibn Omar, which, however, has been differently construed.

manumission is not lawful, neither immediately nor suspensively on the consent of the seller.*

Miscellaneous cases.

When a person sells on condition that if the price be not paid in three days there shall be no sale between the parties, the sale and the condition are both lawful; and if the subject of contract be a slave, and the purchaser should manumit him within the three days before payment of the price, the manumission is valid, because the transaction is in fact a sale with the condition of an option to the purchaser. If the three days should expire without payment of the price, the sale is vitiated but not cancelled; so that if the slave had been delivered, and the purchaser should manumit him after the expiration of the three days, the manumission would be valid, and the purchaser liable for his value; but if the slave were still in the hands of the seller, manumission by the purchaser would not be valid. When, on the other hand, a slave is sold, and the price paid down, but on condition that if repaid within three days there shall be no sale between the parties, the transaction is also lawful, and treated in the same manner as a sale with a condition of option to the seller; so that if the purchaser take possession of the slave, he is responsible for the slave's value in the event of loss, and manumission by him is not lawful; but if the seller manumit, the slave becomes free.

Option lawful, though given after a sale.

An option granted after a sale is equally lawful as if stipulated for at the time of sale. So that if the purchaser should say to the seller, or the seller to the purchaser, after completion of the sale, "I have given you an option for three days," or the like, the option is valid, and as effectual as if stipulated for at the time of contract; and if, after a sale and possession by the purchaser, some days should elapse, and the seller should then say to him, "You have an option," the option would be valid and in

* Because the seller's option prevents the right of property from shifting from him (as will be seen in the next section); and this effect is not impaired by the illegality attaching to the sale by reason of part of the consideration (the wine) being unlawful.

effect while the meeting lasted, the words of the seller being equivalent to the expression, "You have an *ikalut*," or power to dissolve the sale; and if in such circumstances the seller should say, "You have an option for three days," the option would be good for that period.

Abatement of part of the stipulated period.

If a person having stipulated for an option of three days should afterwards abate a day or two days, the abatement is good, and the case becomes the same as if the stipulation had originally been for the shorter period.

Sale of a thing with an option, and liberty to use it intermediately.

A person sells a slave on condition that he is to have an option for three days, and liberty to employ the slave; the sale is valid; and if he should employ the slave, his option is not rendered void. The case would be different if the subject of sale were a vine, and the seller should stipulate for an option of three days, and liberty to eat of its fruit; for such a sale would not be lawful.

Alternative option to the seller and another party.

* If a person should purchase a slave, stipulating for an option to another for three days, in these terms—"that whichever of them should confirm or cancel the sale, it would be confirmed or cancelled accordingly," the sale would be valid, according to our three doctors, on a favourable construction. If one of the parties should confirm, and the other cancel the sale, and it be known which of them acted first, his act would be preferred; but if they should act together, preference would be given to the cancellation.

Sale by an agent under instructions to reserve an option.

A person instructs another to sell his slave, and stipulate for an option to the principal, and he sells absolutely without any option, or with the reservation of one to himself; the sale is suspended. And if the agent should, in obedience to his instructions, reserve an option to the principal, that would be an option to both, and cancellation or confirmation by either would be valid; except that if the agent should confirm, though his own option would be extinguished, that of his principal would remain. So, also, if the instructions were to sell absolutely, or with the con-

* The remaining paragraphs of this section have been taken from chapter vi. section 5, of the original, p. 71.

dition of an option in his own favour, and he should sell, reserving an option to his principal or to a stranger, the option would be good as to himself also, because the stipulation for an option to any other than the contractor, includes in it an option to himself. Further, and in like manner, if the instruction were to buy, and stipulate for an option to himself the agent, and he should buy and stipulate for an option to himself, or to the principal, or to a stranger, in any of the cases the purchase would be lawful as against the principal. But if the instruction were to stipulate for an option to the principal, and the agent should neglect to do so, or should stipulate for an option to himself, the contract would not be lawful as against the principal, but would be binding on the agent himself. And if one should instruct another to purchase a slave for him, and stipulate for an option to himself the principal, and the agent should exactly follow his instructions, so that the contract would be lawful as against the principal, and the agent should then approve the sale, his own option would be at an end, but that of the principal would remain; and if the latter approved of the sale, the slave would become his property, but if he rejected it, the slave would belong to the agent; so that if after that the slave should perish in his hands, he would perish as his property; but if the agent had not approved the sale in the first instance, and the principal should say to him, "Restore the slave, I have no further occasion for him," and the slave should after that perish in the hands of the agent, he would perish as the property of the principal.

Section II.

Effect of an option by stipulation on the right of Property.

When an option is reserved to the seller, the right of property in the thing sold does not pass from him, but such right in the price passes from the purchaser. Upon these points our doctors are agreed. But does the price vest in the seller? According to Aboo Huneefa it does not, but in the opinion of both the disciples it does vest

Effect of option, when the seller's;

in the seller. If an option be reserved to both the contracting parties, the legal effect of sale, that is the reciprocal vestiture of the thing sold and the price, is suspended. When the option is reserved to the purchaser, the right of property in the price does not pass out of him, but the thing sold passes from the seller, with the same difference of opinion between the master and his disciples as to its vesting in the purchaser. Upon this original difference of opinion are founded differences in many other cases, a few of which may be adduced in this place for their bearing on other points of law, which they may serve in some degree to illustrate.

when the purchaser's.

Differences between Aboo Huneefa and his two disciples.

1. When a person purchases his own wife on condition that he shall have an option for three days, the marriage is not vitiated according to Aboo Huneefa, but it is vitiated in the opinion of his disciples;* and carnal intercourse with her during the period of option does not preclude the purchaser from returning her in exercise of his right of option, unless she were a virgin, or be injured by the intercourse, according to Aboo Huneefa, while in the opinion of the disciples it would have that effect whether she were a virgin or not. It is to be observed, that if the woman were not the purchaser's wife, carnal intercourse with her would, in all their opinions, extinguish the option, whether she were a virgin or not.

2. If the purchased woman should bear a child during the period of option, in consequence of previous intercourse with the purchaser by virtue of marriage, she would not become his *oom-i-wulud* according to Aboo Huneefa, but would, in the opinion of his disciples. This difference supposes her to be still in the possession of the seller; for if the purchaser had taken possession of her, and she should in such circumstances bring forth a child within the three days, the option would fall to the ground,

---

* Marriage is cancelled by a supervening right of property, that is, by either of the parties becoming wholly or in part the property of the other.—*Fut. Alum.* vol. i. p. 397. See also *Hamilton's Hedaya*, vol. i. p. 172.

and the right of property in her become vested in the purchaser, according to all their opinions, by reason of the blemish sustained by childbirth.

3. When a person purchases, with an option of three days, a female slave who had previously borne him a child, she does not become his *oom-i-wulud,* by the mere fact of the purchase according to Aboo Huneefa, but in the opinion of his disciples she immediately becomes his *oom-i-wulud,* the option is extinguished and the sale absolute, and the purchaser liable for the price.

4. In like manner, if the purchaser were the near relation of the slave, he would not be immediately free on the mere contract according to Aboo Huneefa, but would be so in the opinion of the two disciples.*

5. If a person should purchase a female slave with the condition of an option, take her into his possession, and her courses should occur during the period of option, that would not suffice for her purification (according to Aboo Huneefa) if he should confirm the sale; and in his opinion purification would not be necessary if the sale were cancelled on her return to the seller; while according to the two disciples the purification would be sufficient in the first case, and necessary in the other, if the cancellation and return take place after possession by the purchaser; but if they should take place before such possession, purification would not be required. If the option were to the seller, and he should cancel the sale, purification would not be incumbent upon him; and if he should confirm the sale, purification would be incumbent on the purchaser after the confirmation and possession, by waiting for a fresh occurrence of the courses. Upon these points there is no difference of opinion.†

It would seem that in the case of a purchase or sale with a stipulation for an option, the parties cannot be

---

* If a person become possessed of a slave, who is his relation within the prohibited degrees, such slave by that act acquires his freedom."—*Hamilton's Hedaya*, vol. i. p. 432.

† See *Hamilton's Hedaya*, vol. iv. p. 103, section *Istibra.*

called on to make a reciprocal delivery of the price and the thing sold, till expiration of the period.

This option prevents completion of bargain.

According to our doctors, the option by stipulation prevents the completion of a bargain. Hence, if the subject of sale be one or several articles, the party to whom the option has been reserved, whether seller or purchaser, cannot confirm the sale as to part only, whether the thing sold were delivered or not, for that would be a splitting of the bargain before completion, which is not lawful, though after completion it would be lawful.*

SECTION III.

Of confirmation and cancellation of a Sale when subject to an option by stipulation.

Sale may be confirmed within the period of option.

The person for whom an option is stipulated, whether the seller, purchaser, or a stranger, may, according to all our lawyers, confirm or cancel the sale at any time within the period of option, and he may confirm it even without the knowledge of the other party to the contract.

Confirmation by the seller in three ways.

When the seller has the option, confirmation by him is in one of three ways; first, by express words within the period of option, as, "I have allowed the sale," or, "am content with it," or, "have extinguished my option;" secondly, by the death of the seller within the period of option;† and, thirdly, by mere expiration of the period without cancellation or confirmation. And it matters not how the exercise of the option may be prevented, as, for instance, by the party entitled to it becoming mad, or fainting, or falling asleep, or getting drunk during the period.

Effect of his dealing with the price.

When the price is of such a nature as to admit of being particularised by specification, and the seller takes possession, and makes use of it by gift or sale, that amounts

---

* See *ante*, page 24.

† From which it appears that this option does not descend to heirs. See also *Hamilton's Hedaya*, vol. ii. p. 389.

to an approval of the original contract on his part; but if the price be of a nature that does not admit of such specification (as *dirhems*, for instance), his using it after taking possession, whether in a transaction with the purchaser himself or a third party, does not amount to an approval of the sale; while his using it before taking possession would have that effect if the transaction were with the purchaser, and apparently also if it were with a third party. A person sells a slave, with an option for three days, for a price on the responsibility of the purchaser, and during the period of option makes a gift to him of the price, or releases him from it, or buys something else from him in exchange for it; the purchase, release, and gift, are each valid, and the option is extinguished. So, also, if he buy something from a third party in exchange for the price, the option is extinguished, though the latter sale is not valid.* But if the price were in money, and the purchaser should pay it, and the seller take possession and expend it within three days, his option would not be extinguished.

Cancellation by the seller by word;

Cancellation by the seller, when he has the option, may be either by word or deed; by word, as if he should say, "I have cancelled the sale;" but to the validity of this mode of cancellation the presence of the purchaser is necessary, according to Aboo Huneefa and Moohummud (from whom Aboo Yoosuf differed in this respect), unless the cancellation be with consent, or by decree of the judge. By presence, nothing more than knowledge is intended; for if the purchaser were absent at the time of cancellation, but should receive intelligence of it before the expiration of the period of option, the cancellation would be valid. And a cancellation in his absence may be recalled, and the sale confirmed, if the intelligence of the cancellation had not reached him. Should he not receive information of a cancellation till after the expiration of the period of option, the sale would be complete by such expiration.

---

* See *ante*, page 6.

By deed. Cancellation by deed is when the seller exercises during the period of option any right of ownership over the thing sold, as if he should manumit a slave, or make him a *moodubbur* or *mookatib*. So, also, if he sell the thing sold to another party, or make a gift or pledge with delivery of it. Gift or pledge without delivery would not be a cancellation of the sale. But a lease, though unaccompanied by delivery, would, according to most of our lawyers, have that effect.

Purchaser's lien for the price, on cancellation by the seller. A person sells land on condition of an option for three days, and mutual possession is taken of it and the price; he then cancels the sale before the expiration of the period of option. In such circumstances, the land, having been on the purchaser's responsibility for its value, remains as a security to him for the price, and he may retain possession of it till that is repaid. But if the seller should permit the purchaser to cultivate the land, and the purchaser should avail himself of the permission, the land would then become an *amanut*, or trust, in his hands, which the seller might resume at pleasure before payment of any part of the price that might still remain due, the purchaser having no longer any lien.

Effect of loss of the thing sold. When the thing sold perishes before delivery the sale is void, whether the option were to the seller or purchaser, or to both of them.* If it perish after delivery, and the option were to the seller, the sale is in like manner null, and the purchaser is liable for the value of the thing sold, or for its like if it happen to be of the class of similars; but if the option were to the purchaser the option is extinguished, and the sale obligatory, the purchaser being liable for the price.

Of its destruction by a stranger. Destruction by a stranger of the thing sold when the seller has an option does not cancel the sale, and the option remains, whether the thing sold were in the hands of the seller or the purchaser. If the seller please, he may cancel the sale and pursue the aggressor on his responsibility; and in like manner, if the destruction were by

* See *ante*, note, page 31.

the purchaser, the seller may cancel the sale and sue him for the loss, or confirm it, and proceed against him for the price.

If the thing sold sustain damage in the hands of the seller, either by an act of Providence or its own act, the sale is not cancelled, and the seller's option remains; the purchaser, however, is at liberty to abandon the sale on account of the supervenient change in the thing sold before delivery, though he may take it if he please at the full price. If the damage were induced by the act of the seller, the sale is rendered void; if by the act of a stranger, the sale and option remain good, and the seller may cancel the sale and proceed against the aggressor for compensation, or confirm it and have recourse to the purchaser for the price, who has his remedy over against the aggressor. So, also, if the damage were occasioned by the act of the purchaser, the sale and option remain good, and the seller may cancel the sale, and pursue the purchaser for compensation, or confirm it and and sue him for the price. And, in like manner, when the thing sold is damaged in the hands of the purchaser by his own act, or the act of a stranger, or providential interference, the seller retains his option, and may either confirm the sale, taking the full price from the purchaser, or he may cancel it, taking back what may remain of the thing sold, with a compensation for the damage from the purchaser, or the stranger where damage was occasioned by him, the purchaser having a right of recourse against the latter when made responsible in the first instance.

Of damage in the hands of the seller.

Of damage in the hands of the purchaser.

A person purchased his own son with a condition of option to the seller, and then died; the seller afterwards confirmed the sale, whereupon the son became free, but was not entitled to inherit from his father.*

Purchase of a son, with option to the seller.

If a person sell a female slave with an option for three days, and the slave gain something, or brings forth a

Increase during the period of option.

---

* Slavery is an impediment to the right of inheritance, and the son was still a slave at the father's death.

child, the increase accrues to the original, and belongs to the purchaser or the seller according as the sale is confirmed or cancelled.

Confirmation by the purchaser.

When the purchaser has the option, the sale is confirmed in one of the three ways already mentioned, and further by the exercise on his part of the right of ownership over the thing sold. On this point, it is a general rule that any act which is necessary for the purpose of trial, and is lawful to a person who is not the proprietor, when done once by a purchaser, is not construed into evidence of an election on his part, so as to extinguish his right of option, while every act not necessary for the purpose of trial, or which, though necessary, yet is not lawful to any but a proprietor, is considered evidence of election on the part of the purchaser when done by him. Hence sale, manumission, whether absolute or by *tudbeer* or *kitabut* or only partial, pledge, gift even without delivery, and lease, being acts peculiar to a proprietor, amount to confirmation when done by a purchaser having an option. So also carnal intercourse with a female slave, or kissing or embracing her with desire, or looking on her nakedness with desire, amounts to confirmation of sale by a purchaser who has an option; but the same acts when unaccompanied with desire, or looking upon any other part of her person though with desire, because that may be necessary for the purpose of examination, do not extinguish the option of the purchaser. Nor has calling the slave to his bed, nor giving her in marriage, that effect, until followed by coition.

General rule as to his acts.

Acts which do not extinguish his option,

If the subject of sale be a beast of burden (*dabbu*), and the purchaser having an option should ride it to try its paces or its strength; or a garment, and he should put it on to ascertain its size; or a female slave, and he should set her to work on trial; none of these acts would have the effect of extinguishing his option. But if in riding the animal he exceed what is sanctioned by usage, or ride him on any necessary occasion of his own, that would indicate satisfaction with his purchase, and put an end to his option; and a second trial, either of the beast or

unless carried to excess.

the slave, would have that effect, unless in a manner quite different from the first.

Effect of damage in the possession of the purchaser.

If the option be to the purchaser, and goods taken possession of by him sustain an injury which cannot be repaired, the contract is obligatory and the option void, whether the injury were occasioned by the act of the seller or another. If the injury be susceptible of cure, as sickness for instance, the option remains, and the purchaser may confirm or cancel the sale. But actual cure within the period of option is necessary to its validity; for if the period should expire and the injury or its effects still remain, the right to cancel is void, and the sale becomes obligatory.

Of an increase to the thing sold.

If the thing sold should increase during the period of option, while in the hands of the purchaser, and the increase be united to, and have issued from, the original, as the fat or improved condition or restored health of an animal, it prevents cancellation, according to Aboo Huneefa and Aboo Yoosuf; and if the increase be united to the original, but have not issued from it, as the dye or sewing of cloth, or buildings, or plants on land, it also prevents cancellation in the opinion of all our lawyers. So, also, if the increase have issued from the original, but is separated from it, as the young, or milk, or wool of an animal, it has the effect of preventing cancellation. But an increase which is separated, and did not issue from the original, such as the gain acquired by a slave, does not prevent cancellation, according to the opinion of all our lawyers.

Acts with regard to land, that extinguish option;

If a person purchase land with crops or plants upon it, and water the plants, or cut, or gather, or expose to sale any part of them, his option is extinguished. So also if he were to prune or impregnate the palm-trees on the land, or sow or cultivate the land, his option would be void, and the acts be evidence of satisfaction with his purchase.

with regard to a mansion.

Occupying a purchased mansion, or suffering another to occupy it, whether at a rent or not, or making new erections, or repairing, or plastering, or pulling down any of the old, amount to a confirmation of a sale; and even if a wall should fall down without the intervention of any one, the purchaser's option is at an end; but continuing to reside in a house which he already occupies does not extinguish his option.

Assertion of a right to pre-emption.

If a house next to a house purchased with an option to the buyer be for sale, and he should claim a right to pre-emption, that would amount to an extinction of his option; and it is not necessary that he should obtain the house, for the mere assertion of a right to pre-emption is sufficient.

Acts with regard to animals.

If a person purchase a cow or goat with an option, and milk her, that extinguishes his option; and if a hen be purchased with an option, and lay an egg, the option is at an end, unless the egg be addled. So, also, if an animal bring forth its young during the period of option, the option is extinguished, unless the young be still-born; and also in that case if the mother sustain any injury in parturition.

Case of a seller refusing to take back the thing sold.

* A person purchases a thing on condition that he shall have an option for three days, and within the time brings the thing to the door of the seller to return it, but the seller conceals himself, whereupon the purchaser applies to the *Kazee* to appoint an adversary instead of the seller, to whom restitution may be made of the thing purchased. Opinions differ as to the duty of the *Kazee* in such circumstances. Some think that he ought to comply with the application, but another authority is opposed to this; and there are two reports as to what the *Kazee* should do when he refuses to nominate an adversary; one, that he should send a messenger to the seller's door to intimate that if he do not appear the sale will be cancelled; and the other, that the *Kazee* should not interfere at all, as the purchaser ought to have provided against the contingency by getting an agent appointed, to whom restitution should be made in case of the seller's absence.

---

* This and the following paragraph are from page 60 of the original.

When a person purchases with an option for three days a thing that is susceptible of damage, though, according to analogy, he cannot be required to exercise his option till the expiration of the time, yet on a favourable construction of law, and for the purpose of preventing injury to both parties, the purchaser may be called upon to cancel the sale, or take possession of the thing sold, without, however, being obliged to pay the price until actual confirmation of the sale, or some damage to the thing sold. In the case of an absolute sale of a thing liable to injury, of which the purchaser will neither take possession nor pay the price, and withdraws or absents himself, the seller is at liberty to sell it to another party who may lawfully purchase, though he be cognizant of the previous transaction.

Purchase, with option of a thing liable to become quickly bad.

When a sale has been dissolved by virtue of an option, and the thing sold perishes in the hands of the purchaser before its restoration to the seller, the former is liable for the price when the option is his, or its value when the option is the seller's.

Purchaser's liability after cancellation of the sale.

When two persons purchase a thing on condition that both shall have an option, and one is content with the sale, either expressly or by implication, the other has not the power to reject, according to Aboo Huneefa, and his option is at an end. The two disciples, however, considered that he had a right to reject the sale to the extent of his share. And there is the same difference of opinion between the master and his disciples in the parallel cases under the options of Inspection and Defect.

Confirmation by one of two persons having an option.

SECTION IV.*

Of options of Rejection and Selection among several articles.

When a person purchases two pieces of cloth, or two

Option of

* The two first paragraphs of this section are taken from the beginning of section v. in the original, page 70; the remainder from section vi. page 73.

rejection as to one of two things.

slaves, or two beasts, on condition that he shall have an option with regard to one of them for three days, or that the seller shall have such option, the transaction may be in four different ways, in three of which it is unlawful, and in one of which it is lawful with regard to both the things purchased. First, there may be no distinct mention of the individual to which the option is to apply, nor of the price of each separately. Second, the individual may be specified, but not the proportion of the price applicable to each. Third, the proportion of the price may be mentioned without specification of the individual; and fourth, the individual and the shares of the price applicable to each may be distinctly specified. It is in the last case only that the sale is lawful as to both the things sold, and it is absolute as to one, and optional with regard to the other.

As to part of a single thing.

A quantity of any article estimable by measurement of capacity, or by weight, or even a single slave, may be purchased with an option as to half either to the seller or the purchaser; and if the option be reserved to the purchaser, he may reverse the sale as to half, though in so doing there is a splitting of what was one bargain, because the seller has given his consent.

Option of selection or determination.

When one of two or three slaves, or one out of two or three pieces of cloth is sold, with liberty to the purchaser to take which of them he pleases, the transaction is a sale with option of determination or selection; and this option may be reserved to the seller as well as the purchaser; but it is lawful only where the things sold are not of the class of similars, and the choice is limited to a number less than four.

When a sale of this nature takes place, and the purchaser takes possession of both the articles, one is at his own risk for its price, and the other is an *amanut* or trust for the seller.

Option by stipulation may be combined with it.

If the parties should agree to combine the ordinary option by stipulation with an option of selection, the effect would be to legalize the return of both the articles for three days, even after one of them had been selected. If one only of the articles be returned, it is considered to be done in exercise of the right of selection, and the sale of the other would be established, but still subject to the option by stipulation till the expiration of the three days; if the three days had already expired, the option by stipulation would be at an end, and the sale obligatory as to one of the articles, the party being bound to make a choice.

When the option by stipulation is not joined with the option of selection, the latter must be restricted to a fixed period, which cannot be more than three days according to Aboo Huneefa, though it may exceed that number in the opinion of his disciples, provided the period be fixed. **Option of selection is limited to three days.**

When the option of selection is left absolute, without any restriction as to time, it is not lawful according to many authorities. When the ordinary option by stipulation is conjoined with that of selection, and the person having the options happens to die, the former option is at an end, but the latter survives to his heir; so that the heir may select one of the articles, but he cannot return both, and when he has selected one, the other remains as an *amanut* in his hands. **Descends to heirs.**

If the option be to the purchaser, and one of the articles should happen to perish before possession by him, it perishes as an *amanut*, and he may either take or reject the one that remains; while if they should both so perish the sale would be void. And if one of them should perish after possession by the purchaser, the loss would be his, and the remaining article an *amanut*, which he must restore; while if both should perish, one after the other, the selection would be held to apply to the first that perished, and he would be liable for its price; and if they should perish together, he would become liable for half the price of each. If, instead of perishing altogether, one of the articles should only receive some damage in the hands of the seller, and before possession by the purchaser, the damaged article could not be considered the one selected for sale, but the purchaser would have his option of taking either of them at its full price, or rejecting them entirely. **Effect of loss or damage when the option is the purchaser's.**

And the rule would be the same if both articles should receive damage before possession; while, if the injury take place after possession of the articles, and while they are in the hands of the purchaser, the damaged article is considered the one selected for sale, and the other is in trust. And if both the articles be damaged, the sale is binding as to whichever was first damaged, and the other is to be returned to the seller, without, however, any responsibility on the part of the purchaser for the damage.

Effect of dealing in such case.

If the purchaser should deal as a proprietor with one of the articles, the dealing would be lawful, and tantamount to a selection upon his part, and he would become liable for its price (the other being the *amanut*): but if the seller should deal with either of them, his act would necessarily be suspended until the purchaser had made his selection, and be then valid only with regard to the article rejected by him.

Effect of loss or damage when the option is the seller's.

If the option of selection be to the seller, he can compel the purchaser to take whichever of the articles he pleases, and the purchaser has no right to reject, because the sale with regard to him is absolute. If one of the articles should perish, whether before or after possession, it would perish as an *amanut*, and the seller would be at liberty to compel the purchaser to take the surviving one, or he might cancel the sale. If one or both of the articles be injured, whether before or after possession, the option of the seller remains, and he may compel the purchaser to take whichever of them he pleases. If he insist on his taking the one that is perfect, the purchaser has no option. And the rule is the same, though he should insist on his taking the injured article, if the injury occurred after possession; but if it happened before possession, the purchaser has a right to reject the injured article if he please. And if the seller should attempt to force it upon him, and he should refuse, the seller cannot then revert to the other article, and insist on his taking that, but he may cancel the sale and reclaim both the articles.

Effect of disposal in such case.

Any disposal by the purchaser before the seller has exercised his right of selection would not be lawful; but a disposal of one of them by the seller would be quite lawful, while he would still retain the option of forcing the other on the purchaser, or cancelling the sale. A disposal of both of the articles by the seller would also be lawful, but it would be a cancellation of the first sale.

The option of selection is extinguished by whatever would extinguish the option by stipulation. **Extinction of this option.**

SECTION V.*

Of Disputes regarding Options by Stipulation.

In a dispute as to the fact of option, the word of him who denies, and the evidence of him who asserts it is preferred. **Dispute as to the fact, or period of option;** If the question be as to the period, the word of him who asserts the shortest period is preferred; and in a dispute with regard to its expiration, preference is given to him who denies its expiration. If the parties differ as to the allowance or confirmation of the sale, **or confirmation of the sale.** and the question arises within the period, the word of him who has the option, and the evidence of the other, is preferred; but if the question do not arise till after the expiration of the period, the word of him who claims the allowance of the sale, and the evidence of him who insists for cancellation, is preferred. While if both the parties had an option, the word of the person claiming cancellation, and the evidence of the other, would be entitled to preference in the first case, and the word of the claimant of confirmation, and the evidence of the claimant of cancellation, would be preferred in the second case. All this, however, is on the supposition that the evidence adduced by the parties does not fix the date of the fact which they offer to prove; for if both should adduce evidence of dates, the evidence of him who alleges the prior date is preferred, whether it apply to the allowance or cancellation of the contract.

A case is put in the *Jama Kubeer*, on the authority of Moohummud, which may serve to illustrate some of these **Illustration.**

* This is section iv. in the original.

rules. A person sold a slave for a thousand *dirhems*, on condition that he should have an option for three days, and the purchaser took possession. The period having expired, one of the parties, it matters not which, declared that the slave had died within the period, and that the sale was dissolved, and the value of the slave obligatory on the purchaser; while the other answered, "Nay, but the slave is still alive, and has absconded." In such circumstances, the word of the latter is to be preferred; and if both the parties adduce evidence, his evidence is entitled to preference also. If the parties agree as to the death of the slave, but one of them alleges that it occurred within the three days, while the other insists that its occurrence took place after their expiration, the word of the former, and the evidence of the latter, is to be preferred. If they should further agree as to the slave having died after the expiration of the three days, and in the possession of the purchaser, but differ as to the cancellation or allowance of the sale; one adducing evidence that the seller dissolved the sale within the three days, and the other, that he allowed it, the evidence of the former is to be preferred: but it has been said, that though this would be agreeable to analogy, yet that, on a favourable construction, preference is given to the evidence of him who claims confirmation of the sale. If they should agree as to the death of the slave within the three days, and the other circumstances of the case were the same as last stated, the evidence of the party claiming allowance of the sale would be preferred. And if one of the parties should maintain that the death occurred after the three days, but that the seller had allowed the sale previously to their expiration, while the other maintains the occurrence of the death within the three days, and previous dissolution by the seller, the word of the claimant of dissolution, and the evidence of the other party, is to be preferred. While, if one of them should maintain that the death occurred after the three days, and that the seller dissolved the sale within the period, but the other, that the slave died within the period, and that the seller had previously allowed the sale, the word of the claimant of dissolution, and the evidence of his adversary, would be preferred.

Dispute as to the identity of the article to which the option applies.

*When a person has purchased a thing with an option for three days, and having taken possession comes back to restore it in right of the option, and the seller denies that it is the article which he sold, the word of the purchaser, with his oath, are entitled to preference. But if the thing had never passed into the possession of the purchaser, and he should afterwards wish to confirm the contract with regard to some specific article still in the seller's hands, though there is no distinct authority in any of the books applicable to the case, it seems more proper that in such circumstances the word of the seller should be preferred. If, on the other hand, the option were to the seller, and the thing sold, having passed into the possession of the purchaser, should be returned by him during the period of option, and the other should insist that the returned article was not the one which he sold and the purchaser took possession of, the purchaser maintaining that it was, the word of the purchaser, with his oath, would be entitled to preference. While, if the article had not passed into the purchaser's possession, and the seller should desire to make the sale obligatory, with regard to a particular article, which the other declares he never bought, here also the word and oath of the purchaser are preferred.

* The remainder of this section is taken from section vii. of the original, page 76.

CHAPTER VII.

OPTION OF INSPECTION.*

SECTION I.

Of its Establishment and Legal Effect.

Purchase of an unseen thing is lawful, but subject to option.

A PERSON may lawfully purchase a thing which he has not seen, but when he does so he has an option on seeing the thing, and may either take it at the full price, or reject it, whether it correspond with the description given of it to him or not. This option arises from the contract itself, and does not depend on any stipulation. It does not prevent the establishment of a right of property in the things exchanged, though it prevents such right from being conclusive; and it cannot be extinguished before inspection even by express acquiescence. Insomuch that, though a sale may be cancelled before inspection, according to all our lawyers, it cannot be lawfully confirmed before inspection; and if so confirmed, the purchaser's option would remain exactly as before; so that on seeing the thing he would still have the power of allowing or rejecting the sale.

Seller's option as to the price.

As the purchaser has an option on inspection of the thing sold, so also has the seller the like option with regard to the price, when it is something specific.

Condition of purchaser's option.

It is a necessary condition to the establishment of this option in the purchaser, that the thing sold be such as can be particularised by specification, and also that it be

* Arab. *Khiyar-oor-Rooyut.* This option is founded on a saying of the Prophet, viz., "He who purchases a thing that he has not seen, has an option when he sees it."—*Hidayah*, vol. iii. p. 52.

actually specified. Hence the option cannot, in any case, apply to *dirhems* or *deenars;* but it is applicable to commodities estimated by weight or measurement of capacity, when distinctly specified; and also to pieces or vessels of gold or silver. When a person is entitled to any property undeterminately under the obligation of another, such as the goods advanced for in a *sulum* contract, the option of inspection is not applicable. Nor does it apply to any commodities estimated by weight or measurement of capacity, when not distinctly specified.

To what contracts this option is applicable.

This option is established in all contracts that are cancelled by restitution, such as lease, composition for a claim to property, partition, purchase, and the like; but it is not established in contracts that are not cancelled by restitution, such as *Muhr, Khoola,** the composition for blood, and the like, where the thing to be restored after cancellation is ensured for itself,† and not for what is opposed to it.

It would seem that the option of inspection, as well as the option of defect, hereafter to be explained, may be established with regard to a defective sale.

How long it remains in force.

There is a difference of opinion among the learned as to the option of inspection being absolute, or limited to a particular time. Some think that it is restricted to the time when cancellation of the contract first becomes possible after inspection of the thing sold, and that if the contract is not then cancelled, the option of inspection falls to the ground, without any confirmation of the sale, either expressly or by implication. But the better opinion seems to be that it is not restricted in point of time, and that it remains in force until something takes place to render it void, and that the seller cannot call upon the purchaser for the price until his option is extinguished.

Does not

The option of inspection does not descend to heirs, so

---

* These terms are explained, page 22.

† That is, the holder is responsible for the identical thing, which must be restored if in existence, or for its value in the event of loss.

descend to heirs.

that if the purchaser should die before inspection, his heir has not the power of returning the article purchased.

Seller's option

If a person sell a thing which he has not seen, as, for instance, if he inherit something and sell before seeing it, he has no option according to Aboo Huneefa. But if he sell one specific thing for another specific thing which he has not seen, and also for an obligation,* he may, on seeing the specific part of the consideration, cancel the sale in proportion to it, but no farther, because the option of inspection is not applicable to obligations.

When the purchaser has an option as to a thing seen before purchase.

When a person purchases a thing which he had previously seen, he has still an option if it have undergone any change; but otherwise he has no option, unless he were ignorant at the time of the contract that he had previously seen it. If the parties differ as to the fact of a change, the purchaser maintaining and the seller denying it, the word of the latter, with his oath, are to be preferred, and the burden of proof is on the former. This is true when the interval since the purchaser's inspection is so short that a change could hardly have taken place within the period; but if the interval be long, as if the purchaser had seen a female slave in her youth, and should purchase her twenty years after, and the seller insist that she had not changed, the word of the purchaser would be entitled to preference. If they differ as to the fact of inspection at the time of purchase, the seller maintaining, and the purchaser denying it, the word and oath of the purchaser are to be preferred. If the difference be as to the identity of the article returned, the seller saying that it is not the one he sold, while the purchaser insists that it is, the word of the latter is also preferred. And, in like manner, in every other case where the contract can be cancelled by the word of the purchaser alone, without the consent of the seller, or decree of a judge; but whenever such consent or decree is necessary to the cancellation, preference is given to the word of the seller, as, for instance, in all cases of return by reason of defect.

---

* Arab. *deyn*, see note, page 7.

When a person purchases a thing which he has already seen, but is ignorant of the fact at the time of sale, as, for instance, a piece of cloth which he had seen in the hands of a party, who afterwards covers it up in a towel and sells it to him; or a slave girl who is afterwards sold with her face covered, the purchaser being ignorant that the cloth and the slave are the same which he had previously seen, he has an option on their being exposed to his view. And if one should purchase a large leathern bag of water, he has an option on seeing the contents, for waters differ in their qualities, some being better than others. A purchase in ignorance of previous inspection.

The option of inspection prevents the completion of the bargain, as already observed of the option by stipulation. Hence, if a person purchase a package of *Zutee* cloths, and without seeing take possession of them, and one of the pieces then happens to sustain damage, he is precluded from returning any of them under his option of inspection; and if a contract be allowed as to part of the thing sold without the rest, as, for instance, if one should purchase two pieces of cloth, or two slaves, or the like, and see them after taking possession, and then declare with regard to one of them, "I am content with this," it would not be lawful, and his option would still remain as before. If a person purchase two things and inspect them, and then take possession of one of them, that would be sufficient assent as to both, according to Aboo Huneefa, though the inspection of one is not sufficient for both; or if two persons, having purchased a thing which neither of them had seen, should take possession, and then inspect it, whereupon one is satisfied, but the other wishes to cancel the sale, it could not, according to Aboo Huneefa, be cancelled without their joint agreement to that effect. So, also, if the case were reversed, and there were two sellers and one purchaser, the option being with the former, and one of them should wish to cancel the sale, and the other to confirm, their joint agreement would be necessary to its confirmation. A person having seen one of two pieces of cloth purchases them both, and Option of inspection prevents completion of a bargain.

then sees the other; he has still the option of rejecting or taking both; and if two persons should purchase a female slave that had already been seen by one of them, and both take possession, whereupon she is seen by the other who had not previously seen her, and they then agree on returning her, it is lawful for them to do so. And if the one who had first seen her should declare his contentment with the sale before her rejection by the other, the latter would still have the right to return her, the confirmation by one being no more than his inspection.

Sale, how cancelled.

Rejection under an option of inspection, whether before or after possession, is cancellation of the sale, and does not require the decree of a judge, nor the assent of the seller, and the cancellation is effected by the mere words, "I have rejected;" except that, according to Aboo Huneefa and Moohummud, the knowledge of the seller is requisite to the validity of the reversal. All are agreed that assent to the sale is valid, whether the seller be present or not. Assent is of two kinds, express or implied; express, as if the purchaser should say after inspection, "I am content," or, "have approved;" and implied, when the purchaser, after purchase, inspects and then takes possession of the thing sold. If the purchaser should first take possession, and then inspect the thing, his option remains entire until he actually affirm the sale, or acts in a manner that indicates his assent to it.

How affirmed.

Acts of ownership that extinguish this option.

The option of inspection is extinguished by every act of ownership over the thing purchased, or injury to it, which would have the effect of extinguishing the option by stipulation. Hence, if the act be such as does not admit of being reversed after it has taken place, as manumission, or *tudbeer*,* or such as induces a right to a third party, as an absolute sale, pledge, or lease, it extinguishes the option, whether the act take place before or after inspection; and if the purchaser of a thing should sell it before inspection, but after taking possession of it, and

* See *ante*, note, page 28.

the thing be subsequently returned to him on account of a defect under the decree of a judge, or if any other act of ownership by a purchaser be entirely cancelled, as, for instance, a pledge by its redemption, or a lease by expiration of its term, his option of inspection does not revive. But if the act do not involve the right of a third party, as a re-sale with a stipulation of option to the purchaser himself, or a gift without delivery, or a mere exposal of the thing to sale, his first option is not invalidated unless the act take place after inspection; and the exposal to sale of only part of the purchased article, though after inspection, would not invalidate the option, according to Aboo Yoosuf, whose opinion on the point is preferred to that of Moohummud. But a re-sale, with an option to the new purchaser, or a gift or invalid sale with delivery, though before inspection, would have the effect of extinguishing the original option. And if part of the thing purchased should perish, or if it should receive any damage or accession, whether united or separate, in the hands of the purchaser, his option would also become void.

Effect of a claim of pre-emption.

If a person purchase a house which he has not seen, and another contiguous to it is sold, which he takes under a claim of pre-emption, this does not invalidate his right of option with regard to the first.

***Where* the thing purchased is to be returned.**

When a person having purchased a thing, and carried it to his own house, wishes to return it on account of a defect, or by virtue of an option by stipulation, or for want of inspection, he must return it to the place of contract, otherwise it is no return, whether the value of the thing be improved or deteriorated thereby; and the trouble of returning it is incumbent on the purchaser.

Extinction of option as to land.

If a person purchase land, and grant permission to the cultivators to sow it, and they do so, his option is at an end, their act by his direction being the same as his own. And though there be cultivators already on the land, and they should sow it without his interference, if he then, on inspecting the land, desire to return it under his option, he is not at liberty to do so. But the mere letting of the land before seeing it, for the purpose of being sown, does not extinguish his option till the sowing actually take place.

Case of a mansion purchased at a distance.

A person purchases a mansion in another town, the seller saying to the purchaser, "I have delivered it to you;" but the purchaser refuses to pay the price for want of inspection and actual delivery, he is entitled to return the mansion under his option for the first cause; but if he wish to retain it, the seller should be directed to accompany him to the city where the mansion is situated, or to send an agent with him to receive the price, and give actual delivery of the mansion.

Contingencies that extinguish option in the case of slaves.

A wound received by a slave, and carnal intercourse with a female slave, while in the possession of the purchaser, and whether the wound be inflicted by the purchaser or a stranger, or the intercourse be had unlawfully or by mistake, and by the purchaser or a stranger, prevent the return of the slave under an option of inspection, without the consent of the seller; and the effect is the same if a female slave give birth to a child while in the possession of the purchaser, and whether the child live or die. But if the subject be a beast of burden or a sheep, and it produces a young one, it is only in the event of the young one living, or being killed by the purchaser or another, that the right of returning it would be lost; for if the young one should die a natural death the purchaser would retain his right of returning its mother under his option of inspection.

Case of fever.

If a slave should fever, and the fever leave him, the purchaser has his option on seeing him. And in case of dispute between the parties, and the matter being carried before the *Kazee,* if the fever be still on the slave the option ought to be cancelled, and the sale confirmed. Though the slave should subsequently recover, the purchaser cannot return him after the decree of the *Kazee.*

Section II.

Of the circumstances in which Inspection of a part is equivalent to Inspection of the whole in extinguishing an Option.

General principle. The general principle on this head is, that when the part which has not been seen is an appendage to that which has been seen, the purchaser has no option with regard to the former; but when the unseen is itself the original or principal part of the thing purchased, then it is to be considered, whether the inspection of what has been seen be or be not a sufficient indication of the condition of the unseen. And if it be so the option is void, while if it be not so the option remains subsisting.

What is necessary in the case of human beings: When a slave, whether male or female, is the subject of sale, and the purchaser has seen the face and is satisfied, his option is at an end; and sight of the greater part of the face is in this respect the same as if the whole were seen; but the sight of the whole body without the face is not sufficient to extinguish the purchaser's option, when any of the race of Adam is the subject of the contract.

of the lower animals. With respect to a horse, mule, ass, or the like, inspection of the face is not enough; and the purchaser's option remains until he has seen the face and the hinder part. Professional persons, and such as have skill in cattle, are said to consider that inspection of the legs is also necessary, and a condition of the extinction of option. Sight of the hoof, forehead, and tail alone, are clearly not sufficient.

Of animals purchased for a particular purpose. If a sheep be purchased for breeding, the udder and whole body must be seen; and a sheep purchased for its flesh must be handled, so that if only seen from a distance the purchaser's option remains. When a milch cow or camel is purchased, and the whole body is seen without the udder, the purchaser has still an option. **Of objects of taste, smell, or hearing.** Articles of food must be tasted, and odoriferous things must be smelt; and of drums for war, the sound must be heard; and if things to be tasted are tasted at night, though not seen, the option is extinguished.

Of moveables, other than animals.

If the thing sold be moveable, but not an animal, and the purchaser's object had reference to some part of it in particular, that part must be seen in order to extinguish his option; but if there be nothing of that description, then the sight of any part of it when he is satisfied is sufficient to extinguish his option with regard to the remainder, provided it is found to correspond in quality with the portion he has seen; if it be different he has an option. When the subject of sale is a single piece of cloth folded up, and the purchaser has seen only the outside, his option is not extinguished until he has seen what is within also. It has been said with regard to a bed, that the whole of it must be seen; and with respect to a stuffed pillow, or cushion, if it be stuffed with the usual materials, the sight of the outside is sufficient to negative the purchaser's option; but if the stuffing be different to what is usual, the option remains.

Of things in pairs, and oil in a bottle.

When a person purchases two boots or two shoes, or two leaves of a door, and sees only one of them, he has an option on the other being exposed to his view. And if one purchase oil in a bottle, and see the bottle, but neglect to pour out some of the oil on the palm of his hand or finger, this is no sufficient inspection, according to Aboo Huneefa. Nor is it enough to see the thing purchased through a piece of glass, nor reflected in a mirror or reservoir of water. And if fish in the water that can be taken without fishing for them be purchased, and then seen while still in the water, option is not extinguished; but inspection of a thing through a fine veil is accounted sufficient.

Of immoveable estate.

With regard to immoveable estate, when the purchaser of a mansion sees the outside of it, and is content, his option is at an end; but if there be buildings within the circuit of the mansion, the interior of them must be seen also. So that if the mansion should contain summer and winter apartments, it is essential that these, as well as the *suhn*, or court of the mansion, should be seen. But inspection of the kitchen, privy, or the upper part of the house is not requisite, except in some cities like Samarkand, where the purchaser of a house has usually a view to the upper story. Some persons, however, maintain that inspection of the whole house is in all cases necessary; and this opinion appears more probable, and agreeable to analogy.

In the purchase of a granary, it is sufficient if the outer wall be seen; and in the purchase of vines, or other trees, the sight of their tops is enough: so that if the purchaser be satisfied, his option of inspection no longer remains. Of a garden, the outside and inside must both be seen.

With regard to trees.

When the subject of sale is something estimated by weight or measurement of capacity, and part of it only is seen at the time of purchase, then, if the whole be in one vessel, the purchaser has no further option, unless the remainder differ from what was exposed to his view. In the event of such difference, he has an option; but it is on account of the defect, not for want of sufficient inspection. And though the articles be in different vessels, yet if the whole be of the same kind and quality, the purchaser has no option according to the learned men of Irak, whose opinion is most approved; but if they should be of different kinds, or of the same kind and different qualities, the purchaser would retain his option without any difference of opinion.

Things estimated by weight or measurement of capacity.

When the things sold are articles of tale, the unities of which differ considerably from each other, as pieces of cloth contained in a leathern bag, or melons in a basket, each one must be seen; and when a part only is seen, the purchaser has an option as to the remainder; but if he desire to reject, he must reject the whole. In articles of tale the unities of which are nearly alike, as walnuts or eggs, inspection of part is sufficient, when the remainder is of the same or superior quality; and where inferior, and the purchaser avails himself of his option by returning them, he must return the whole.

Articles of tale.

In all the above cases, in the event of any dispute between the parties as to the quality of the remainder of the articles, the purchaser insisting that they are of a different quality from the portion seen, and the seller

Disputes as to quality.

retorting that they are of the same quality, the word and oath of the latter are to be preferred, and the burden of proof is on the former.

Of articles under the ground.

When the things purchased are covered with earth, as onions, garlic, and carrots, inspection of part is not sufficient, according to Aboo Huneefa, and the purchaser's option remains till he has seen the whole; but, according to both the disciples, when a part is dug up that may serve as a sample of the whole, and the purchaser is satisfied, his option is extinguished. It is generally admitted, however, that this case is not reported in the Zahir Rewayut, and it is stated in the *Amalee* of Aboo Yoosuf, that he made the following distinctions in cases of this description:—Thus, if the things when dug up be estimable by weight or measurement of capacity, and the seller digs up a part, or the purchaser does so with his permission, then, if the portion dug up be a quantity sufficient to be estimated by the measure or weight in use for such things, and the purchaser sees such portion and is satisfied, the sale is binding as to the whole when the remainder is found to correspond. If, again, the portion dug up be too small to be so estimated, the purchaser's option remains, that is, if he had the seller's permission for digging, or the seller had dug up the portion himself; but if the purchaser should dig without the permission of the seller, and the portion dug up be anything having price, the sale is binding on him as to the whole, whether he be satisfied or not; and though less should be found in another part of the land, or nothing should be found at all. If, however, what is dug up be so small in quantity as to have no price, the purchaser's option is not extinguished. In all these cases the *Futwah* is in accordance with the opinion of Aboo Yoosuf. When the articles concealed by the earth are such as when dug up are sold by tale, as radishes, for instance, and part only is seen by the purchaser, his option is not extinguished as to the remainder, provided the digging were by the seller, or with his consent; but if the purchaser should dig without his consent, and what is dug up be of some price, his option is extinguished as to the remainder; all this also is approved.

All the above cases are on the supposition that the thing concealed is known to exist in the earth. If, then, the sale should take place before vegetation, or after vegetation may have actually taken place in the earth, but while the fact is still unknown, the sale is not lawful, or if something which may be in actual existence in the earth be sold, as onions, and the seller were to pull up some from one place, saying, "I sell to you on condition that what is contained in the whole ground is like this, on the average," the sale would not be lawful.

Case.

The following case is given on the authority of Moohummud. A person purchased ten *jureebs** of carrots in the ground, and taking possession of the ground sent his servant to dig up the carrots; he dug up the whole, and brought them to his master. Moohummud being asked whether the master had any option of inspection, answered in the affirmative; and it being observed that the seller would sustain a loss of one-third by the digging up, replied, that notwithstanding the loss, the purchaser was entitled to the option.

Course to be followed when one or both of the parties is unwilling to dig.

If, in a sale of carrots, neither of the parties should be willing to dig, the seller for fear that the purchaser may not be satisfied, and that he will therefore have to bear the loss, and the purchaser, for fear that the articles may not be good, and that he will not have the power of returning them, either of the parties may lawfully take the initiative, and if neither will do so the judge should cancel the sale.

---

* The *jureeb* is an area of 60 by 60 *zira*, each *zira* being seven *kubza* (hands), which was one *kubza* more than the ordinary *zira*.—*Fut. Alumgeeree*, vol. ii. page 339. The *zira*, or cubit, is the length from the elbow to the extremity of the middle finger of a man's arm. —*Freytag*.

Section III.

Of Purchase by a blind Man, an Agent, or Messenger.

Option of a blind man.

Sale and purchase by a blind man are lawful according to our three doctors; and he has an option when he purchases, but not when he sells. Turning over and feeling are to him instead of sight in matters within the cognizance of touch, and smelling and tasting when the things relate to these senses respectively. Description is not an essential condition, according to the most authentic reports. When the thing sold is cloth, a description of its length, breadth, and degree of excellence, are necessary in addition to handling; and feeling and description are also both required with regard to wheat. Description alone is sufficient with regard to fruit on the tops of trees, according to the most authentic reports. A blind man's option is not extinguished with regard to immoveable estate until it is described to him; and the rule is the same with regard to cattle, slaves, trees, and everything else which cannot be sufficiently known by touch, smell, or taste.

When cognizance has been had before the contract.

When a blind man has had these means of cognizance before a contract, they are equally effectual, and he has no option. If a blind man, to whom a thing has been described, and who has expressed his satisfaction with it, should recover his sight, his option does not return; and when a person in the enjoyment of his sight makes a purchase, and then becomes blind, his option is transferred from sight to description; but if a blind man should say before the description, "I am satisfied," his option would not be extinguished.

Appointment of an agent or messenger to take possession.

A purchaser may appoint or employ an agent, or messenger, to take possession on his behalf of his purchase by such forms as these, "Be my agent* in taking possession of the thing sold," or, "I have appointed you to take possession of it, or, "Be messenger† on my behalf in taking

* Arab. *vukeel.*

† Arab. *russool.*

possession," or, "I have directed or sent you to take possession." If an agent so appointed should take possession after seeing the article, the purchaser has no power to reject it, according to Aboo Huneefa; but he would, according to the same authority, if a mere messenger had seen and then taken possession of the article. The two disciples, however, reject this distinction, and consider that the purchaser retains his option in both cases, and may either reject or keep the article according to his pleasure.

Effect of inspection by him.

With regard to an agent for purchase, all are agreed that inspection by him is like inspection by the principal himself, who, therefore, when he sees the article, has not the power to reject it; and it is likewise agreed that a messenger employed to purchase has not the power of extinguishing his employer's option, and that inspection by him is not like inspection by the principal.

Effect of inspection by an agent or messenger employed to purchase,

When a person employs an agent or a messenger before purchase to look at an article, and then purchases it himself, he has his option of inspection. And when an agent for purchase purchases a thing which his principal had previously seen, the agent being ignorant of the fact, he has an option of inspection, that is, when he was not appointed to purchase a specific thing. But if appointed to purchase a specific thing which the principal had previously seen, though the agent had not seen it, he would have no option of inspection.

or only to inspect.

CHAPTER VIII.

OPTION OF DEFECT.

SECTION I.

Of the establishment of the Option, its effect and conditions, and of knowing and distinguishing defects.

This option how established.

THIS option, like the last, is established without stipulation. When a person purchases a thing with a defect of which he had no knowledge at or previous to the sale, whether the defect be trivial or flagrant, provided that it cannot be easily removed, he has an option, and may either retain the article at its full price or reject it; but he cannot retain it, and seek compensation for the defect. If he become acquainted with the defect before possession, he may cancel the sale and reject the purchased article, without the consent of the seller, or the intervention of a judge; but after possession the contract cannot be cancelled, except by consent or a decree. When the article is rejected with the seller's consent, the contract, though cancelled as regards him and the purchaser, is subsisting so far as the rights of third parties are concerned; but when rejected under the decree of a judge, the contract is cancelled as regards the parties themselves and all others.

To what contracts applicable.

Every contract that is cancelled by restitution, and when the thing to be restored, after cancellation, is ensured for what is opposed to it,* may be cancelled for any defect, whether slight or flagrant; while contracts which are not cancelled by restitution, and where the thing to be restored after cancellation is ensured for itself, and not for what is opposed to it, such as *Muhr*, the exchange for *Khoola*, and *Kisas*, or retaliation, can be cancelled only where the defect is flagrant. It should be observed, however, with regard to *Muhr*, that where the things of which it is composed are not such as are estimated by weight or measure of capacity, they may be rejected for a slight defect.

Flagrant and trivial defects.

When two valuators agree about the value of a thing in its perfect condition, and also agree that in its present condition it is below that value, the defect is said to be flagrant; but where, on the other hand, one of them insists that the thing is still worth what the other alleges to be its full value in a perfect state, though he maintains its present worth to be somewhat less, the defect is said to be slight or trivial.

Its defect.

Notwithstanding the option for defect, there is a present though not conclusive establishment of property in the purchaser, and his option descends to heirs, and is not restricted as to time.

Conditions of its establishment.

The following conditions are required to the establishment of this option. First, the existence of the defect at the time of sale, or subsequently to it, but before delivery. Secondly, its existence with the purchaser after he has taken possession of the thing sold; for its existence with the seller alone is not sufficient to establish the right of return in all cases. Thirdly, ignorance on the part of the purchaser, at and previous to the sale, of the existence of the defect; for if he knew it at either time he has no option. Fourthly, the absence of any stipulation for waiving, or releasing the seller from liability for defects in the thing sold; for if there be any condition to that effect the purchaser has no option. And lastly, with regard to the three following defects, absconding, theft,

* That is, the holder, in the event of its loss, loses his right to what is opposed to it.

and incontinence of urine in bed, which are peculiar to slaves, understanding, and unity or sameness of state, are necessary conditions.

Definition of defect. According to Koodooree, everything that induces an abatement of price in the thing sold according to the custom of merchants, is a defect; and to determine what is or is not a defect in a particular case, reference is to be made to persons of experience, that is merchants, and workmen, where the thing sold is a manufactured article.

Defects in slaves. In slaves, not only disease, and the various infirmities to which man is liable, but almost every departure from the ordinary state of humanity, is accounted a defect. Thus, to be blind, or one-eyed, or deaf, or dumb, or to squint, or have more or less than the usual number of fingers, are all defects in slaves, whether male or female. To have a fetid breath, or unpleasant odour from the person, are defects in a female but not in a male slave, unless so excessive as to be evidence of internal disease. The loss of a tooth, and black or green teeth, are defects in both; but accounts differ as to yellow teeth, whether they are to be considered a defect or not. Being left-handed is a defect when it amounts to an incapacity of using the right hand; but not when it is slight, and the person is more properly to be considered *ambi dexter*. So also to be weaksighted, or have the toes turned in, or be bow-legged, or wide and straddling between the feet, or to have the hair of the head or body partly white and partly black, are all defects. A colour of the hair between yellow and red is accounted a defect in Turkish and Indian women; but not in Greek and Sclavonian, for it is the general colour of the hair in these races. Of hair, in general, black is the prevailing colour, and any other may be a defect when it is so considered by merchants, and detracts from the price.

In females. In a female slave, any malformation of the generative organs is a defect. So also stoppage of the courses in a female who has attained the age of puberty, which, in this case, is considered to be seventeen years. And if a person should purchase a slave who has borne a child while in the possession of the seller, or another party, and the purchaser was ignorant of the fact, he may, on becoming acquainted with it, return the slave, according to a report which is considered authentic, and has been adopted for the *Futwa*. But the mere fact of production is not accounted a defect in the lower animals, unless it have occasioned some injury. Pregnancy is also a defect in a female slave. So also is fornication, whether it be more or less; but in a male slave it is a defect only when excessive, so as to interfere with his service to his master. It is also a defect in a male slave, if he bear the mark of the *hudd* or specific punishment for that offence; and even to be illegitimate* is a defect in a female slave, but not in a male. There is this difference between fornication and other defects in a female slave, that, while the others must return or shew themselves in the possession of the purchaser, it is sufficient with regard to this, that the slave, if of mature age, was once guilty of it while in the possession of the seller, and the repetition of the offence in the possession of the purchaser is not necessary to entitle him to reject her.

Impotence, and being an eunuch, are defects in a male slave: and if a person purchase a slave on condition of his being an eunuch, but find him otherwise, he cannot return him; though if he should purchase him on condition of being entire, and find him an eunuch, he has the right to return him. Wine drinking, when carried to an injurious excess, debt (unless paid or released), and responsibility incurred for an offence, are defects in slaves, whether male or female; but with regard to the last defect, it is to be understood of an offence committed by the slave between the date of contract and delivery; for of offences committed previously to the contract, the seller adopts the responsibility by the act of sale, and may, by paying the proper compensation, prevent the purchaser's right to return the slave. Some — In males.

* Legitimacy, by the Moohummudan law, is not confined to persons born in marriage, but extends to the children of female slaves, acknowledged by their masters. See note, page 17.

kinds of gambling are accounted defects in a slave, as gambling at draughts, chess, or the like; and if a purchased slave be a gambler of this description, he may be returned; but not so where he gambles only for nuts or melons, which is not usually considered a blemish. To be of any other religion than the Mussulman is a defect in a slave; and if a slave be purchased on condition of being an infidel, he cannot be returned because he proves to be a Mussulman, though he may be returned in the converse of the case, when purchased on condition of being a Mussulman but proving to be an infidel. So, also, when a slave is purchased on condition of being a Christian but proves to be a Mussulman, the purchaser has no option.

Absconding, theft, and incontinence of urine.

Absconding, theft, and incontinence of urine in bed, are not defects in a child without understanding; and the test of understanding in this respect is ability to feed himself and put on his clothes. Unity of condition is also necessary to establish the purchaser's right of rejection. Thus, if the defect had appeared in childhood, while the slave was in the seller's possession, and should again exhibit itself in the purchaser's possession while the slave is still a child, or if at both the times the slave were of mature age, the purchaser would have the right of return; but if the slave were a child in the first instance, and the defect did not again exhibit itself till he had passed the age of childhood, the purchaser would not have the power of returning him.

Absconding described.

When a slave conceals himself, or is absent from his master contrary to orders, he is said to abscond; and absconding, without any actual travel or journey, is a defect according to all our doctors. When a slave absconds from his master, or any person with whom he was on lease, or loan, or deposit, and goes out of the city, it is a defect by general agreement; but where he does not leave the city, opinions differ; according to what is most likely to be correct, it is a defect if the city be large, like Cairo, but not so if it be so small that neither houses nor inhabitants are concealed in it. Going from a village to the town, and *vice versâ*, are absconding; but it is not absconding where a slave leaves an usurper to go back to his master. If, however, he leave the usurper, and neither return to him nor go to his master, knowing his residence, and being able to go to it, it is accounted a defect.

Theft is a defect though to an amount less than ten *dirhems*;* and there is no difference whether it be from the slave's master or another person, except in the article of eatables, the theft of which from a master, to eat, is not accounted a defect; but the theft of eatables from a master, to sell, or from another person for any purpose, is a defect. Digging or breaking into a house, though nothing be abstracted, is a defect. **Theft.**

Madness in childhood is a defect for ever; that is, if a slave be mad while a child, in the possession of the seller, and madness should again exhibit itself in the possession of the purchaser, whether the slave be yet a child, or be full grown at the time of its reappearance, he may be returned for the defect; but it is necessary that the madness should reappear in the possession of the purchaser, and continue for more than a day and a night, otherwise it is no defect. **Madness.**

Marriage in a slave, male or female, is a defect, but it is cured by an absolute divorce, previous to rejection by the purchaser: a revokable divorce, however, is not sufficient for this purpose. And if a person purchase a female slave, and find that she is subject to repeated attacks of pain in the eyes, or toothache, and the complaint is not new, but of long standing, he may return her on account of the defect. It would seem that the rule applies also, at least in the case of toothache, to a male slave; while with regard to a female, even a difference of colour in the eyes is accounted a defect. If a person should purchase a female slave on condition of her being beautiful, and find that she is ugly, he is entitled to return her; but not so if the condition be that she shall be little, and he find that she has arrived at puberty. To eat much is a defect in a **Marriage.** **Chronic pains.**

* This is the lowest value for which amputation of the hand can be inflicted.

female slave, but not in a male: to eat little is a defect in neither.

Scars. A person purchases a female slave having a scar, which he does not know to be a defect, but afterwards discovers that it is so; he may return her. Or, as the case is put more fully in another authority;* a person wishing to purchase a slave sees a scar upon her, but does not know that it is a defect: he afterwards finds that it is so, and is entitled to return her, because the matter is one on which men may reasonably doubt, and his taking her does not necessarily argue contentment with the defect. The general rule with regard to scars seems to be, that if the defect be manifest, not concealed from men, the purchaser has not the power of rejection, but if it be not a manifest defect, he has such power.

Defects in cattle. † In cattle, it is a defect to eat little, though not so in the human race; and to eat much, even to excess, is not a defect in the former.

In an ass. In an ass, it is a defect not to bray: but he cannot be returned for being slow in his paces, unless swiftness were made a condition of the purchase.

A cow. If a cow does not give milk, and cows like her are purchased for their milk, she may be returned by the purchaser; but not so if her like are purchased for their flesh; and it is also a defect in a cow if she has a trick of seizing her udder and pressing out the milk.

A cock. It is a defect in a cock to crow at unseasonable times, and he may be returned for it. And to be maimed of an ear is a defect in a sheep, for which it may be returned if it were purchased for sacrifice; and the rule is the same with regard to all other blemishes that prevent sacrifice.

Horses. In horses, swellings, tumours, and excrescences about the feet, pasterns, and hoofs, are defects; so, also, to be wide between the thighs, while the feet approach closely together, or to be stubborn, standing still, and not willing to be led, or refractory, not standing under or obeying the

* The Futawa of Kazee Khan, MS.

† The remainder of this section is taken from section ii. of the original.

bridle, and to have a trick of drawing away the head from the halter or reins, though tied upon it, or even of moistening the nose-bag in which provender is put with water flowing from the mouth, are all defects, provided, however, with regard to the last, that it be such as to diminish the price.

Tusreea.

Tusreea, or tying up the udder of an animal that the milk may collect in it, is not a defect which entitles a purchaser to return her. Nor, if a seller should blacken the fingers of his slave and place him at a desk, that a purchaser may suppose him to be a writer, or dress him so that he may pass for a baker, does this in either case give the purchaser a power of cancelling the contract.*

Boots found to be tight.

If a person purchase a pair of boots, and find them too tight for his feet, he may return them, provided he bought them for his own use. When purchased not expressly for that purpose, but generally, opinions differ as to his right to return them, some judges having decided for the right, and others against it.

A polluted garment.

When a person purchases a polluted garment, not knowing it to be so, but afterwards comes to the knowledge of the fact, he is not entitled to return it, according to the most approved decisions, if it can be washed without injury; but if there be oil in the garment it is a defect, as the stain of oil can seldom be entirely removed.

General rule as to commodities of weight or measure of capacity.

If a person purchase wheat distinctly pointed out, and afterwards find it to be bad, he has no right to return it on account of the defect. So, also, in the case of a silver vessel distinctly specified, which is found to be bad, provided the badness be other than an adulteration of the metal, or a fracture of the vessel, there is no right of return; and generally with regard to articles estimated by measure of capacity or weight, badness of quality is not a defect of which a purchaser can avail himself. But if wheat be actually infested by weevils, or rotten, it may be returned. A person purchases five hundred *kufeezes*†

Wheat mixed with earth.

---

* These are more properly fraudulent devices than defects.

† The *kufeez* is a measure of about 19 ℔.—*Galloway on the Law and Constitution of India*, p. 111.

of wheat which is found to contain earth: if the earth be like that what is usual in the like quantity of wheat, and would not generally be considered a defect, he is neither entitled to return the wheat, nor to claim compensation for the loss; but if the earth be not like what is usual in such wheat, and would generally be considered a defect, he is entitled to return the whole, but he cannot separate the earth from the wheat and keep the latter, claiming a proportionate abatement from the price. If, however, he should have actually made the separation, and have conducted the operation with such care that nothing has been lost in winnowing, so that if the wheat and earth were again mixed together they would still amount to the original measure, in that case he may insist on returning the whole; but otherwise he is not entitled to do so, but he may claim compensation for the defect, that is for the loss on the wheat.

Other grain so mixed, or oil, &c. The same rules apply to sesame, and other grain, when found to contain earth. In like manner, when oil is found to be mixed with black viscous mud, the purchaser cannot insist on returning the mud alone; but if tin or lead be found in musk, the purchaser is entitled to separate them, and return the former by itself, however small or great the quantity may be. Aboo Yoosuf has laid down the following general principle for this class of cases, which has been adopted by many learned men; viz., that whatever may be neglected in a small quantity, is not to be separated when the quantity is great, as earth in the above examples, and that whatever may not be neglected in a small quantity, like tin or lead in musk, the same may be separated when the quantity is great.

General principle.

Bundle of pot herbs containing grass. When a quantity of pot herbs is found to contain grass in the inside, such as is considered to be a defect, it may be returned. So, also, if a person should buy a basket or hamper of fruit, and find grass at the bottom, or a heap of anything, and find moss below, he is entitled to return it.

Books containing errors. A person purchases a book, and finds errors in the letters, or he purchases it on condition of its being pointed according to syntax, and finds that there are errors in the pointing; these are defects for which the book may be returned. So, likewise, if he purchase *the* book, or Kooran, on condition of its being complete, and find some of the verses, or even a single verse, wanting, this also is a defect for which it may be returned; and it is stated in another place, that if a person purchase a book for his son, and be informed by his teacher that it contains many errors, and the errors are in the writing, he may return it and reclaim the price.

A house. It is a defect in a house if the bolt of its lock shoot into a wall belonging to another party, or if there be a large hole in the wall, or if one wall be held in partnership with another person, or a wall be a mass of clay or mortar, and such as is generally considered to be a defect.

Land. If a man purchase land and find a way in it used by the public, he may reject the land; and if one should purchase a garden and find in it a passage or stream of water belonging to another person, or that it is full of ant nests, or cannot be watered without damming up a channel, in all these cases he is entitled to reject it.

SECTION II.

Of what prevents, and what does not prevent, a return on account of defect, and for what defects compensation may, and for what it may not, be claimed.

General principle. It is a general principle, that any exercise of ownership by a purchaser after knowledge of a defect, annuls his right to reject the thing sold. Thus, if a person should purchase a beast of burden, find him to be wounded, and apply a remedy to the wound, or ride him for any occasion of his own, he cannot afterwards reject him on account of the defect. Or if he should ride him, though only to try his paces, or should put on a garment to ascertain its size, that is an acquiescence in the defect. But riding a beast for the purpose of returning or watering him, or purchasing his provender, is not an acquiescence, unless the animal be over-fatigued by reason of the roughness of the way or its own weakness. To place on him the provender of another animal would be an acquiescence. To employ a slave once, unless against his will, is not acquiescence in a defect; but to employ him twice is so. Nor would a slight punishment inflicted on a slave by a purchaser, after discovery of a defect, prevent his rejection, unless it left a mark; but if it leave a mark, the purchaser cannot reject the slave, or even seek compensation for the defect. Inhabiting, or repairing, or demolishing any part of a house by a purchaser, after discovery of a defect, annuls his option. If a person should purchase a cow or an ewe, and after coming to the knowledge of a defect should milk her, and either drink the milk himself or give it to the animal's young one, or should send the young one to her, it amounts to an acquiescence in the defect; but not so if the young one suck its mother without the purchaser's intervention. And exposing the thing purchased to sale, or pledging it, or letting it to hire, after discovery of a defect, amounts to acquiescence, and debars the purchaser from his right to return the article, or even to claim compensation for the defect. So, also, making a gift of it, though without delivery, after discovery of the defect, would bar his right of rejection.

Acquiescence in one defect does not bar the right to reject on account of another.

The acquiescence in a particular defect, implied in the above cases, does not debar a purchaser from his right of option on account of another defect which may be subsequently found in the thing sold. Thus, in the case first put, though the animal be cured of the wound by the remedies applied by the purchaser, it may still be rejected for another defect of which it has not been cured; but a return of the original defect does not restore the option.

But the right does not revive on the return of the first defect.

Thus, when a person purchases a female slave having a whiteness in one of her eyes of which he is not aware, takes possession of her, and then discovers the blemish, he is of course entitled to return her; but if he delay to do so until the whiteness has disappeared, and the eye regain its lustre, he loses his right, nor does it revive though the whiteness should return; but if he find another defect in the slave he may reject her. So also if she had lost a front tooth, or had a blackness in one of her teeth, and the purchaser was not aware of the blemish when he took possession, but afterwards becomes acquainted with it, and then neglects to take advantage of it until the tooth grows or the blackness disappears, he loses his right of option entirely on account of that defect, and does not regain it though the new tooth should fall out or the blackness return; but he may reject the slave on account of any other defect he may find in her.

Acts done before discovery of a defect that bar the right to return.

A person purchases a cow, and having drunk of her milk becomes acquainted with a defect; he is prevented from returning her, but is entitled to compensation for the defect. In like manner, one carnally enjoys a purchased slave, and afterwards becomes cognizant of a defect, but cannot reject her, though he may claim compensation for the defect, whether she were a virgin or not, unless the seller prefer to take her as she is. And the result is the same if he only kiss or touch her with desire; but sexual intercourse, or either of these acts, after knowledge of the defect, would amount to acquiescence, and preclude alike rejection or compensation for the loss. Even if a stranger were to have illicit intercourse with the slave while in the possession of the purchaser, it would bar his right of rejection, though he would be entitled to compensation on account of the original defect, unless the seller were willing to take her back as she is; while if the stranger's intercourse with her had been under a semblance of right, when he would be subjected to the *ikr*, or prescribed ransom, even the seller's consent to take her back would not enable the purchaser to return her on his hands.* A person purchases a piece of cloth, and cuts it up without sewing it; he then discovers a defect, and may claim compensation on account of it; but he is not entitled to reject the cloth, unless the seller be willing to take it as it is; and if the purchaser sell the cloth, that would cancel his right to return

* Because the ransom is an accession.

it, and also bar his claim to compensation, whether he were cognizant of the defect or not;* while if he should sew the cloth, and then discover the defect, though he would still be entitled to compensation for the defect, not even the consent of the seller would enable him to return the cloth on his hands.†

Further acts which have the same effect.

A person purchases a vine and eats the fruit; he then discovers a defect, but cannot return the vine, though the seller should consent; or he purchases an axe, puts it into the fire, and then discovers a defect, but he cannot return it. And even if he should purchase a piece of iron for the express purpose of making it into carpenters' tools, place it in the forge, and then find a defect which renders it unfit for his purpose, he can only claim compensation for the defect, and is not entitled to reject the iron. But if gold were put into the fire, and a defect were then discovered, it might be returned. The sharpening of a handsaw, before the discovery of the defect, would disentitle the purchaser from returning it; but the sharpening of a knife would not have the same effect, unless it were sharpened with a file, which would injure it. A person purchased a large stone pot or cauldron, the seller telling him to use it in cookery, and if there should appear to be any defect in it he would take it back and return the price; the purchaser did so, but it was held, nevertheless, that he could not return the pot without consent of the seller, and was only entitled to compensation for the defect.

Effect of an accession to the thing purchased, in preventing its return.

An increase or accession to the thing purchased may also have the effect of preventing its return on account of a defect. Accessions are of two kinds, united and separated. United accessions are also of two kinds; first, such as do not issue from the thing sold, as a dye superadded to it, or the like, and those by general agreement preclude its return for a defect, though the seller be willing to take it back; and second, such as issue from the

* The general rule as to compensation is explained a little further on.

† Because the sewing is an accession.

thing itself, as its fatness, or improvement in condition and beauty, and these do not preclude its return on account of a defect. If the purchaser should prefer to keep the thing sold, and seek compensation for the defect, but the seller refuse compensation, saying, "Return me the thing sold, that I may return you the full price," the seller is not entitled to do so according to Aboo Huneefa and Aboo Yoosuf, though Moohummud differed from them on this point. Accessions separated from the thing sold are also of two kinds; the first, such as have issued from the thing sold, as the young of an animal, or the fruit of a tree, or what comes within their meaning, as *irish** or *ikr*,† and these prevent the return of the thing sold for a defect, and also prevent cancellations for other causes; and the second, such as have not issued from the thing sold, as gain, or corn, which do not preclude return on account of defect, nor cancellation for other causes. The mode of rescinding the contract is to cancel it, as to the original thing sold without the accession, and to surrender the accession gratuitously to the purchaser. All that has been said with regard to accessions is on the supposition that the accession is still in existence, and in the hands of the purchaser; for if the accession have perished by an act of Providence, the original may be returned on account of a defect, in the same way as if the accession had never been; but if it perish by the act of the purchaser, it is optional to the seller to accept the return of the original, and restore the price, or to reject it; while if the act were a stranger's, though the purchaser cannot insist on returning the original, he is entitled to compensation for the defect.

If the increase should take place before possession, and the purchaser take possession of both original and increase, and then find a defect in the former, he may return it at a due proportion of the price, retaining the increase; and if he find a defect in the increase, he may return it alone at its proportion of the price. Increase before possession.

---

* A fine for damage. † Prescribed ransom for vitiated virginity.

Effect of diminution,

If a person should purchase wheat with dust in it, and the dust is removed so as to reduce the original quantity, he can no more return the wheat on account of a defect; and the result would be the same if it were moist, and should become dry while in his possession, or if the thing purchased were green timber and it should shrink.

by subsequent assessment of khiraj.

A person purchases land on which no *khiraj* or tribute has been imposed, and finds a defect, after which the land is assessed; he cannot return it. But if he should purchase a mansion, and a claim were subsequently made to a channel of water flowing through it, and the claim be supported by evidence, this is tantamount to a defect, for which the purchaser may reject his purchase, unless he prefer to retain it at the full price; and if he have erected buildings upon the premises, he may remove them, but he is not entitled to compensation for their value. And when a person has purchased a piece of land and built a *Musjid** upon it, or has appropriated it to a charitable, or other use or purpose, and afterwards discovers some defect in the land, he is precluded from returning it to the seller, but is entitled to compensation for the defect.

Defect in one of two things purchased together.

When a person has purchased two slaves, or two pieces of cloth, or the like, by one bargain, and taking possession of one of them finds a defect in the other of which he has not taken possession, he has the option of rejecting both, or taking them at the full price; but he cannot take the perfect one and reject that which is blemished at its proportion of the price. And the result would be the same if the defect were found in the one of which he took possession; he must either take or reject them both together. But if he had taken possession of both in the first instance, and had then found a defect in one of them, he would be entitled to reject the defective one specially, and could not reject them both without the consent of the seller. It is only, however, when the subjects of sale can be used separately, like two slaves, that the purchaser can have the option of rejecting one of them; for if they are

* A *mosque*; literally, *a place of prostration*.

two shoes, or two boots, or two leaves of a door, and he should find a defect in one of them, he must either return or keep them both together. With regard to a pair of bulls, it may seem that if a defect were found in one of them after possession, the defective one might be returned without his fellow; but here also our learned men have said that if one of them will not work without the other, they must be treated as if the subject of sale were single, and the blemished one cannot be returned alone.

In a clump of trees.

If a person should purchase a clump of trees, and before taking possession discover that some of them are blemished, he cannot reject those specially, but must take or reject the whole. And if the land be purchased with the trees, the rule is the same, though the discovery should not be made till after delivery; but if the trees be purchased without the land, and the fact that some of them are blemished is not discovered till after possession has been taken by the purchaser, he is entitled to reject those that are blemished.

In part of a single thing.

If the subject of sale be one thing, and part of it is found to be blemished, the purchaser is not entitled to return the blemished part specially, whether the discovery be made before or after he took possession. And if the subject of contract be a commodity estimated by weight or measure of capacity, and the quantity purchased be measured or weighed in one operation, and part of it is found to be damaged, the purchaser is not entitled to return the damaged part alone, whether he discover the blemish before or after taking possession. Where the quantity purchased is contained in several vessels, and the contents of one vessel are found to be blemished, that vessel may be returned alone, according to some opinions, in the same way as if the articles were of two kinds, as wheat and barley for instance. But there seems to be an equal weight of authority against this distinction. It is also to be observed that if some of the grains appear to be inferior in size to the rest, and the purchaser should propose to pass the whole through a sieve, and reject all that falls below it, keeping only the remainder, he would not be entitled to do so. So, also, with regard to walnuts and eggs, the smaller ones cannot be rejected and the rest kept.

In parcels, or hanks of silk, &c.

When a person purchases several parcels of silk, each of which he finds to be partially damaged, and wishes to separate what is good from what is damaged, and to return the latter specially, he is not allowed to do so; but if he should find the damage confined to one parcel, the whole of which is damaged, he may return that specially, and keep the remainder. So, also, if one should purchase by tale some clews or hanks of cotton or thread, and find in every one of them some damage, he is not allowed to separate the damaged threads and return those specially; but if he find some of the clews or hanks damaged entirely, he may return these, and keep those that are not damaged.

A claim to part of a commodity of weight or capacity.

When a third party is entitled to part of a commodity estimated by weight or measure of capacity, and the claim is made after the purchaser has taken possession, he has no option with regard to the remainder; but if the claim be made before possession by the purchaser, he is at liberty to reject the remainder. While if the thing purchased were a piece of cloth, he would be equally at liberty to reject the remainder, though the claim were not established till after he took possession.

Return is barred by a supervenient injury, but compensation may be claimed.

When a purchased article sustains an injury, whether by an act of Providence or otherwise, in the possession of the purchaser, and he afterwards becomes acquainted with a defect which existed in it while in the hands of the seller, he is entitled to compensation for the original defect; but is precluded from returning the article to the seller, unless he consent to receive it. With such consent the return is allowed, except in circumstances where it is prohibited by the right, or, as it may be termed, the policy of the law itself.

Mode of estimating defects.

Whenever recourse is had for compensation on account of a defect, the thing sold is first to be valued in its original state free from the defect; it is then to be valued with the defect, and if the two values differ by, say a half, the purchaser's recourse to the seller is for half the original price.

When a person has sold a thing after knowledge of a defect, the following is the general rule for determining whether he be entitled to compensation or not. Wherever, if the thing sold were still under the power of the purchaser, he would have a right to return it to the seller, with or against his consent, then he has no claim to compensation after the sale, or other the like cause by which his power over it has terminated; and, on the other hand, wherever he would have no such right to return the thing to the seller, with or without his consent, if it were still under his power, he is entitled to compensation, notwithstanding the sale or other cause by which his power over it has terminated.

Rule as to compensation when a return is rendered impracticable by acts done after knowledge of a defect.

A person purchases a slave, takes possession of him, and then, without being aware of a defect, in conjunction with another, slays him. He then becomes acquainted with the defect, but has no right of recourse against the seller on account of it. Nor if a stranger should slay the slave intentionally, or by accident, has the purchaser any claim to compensation for the defect. And though the purchaser were himself alone the slayer, still he would have no right to compensation for the defect, according to the Zahir Rewayut, though Aboo Yoosuf by another report differed from this opinion.* If, on the other hand, the purchaser should emancipate the slave gratuitously, or the slave should die a natural death, and the purchaser should then become acquainted with a defect, he may have recourse to the seller for the damage; and *tudbeer* and

By acts done before knowledge of a defect.

* When the slave is slain by a stranger, liability is incurred to his owner for the value of the slave, not exceeding 10,000 *dirhems*, which is the amount of the fine for blood; and the purchaser may be said to receive compensation for the defect, or, at least, the question of compensation is complicated by this liability. When the purchaser is himself the slayer, there is nothing of this kind to prevent his recourse for compensation; and it seems that Aboo Yoosuf therefore thought him entitled. The *Zahir Rewayut* proceeds on the ground that there is responsibility in all cases of homicide, though, when a slave is slain by his master, it is necessarily waived, by reason of the person by and to whom it is due being identical. — See *Hamilton's Hedaya*, vol. ii. p. 414.

isteelad are in this respect like gratuitous emancipation. But if the emancipation were for some consideration in property, or by way of *Kitabut,* and the purchaser should then become cognizant of a defect, he would have no claim for compensation on account of it. A person purchases a fish and finds it to be damaged, but the seller being absent he sells it, as the fish would putrify if he waited for his return; he cannot, however, have recourse to the seller for any loss on account of the damage, and is without remedy.*

By destruction or consumption of the thing sold,

When a person purchases grain of any kind, or a garment, and destroys the grain, or tears the garment, and then becomes aware that it was defective, he has no claim to compensation for the defect without any difference of opinion. And even if he should tear the garment in putting it on, or eat the grain, and then become cognizant of a defect, still his claim to compensation is barred, according to Aboo Huneefa, whose opinion appears to be correct.

or by a partial sale.

When a person having purchased a slave, sells a share in him, and retains the remaining share to himself, he can neither reject the retained share for a blemish subsequently discovered, nor seek compensation for the blemish on account of the share which he has sold. Upon this point there is no difference of opinion. But is he entitled to compensation on account of the share that he has retained? According to the Zahir Rewayut, he is not entitled to such compensation, and the decision is held to be valid. If, however, one should purchase flour, bake part of it, and then discover that it is bitter, it would seem that he may return the remainder for a proportionable share of the price, and claim compensation on account of the part that has been baked. And in like manner with regard to grain of any kind, if the purchaser, after eating a portion should find it to be damaged, he may claim compensation for the damage in what he had eaten, and return the remainder for a rateable share of the price.

---

* This case more properly falls under the rule in the preceding paragraph.

If a person purchase eggs, melons, cucumbers, gourds, or walnuts, and break them, not knowing them to be bad, but find them to be so, he is entitled to a return of the full price, if, as in the case of bitter gourds, or rotten eggs, the thing be of no use (for not being property or *mal*, the sale itself was void); but if the article, notwithstanding its badness, be of some utility, as, for instance, if it can be eaten by the poor or even by cattle, his remedy is for a share of the price proportioned to the defect; and if he should eat any part of it after merely tasting it, he can claim nothing. If a few only of the things be bad, as one or two in a hundred walnuts, the sale is lawful; but if many of them be bad it is unlawful, and the purchaser may have recourse for the full price. With regard to ostrich eggs, which are broken and found to be addled, some of our learned men have said that compensation can be claimed only as for a defect, the shell being of use; and upon this point there should be no difference of opinion. But when an ostrich egg is broken and found to contain a dead bird, moderns have differed; some of them being of opinion that the sale is unlawful, as two things are purchased, one of which is carrion; while others have maintained, that the carrion being contained within the shell as its bed, there is but one thing in reality, and that the sale is lawful.

Case of things broken or destroyed in trial, and proving to be bad.

A person purchases a slave, and having taken possession of him sells him back to the seller, who then finds an old blemish in him; according to Aboo Yoosuf (and Aboo Huneefa was of the same opinion), he may return the slave to the purchaser.*

Case of return for an old blemish.

A person purchases a *deenar* for *dirhems*, and after reciprocal possession sells the *deenar* to another, who finds it to be defective, and returns it to him without any order of the judge; the first purchaser may also return it to his seller on account of the defect. And on the same principle, when a person receives payment of a debt in *dirhems*,

Return of base money to an original seller by a first purchaser, on a return being made to himself.

* This and the two next cases are from pages 108 and 109 of the original.

and pays away these *dirhems* to a creditor, who finds them to be base (*zooyoof*), and returns them to him without the order of a judge, he is entitled to return them to the party from whom he first received them.

Of other things.

When a second purchaser who finds a defect in the thing purchased, but is precluded from returning it by a supervenient defect during his own possession, has recourse for compensation to the person from whom he purchased, the latter cannot go back to the original seller, according to Aboo Huneefa; though both his disciples differed from him on this point. A person purchases a slave, and taking possession of him, sells him to another in whose hands he dies, and it is then discovered that the slave had a defect while in the possession of the original seller, whereupon the second purchaser has recourse to the first purchaser for compensation, on account of this defect; in such circumstances, the first purchaser has no right of recourse against the original seller, because the second sale is not cancelled by the mere recourse for compensation, and its subsistence is a bar to the first purchaser proceeding against the original seller. If a person should sell a thing which is returned for any cause that induces a complete cancellation of the sale, and he then discovers a defect which existed in the thing when it was in the possession of the seller to himself, he may return it to such seller.

Section III.

Of Suits regarding Defects and the Production of Evidence.

Defects are of two kinds, manifest and latent. The former are such as the judge can ascertain by mere inspection, as sores, blindness, superfluous fingers, and the like. The latter are such as cannot be ascertained by mere inspection.

Manifest defects.

Manifest defects are either old, as superfluous fingers, and the like; or new, which again are divided into three classes, according to the probability of their occurrence in the period between the sale and the time of litigation; the first class being such as could not have happened within that period, as the marks of small-pox for instance; the second, such as might have occurred within that period, as wounds; and the third, such as could not have occurred previous to the sale. Latent defects are also of two kinds; such as may be known from existing marks or indications, as womanhood (opposed to virginity,) pregnancy, and disease in a part of the female person of which a man cannot take personal cognizance; and such cannot be known by existing marks, as theft, absconding, and madness.

Latent defects.

Suit relating to manifest defects.

If a suit should relate to a manifest defect which the judge can ascertain by inspection, he is to make the requisite inspection, and if he should find the defect existing, he is to hear the suit, but not otherwise. If it should further appear that the defect is either an old one, or a new one that could not have happened since the date of the suit, the purchaser has the right of rejecting the thing sold; because the actual existence of the defect is established by inspection, and it may be inferred with certainty that it must have existed at the time that the subject of sale was in the hands of the seller. It may, however, be objected by the seller, that the purchaser has lost his right by acquiescence in the defect, or some other cause, and in such case the word and oath of the purchaser are to be preferred. With regard to his oath, all reports agree that the seller is entitled to demand it, but according to most of our learned men, the judge should not require it unless on the demand of the seller. The form of administering the oath which is adopted by most judges, and is accounted proper and valid, is as follows: "By God, your right to reject for the defect has not been lost for the reason alleged, neither expressly nor by implication." If it should appear that the defect might have occurred since the date of the sale, and also might have occurred previously to it, or the case should present any difficulty, the judge is to ask the seller if the defect existed in the property when it was in his hands; and if he should answer in the affirmative, the purchaser is entitled to reject the article, unless the seller allege an extinction of his right to do so, and the allegation is established either by the purchaser's refusal to take the oath, or by evidence. If, however, the reply of the seller should be in the negative, his word and oath are to be preferred, unless the purchaser can produce evidence to the existence of the defect in the hands of the seller. The approved form of administering the oath in this case is as follows: "By God, he has not the right of rejection against you on account of this defect which he claims." When it appears that the defect is one which cannot be supposed to have happened previous to the sale, the judge is not to decree for a return against the seller.

Suit relating to a latent defect indicated by existing marks.

When the suit has relation to a defect, which, though latent, is indicated by marks still existing on the person, and they are such as may be ascertained by a man, the judge is to make inspection in person, if he have any knowledge of diseases; otherwise he is to inquire of persons acquainted with such matters, and to rely upon the statement of one or two such persons, being respectable (one is sufficient, but it would be more cautious to have two), and upon the information thus obtained, the present existence of the defect may be established so as to justify the hearing of the cause. The judge is then, according to what appear to be the best authorities, to consider if the defect be one that might have occurred since the date of the sale, according to the information of the one or two respectable persons to whom the matter may have been referred, and if it appear to be of that description, or if they should have found it difficult to come to a decided opinion on the point, and have differed respecting it, in none of these cases is he to pronounce for the rejection of the thing sold by the purchaser, but he should put the seller on his oath. If the defect be one that could not have occurred within that period, and its existence is established by the statement of only one person, the judge is in that case also to follow the same course, and to put the seller upon his oath, while if the existence of the disease be established by the statement of two persons, the judge may at once decree in favour of the purchaser's right of rejection. If the defect be one which women only can speak to, as pregnancy, or the like, the judge is to submit it to the inspection of one or two respectable women (one would suffice, but two would be more cautious), and if the person or persons referred to should say that the woman in question is pregnant, the existence of the defect is sufficiently established for entertaining the suit. Then, if the same person or persons should say that the pregnancy has occurred since the sale, the judge is not to decree against the seller, but to put him on his oath; when if he should refuse to swear, decree is to be given against him for rejection. And though the person or persons referred to should state that the pregnancy existed while the woman who is the subject of sale was still in the possession of the seller, yet if the statement be made after possession by the purchaser, the same course is to be followed, and the seller put on his oath. And even though the statement should be made before possession by the purchaser, the judge is not to pronounce for immediate rejection on the statement of only one person. Whether he should do so on the statement of two persons, is liable to some doubt, but the weight of authority is against his relying on their statement, and in favour of his first referring the matter to the oath of the seller in this case also.

Suit relating to latent defects that are not indicated by existing marks.

When the defect complained of is latent, and cannot be ascertained from existing marks on the person, as absconding, madness, theft, and incontinence of urine in bed, its present existence is first to be determined, and this is to be done by the judge inquiring of the seller as to the fact. But it is a necessary preliminary that the purchaser's complaint be properly laid. Thus, he must not only allege that the defects charged existed while the thing or person purchased was in the possession of the seller, but that they also exist now that the thing or person is in his own possession. In the case of madness, this is sufficient. But with regard to the other defects mentioned, he must further allege a continuance of the same state or condition, that is, he must allege that the person was a *minor* at the time of their occurrence while he was in the possession of the seller, and also at the time of their occurrence when he was in his own hands, or that he was *major* at both the times; for if he were *minor* at one time and *major* at the other, the suit could not be sustained. The suit being properly laid, the seller is to be asked, as already mentioned, whether he admits the present existence of the defect or denies it. If he deny it, he cannot be called upon further to answer till the purchaser has proved the fact, that is, for instance, if the defect complained of be absconding—that the slave absconded from him. If the seller admit the present existence of the defect, that is, in the instance put, that the slave has absconded from the purchaser, he may then be interrogated as to the existence of the defect with himself, and, if he admit the fact, the slave is returned on his hands, according to the complaint of the purchaser; but if he deny it, the purchaser is then to be called upon for evidence, that the slave had absconded when in the seller's possession. If he prove it, the slave is returned to the seller; and if the purchaser is unable to produce evidence, the seller is put upon his oath. In like manner, where the purchaser has proved the present existence of the defect, an oath is to be administered to the seller in these terms: "By God, the slave never absconded while in your possession." When the seller neither admits the present existence of the defect, nor is the purchaser able to prove it, there is a difference of opinion between the *Imam* and his disciples, as to the seller's liability to be put upon his oath; the former thinking that he is not liable, but both the latter considering that he is. The purchaser is not to be sworn as to his acquiescence in the defect, according to Aboo Huneefa and Moohummud, without the demand of the seller. When called for by the seller, the form of oath which has been adopted by most judges, and is accounted valid, is as follows: "By God, your right to reject has not been lost for the cause alleged by the seller, neither expressly nor by implication."

Miscellaneous cases.

Disputes may occur relative to defects or blemishes in things sold which it would not be easy to bring within any of the preceding rules; and a few of the cases reported in the law books may be adduced in this place, if only to illustrate the procedure of Moohummudan courts of justice in matters of this kind. The following case is given by Moohummud in the *Amlaa*, or Opinions:—When a person purchases two slaves for a thousand *dirhems* in one bargain, and after taking possession of them both, finds one of them to be blemished, but the seller and he differ as to the respective values of the slaves on the day of sale, he alleging that the value of the blemished slave was double that of the other, while the seller maintains the reverse; in these circumstances, no respect is to be had to the assertion of either, but the judge is to take into consideration the value of both the slaves on the day of litigation, and if they be then equal in value, he is to cause the blemished slave to be returned for half the original price; not, however, until he has put each of the parties on his oath as to the allegation of his adversary. If both the parties should adduce evidence each to his own allegation, it is to be received as to the excess insisted on by him over the amount stated by the other, and in that case the rejected slave would, according to the witnesses of the purchaser, be valued at the same sum as the other slave would be valued at according to the witnesses of the seller, and the result be the same, the purchaser having to make his rejection at half the price, or five hundred *dirhems*. And if one of the slaves should die, and a blemish be found in the survivor, and the parties should dispute about the respective values of the slaves, neither party being able to adduce evidence, the word of the seller is to be preferred as to the value of the dead slave, and the value of the survivor to be taken as it may be on the day of litigation. If both parties offer evidence as to the value of the dead slave, the evidence of the seller is also to be preferred, while if they both offer evidence as to the value of the survivor, preference is to be given to that of the purchaser.

Disputes as to the respective values of two slaves, one of whom is blemished.

As to time of sale.

A person sold a slave to another, who took possession of him, and then charged him with a blemish, saying, "I purchased him to day, and such a blemish could not happen in one day;" the seller, however, alleged that he had sold him a month ago, and that such a blemish might happen in that time; preference was given to the word of the seller.

As to some use made by the purchaser of the subject of sale.

A person purchased a beast, and wishing to return him on account of a defect, the seller said, "You rode him on some occasion of your own after you were aware of the defect;" when the purchaser replied, "Nay, but I rode him only to return him to you;" the purchaser's word was preferred; and if the seller should say, "You rode him for watering without any necessity," it is also proper that the word of the purchaser should be received.

As to the identity of an existing blemish with one previously admitted.

A person sold a slave girl to another, and said, "I sold her with a scar on such a place;" the purchaser afterwards brought her back, having a scar on the place indicated, and wished to return her, but the seller said, "This is not the scar which I acknowledged—you have already released me from that, and this is a new one that has occurred in your hands;" the purchaser's word was preferred. But if the seller had said, "I sold her with a blemish," and the purchaser should bring her back having a blemish, and the seller should then say, "This is not the blemish that she had, which was so and so," his word is to be preferred. While, if he had said, "I sold her with a blemish on her head," and the purchaser should bring her back, intending to return her on account of a blemish on her head, the word of the purchaser would be preferred as to that being the identical blemish, if the seller should deny it. The inference to be drawn from these and other similar cases (says the author) is, that when the seller has indicated a particular place as the site of the blemish, the purchaser's word is to be received; but when no particular place is indicated, the blemish being stated generally, preference is given to the word of the seller.

As to identity of the subject of sale.

A person purchased a servant and took possession, but afterwards brought him back to return him on account of a defect, when the seller said, "This is not my servant," and the purchaser replied, "It is your servant whom I purchased;" the word of the seller, with his oath, was preferred.

When the Imam,* or his agent, sells booty that has been secured, and the purchaser finds a defect in it, he is not immediately to return it; but the Imam should appoint some person to contest the matter with him. Such person cannot acknowledge the defect, nor is he liable to be put on oath if he deny it, his duty being merely to adduce evidence; and if he should acknowledge the defect he ought to be dismissed. If the defect be established, and the thing returned on account of it, it is to be restored to the general mass of the booty, when the case occurs before partition; and if it does not occur till after partition, the thing is to be sold on account of its price, and the difference, if any, to be made good by or to the *Beit ool mal*, or general treasury.

Defects in booty sold by the Imam or his agents.

When a *Mookatib* purchases his father or son, he is not entitled to reject him, or seek compensation for a defect; but if the *Mookatib* prove unable to pay his own ransom after becoming acquainted with the defect, his master may reject, the *Mookatib* giving him authority for that purpose. If the master should sell the *Mookatib* on account of his inability, or he should die, the master may make the return on his own authority, while if the *Mookatib* should release the defect before he became unable to complete his ransom, the master would have no right to reject; and if the master should grant a release before the *Mookatib's* inability became evident, the release would be lawful. The law is the same in the case of a *Mookatib's* purchase of his mother. If he should purchase his brother or sister, or paternal uncle; these relatives also, according to Aboo Yoosuf and Moohummud, come within the operation of the contract of *Kitabut*, and the rules applicable to the purchase of a father or son, while Aboo Huneefa considered that these relatives do not fall within the operation of the *Kitabut*, and may therefore be re-

A *Mookatib* is not entitled to reject his father, son, or mother, for defects.

Other relatives.

* The leader or chief of the Moohummudans.

turned by the *Mookatib*, on account of defects. If a *Mookatib* should purchase his *Oom-i-wulud*, and his son be with her, he has no power to return her on account of a defect; but he may seek compensation for it, and this is his exclusive right, so that he alone can give a release for it before he becomes unable to complete his ransom; and a release granted by his master would not be valid. Though the *Oom-i-wulud* should be without her child, still the *Mookatib* has no right to reject her, according to Aboo Yoosuf and Moohummud, though in the opinion of Aboo Huneefa he would in that case have the power to do so.

Purchase from a *Mookatib* by his master.

When a person purchases a slave from his *Mookatib*, he is not entitled to return him on account of a defect, nor can he litigate the matter with the vendor to the *Mookatib*. If a *Mookatib* or a freeman should purchase a slave, and enter into an agreement of *Kitabut* with him, he can neither reject him for a defect, nor seek compensation on account of it.

A gift of the price bars rejection for defects.

A person sells a thing to another, and before receiving the price makes a present of it to the purchaser; the latter is barred from returning the thing on account of a defect; but if the price be first received and then presented to the purchaser, he may reject on account of a defect.

SECTION IV.

Of a Release from Defects, and security for them.

What is included in a general release.

A release of defects, or exemption from responsibility on account of them, is lawful in a sale of animals or other property, and all defects are included in the release, whether known or unknown to the seller, whether demurred to or not demurred to by the purchaser, and whether the kind of defect has or has not been specified or pointed out. According to Aboo Huneefa and Aboo Yoosuf, the release extends to defects existing at the time of sale, and also to such as may happen up to the time of delivery; but, according to Moohummud, it is limited to the former. A condition that the seller shall be "free from every defect in it," that is, the subject of sale, does not comprehend defects supervenient to the time of sale, according to all their opinions; and a condition that he shall be free "from all defects in it, and that may happen," would vitiate the sale.

Special releases: how construed;

A release from all defects comprehends diseases as well as blemishes; but disease implies sickness, and an exemption on account of diseases does not extend to a cautery on the skin, or superfluous fingers, or the scar of an old wound. A release from all *ghaillut* (misfortune) means theft, absconding and wickedness; and in an exemption on account of black teeth, red and yellow are included. If a slave be sold with an exemption on account of all sores, it comprehends contusions as well as the scars of wounds already healed, but not a cautery, to which the term sore is inapplicable. In like manner, exemption on account of fractures on the head does not include open wounds on the head, which are not fractures. A man said to another, "you are released from every right I have against you;" the words were held to extend to defects, but not to every possible contingency.

continued.

If the purchaser of a slave say to the seller, "I have released you from every defect in his eye," this is no release if the slave be found blind of an eye. So, also, a release from every defect in his hand does not exempt the seller if the slave be found to have lost a hand; but the loss of one or two fingers would be within the terms of the exemption. The loss of two fingers is two defects, and would not be included in a release from a single defect; but if all the fingers with half the hand were cut off, it would be considered but one defect.

Effect of stipulation for exemption as an admission of defects.

A stipulation to be exempt from responsibility, on account of all defects, is not an admission that there are defects; contrary to the case of a stipulation for release from a single defect, or from two defects, which would be an admission.

Guarantee by a third party: how construed.

A person purchases a slave from another, and a third party becomes security for his defects; a blemish is subsequently found, and the slave is returned to the seller, but the surety is not liable, according to the analogy of a saying of Aboo Huneefa, that this is a security for the fulfilment of a bargain.* According to Aboo Yoosuf, however, it is a security for defects, being like the security against all contingencies, which is restricted by custom to the establishment of a right.† And, in like manner, if the person should become surety for the theft or emancipation of the slave, and he should prove to be free or stolen, the surety would be liable. So, also, if one should become surety for blindness or madness, and either of these should be found in the slave, recourse may be had against the surety for the price; and if the slave should die in the hands of the purchaser before his return to the seller, and a decree should be passed against the latter for compensation on account of the defect, the purchaser might also in that case have recourse against the surety for the amount. A person purchases a slave, and another becomes security for such a share of the price as may correspond to any defect that may be found in him; in such case, in the opinion of Aboo Huneefa, as well as Aboo Yoosuf, the undertaking would be lawful, and in the event of the defect exhibiting itself, and the subject of sale being rejected in consequence, the purchaser might have recourse against the surety for a corresponding part of the price, in the same way as against the seller himself.

SECTION V.

Of compounding Defects.

Composition for defects is lawful.

When a person has purchased a slave for a thousand *dirhems*, and after taking possession of him and paying

---

* Such a security is null. See *Hamilton's Hedaya*, vol. ii. p. 596.

† Ibid. p. 597.

down the price, discovers that he is defective, and the seller denies that he sold him with the defect, but subsequently compounds for a certain amount of *dirhems*, to be returned either immediately or at a future date, the transaction according to Moohummud is quite lawful; and though the consideration agreed upon were a *deenar*, the composition would still be lawful if the *deenar* were paid down before the separation of the parties; but if they should separate before payment of the *deenar*, the composition would be void.* A composition after a resale and receipt of the price by the purchaser would not be lawful, though the composition were for a sum in *dirhems*. But if the slave should die in the hands of the second purchaser, and the latter come back to the first purchaser for compensation on account of a defect, and he should then compound with the original seller, though the composition would be void according to Aboo Huneefa, it would be lawful in the opinion of both his disciples.

but not after resale by purchaser.

Miscellaneous cases.

A purchaser complained of a defect in the eye of a female slave, and the seller compounded for the eye, the composition was held to be lawful, though there was no mention of the particular defect; mention of its position being considered equivalent to a specification of the defect itself.

The purchaser of a piece of cloth having given it to a fuller to be cleaned finds it to be torn, and not knowing whether the rent was made by the fuller, or whether it existed in the cloth while in the possession of the seller, enters into a composition to keep the cloth and receive a *dirhem* from each of the seller and fuller; such a transaction is lawful; and it would be so also, if the terms of the composition were that the seller should take back the cloth, receiving a *dirhem* from each of the purchaser and fuller. The purchaser of a slave girl finding her to be defective, compounds with the seller on the terms that the latter shall return a portion of the price and the purchaser

---

* For the reasons of the distinction between the cases, the reader is referred to Book ii. chapter iii. section 3.

keep the slave; such a composition is lawful; but it would not be lawful if the terms were that the purchaser should return the slave with a sum in money to the seller; though, if the price had been paid in full, the purchaser might sell back the slave for less than he originally paid for her. And where the purchaser of a piece of cloth had cut it up for a *kumees* or shirt, but before sewing it found a defect in the cloth which the seller acknowledged had existed when it was in his possession, and the parties then agreed that the seller should take back the cloth and the purchaser abate two *dirhems* in the return of the price, this was held to be lawful; the sum retained by the seller being opposed to the loss sustained by the act of the purchaser.

Composition is annulled by subsequent removal of the defect.

The removal of a defect annuls a composition made on account of it, and the purchaser must restore to the seller what he received in exchange for it, or any abatement that may have been made from the price on its account; but if the removal of the defect does not take place till after the thing sold has passed from the property of the purchaser, he is not bound to make restitution. And if after a purchase the parties should agree that the seller shall be released from all responsibility on account of defects on payment of a *dirhem*, the composition is good, though no defect be found; but if the seller should say, "I have bought the defects from you," it would not be lawful.

Exception.

Miscellaneous cases.

A purchaser alleges a defect in a slave girl, which the seller denies; they enter into a composition notwithstanding, that, for a consideration in property, the purchaser is to release the seller from all responsibility on account of this defect; it subsequently appears that there was no such defect, or that if there was it had been cured; in such circumstances, the seller is entitled to get back from the purchaser what he paid in exchange for the composition. So, also, if a purchaser should complain of a whiteness in the eye of a slave girl, and the seller compound for it by abating a *dirhem* from the price, but the whiteness subsequently disappears, and the eye regains its lustre, the purchaser must restore the *dirhem* to the seller. And in like manner, if the purchaser of a slave girl should find that she is married, and wishing to reject her, the seller enters into a composition with him for a sum in *dirhems*, but the husband of the slave subsequently divorces her, the purchaser must restore the *dirhems* to the seller.

A person purchases an ass, and finding an old defect in him, wishes to return him to the seller, but they agree upon a composition for one *deenar*; the purchaser subsequently finds another defect, and is entitled to return the ass on account of it, returning with him the *deenar* which he had already received.

SECTION VI.

Of Defects in Sales by and to Executors or Agents.

Sale by an executor. When an executor sells the property of his testator, the obligations of the contract are binding upon him personally, and the thing sold may be returned on his hands for a defect. And if a person should purchase a slave for a thousand *dirhems*, and take possession of him, but die before paying the price, leaving debt beside to the amount of another thousand, and no other property than the slave, and if in these circumstances the executor should discover a defect in the slave, and return him on account of it to the seller without the decree of a judge, that would be no dissolution of the sale so far as the creditor is concerned, and the executor must take five hundred *dirhems* from the seller and pay them to the creditor on account of his debt. The result would be the same if the executor should agree to a dissolution of the sale without any defect. If the seller should refuse to take back the slave, and the matter were brought into litigation before the judge, it would be his duty, when made aware of the debt to the other creditor, to sell the slave instead of returning him to the seller, and to divide his price between the seller and the creditor; and the seller would not be responsible for any loss on account of the defect, neither before the sale by the judge nor after it. If the judge should not be acquainted with the debt due to the other creditor, and the matter were litigated before him by the executor and seller as a question of defect, he should return the slave to the seller on account of the defect, and annul his right to the price from the deceased. If after this the creditor should adduce evidence of his debt, the seller would then be put on his option to keep the restored slave and account to the creditor for half the price, which would be tantamount to an equal division of the price between them, or surrender the slave to the judge to be sold, and the proceeds to be divided among them according to their respective claims.

Sale by an agent. When an agent for sale has sold an article and is involved in litigation on account of a defect in it, if he should take back the thing sold without the decree of a judge, he is bound personally, and not his principal, and the thing sold becomes the agent's property; nor is he entitled to contest the matter with his principal; and if he should do so, and adduce evidence of the existence of the defect while the thing sold was in the hands of his principal, his evidence would not be received. But if the return of the thing sold were under the decree of a judge upon evidence, it would be obligatory on the principal, whether the defect were old or recent. If the decree were on the agent's refusal to take an oath, the effect would be the same; but if the decree were on the agent's acknowledgment, and the defect were one the like of which does not happen within such a time, the return would be obligatory on the principal; while if the defect were not of that character, the return would be to the agent, who might, however, litigate the matter with his principal; and if he could adduce evidence that the defect existed while the thing sold was in his possession, he would be ultimately able to throw it back on his principal's hands. He would also have the benefit of his principal's oath if he had no evidence, and be entitled to throw the thing on his hands if he refused to swear.

Rejection by and to an agent. To reject on account of a defect belongs to the agent, and rejection is also to be made to him while he lives and is of sound understanding, and a person liable for his engagements; but if he be not a person of this description, as for instance, if he be an inhibited slave, or an inhibited youth,* rejection should be made to the principal himself; and though the agent were of the class referred to, yet if he should happen to die, restitution ought also to be made to the principal.

Agent for purchase. An agent for purchase, who has purchased a slave girl for his principal, but has not delivered her over before he discovers a defect, may return her to the purchaser whether his principal be present or absent; but if he have made delivery of her to the principal, he has no longer any power to return her without the principal's order. If the seller should insist in the former case that the principal had acquiesced in the defect (the principal being abroad at the time of dispute), and should demand the oath of the agent or his principal, he would not be entitled to have it according to us. If the agent should, without his oath being called for, return the slave girl to the seller, and the principal should then appear and declare his acquiescence, with a view to get back the slave from the hands of the seller, he would be entitled to reclaim her. If the seller should adduce evidence of the principal's acquiescence, his evidence would be received; and the agent's acknowledgment of the principal's acquiescence would also be valid, and preclude further litigation on his part. While an acknowledgment by the agent of a release by his principal of the defect, would be credited only as against himself, and would bind him with the thing sold, unless the principal were content to take it, or evidence were adduced of his acquiescence. **Agent for litigation.** If we put an agent appointed to dispute the defect in place of the agent for purchase, and the seller were to insist that the purchaser himself had acquiesced in the defect, the agent would not be entitled to return the thing sold before producing his principal to be put on oath.

---

* A youth under puberty; who may, however, when he understands purchase and sale, be appointed an agent for either." —*Hamilton's Hedaya*, vol. iii. page 5.

Return to and by agent for purchase.

When an agent for purchase has purchased and made delivery to his principal, and the latter finds a defect in the thing bought, he is to return it to the agent, who will then return it to the seller. If the agent himself should find a defect in the thing sold before taking possession, he may lawfully release the seller on account of it, and his release is binding on his principal; but if the release were after possession, it would be binding on the agent alone, and not on his principal.

A purchaser from an agent makes the return to him of a thing on account of defect, though the price had actually reached the principal.

When an agent purchases a slave for the purchase of which he was expressly appointed, and discovers a defect before taking possession, he is entitled to reject the slave, whether the defect be trivial or flagrant. He may also acquiesce in the defect if it be of the former description, so as to bind his principal; but if it be flagrant, the sale is binding on himself only, on a favourable construction of the law, unless the principal be willing to take the slave.

CHAPTER IX.

OF LAWFUL AND UNLAWFUL SALES.

SECTION I.

Of the Sale of Obligations for Obligations, and the Sale of Prices and Annulments of the Contract by Separation of Parties before Possession.*

The sale of an obligation for an obligation when lawful.

THE sale of an obligation for an obligation is lawful, when possession, either actual or implied, of both the articles exchanged is taken at the meeting before the separation of the parties, or when actual possession of one of the things has been taken and implied possession of the other. And it makes no difference whether the contract be a *surf* † or not. Thus first as to actual possession of both the things exchanged, and when the transaction is a *surf*. If a person should buy a *deenar* for ten *dirhems*, and neither of them is at first produced,‡ but both are subsequently paid down in cash at the meeting before the separation of the parties, the sale is lawful. So, also, when it is not a *surf*, as if one should purchase *fooloos*, or

Actual possession of both.

* Arab. *Deyn*. See *ante*, note on page 7.

† Explained page 7.

‡ Arab. *bu huzrut-i-hima*, literally, *in the presence of both*. This qualification is necessary to prevent the things exchanged from being determinate. The contract may be supposed to take place at the commencement of the meeting, when it is duly constituted and lawful in all respects, though the things exchanged are then undeterminate; but, to preserve it in its state of validity, possession before the parties separate is necessary, for the contract which was at first valid will become void by their separating without possession.

grain of any kind, for *dirhems*, and neither of the things is produced, but both are subsequently paid down or delivered at the meeting before the parties separate, the sale would be lawful. Next as to implied possession of both the things exchanged, and when the transaction is a *surf*. If ten *dirhems* and one *deenar* be reciprocally due by and to two persons, and each of them should buy his debt from the other in exchange for what is due to himself; or when the transaction is not a *surf*, as if the debt due to one be *fooloos* or grain of any kind, and the debt due by him to the other be *dirhems*, and each of them should buy the debt due by him in exchange for that which is due to him by his fellow, and the parties should then separate; here, also, the sale would be lawful. Again, as to actual possession of one of the things exchanged, and implied possession of the other. If a person by whom a debt of ten *dirhems* is owing to another, should purchase his debt of ten *dirhems* for a *deenar*, which he pays down, and the parties should then separate from the meeting, such a contract would be lawful. So, also, if a person being indebted to another in a certain quantity of wheat, should purchase the wheat for *dirhems*, which he pays down at the meeting, the sale would in like manner be lawful.

Implied possession of both.

Actual possession of one, and implied of the other.

When possession of one only is taken, it must be actual.

When possession of only one of the things exchanged is taken before the separation of the parties, it is only when the possession is actual, and the transaction is not a *surf*, that the sale is lawful. Thus, if a person should purchase a *deenar* for ten *dirhems* (when the transaction would be a *surf*), and should take possession of the *deenar* without delivering the *dirhems*, or *vice versâ*, and the parties should then separate, the sale would be void; but if he should purchase *fooloos* or grain of any kind for *dirhems* (when the transaction would not be a *surf*), and the parties should separate after actual possession is taken of one of the subjects exchanged, the sale would be lawful. If, on the other hand, only implied possession were taken of one of the things exchanged, the sale would be unlawful, whether it were a *surf* or not. As if one indebted to another for a *deenar* should purchase the debt for ten *dirhems* (when the transaction would be a *surf*), and the parties should separate before possession were taken of the ten *dirhems*, the sale would be void. So, also, when a person is indebted in *fooloos* or any kind of grain, and buys the debt of his creditor for a sum in *dirhems*, but the parties separate before the payment of the *dirhems*, the sale is in like manner void. These rules are quoted from the *Zukheera*, and the author adds that they are worthy of remembrance, though very generally forgotten by mankind.

Sale of prices—*dirhems* and *deenars*.

When a person purchases a thousand *dirhems* for a hundred *deenars*, and pays down the *deenars* without receiving payment of the *dirhems*, but happening to be indebted to the seller of the *dirhems* in a thousand *dirhems* on a previous transaction, the latter says to him, "I will make the thousand *dirhems* which you already owe me this thousand that I now owe you on the present *surf*," and the other party is content, such a transaction would be lawful on a favourable construction of the law. But a balancing of accounts by a purchase subsequent to the *surf*, as if one should purchase *dirhems* with a *deenar*, and pay down the *deenar*, but should not receive payment of the *dirhems* until some time after when he purchases a piece of cloth from the seller of the *dirhems*, and the latter says to him, "I will make the *dirhems* which you now owe me the *dirhems* which are due to you on the *surf* sale," and the parties are mutually content, such a transaction, according to the best and most approved authorities, would not be lawful.

A previous debt may be set off in a *surf*, but a debt due on a *surf* cannot be set off in a subsequent bargain.

***Fooloos* for *fooloos*.**

When one specific *fuls* is sold for two *fooloos* also specific, the sale is lawful, by reason of the specification of both the things exchanged; so that if one of them should perish before possession, the contract would be void; and if one of the parties should desire to substitute a similar in the place of the perished article, it would not be in his power to do so. But if a person should sell one *fuls* undetermined for two *fooloos*, also undetermined, the sale would not be lawful, though reciprocal possession should take place at the meeting, and if one specific *fuls* were sold for two undeterminate *fooloos*, or *vice versa*, it would only be in case the *fooloos* left undeterminate should be taken possession of at the meeting, that the sale would be lawful.

Fooloos for *dirhems*, with an option.

When parties interchange *fooloos* for *dirhems*, with the stipulation of an option to each, and take possession mutually before they separate, the sale is void;* but where the option is reserved to only one of the parties, though Aboo Huneefa still considered the sale to be void, both his disciples were of opinion that it would be lawful. And, in like manner, a sale of *fooloos* for *fooloos*, with a right of option to both parties would be invalid, though mutual possession were taken before separation; but where the option is reserved to only one of them, the sale is valid according to the disciples, though otherwise in the opinion of their master. And if a person should sell a specific *fuls* for two *fooloos* also specific, with a condition of option, the sale would be lawful. When *fooloos* have ceased to be current, and a person makes a purchase with them in a place where they are not readily received, it is only when the *fooloos* are specific, that the sale is lawful; for if they be not specific the transaction is not lawful.

Dirhems of three kinds.

Coined *dirhems* are of three kinds. In one of these the alloy preponderates, two-third parts, or three-fourth parts, or five-sixth parts, being of copper to one of silver; in another the silver preponderates, two-third parts or three-fourth parts being of silver to one of copper; and in the third kind the silver and copper are equal, or each one-half.

First kind.

The first kind of *dirhems* is treated as if composed of two separate things, copper and silver, neither being merged in the other, but each regarded separately; and if pure silver, or what is regarded as pure silver, be purchased with *dirhems* of this description, and the weight

* Because the transaction is a *surf*, in which it will be seen hereafter (Book ii. chapter 1), that an option cannot be stipulated for to either party. It is implied that the *Fooloos* are undeterminate.

of the pure silver be less than, or only equal to, the silver contained in the *dirhems*, or if the relative weights be unknown, the sale is not lawful according to our doctors; while, if the pure silver be more in weight than the silver contained in the *dirhems*, the sale is lawful, the excess being a counterpoise to the copper; but the conditions of a *surf* must be observed in the transaction, and a failure in this respect* would vitiate the sale with regard to the copper as well as the silver. If gold were purchased with this first kind of *dirhems*, the sale would be lawful, however it might be,† but a failure to observe the conditions of *surf* would in this case also invalidate the whole sale. And if some of this kind of *dirhems* be sold or exchanged for others of them, the transaction is lawful, whether those on both sides be equal, or one side be in excess of the other, but mutual possession of both is a condition of the legality of the contract. When *dirhems* of which two-thirds are copper and one-third silver cease to pass current, they are like non-current *fooloos*, so that they become determinate by specification; and the validity of the contract depends on their being specific, and it becomes void on their perishing before delivery. With regard to the second kind of *dirhems*, in which the silver preponderates (being in the proportion of two-third parts to one-third of copper), the sale of them for pure silver is not legal, unless the quantities opposed to each other be equal, and when some of them are sold or exchanged for others of the same class, the sale in like manner is not legal unless as similar for similar. With regard to the third kind of *dirhems*, in which the silver and alloy are equal, the sale of them for pure silver is regulated in the same way as if, instead of these *dirhems*, *dirhems* of the first class were substituted. But a loan of them is not lawful except by weight, nor is a sale for these *dirhems* lawful but by weight, unless they are pointed out, which would be sufficient to explain their quantity and quality, in the same

Second kind.

Third kind.

---

* Literally, *if disturbed by any of these conditions.*

† That is, though one be in excess of the other.

way as if the *dirhems* were pure; but the sale would not be dissolved by their loss before delivery.

Dirhems of the second and third kinds, how to be used in commerce.

Dirhems, of which two-third parts are silver and one-third part is copper, are like impure or base *dirhems*.* When anything is sold for them the sale is not lawful unless by weight, except when they are pointed out, as if the whole were base silver. When the *dirhems* are pointed out, the sale is lawful without weight; and if the *dirhems* were half silver and half copper, the answer in this respect would be the same as if they were two-third parts silver and one-third part copper. When a person has purchased some merchandise with these *dirhems*, and they cease to be current by men abandoning their use in commerce, the sale is void according to Aboo Huneefa; and if the thing sold be still in existence, the seller is entitled to take possession of it; and if it has perished the purchaser is liable for its value. The disciples, however, considered the sale to be lawful, with this difference of opinion between them, that while Aboo Yoosuf thought the purchaser liable for the value of the *dirhems* as they stood on the day of taking possession, Moohummud considered that he was liable for their value as on the latest day of their currency.

When *dirhems* of the different kinds are interchanged for each other.

When *dirhems* are of different kinds, some having two-third parts of copper to one of silver, some having two-third parts of silver to one of copper, and some having the silver and copper equal, there need be no fear in selling one of these kinds for another kind with an excess, if the sale be from hand to hand. But if one kind of them be sold for the same kind with excess, it is not

* Arab. *bu munzilut* (in the stage or place of) *zooyoof* and *nubhirjah*. I have not been able to find an exact definition of these terms; but I suppose that they are applicable to all *dirhems* in which the silver preponderates over the alloy, or all of the first class. The second and third classes, that is *dirhems* in which the alloy is equal to, or preponderates over, the silver, are employed in the same way as those that are called *sitook* (see *post*, Book ii. chap. 2, sect. 1); and this corresponds with the description of *sitooka*, given in the translation of the *Hidayah*, vol. iii. page 152, for which, however, there seems to be no authority in the printed edition of the original.

lawful as to those in which the silver preponderates, except as similar for similar; while of those in which the copper preponderates the sale is lawful, whether the things opposed to each other be equal, or one be in excess, but delivery from hand to hand is here also a necessary condition. On the analogy of this rule it is said, with regard to Adawlee *dirhems* extant in our times, that the sale of one of them for two is lawful when it is from hand to hand; but our doctors do not allow this as regards them or the Atarif *dirhems*, for if excess were allowed in them the door of usury would be opened.

SECTION II.

Of the Sale of Fruits, Leaves, and Growing Crops.

When the sale of fruit on a tree is lawful.

The sale of fruit before its appearance is not valid, by general agreement; when sold after it has appeared, and is of some use, the sale is valid. And when sold before it is of any use, as being yet unfit for food to man or beast, its sale is also valid according to the most authentic opinions;* but it is incumbent on the purchaser to remove the fruit immediately, if sold in absolute terms, or with a condition to that effect. A condition that it shall be left on the tree would vitiate the sale, if the fruit has not attained its full size.† When it has attained its full size, and is sold, either in absolute terms, or with a con-

* "The sale of fruit on a tree is valid, *whether the strength of the fruit be ascertained or not; that is, whether it may or may not have reached such a degree of strength as may preserve it from common accidents.*"—*Hamilton's Hedaya*, vol. ii. page 374. All that appears in the printed original to correspond with the words in italics, may be more literally translated thus: "whether its goodness have begun or not;" which the commentator explains as "goodness for food to man or beast."—*Hidayah and Kifayah*, vol. iii. page 23.

† "Since it implicates together the right of property of the two parties." "Besides, in this case it must necessarily follow that one deed is interwoven with another; in other words, that either a loan or a lease is implicated with the sale which is unlawful."—*Hamilton's Hedaya*, vol. ii. pages 374, 375.

dition that it shall be removed, the sale is valid; but if sold with a condition that it shall be left, the sale is invalid by analogy, according to Aboo Huneefa and Aboo Yoosuf, and valid on a favourable construction of law, according to Moohummud, with whose opinion the *futwa* is said, by one authority, to correspond, while by another, the opinion of the two elders is said to be valid. If the whole fruit be sold, and part only has appeared, the sale is invalid, according to the obvious and most authentic construction of law, though some judges have decided in favour of its legality from a regard to the practice of mankind.

Rule as to the aftergrowth of fruit left on the tree.

If a person should purchase fruit unconditionally, and leave it on the tree with permission of the seller, he may lawfully avail himself of its aftergrowth; but if he leave it without such permission, and it should increase in substance, he must bestow the excess in charity. If left after it has ceased to grow, he is not called upon to bestow anything in charity. If one should sell fruit unconditionally and leave it on a date tree, giving at the same time a lease of the tree for a fixed period, the lease is void; but the purchaser is still at liberty to avail himself of its aftergrowth.*

Effect of increase.

If a person should purchase fruit exempt from any obligation for its removal, and the fruit should increase before it is vacated by the seller, the sale is vitiated; but if the increase should not take place till after the fruit has been vacated, the sale is not vitiated, and the seller and purchaser become partners, the word and oath of the latter being preferred as to the quantity of the increase, because he is in possession. And the rule is the same with regard to artichokes and melons. Of these, however, the purchaser may secure the increase to himself by purchasing the plants, when the aftergrowth would be an accession to his own property.

* For the lease, being a nullity, cannot affect the permission, which therefore remains good. The sale and lease cannot stand together; and the latter must give way, as the former is entitled to preference. See *post*, chapter xii.

Leaves of the mulberry-tree.

A person purchases leaves of the mulberry-tree* without any mention of the place where they are to be cut off, but it is sufficiently known by custom; the sale is lawful. And if the purchaser should leave the branches, he may cut them in the second year; and if he leave them for a considerable time, and then desire to cut them, he may lawfully do so, provided that the tree be not injured by the cutting.

Of the white mulberry.

If a person purchase the leaves of the white mulberry † after they have appeared on the tree, but fail to cut them till the proper time has passed, he is not on that account entitled to cancel the sale, if he had purchased the leaves and branches together, and the part to be cut off had been explained; and he may be compelled to remove them, unless doing so would be injurious to the tree, in which case the seller would have an option of rescinding the sale. If the leaves had been purchased without the branches, under a condition for their immediate removal, the sale would also be lawful; but if the terms were that the leaves should be removed gradually, the sale would not be lawful. And the result would be the same if the purchase be made with an express stipulation that they are to be left on the tree. If the leaves be purchased without any condition, and be removed on the day of sale, the transaction is lawful; but if the day be allowed to pass without their removal, that would vitiate the sale. The device for obviating the difficulty in this case is for the purchaser to buy the whole tree and its roots, and then after taking the leaves to resell the tree to the vendor.

Of the osiers of the willow.

A sale of the osiers of the willow is lawful, though they are growing or increasing from time to time; and the sale of leeks is lawful though they are growing from the lowest stage till they are fit for use, from a regard to usage; but things, with respect to which there is no

---

* Arab. *Toot.*

† Arab. *Firsad.* This name is said to be peculiar to the sweet and white mulberry.—*Freytag.*

usage, cannot be lawfully sold, if growing or increasing from time to time.

Sale of a bed of cucumbers.

If a person being possessed of a bedof cucu mbers should sell it before the appearance of the cucumbers, the sale would be lawful as regards the plants, and the cucumbers that might grow on them thereafter would then be an issue from the purchaser's own property. If he should wish to leave the plants in the bed, and to reserve legal power over them, he must buy the plants for a part of the price, and take a lease of the land for a fixed term in consideration of the remainder; but the sale must precede the lease, for if the latter were prior the transaction would be illegal. A sale of the plants with a loan of the land also would be lawful, with this difference, that the loan would not be binding, and might be recalled. When two parties are partners in a bed of cucumbers, one of them cannot lawfully sell his share to a stranger, because extracting the plants may injure the property of another, and no one is obliged to submit to injury. If the partner consent, the whole of the bed should be purchased from both the partners, and the sale then cancelled as to the share of one of them.

A growing crop;

A person sells a growing crop, consisting of pot herbs, on condition that the purchaser shall cut them, or send cattle to eat them off the ground, the sale is lawful; but if the condition were that the herbs should be left in the ground until maturity, the sale would not be lawful; and the rule is the same with regard to trefoil or clover.

held in partnership.

Two persons holding land in partnership, on which there is a growing crop, their joint property, one of them sells his share in the crop without his share in the land, to a stranger; the sale is lawful if the crop be ripe, but not so if it be unripe, except with the consent of the partner, whether the sale be in absolute terms, or on condition that the crop shall be cut; and if the condition be that it shall be left in the ground, the sale is not lawful even with the consent of the partner. But if one of the partners should sell his share of the land with his share of the crop, the sale would be quite lawful, the purchaser coming into the stead of the seller. And in the first case, where the sale of the share in the crop is unlawful, it would become legal if allowed to remain uncancelled until the crop is ripe. When one of the partners sells his share in the crop to the other, without his interest in the land, the sale is not lawful if the crop be unripe; and the rule is the same with regard to cotton and all kinds of crops held in partnership between two persons, one of whom sells to the other his share in the crop without the land; but where half the land with half the crop are sold, whether to a co-partner or to a stranger, without his consent, the sale is lawful.

A tree in partnership.

When a single tree is held in partnership between two persons, and one of them sells his share in it to a stranger, the sale is not lawful; and when there are three partners, one of whom sells his share to only one of his partners, the sale is not lawful; but a sale to them both would be lawful.

Sale of share in a crop held jointly by the owner of the soil and the cultivators.

When a crop belongs to the owner of the soil and to the cultivators jointly,* and the former sells his share to the latter, the sale is not lawful; but a sale by the latter of their share to the former would be lawful, for there would then be no necessity for delivery of the share; and if the crop be ripe, either party may sell his share to the other. It would seem, however, that a co-sharer in the crop for only a third cannot lawfully sell his share to the landlord or another.

Sale of the land by the owner.

When the landlord sells land on which there is a crop held jointly between himself and the cultivators, two cases are presented for consideration. First, when the crop consists of pot herbs which are not ripe, and in this case, the sale of the land is dependent on the permission of the cultivator whether the land be sold with or without the crop; when, therefore, the land is sold with the whole crop, and the sale is sanctioned as to both by the cultivator, it is lawful, and the price is to be divided rateably between the

* This refers to the contract of *Moozariut*, where one of the parties is a proprietor of land, and the other a cultivator, and they agree to divide the produce between them in certain proportions.

land and the crop, the part of it apportioned to the former belonging exclusively to the landlord, and the part of it apportioned to the latter being divided equally between him and the cultivator. Where the cultivator refuses his sanction to the sale, the purchaser may either cancel it at once or wait till the crop is ripe. When the landlord sells the land alone, and the sale is sanctioned by the cultivator, the purchaser is entitled to the land, and the crop remains as before the property of the seller and of the cultivator, while if the latter refuse his sanction, the purchaser is at liberty to cancel the sale; and if the landlord should sell the land with his share in the crop, and the sale is sanctioned by the cultivator, the purchaser would take the land and the landlord's share in the crop at the full price, while if the cultivator should refuse his sanction, the purchaser would be at liberty to cancel the sale; but in this instance, the cultivator would have no right to do so if he should desire it. The other case presented for consideration is where the crop is ripe at the time of sale. Here, if the land be sold alone, or together with the landlord's share of the crop, the sale is lawful without any dependence on the sanction of the cultivator. If the land be sold with the whole of the crop, the sale takes effect immediately as to the land and the landlord's share of the crop, while with regard to the cultivator's share it is necessarily dependent on his sanction; if he allow the sale he is entitled to a rateable share of the price, and if he refuse his sanction the purchaser has an option, provided he were not aware of the joint ownership in the crop.

Sale of land under crop. Land on which there is a crop may be lawfully sold without the crop, or the crop may be sold without the land; and half the land may be sold without the crop, but half the crop cannot be sold without the land, except where the crop is held in joint-ownership between the landlord and cultivators. In that case, as already mentioned, the latter may sell their share to the former, but a sale by the landlord of his share to the cultivators would not be lawful, unless the seed were furnished by the latter, when it would seem that the sale to them ought also to be lawful. Where the crop is ripe, either of them may sell his share to the other.

When the landlord sells his share of the crop to a stranger without the land, or the cultivator sells his share in it to a stranger, the crop in both cases being unripe, and the sale in consequence unlawful on account of the damage which may accrue to the partner, but the latter afterwards sells his share to the same purchaser, the first sale becomes lawful.

Sale of a share in the crop, at first unlawful, is rendered lawful by subsequent sale of partner's share.

A person gives up his land to another on an understanding that he is to plant it, and that they are to divide the produce between them equally. The land is planted accordingly with mulberries, and after a while the owner of the land sells it with his share in the plants to a third party; the sale is valid; and a subsequent sale by the purchaser, though invalid according to Moohummud, would also be valid in the opinion of Aboo Huneefa and Aboo Yoosuf, who considered the sale of immoveable property before seizin to be lawful, and the *futwa* is in accordance with their opinion.

Sale of land under wood.

A single cutting from leeks after they have grown up, may be lawfully sold, but not so many cuttings. And the rule is the same with regard to all potherbs, a single cutting of which after they are grown up may be lawfully sold, but the sale of so many cuttings is not lawful. So, also, with regard to green corn which is cut in that state as food for horses, and trees when intended to be immediately cut or rooted up.

A cutting from leeks.

Growing grass, though on land which is private property, cannot be lawfully sold or let to hire.* The owner

Growing grass.

* Because it is partnership property, according to the saying of the Prophet: "All men are partners in three things—water, grass, and fire."—*Inayah*, vol. iii. p. 98. Mr. Hamilton restricts the prohibition to "grass growing on a common" (*Hedaya*, vol. ii. p. 435); but there is no warrant for this in the printed edition of the original; and in both its commentaries, the *Kifayah* and *Inayah*, the doctrine is stated in almost the same words, and with the same qualifications, as are above mentioned. It is further expressly stated, in another place, in the *Kifayah* (vol. iv. p. 1103), that "its master (*Sahib*) does not become proprietor of the grass by its being on his land."

of the land may, however, prevent persons from entering on his land to take the grass. In that case, the person prevented may say to the landlord, "I have a right in your land; either permit me to enjoy it, or mow the grass and deliver it to me." This, however, only when the grass is a natural growth; for if the proprietor of the land has watered, or otherwise prepared it for vegetation, and the grass has grown on it in consequence, he may, according to the best authorities, sell the grass as his own property, and even reclaim it from a person who should mow it without his permission. And even the object of letting the grass may be attained by giving a lease of the land for cattle to stand or remain upon, or any other advantage, at what may be considered a fair rent. In grass is included all kinds of herbage pastured by cattle, whether green or dry, with the exception of trees; for grass has no stem or trunk, which is the distinguishing characteristic of the latter. The natural growth of trees may, therefore, be lawfully sold. It is to be observed that mushrooms are on the same footing as grass.

The sale of the eggs of game on one's land not taken is unlawful.

SECTION III.

Of the Sale of Things under Pledge, or Let to Hire, or Usurped, and of Absconded Slaves, and Khiraj Lands.

Sale of a thing under pledge.

There is some difference among the learned with regard to the sale of a thing that is pledged;* but according to the general and most authentic opinion, the sale is in suspense. So that if the pledger should pay the debt, or the pledgee should release him from the debt, or should restore the pledge to him, or allow and be content with the sale, the sale would be complete, and there would be no necessity for a renewal of the contract. If the pledgee should refuse his sanction to the sale, and the purchaser should in consequence apply to the judge for delivery of the thing sold, it would be his duty to cancel the sale.

---

* Arab. *murhoon.* Land is not properly the subject of pledge; but a conditional sale of land, corresponding to the English mortgage, though condemned as an evasion of the prohibition of usury, is yet held to be strictly legal. See *post*, chapter of "Abominable Sales."

The sale of a thing let to hire is like that of a thing in pledge, and according to the general and more correct opinion, the sale is in suspense. In both cases, the purchaser has an option if he were not aware that the thing bought was in pledge or let to hire at the time of his purchase; and it appears that, according to the *Zahir Rewayut*, he has such option even though he were aware of the fact. There is some difference in the reports as to the right of the tenant to cancel the sale; but the weight of authority and the *futwa* seem to be against his having any such power. And most of the learned are of opinion that even though the period of the lease should be long, the sale would still take effect on its expiration. There is a like difference of opinion as to the right of the pledgee to cancel the sale, but according to the most authentic and valid opinions he has no such right. **Sale of a thing under lease**

A person sells a mansion already in lease, without the consent of the tenant, who subsequently makes an addition to the rent, and the contract of lease is renewed. This gives immediate effect to the suspended sale; for the grant of a new lease comprehends a cancellation of the first, and removes the only impediment to the operation of the sale. **becomes operative by renewal of the term.**

When the lessor sells the subject of a lease to a third party without the permission of the tenant, and afterwards sells it to the tenant himself, the second sale is lawful, and cancels the first; but if he should sell the property first to one person and then to another, both sales being sanctioned by the tenant, the first sale would be lawful and the second void. The lessee of a slave who is sold by his owner and delivered to the purchaser, cannot make the latter responsible; but the case is different with a pledgee, who may in such circumstances claim the value of the slave from the purchaser. **Sale to the tenant after a sale to a stranger.**

When a person who purchases from a pledger sells or manumits a slave, and the pledgee sanctions the original sale, the second also, and the manumission, are thereby rendered effectual, without any difference of opinion. And when a pledger sells a pledge without permission of the pledgee, and then sells it to the pledgee himself, the **Effect of sanction by the pledgee of previous disposals by the pledger.**

second sale is lawful and cancels the first. Or, if the pledger should first sell the pledge to one person and then sell it to another, in both cases without the consent of the pledgee, and the pledgee should afterwards sanction one of the sales, the sale so sanctioned would become operative, and the price be paid to the pledgee to the extent of his debt; but if, instead of a second sale, the pledger should make a pledge or a lease of the thing pledged, and the original pledgee should sanction the second transaction, the effect would be to render the first sale operative, and to render the pledge or the lease void.* A person sells a slave who is in pledge, and the purchaser manumits him without receiving possession from the pledgee; the slave is free, and the purchaser becomes liable to the pledgee for his value; but the seller has no right against him for the price. A pledger sells the pledge, and gets possession of the price, he then sells to another person still before releasing the pledge, but subsequently releases it; in such circumstances, the first purchaser is to be preferred.

Sale by owner of property that has been usurped.

When usurped property is sold to another person than the usurper, the sale is in suspense; if the usurpation be acknowledged by him, the sale is complete and binding on the usurper; and though denied by him, the result is the same, provided the rightful owner has evidence; if he have no evidence, and the thing sold perishes before it can be delivered, the sale is dissolved.

Sale by the usurper;

When a person sells the property of another, and then purchases it from the rightful owner and delivers it to the purchaser from himself, that does not legalize the wrongful sale, which on the contrary is not merely invalid but actually void. But a sale is rendered lawful when the cause of property in the vendor is made to precede it; insomuch that if the usurper of property should sell it, and then make compensation for his wrongful act to the owner, the sale would be lawful; while if he should purchase the property from the owner, or receive it in a gift, or inherit it from him, none of these acts would give

how legalised.

---

* See *ante*, note, page 142.

legal effect and operation to a sale previously contracted by him. But when the usurper of a slave directs a person to purchase him from his master on the usurper's account, and it is done, he becomes lawfully possessed by the mere act of purchase;* and so, also, if a stranger should direct the usurper to purchase the slave on his account, and he should do so, the stranger would become legally possessed by the mere act of purchase.

Effect of a composition with the owner.

The following case is cited from Moohummud. A person usurped a slave from another, and sold and delivered him to a third party, he then compounded with the slave's master for a consideration; in these circumstances Moohummud was of opinion, that, if the consideration were *dirhems* or *deenars*, the sale would be lawful; but if it were a specific chattel the composition must be considered as a second sale, which would render the first void. And when the usurper of a slave manumits him, and then makes compensation for his value, that does not legalize the previous manumission.† Nor if the purchaser of a slave from one who had usurped him should manumit the slave, and the lawful owner should then sanction the sale, would that, according to analogy and the opinion of Moohummud, give legal effect to the manumission, though Aboo Huneefa and Aboo Yoosuf, on a more favourable construction of the law, thought it ought to have that effect; while, if the purchaser from the usurper should sell the slave, and the lawful owner should then confirm the original sale, that by the purchaser would remain inoperative, without any difference of opinion. When the usurper sells to a person who again sells to another, and there are thus several changes of hands, and the lawful proprietor then sanctions one of the contracts, that which he so sanctions becomes legal and effective. But if the owner were to exact compensation from the

---

* See *ante*, page 39.

† "The right of property established in an usurper, in virtue of his payment of compensation, is defective; and a defective right of property is sufficient to legalize sale, but not emancipation."—*Hamilton's Hedaya*, vol. iii. p. 544.

usurper for his wrongful act, that would legalize the sale by him, and render all the subsequent sales entirely void.*

Sale of an absconded slave.

The sale of an absconded slave is not lawful.† If the slave should return and be delivered to the purchaser, that would legalize the sale, according to many authorities; and some have gone so far as to maintain that if the seller should refuse to deliver the slave, or the purchaser to take him, the party refusing may be compelled by the party willing, and that a new sale would not be necessary. But the weight of tradition and authorities seems to be against the legality of the sale, and in favour of a new sale in the event of the slave's return. If a person should come to the master of an absconded slave, and say, "Your slave that absconded is in my possession, and I have already taken him, sell him to me," and the master should sell him, the sale in such circumstances would be lawful. But though the master should allow the sale, yet if at the time of taking possession the party had called on persons to witness that he did so for the purpose of restoring the slave to his owner, in that case he would not become possessed as a purchaser;‡ and if the slave should die before the purchaser returned to his home the sale would be cancelled, and he might return to the vendor for a refund of the price; but if he had not called upon persons to witness, as before mentioned, his previous possession would become constructively possession under the sale. If the person should say, "Your slave is with such an one who has already taken possession of him, sell him to me," and the owner should credit the assertion and sell, the sale would not be lawful; it would, however, be

---

* It seems from this that the sanction or compensation gives no retrospective effect to the sale by the usurper, which is legalized as only from the date of sanction or compensation, and *that* being subsequent to the other sales, they are in consequence excluded, and become void.

† It has been expressly prohibited by the Prophet.—*Hamilton's Hedaya*, vol. ii. p. 437.

‡ Because his possession would be a trust (*Ibid.* p. 264), which is not convertible into possession under a purchase.—*Ante*, p. 38.

a sale, though invalid, and when followed by possession on the part of the purchaser, he would become the proprietor.

If a person should purchase a slave who absconds before delivery, he may cancel the contract if he please, and the seller cannot call upon him for payment of the price until he is in a condition to make delivery of the slave.

Slave absconding between sale and delivery.

The sale by a person to his infant son of an absconded slave is not lawful; but a gift to him of the slave is lawful.* So also a gift of him to an orphan, being under one's protection, and the emancipation of an absconded slave in expiation of a vow is lawful, when the emancipator knows that he is alive, and where he is to be found. And when an usurped slave absconds from the hands of the usurper, and the lawful owner then sells the slave while he is yet absconding to the usurper, the sale is lawful.

Sale or gift of an absconded slave to an infant.

The sale of *Khiraj* or tribute lands is lawful, by which is meant lands of Sowad,† and in like manner the sale

Sale of *khiraj* lands.

---

* See *ante*, note, p. 22.

† Viz.: "*Irak.* Then what is watered of it from its great rivers is *Khirajee.*" — *Futawa Alumgeeree*, vol. ii. p. 338. "And besides this, every country, conquered by force, the inhabitants of which have embraced the faith, and on whom it has been conferred, is *Khirajee*, if the water of *Khiraj* flows to it; and every country which has peaceably submitted to the *Jiziyut* or capitation tax, is also *Khirajee.*"— *Ibid.* The description contained in these extracts, which I have rendered literally, applies to the Moohummudan conquests everywhere. And in the British territories, in India, all the land is considered liable to *Khiraj*, or revenue, as it is there called, unless the revenue of it has been granted away by the State. As *Khiraj* lands have been classed by the compilers of the *Futawa Alumgeeree* with dependent rights, and it has sometimes been supposed that the Moohummudan sovereigns of India claimed a proprietary interest in the land, I subjoin an extract from a work of high authority, in confirmation of the right to sell, stated in the text, viz.: "The land of the Sowad of Irak, is the property of its inhabitants. They may alienate it by sale, and dispose of it as they please; for when the *Imam* conquers a country by force of arms, if he permit the inhabitants to remain in it, imposing the *khiraj* on their lands and the *jizeeah* on their heads, the land is the property of the inhabitants, and since it is their property, it is lawful for them to sell it or dispose of it as they choose."—*Suraj-ool-Vuhaj.* That is, by any mode of transfer legal by the Moohummudan law.—*Galloway on the Law and Constitution of India*, p. 38.

of *Kateea* lands is lawful, or lands separated by the Imam and set apart for a particular tribe.

Ikharut and *ikarut* lands.

With regard to the sale of *Ikharut* and *Ikarut* lands, the former of which means bad land taken by the direction of the owner and improved and sown, and the latter means lands in the hands of cultivators, we will say, that if sold by the owner the sale of them is lawful, but if sold by the improver or cultivator the sale is not lawful.

Land under a contract of *moozariut.*

If land be under a contract of *Moozariut* the cultivator has a preference, according to one authority, during the term of the contract, by whomsoever the seed be provided; and if he sanction the sale he has no claim for hire on account of his labour, the purchaser being entitled, according to another authority, to both the landlord's and the cultivator's shares in the crop. While if the latter should refuse his sanction to the sale it would be unlawful, provided the land were under crop at the time; but if free of crop it would seem that the sale of the land without his consent would be lawful; and the rule is the same as to gardens in which the fruit has not appeared.

A village in which there is a *musjid.*

If a person should buy a village in which there is a *Musjid* or a tomb, without excepting these, the sale is vitiated. With regard to the *Musjid,* however, it is a condition that it be in a state of repair fit for use; for if the place around it be waste and ruined, and men can dispense with the use of the *Musjid,* the sale would not be vitiated.

An estate partially under *wukf.*

When a person purchases an estate, a portion of which is under *wukf,** it would appear that the sale is lawful. So also if land, the property of the seller, and land under *wukf* be sold together, without distinguishing what share of the price is applicable to the former and what to the latter, it would seem that the sale is legal and valid as to the former.

Property in which there is a highway.

The existence of a highway through property does not vitiate its sale, though it is a defect; but if the way be without any distinct mark or boundary to determine its

* An appropriation for a religious or charitable purpose.

quantity or limits, that would, according to one authority, vitiate the sale.

When a village is sold, in which there is a *Musjid*, which is excepted from the sale, it becomes a question whether mention of its boundaries be or be not a condition of the legality of the sale. Opinions differ upon this point; but according to the most approved it is not necessary. And the same rule applies to the exception of large reservoirs of water and highways; but the boundaries of a tomb should be mentioned, unless they are sufficiently indicated by its being a hill or rising ground.

Not necessary that the boundaries of an excepted *musjid* or highway should be specified.

If there be sulphur, or stone, or salt, or pistachio nut trees, in a mountain which is not the property of any one, these may be lawfully carried away and sold; but if the mountain be private property the removal of any of these is unlawful.

Of things found in a place not private property.

Section IV.

Of the Sale of Animals.

The sale of fish in the sea, or a large river, or in a well,* is not lawful. If a person be the proprietor of a pond into which fish enter, and the pond was originally prepared with that view, what enters into it is his property, and no one has a right to take it without his permission. If they can be taken without the artifice of the fisherman, the sale of them is lawful, but otherwise it is not lawful. If the pond were not originally prepared with the view referred to, the proprietor of the pond has no right to the fish, and the sale of them by him is unlawful, unless he shut up the pond. When he does so, whatever has entered into the pond is also his property, and the legality of its sale by him will depend on the same distinction as in the former case. Though a pond were not originally prepared for fish to enter it, yet if they are caught elsewhere and let loose in the pond they become the property of

Sale of fish in the sea,

and in a prepared pond.

* Arab. *Beer*, a well, a pit; probably a large and deep well, from which, though water may be drawn, it might be impracticable to bring up fish.

the owner of the pond, and may be lawfully sold or not, as in the preceding cases, according as they can or cannot be retaken without artifice. The same distinctions apply to fish when caught and put into a reservoir of water.

Option of inspection.

Whenever the sale of fish in the water is lawful, the purchaser has an option on taking possession and seeing it.

Fish in a large stream.

If fish be in a large stream or channel, the sale of it in that state is not lawful, though the seller should be able to deliver it after the sale. So also though he had once possessed the fish, yet if it escape from his hands and fall into the stream or channel he cannot lawfully sell it; but in this case, according to one authority, if the fish can be retaken and delivered before the parties have cancelled the contract, the sale is lawful. This distinction, however, is rejected by the learned men of Bulkh, who say that the sale is unlawful though the seller should be able to deliver the fish.

Pigeons.

With regard to pigeons, if their number be known and they can be delivered, the sale of them is lawful. There could be no difficulty or question as to the legality of the sale, when the pigeons are in their holes, and the egress shut up; but there is no doubt that the sale of them when on the wing is also lawful, if it be known from their habit that they will return to their cots.

Sale of birds or fish that, though at liberty, return to be fed.

The sale of birds or fish in the water, or birds in the air, which regularly return to be fed, is lawful, and delivery may be made when they return. And the case is the same with regard to a deer which is tame and comes to be fed; but if after being fed it should return to the woods and a state of nature, so that it cannot be taken without hunting, the sale of it would be unlawful.

Of a stray horse.

The sale of a stray horse, which cannot be retaken without artifice, is not lawful.

Bees.

The sale of bees, when collected together, is not lawful according to Aboo Huneefa and Aboo Yoosuf, unless there be honey in their hives, when the hives with their contents, including the bees, may be lawfully sold. According to

Moohummud, the sale of the bees when collected together* is lawful, and his opinion is adopted for the *futwa*.

Leeches.

The sale of leeches is lawful according to the most approved opinions; and all are agreed that a person may be lawfully hired for the purpose of procuring them.

Silkworms and their cocoons.

The sale of silk cocoons is lawful according to Aboo Yoosuf and Moohummud, and the *futwa* is agreeable to their opinions; and the sale of the silkworms is also lawful according to Moohummud, with whose opinion the *futwa* corresponds.

Reptiles.

The sale of reptiles of the earth, as snakes, scorpions, white lizards, and the like, is not lawful; nor the sale of any animal of the sea or water, except fish, as frogs, crabs, &c.: even the use of their skins or bones is unlawful; but it is stated in one authority that the sale of snakes, when they can be of use in medicine, is lawful; and the more valid opinion is that everything that is of use may be lawfully sold.

Of trained animals.

The sale of trained dogs is lawful: so, also, of cats and other beasts or birds of prey, whether trained or not. If an untrained dog be capable of training, the sale of him is lawful, otherwise it is not; and the same may be said of the lion, the sale of which, when capable of being trained and used in hunting, is lawful. As hunting leopards and hawks are always capable of being trained, the sale of them, under any circumstances, is lawful. The sale of the elephant is lawful; and with regard to apes, there are two accounts of Aboo Huneefa's opinion, and according to one of them, which has been approved, he thought the sale to be lawful. It is also stated in one authority, which is said to be approved, that the sale of all animals, with the exception of the hog, is lawful.

Elephants and apes.

Houses in Mecca and Baghdad.

The sale of the structures of houses in Mecca is lawful, but not the sale of their lands.† The sale of mansions in

* Arab. *Mujmooa*. Collected in their hives, I suppose is meant; and in the *Hidayah*, the word employed is "secured."—See *Translation*, vol. ii. p. 436.

† In the *Hidayah*, the sale of the ground in Mecca is stated to be only abominable, but a saying of the Prophet is quoted, which amounts to a positive prohibition.—*Translation*, vol. iv. p. 119.

Baghdad and of shops in the market belonging to the sooltan is not lawful, nor can they be made the subjects of claims of pre-emption.

SECTION V.

Of the Sale of Game by a Moohrim, and of things that are forbidden.

Sale of game when unlawful.

The sale of game* by a *Moohrim*,† or of forbidden game,‡ or of game within the sacred territory,§ whether the vendor be a *Moohrim* or not, are all alike unlawful; but if two lawful persons‖ within the sacred territory sell game to each other that is without the territory, and make delivery after they have come out of the territory to lawful ground, the sale is lawful according to Aboo Huneefa, though not so in the opinion of Moohummud. And if a person having game belonging to another person in his hand should become a *Moohrim*, and the proprietor being in a lawful condition should sell the game, the sale would be lawful, and the *Moohrim* be compelled to deliver it; while if he destroyed it he would be bound to make compensation. If a *Moohrim* were to appoint a lawful person his agent for the sale of game, and the agent should sell it in consequence, the sale would be lawful according to Aboo Huneefa, but void in the opinion of both his disciples. And if a lawful person should appoint a *Moohrim*

---

* Wild animals, not within the power of man, whether used for food or not.—*Futawa Alumgeeree*, vol. v. p. 613.

† A pilgrim, while he remains at Mecca. "On the first morning of the succeeding month (Zee'lhijja), the prescribed ceremonies commence." "It is from this time, and during the remainder of their stay in the holy territory, that the devotees bear the title of *Moohrim*." —*Hamilton's Hedaya*, Preliminary Discourse, p. 59.

‡ That is, unlawful game, explained a little further on.

§ Arab. *Hurum*: the territory in the neighbourhood of Mecca, where no animal of the *game* species is ever put to death."—*Hedaya*, vol. iv. p. 64.

‖ That is, persons not *Moohrim*.

his agent for the sale or purchase of game, it would not be lawful. If a person after appointing an agent for the sale of game should become a *Moohrim*, and the agent should then effect a sale, it would be lawful in the opinion of Aboo Huneefa, but void in that of his disciples; and if a lawful person should purchase game from another lawful person, and possession is not taken till one of the parties become a *Moohrim*, the sale is dissolved.

Sale of animals improperly slaughtered. The sale of an animal slaughtered by a *Mujoosee*,* or apostate, or any other than a *Kitabee*,† is not lawful; nor the sale of any slaughtered animal over which the *tusmeea*‡ has been intentionally omitted. The rule is the same with regard to animals slaughtered by a youth without understanding, or by an insane person. The sale of game slaughtered by a *Moohrim*, or game slaughtered within the sacred territory, though by a person not a *Moohrim*, are alike unlawful.§

Slaughtered by *kitabees*. The sale of animals slaughtered by *Kitabees* is lawful. The sale of carrion by infidels among themselves is unlawful; but the sale to each other of animals slaughtered by them is lawful, and slaughtering with them is strangling or beating to death.

Sale between *Zimmees*, one of whom becomes a *Mooslim*. When two *Zimmees*‖ sell wine or a hog to each other, and both or one of them adopts the faith before possession, the sale is dissolved; by which is meant the establishment of a right to cancel it; but if possession of the wine or hog take place before both or either of the parties become *Mooslim*, the sale is lawful, whether the price were received or not.

Purchase of a *Mooslim* slave by a *Zimmee*. The purchase of a *Mooslim* slave by a *Zimmee* is lawful, but he may be compelled to sell the slave, whether the seller was a minor or adult; and if one infidel buy from

---

* Magi, worshipper of fire.

† From *kitab*, a book, and means persons having a revealed religion, as Christians and Jews, as well as Mussulmans.

‡ The *formula* Bismillah, &c. In the name of the most merciful God.

§ Game slain by a trained animal let slip, or an arrow shot, without the *tusmeea* is also unlawful.

‖ Infidel subjects of a Mooslim power.

another infidel a *Mooslim* slave by a defective contract, he may be compelled to restore him to the seller, who would then be compelled to sell him. If a *Zimmee* manumit a *Mooslim* slave, or enter into a contract of *tudbeer* with him, the transaction in either case is lawful. So, also, if the slave be a female and the *Zimmee* get her with child; but he would be subjected to a beating. And in like manner if he entered into an engagement of *Kitabut* with her, the contract would be lawful, and not subject to be dissolved. So, also, if he purchase a copy of the *Kooran*. When a *Zimmee* purchases a share in a *Mooslim* slave, the same course is to be observed as if he had purchased the whole.

When one party to a contract is a *Mooslim* and the other a *Zimmee*.

When one of the contracting parties is a *Mooslim* and the other a *Zimmee*, nothing is lawful between them that is not lawful between two *Mooslims*. If a *Mooslim* should make a gift to an infidel of a *Mooslim* slave, and make delivery, the gift is lawful, and the infidel may be compelled to sell the slave.

Sale of bones of dead animals.

There is no objection to the sale of the bones of elephants and other large dead animals, except the human species and swine, unless there be some remains of flesh sticking to the bones, which being impure would render the sale unlawful. According to the decisions of the people of Samarcand, the flesh of dogs and asses properly slaughtered by them may be lawfully sold. On this point there is a difference of opinion among the learned, founded on the different views which they take of the purity of such flesh when duly slaughtered. There is no doubt with regard to the hog that, though duly slaughtered, the sale of his flesh would be unlawful. According to one valid report, the flesh of beasts of prey and asses may be lawfully sold when properly slaughtered; but if the animal have died a natural death so as to be carrion, there is no doubt that the sale of its flesh is unlawful. With regard to the skins of beasts of prey, asses and mules, the sale of them when tanned, or if the animal was duly slaughtered, is lawful, but otherwise it is not. This is founded on the fact that all skins, except those of men and swine,

Flesh of dogs and asses.

Sale of the flesh of the hog unlawful, though duly slaughtered. Also of carrion.

are purified by the throat of the animal to which it belonged having been cut, or the skin itself being tanned; and when once rendered pure its use is lawful, and consequently its sale. As to the hair, wool, bones, and horns of dead animals or carrion, there is no objection to their use, and consequently their sale is also lawful. As to tendons or ligaments, there are two reports; and according to one the use and sale of them is lawful. The hair or bristles of a hog cannot be lawfully sold, but they may be used to point threads. And the sale and employment of the human hair for any purpose are alike unlawful. If one should receive some of the hair of the Prophet from a person who may be possessed of it, and give it as a great and precious present to another, not in the manner of a sale and purchase, there is no harm in doing so. Opinions differ as to the legality of the sale of a woman's milk, some considering it unlawful whether the woman be free or a slave; but according to Aboo Yoosuf, whose decision is approved, the sale of a slave's milk is lawful.

Sale of the hair, wool, bones, and horns of carrion.

Hair or bristles of a hog.

Of a woman's milk.

Sale cannot be contracted for the young of which a female is pregnant, nor for her future fœtus, nor for the produce of any male animal.* The sale of a free person, or of wine, a hog, or carrion, are all unlawful. Manure and the globular dung of animals may be lawfully sold or applied to useful purposes: but the sale of human excrement, or its employment, is not lawful, unless mixed up with earth, and in such proportions that the earth shall predominate. The sale of pigeons' dung when in considerable quantity is lawful.

Sale of a *fœtus*, or the produce of an animal.

Dung.

When a thing that is lawful is mixed with one that is unlawful, as if wine or a mouse were to fall among butter or dough, there need be no apprehension in selling it, when the unlawful does not predominate, or both are equal, and there need be no fear in turning it to any use other than eating it. But it is said that a drop of urine or blood falling into vinegar or olive oil would render

Sale of lawful things mixed with unlawful.

* The sale of these was expressly forbidden by the Prophet.—*Mishcat-ul-Musabih*, p. 20.

the sale of it unlawful. And wherever the unlawful ingredient predominates, the sale or gift of the mixture is unlawful. Thus if the fat of carrion were to fall into olive oil, the sale would be lawful if the oil predominate; but unlawful if the fat predominate.

Instruments of music or amusement.

The sale of a harp, or lute, tambourine, flute, drum, and chess or draught board, are all lawful, according to Aboo Huneefa; but not so in the opinion of his disciples, until they have been broken. A distinction, however, has been taken, and it is said that when these instruments are sold to one who does not use them, nor intends to sell them to one who does, the sale of them is lawful; but otherwise not before the instruments are broken. If a person should destroy such things by the direction of the judge, he is in nowise responsible, nor, according to Aboo Yoosuf and Moohummud, is he responsible though he should destroy them without such direction; and the *futwa* is in correspondence with their opinion.

Sales for special considerations.

If one should sell a slave in consideration of what the seller's camel may graze on the purchaser's land, or for so much water as it may drink from his well, the sale is lawful. And in like manner if the slave were sold for one among the purchaser's handmaidens without specifying her, sale would be contracted.

Sale of forbidden drinks.

According to Aboo Huneefa, the sale of all forbidden drinks but wine is lawful, and the destroyer of them is responsible for his act; but according to Aboo Yoosuf and Moohummud the sale of them is unlawful, and the destroyer of them does not incur any responsibility. There seems no objection to the sale of fruit-juice to one who makes it into wine, nor of land to one who takes it for a Christian Church or a Jewish Synagogue.

Sale of a *Mookatib*, &c. not lawful.

The sale of a *Mookutib*, *Moodubbur*, *Oom-i-wulud*, and slave partially emancipated, are all unlawful; and if any of the three last be sold and delivered, the purchaser does not acquire a right of property in them. With regard to *Mookatibs*, when sold with their own consent, there are two reports, and the more probable is in favour of the legality of the sale, most of the learned concurring in opinion that the sale is not invalid when with the *Mookatib's* sanction. If any of the persons above mentioned, or one who is free, should happen to perish in the hands of the purchaser, he is not responsible. If anything having value* be sold for a *Mookatib* or *Oom-i-wulud*, and the purchaser takes possession, it becomes his property, but improperly. An *Oom-i-wulud* may be lawfully sold to herself; and in like manner the sale of a *Moodubbur* to himself is lawful. **Things sold for them.**

If a thing be purchased for carrion, or blood, there is no transfer of property to the purchaser for want of the characteristic of sale; and the rule is the same where the purchase is made for the skin of carrion, except perhaps where the skin is used by mankind for tanning, when it would seem that a contract takes place. When a slave is purchased for carrion or blood, and taken possession of by the purchaser, a question has been raised as to the responsibility of the latter for the slave's value in the event of his death. Aboo Huneefa thought he would not be responsible; but the disciples thought that he would. **Sale for carrion or blood.**

The children of the female slaves above mentioned are of the same rank or *status* as their mothers,† and a child purchased by a person in a state of *kitabut* is like his parent; but with regard to other relatives within the prohibited degrees they do not enter into the *kitabut*, and may be lawfully sold, according to Aboo Huneefa, though the disciples considered the sale to be illegal. **Children of female slaves have the same *status* as their mothers.**

SECTION VI.

Of Reba or Usury, and the Rules regarding it.

Reba is defined to be an excess of property, to which no consideration is opposed in an exchange of property for property; and it is forbidden ‡ in every commodity **Definition of Reba.**

---

* In law is implied. See note, page 3.

† And cannot be sold but with the same restrictions.

‡ It is forbidden by these express texts of the *Kooran:* "God hath permitted selling and forbidden usury: But whoever returneth to usury they shall be the companions of hell fire, they shall continue

In what articles it is forbidden.

estimated by measure of capacity or weight when sold for its kind. The causes of this illegality of *Reba* are quantity and sameness of kind,* by the former of which is understood measure in commodities that are estimated by measurement of capacity, and weight in those that are estimable by weight. Hence, when any measurable commodity, such as wheat, barley, dates, or salt, or any weighable commodity, like gold or silver, is sold for its kind, equal for equal, the sale is valid; but if one of them be in excess, the sale is not valid. In this respect no account is taken of the quality of the things exchanged, goodness and badness being alike; so that in articles exposed to the objection of *Reba* the sale of good for bad is not valid, except as similars for similars. It is to be observed, however, that superiority of quality is not to be disregarded so far as concerns the property belonging to minors or to *Wukfs;*† insomuch that a guardian cannot lawfully sell good for bad even in commodities to which the objection of *Reba* is applicable. It is also to be observed that one handful may be lawfully sold for two handfuls (and the rule is the same with regard to anything less than half a *Saa*‡), or that one apple may be sold for two apples, and in like manner one egg may be sold for two eggs, or one date for two dates, or one nut for two nuts; and even one *fuls*

therein for ever:" "God shall take his blessing from usury."—*Sales' Kooran*, vol. i. p. 50.

* The principle or origin of this is the well-known saying of the Prophet: "Wheat for wheat, like for like, hand to hand, and excess is usury;" and he enumerated six articles, as being all alike, viz., wheat, barley, dates, salt, gold, and silver.—*Hidayah* and *Kifayah*, vol. iii. p. 158. The saying of the Prophet is not rendered in Mr. Hamilton's *Translation*, though it occurs in the printed original, and a definition of usury is given in the former which is not found in the latter.

† See *ante*, note, page 154.

‡ That is, when both the things exchanged are each less than half a *saa*: for if one of them be less, and the other equal to, or more than half a *saa*, the sale is not lawful.—*Kifayah*, vol. iii. p. 127. See *post*, note, page 168. A half *saa* of wheat is the proper portion of a poor person on the festival of *Fitr* or breaking of Lent. The *saa* was 8 *rutls* of Baghdad, each of which was 20 *astar*, each of which was 4½ *mithkal*.—*Futawa Alumgeeree*, vol. i. p. 269. The *mithkal* and *rutl* have been explained pages 19 and 43.

may be validly sold for two *fooloos*, distinctly specified, according to Aboo Huneefa and Aboo Yoosuf, though Moohummud entertained the contrary opinion.

Not limited to eatables. Any articles of the above description, though not used as human food, such as loam or iron, cannot be lawfully sold, according to us, for another of its kind with any excess in one over the other.

Reba of excess, and Reba of delay. When both the qualities of quantity and sameness of kind are found in the commodities exchanged, any excess or delay in the delivery of one of them is unlawful; when one only of the qualities is present and the other absent, excess is lawful but delay is forbidden; when both are absent, excess and delay are both lawful.

What things are measurable, and what weighable. Every commodity with regard to which the Prophet pronounced excess by measure* of capacity to be forbidden is a measurable commodity for ever, though mankind should cease to measure it, such as wheat, barley, dates, and salt; and every commodity with regard to which he pronounced excess by weight to be forbidden remains a weighable commodity, though mankind should cease to weigh it, such as gold and silver. Commodities with regard to which he made no express declaration, but which are known to have been estimated by measure of capacity in his time, retain for ever their quality of measurable commodities, though mankind should in our times sell them by weight; and all commodities with regard to which he made no express declaration, yet are known to have been estimated by weight in his time, remain weighable commodities for ever, though mankind in our age should be in the custom of selling them by measure. Commodities with regard to which there is no declaration of the Prophet, nor knowledge of the custom of mankind in his time, are to be regarded as measurable or weighable, according to the custom of men in our own times; and if by present custom the commodities are both measured and weighed, they are to be regarded as both measurable and weighable.

---

* Arab. *keil*, measuring corn. It seems also to be a measure for dry or liquid goods, but I have not been able to ascertain its quantity.

Equality by weight not sufficient for measurable commodities, nor equality by measure for weighable.

It follows from the above, that if wheat were sold for an equal quantity of its kind by weight, or gold for an equal quantity of its kind by measure, the sale would not be lawful, whatever the present custom may be. And if any measurable commodity be sold by weight, or any weighable commodity by measure, the sale is not lawful, though the thing sold should be equal to that for which it is sold, if the equality be not ascertained by the original legal standard. It has, however, been said by Sheikh Al-Imam, and is universally allowed, that even commodities expressly declared by the prophet to be measurable, may be lawfully sold by weight for *dirhems;* and in like manner, that commodities expressly declared by him to be weighable may be lawfully sold by measure for *dirhems.*

Things sold by *minas*, ounces or *rutls*.

Everything sold by *minas** and ounces,† as oil, and the like, is a weighable commodity, and if a thing which is referred to the *rutl* or ounce, be sold by measure, and both the commodities interchanged be equal in measure, their qualities by measure being ascertained but the quantity by weight unknown, the sale is not lawful; but if they were equal in weight the sale would be quite valid, though one of the commodities should exceed the other in measure.

All wheat is of one kind, and all dates of one kind.

Wheat, though rotten, is of the same kind as sound wheat; so, also, wheat that is weak and grown on soil not irrigated is of the same kind as wheat upon land duly irrigated. And the Persian date is also to be considered as of the same kind, and only differing in quality from the worst description of dates.

Grapes and raisins.

The sale of grapes for raisins in equal quantities by measure is valid, according to Aboo Huneefa, contrary to the opinion of both the disciples. So also with regard to every fruit which has a dried state, such as figs, apricots, pears, pomegranates, and Damascus plums, the sale of them is lawful, fresh for fresh, or dry for dry.‡ There need be

---

* Certain weights, about 2 ℔. (according to some, 6 ℔.)—*Richardson.*

† Arab. *Awakee,* plural of *wookiyyut,* the twelfth part of a *rutl* or ℔.; from 571¼ to 576 English grains.—*Lane's Modern Egyptians,* vol. ii. Appendix.

‡ That is, in the opinion of the three, and fresh for dry, according to Aboo Huneefa.

no apprehension in the sale of *Natif** for dates, one being in excess, except in a place where dates are sold by the weight, in which case the sale would not be lawful with any delay in delivery; but in a place where dates are sold by measure the sale would be lawful with a delay also.

The fruit of all palm trees. It is said by Aboo'l Husn al Kurkhee, that the fruit of the palm trees are all of one kind, but with regard to other fruits, the fruit of each species of tree is a kind by itself. Thus, grapes, pears, and apples, are each of one kind, though the species of each may differ; so that the sale of one kind of grape for another kind of grape, or of one kind of pear for another kind of pear, or of one kind of apple for another kind of apple, is not lawful with any excess.

Moist and dry wheat, &c. The sale of moistened wheat for moistened wheat, and moistened wheat for dry wheat, and fresh or moist dates† for fresh or moist dates, or for dry dates, and of fresh or green beans or pease for fresh beans or pease, and pickled raisins for pickled raisins or for raisins not pickled, is lawful according to Aboo Huneefa and Aboo Yoosuf, but not according to Moohummud, unless it be known that the quantities opposed to each other are equal. **Parched wheat.** With regard to fried or parched wheat, there is a difference of opinion when it is sold for wheat that is not fried or parched; but, according to the more valid opinion, the sale is not lawful, though the quantities opposed to each other be equal by measure; but the sale of parched wheat for wheat of the same description is lawful when the opposed quantities are equal by measure.

Wheat and flour. The sale of wheat for flour and meal is not valid whether the quantities opposed be equal or not; but the sale of flour for an equal quantity of flour by measure is valid. The sale of flour for flour by weight is not

---

* A kind of confection, boiled long with new wine, sugar, and other ingredients.—*Richardson*. It is probable that the confection is made of dates.

† Arab. *Rootbut*, literally, a single fresh or moist date.—*Richardson*. The term is applicable generally to all kinds of green vegetables, dates, &c.

lawful, as the sale of wheat for wheat by weight is unlawful. And the sale of flour for bread and bread for wheat is lawful, whether the quantities opposed be equal or not; because wheat and flour are measurable, and bread is a weighable commodity; hence the sale of one of them for bread is lawful, whether the quantities be equal or one be in excess when both are delivered on the spot; and though the delivery of one of them be postponed, if the bread be immediately deliverable the sale is lawful according to our doctors; and even when the wheat or flour are immediately deliverable, and the delivery of the bread postponed, the sale is lawful according to Aboo Yoosuf, and one report of Aboo Huneefa's opinion, and the *futwa* is agreeable thereto. According to a saying of Aboo Huneefa, there is no harm in the sale of bread, cake for cake, from hand to hand, though differing in size; which has been considered express authority for the sale of bread, however it may be. And where a person sold one round cake deliverable immediately for two cakes to be delivered at a future time, the sale was held to be lawful; but in the converse of the case the sale would not be lawful, though the sale of fragments of bread in any way, whether delivered immediately or to be so at a future time, is quite lawful.

Borrowing bread by weight.

It is not lawful, according to Aboo Huneefa, to borrow bread by weight or by number of pieces. According to Moohummud, it is lawful in both ways, on account of the practice of mankind; while according to Aboo Yoosuf, its sale by weight is lawful, and the *futwa* is agreeable to his opinion, according to one authority, but according to another, it corresponds with the opinion of Moohummud.

Wheat cannot be sold by conjecture.

Wheat cannot be sold for wheat by conjecture, except in small quantities that are not measured;* and the rule applies to all other commodities estimated by mea-

* The case of the handful for two handfuls, on page 164, falls within this exception; but it is given in the Translation of the *Hidayah*, vol. ii. page 490, as an illustration of a general rule, that—"The sale of anything not measured out according to the legal standard, at an unequal rate, is lawful." There is nothing to cor-

surement of capacity or weight. If wheat should be sold for wheat by conjecture, and the quantities were afterwards measured and found to be equal, still the sale would be unlawful; it being a general rule that wherever similarity according to a certain legal standard is a condition of the legality of a contract, a knowledge of that similarity by the standard at the time of the transaction is also a necessary condition.

General rule as to standard.

When grain is purchased for grain similar to it, and the purchaser makes delivery, but leaves what he has purchased without taking possession of it till the parties separate, there is no objection to the transaction according to us; for mutual possession at the meeting is not necessary in the sale of grain for grain, whether of the same or different kind.*

Rule where one of the things exchanged contains a similar of the other, and something more.

If a person should sell olive oil for olives, or oil of sesame for sesame, or a sheep having wool on its back for wool, or one having milk in its udder for milk, or grape juice for grapes, or milk for butter, or a sword mounted with silver for silver, and the article which is unmixed and separate is more than that which is laid up or contained in the other, the sale, according to our authorities, is lawful; but when what is separate is less than, or only equal to, the other, or the relative quantities cannot be ascertained, the sale is not lawful by general consent. All this implies that in the article which contains a portion similar to the other, there is some surplus or *residuum* which has value, for otherwise the sale would be unlawful. And it should be observed that for this qualification there is a report of an express saying of Aboo Huneefa.

Cotton for its thread or cloth.

According to Moohummud, the sale of cotton for its thread is lawful, and the opinion seems to be correct; and the sale of cotton cleared of its seeds for cotton not so cleared is also lawful, where it is known that the former is more than the actual cotton contained in the latter; and

---

respond with this in the printed edition of the Arabic original; and the rule appears to be too general.

* It seems evident that the grain is supposed to be specific and produced.

when cotton cleared of seeds is sold for cotton seeds, it is also necessary that the former should exceed the cotton contained in the seed. There is no objection to the sale of cotton thread for cotton cloth, or any other thread for its cloth, when the cloth is not usually weighed.

Confection of sesame for sesame.

The sale of one *kufeez* of confection of sesame for two *kufeezes* of sesame is lawful, the excess being set against the odour or perfume.

An animal slaughtered or living, sold for flesh of the same kind.

If one should purchase a sheep for mutton,* and the sheep be slaughtered and skinned, and the inside fat and intestines taken out and removed, the sale is lawful only when they are both equal. If the sheep be slaughtered but not skinned, and the mutton is less than, or only equal to, the flesh of the slaughtered sheep, or the relative quantities be unknown, the sale is not lawful, while if the mutton exceed the flesh of the slaughtered sheep, the sale is lawful. And if a living sheep be purchased for mutton, the sale ought, according to analogy, to be unlawful, unless it be known that the latter exceeds the flesh in the former; and such was the opinion of Moohummud; but on a favourable construction it is held to be lawful in all cases; and such was the opinion of both Aboo Huneefa and Aboo Yoosuf. Distinct specification, however, is necessary, and any delay in delivery is unlawful. And if a person should purchase a slaughtered sheep for a living sheep, the sale is lawful by general agreement; or if one should purchase two living sheep for one slaughtered sheep unskinned, the sale would also be lawful. And the sale of two slaughtered and skinned sheep for one slaughtered sheep unskinned is likewise lawful, there being flesh for flesh, and the excess in the two being a set off to the offal in the single sheep; but if the two were not skinned, the sale would be unlawful; for there would be an excess of flesh and offal also, which would be usury. And the sale of two skinned sheep for one skinned sheep is not lawful, for both being flesh the excess would be usury, unless, indeed, the single sheep equalled the two in weight, when the sale would also be lawful.

* That is, the flesh of another sheep.

All flesh is referred to its origin, or the animal from whence it is taken. Hence, as the cow and buffalo are of the same kind, the sale of the flesh of the one for that of the other with any excess is unlawful. Camels also are of one kind, whether Arabian or Bactrian; and in like manner all animals of the class *ghunum*, which comprises sheep and goats, are held to be of the same kind.

Cow and buffalo of the same kind.

So the Arabian and Bactrian camel, and sheep and goats.

Raw flesh may be lawfully sold for that which is cooked when the quantities are equal; and any excess is forbidden, unless there be things in the cooked flesh put in for seasonings.

Raw for cooked flesh.

The flesh and milk of the camel, cow, sheep, and goats, are of different kinds, and one may be sold for the other with excess from hand to hand; but any delay in delivery is not allowed. So also with regard to tail fat,* flesh, and inside fat, being all of different kinds, part of one may be sold for part of the other in excess, but not with any postponement of delivery. Fat of the sides, or the like, follows the flesh, and is, therefore, different in kind from inside or tail fat. With regard to the heads, extremities, and skins of animals, they may be sold in any way, from hand to hand; but a delay in delivery is unlawful.

Milk of different animals different.

Flesh and fat different.

There is no objection to the sale of the flesh of birds, one for two, from hand to hand; but any delay in delivery is unlawful; and it is reported of Aboo Huneefa that he allowed the sale of birds for bird flesh with excess, though of the same kind. One hen may be lawfully sold for two hens that have been killed, whether they be roasted or raw. Nor is there any objection to the sale of one fish for two fishes, for they are not weighed; but where the fish is of a kind that is weighed, the sale is not lawful, except similar for similar. And in every town where flesh is sold without being weighed, there is no objection to the sale of one joint for two joints;† and regard is to

Flesh of birds.

* Arab. *Alyut*, the *fat tail* of the Asiatic ram.—*Richardson*. The species is commonly known as the Cape sheep, and is met with in India, chiefly in the North-Western Provinces.

† Joints of meat are not weighed in Calcutta, even in the European bazars.

be had in this case to the state of the people of the country.

Water. One jug of water may, according to Aboo Huneefa and Aboo Yoosuf, be lawfully sold for two jugs of water; for water with them is neither a measurable nor weighable commodity, and may, therefore, be lawfully sold with excess. And when ice is sold by weight, it may be lawfully sold for ice, provided the quantities opposed are equal.

Cloth. When cloth wrought or embroidered with gold is sold for pure gold, it is necessary to the legality of the contract that the latter should exceed the gold contained in the cloth. Cloth takes its kind from its material and qualities, though it should be comprehended under one general name, as Hurwee and Murwee, or cloth of Herat and cloth of Meroo; and Meroo cloth embroidered in Baghdad is different from that which is embroidered in Khorassan. So also cloth made of flax and cloth made of cotton are of different kinds. There is no objection to the sale of cotton thread for flax, or wool for hair, in the proportion of one to two; but any delay in the delivery of one of them would render the sale unlawful, as the articles are estimated by weight. In like manner silk thread may be lawfully sold for cotton thread; but soft cotton cannot be lawfully sold for dry except similar for similar. If woollen cloth be sold for wool, and the former be in such a state that if unworked it would turn again to wool, equality by weight is to be regarded as necessary, but not otherwise.

There is no *Reba* or usury between a slave and his master, unless the former be drowned to the neck in debt, in which case *Reba* between them would be unlawful;* but debt to a more moderate extent would not have

---

* This alludes to the case of a slave who is *mazoon*, or licensed by his master to trade, when, though the slave and his acquisitions are still the master's property, they are both liable for his debts. His creditors have, therefore, a qualified right in them, and the master dealing with his slave when he is in debt is liable to suspicion.—See *Hamilton's Hedaya*, vol. iii. p. 511.

that effect. A *Moodubbur* and an *Oom-i-woulud* are in this respect on the same footing as an absolute slave; but not so a *Mookatib.* And there is no *Reba* between partners, when they interchange copartnership property; but with regard to other property there may be *Reba* between them, and it is unlawful. Neither is there any objection to *Reba* between a *Mooslim* and an enemy in an enemy's country, according to Aboo Huneefa and Moohummud; but Aboo Yoosuf thought that even in an enemy's country *Reba* was unlawful. And when a *Mooslim* enters an enemy's country under protection, and sells to a *Mooslim* who had embraced the faith in that country, but had not taken refuge with us, *Reba* would be lawful in the transaction, according to Aboo Huneefa; but both Aboo Yoosuf and Moohummud differed from him on this point; and if the convert had once taken refuge with us, and then returned to the enemy's country, *Reba* in a sale to him would without doubt be unlawful. The case would be the same if both the parties had embraced the faith in the enemy's country, and had not taken refuge with us. And a sale which we should consider invalid would, if entered into between them in the enemy's country, be lawful according to Aboo Huneefa and Moohummud; but Aboo Yoosuf thought that it would be unlawful.

SECTION VII.

Of the Sale of Water and Ice.

Water in a well or stream. The sale of water in its well or stream is unlawful.* The device in this case is to let the bucket and rope

* Because existing there in its place, by the creation of God, it is free to all.—*Kifayah*, vol. iv. p. 1103. It has been said (note, page 147) that, according to a saying of the Prophet, "all men are partners in water, fire, and grass." This is to be understood, with regard to water, that all men have a right to its use, for drink to themselves and beasts; and, for that purpose, to draw it from wells, reservoirs, or streams, that are private property, as being in appropriated lands.—*Inayah*, vol. iii. p. 98. The owner may, however, in general, prevent

to hire. When a person has taken water and put it into a water-pot or other vessel, he has thereby secured and become entitled to it, and may lawfully sell or otherwise dispose of it, in the same way as he may do with game after it has been taken. And in like manner rain-water may become property by collecting it. With regard to the sale of water collected by mankind in tanks or reservoirs, it would appear that if the tank or reservoir be plastered, or made of brass or copper, the sale of water in it is in all cases lawful, the proprietor of the reservoir having in a manner secured the water by putting it there. It is, however, a condition that the stream or channel by which the reservoir is supplied be cut off or stopped, in order that the water sold may not be mixed with what is unsold. If the reservoir be neither plastered nor made of brass or copper, there is the same difference of opinion among the learned with regard to the legality of the sale of the water contained in it as exists with regard to the sale of ice in an ice-house in summer. In this case Moohummud was of opinion that if delivery were first made on the offer for sale, and the thing then sold after delivery, the sale would be lawful; but that if first sold and then delivered, the sale would not be lawful. The valid decision, however, seems to be, that the sale is lawful though it should precede the delivery, provided that the delivery take place within three days; but if the delivery do not take place within that time, the sale is unlawful. When the sale is lawful, the purchaser has the option of inspection on seeing the ice at the time of delivery; but if he should not see it till after delivery, and the three days have then expired, he has no option of inspection; while, if the delivery should take place within the three days, his option is good till the completion of three days from the contract.

---

a person from coming on his land to drink; but, in that case, he must supply the person himself. And if he refuse, and the person be thirsty, and apprehensive of injury to himself, he may oppose the proprietor with force of arms, as withholding from him his just right.—*Hamilton's Hedaya*, vol. iv. p. 141.

A *shirb*, or right of water for irrigation,* cannot be lawfully sold alone;† but when sold with the land the sale is lawful. When land is sold with a *shirb* of other land, Moohummud has not recorded any opinion as to the legality of the sale; but it is related on the authority of the learned *Aboo Nusr* that the sale is lawful; and the learned Aboo Jaafur says that there are indications of Moohummud having been of that opinion. A *shirb*.

A person purchases from water-carriers such and such large leathern bags of Euphrates water; the sale, according to Aboo Yoosuf, is lawful when the bags are distinctly specified, from a regard to the practice of mankind. And the rule is the same with regard to water-pots on a favourable construction; but according to analogy the sale should not be lawful when the quantity of the vessels is not known, and this was the opinion of Aboo Huneefa. When a person says to another, "Water my cattle for so many months for a *dirhem*," the transaction is not lawful; but if he should say, "So many leathern bags the month," the sale would be lawful if the bag were shown. If a person should say to another, "I will irrigate your sown field its full," and were to open his channels and water it, he would not be entitled to anything; but if he were to say, "I will water your cattle from my reservoir for so much," the transaction would be lawful.

---

* "This does not fall within the common right of mankind; for if a person desire to water land that he has brought into cultivation with this" (that is, water from wells, and the like, that are property), "the owners of the stream may prevent him, whether injurious to them or not, because that is their peculiar right."—*Hidayah*, vol. iv. p. 1104. See *Translation*, vol. iv. p. 140.

† But it may be inherited, or acquired by bequest, or reserved.—*Ibid.* page 147.

Section VIII.

Of Uncertainty in the Thing Sold, or the Price.

What ignorance vitiates a sale.

Any ignorance of the thing sold or of the price, that affords room for objection to its delivery, prevents the legality of a sale; but an ignorance which affords no room for such objection does not vitiate the contract, as, for instance, ignorance of measure when a heap distinctly specified is sold, but its quantity is unknown, or ignorance of tale when a package of cloth distinctly specified is sold, but the number of pieces contained in it is unknown.

Coin most current in the city is to be generally implied when left unspecified.

When the price is stated absolutely in a contract of sale, the amount only without the denomination of the coin being specified, that coin which is most prevalent in the city is held to be implied, and if the coins be of different denominations the sale is vitiated, unless one of them be specified, or be more current than the rest, when that would be understood. The contract, however, is vitiated only when the coins are of different values; for if the values be equal the contract is lawful.

Some price must be mentioned.

If a person purchase something from another without any mention of the price, the sale is invalid; but if the seller should say, "I have sold you this slave without a price," and the purchaser should answer, "I have accepted him," the sale is void.

Construction of a contract when a specific heap of wheat is sold at a particular rate.

When a person says to another, "I have sold you this heap, every *Kufeez* of it for a *dirhem*," the sale, according to Aboo Huneefa, is lawful as to one *Kufeez* at that rate, and it is not lawful as to the rest, further than that the purchaser, when made acquainted with the whole number of *Kufeezes* before the separation of the parties, has the option of taking the remainder at the rate mentioned, or of rejecting it; but as to one *Kufeez* for a *dirhem* the sale is imperative. Aboo Yoosuf and Moohummud, on the other hand, were of opinion that the sale would be lawful as to the whole quantity at the rate of a *dirhem* the *Kufeez*, whether the number of *Kufeezes* be known or not. And the case would be the same, with the same difference of opinion between the master and his disciples, if the seller had said, "I have sold you this heap, every two *Kufeezes* of it for two *dirhems*," or "every three *Kufeezes* of it for three *dirhems*." If a dispute should not arise between the parties until the seller had actually measured the heap, or part of it, and delivered the quantity so measured to the purchaser, the sale would be obligatory, according to Aboo Huneefa, as to the portion delivered, and void with regard to the remainder.

Applicable to commodities of weight, divisible without injury.

It is to be observed that what has been above stated of a commodity estimated by capacity is applicable, with the same differences of opinion, to commodities of weight, which can be divided without any injury, as honey, olive oil, and the like. But with regard to articles of long or square measure, as if a person should say, "I have sold you this land, every cubit of it, for so much," the sale would not be lawful, according to Aboo Huneefa, as to one cubit, nor as to the whole, further than that if the whole number of cubits were made known to the purchaser at the meeting, he would have an option. But if the parties should separate before he became acquainted with the full number of cubits, the vitiated quality of the sale would be confirmed. According to Aboo Yoosuf and Moohummud, the sale would be lawful as to the whole, at the rate mentioned, and without any option to the purchaser. And the case would be the same, with the like difference of opinion, if the seller should say, "I have sold you this cloth, every two cubits of it, for three *dirhems*." And this rule is applicable to every commodity of weight, which cannot be divided without injury to the seller.

Construction as to articles of long or square measure.

Applicable to certain other articles of weight

Construction as to articles of tale.

Similars of tale.

With regard to articles of tale, a distinction is to be made according as their unities are nearly alike, or differ materially from each other. In the former case, the rule is the same, as has been already stated, with regard to articles of weight or measurement of capacity. In the latter case, when the individuals materially differ, as if the seller should say, "I have sold you this flock of *ghunum*, every sheep of it, for ten *dirhems*," the rule laid down for articles of long or square measure, with the same difference of opinion above specified, is applicable to the case; but if the seller should say, "I have sold you this flock, every two sheep of it for twenty *dirhems*," the sale would not be lawful as to the whole, according to the opinions of our three doctors; and even though the whole number contained in the flock were known at the meeting, and the sale confirmed, it would still be unlawful.

Sale of a whole, with the exception of a part.

If a person should sell a heap with the exception of one *kufeez*, the sale would be lawful as to the whole with that exception; but if a particular flock of *ghunum* were sold, with the exception of one sheep, not specified, the sale would be invalid.

A piece of flesh sold at a certain rate.

If a person say to another, "I have sold you this flesh, every *rutl* for so much," the sale is bad as to the whole according to Aboo Huneefa, but lawful as to the whole, and without any option, according to the two disciples.

Grapes at so much the load.

A person buys grapes, every load for so much (the load being known to the parties); if the grapes be all of one kind, the sale ought to be lawful, according to Aboo Huneefa, for one load, as in the sale of the heap, every *kufeez* for a *dirhem;* but if the grapes be of different kinds, the sale would be unlawful, like that of the flock of *ghunum*. According to the disciples, if the grapes were of one kind the sale would be lawful as to the whole, each load being at the rate specified; and so also though the grapes were of different kinds. This has been handed down to us by one authority; but another makes all our doctors to agree as to the legality of the sale when the grapes are of one kind, and states that where they are of different kinds the *futwa* is agreeable to the opinion of the disciples, and obligatory upon Moohummudans.

Effect of condition as to quantity in the sale of a specific heap.

When the thing sold is a commodity estimated by capacity, and the whole of the measures contained in it is mentioned, the contract has reference to the quantity specified. Thus, if the seller should say, "I have sold you this heap on condition that it is a hundred *kufeezes*, every *kufeez* for a *dirhem*," or, on condition "that it is a hundred *kufeezes* for a hundred *dirhems*" (that is, with or without the specification of a particular price the *kufeez*), and the quantity is found to be as mentioned, good and well it belongs to the purchaser, and he has no option. If the quantity be found to exceed the hundred *kufeezes*, the excess does not enter into the sale but belongs to the seller, the purchaser being entitled to no more than the exact quantity specified for his hundred *dirhems*, and being in this case also without any option; while, if the actual quantity fall short of the hundred *kufeezes*, the purchaser has the option of taking it at a rateable abatement from the price, or abandoning it altogether.* The same rule applies to all commodities of capacity, and also to all of weight when of such a nature that the dividing them would not be attended with any injury.

Applicable to other articles of capacity, and some of weight.

Effect of similar condition where the article is of long or square measure.

If a person should purchase a piece of cloth, on condition that it contains ten cubits for ten *dirhems*, or a piece of land on condition that it contains a hundred cubits for a hundred *dirhems*, and should in either case find the quantity to be less than what he bargained for, he has the option of taking the whole at the full price, or of rejecting it; and though the quantity should exceed the number mentioned, the purchaser is entitled to the whole, without any option to the seller. If in the above case the seller had said, "I have sold you this cloth or this land, on condition that it contains ten cubits, every cubit for a *dirhem*," and the purchaser had found the actual contents to be fifteen cubits, he would have the option of taking the whole at the rate of a *dirhem* the cubit, or of rejecting it; or if he had found the piece to contain no more than nine cubits or less, he would in like manner have the option of taking it at a rateable share of the price.† And the rule is the same with regard to all things

* In this case, the contract turns on the quantity mentioned, which is therefore said to be *usul*, or original.

† Throughout this case, though varied in the second part of it, it will be observed that the contract turns on the actual thing, not on

Applicable to certain articles of weight.

of long or square measure, such as timber, &c.; and also things estimated by weight, the dividing of which would be attended with any injury, such as a brass or copper vessel or the like, as if one should say, "I have sold this vessel on condition that it is ten *minas* for a hundred *dirhems*," and it is found to fall short or exceed the weight indicated, and that whether a price had been specified for each *mina* or not.

Case of a silver vessel sold for gold, on condition of its containing a certain weight.

If a person should sell a silver vessel on condition that its weight is a hundred *minas*, for ten *deenars*, and after mutual delivery and the separation of the parties, the weight is found to be two hundred, the whole belongs to the purchaser for ten *deenars* without any addition to the price; but if the weight be found to be only eighty or ninety the purchaser has an option. If a price were mentioned for every ten of the weight, as if the seller should say, "I have sold it to you on condition that it contains a hundred for ten *deenars*, every ten weight for a *deenar*," and mutual possession should take place, and the weight is then found to be a hundred and fifty, the fact being ascertained before the separation of the parties, the purchaser has the option of adding five *deenars* to the price and taking the whole at fifteen *deenars*, or of rejecting it; but if the fact be not ascertained till after the separation of the parties the sale is void as to one-third of the vessel, and the purchaser at liberty with regard to the remainder to take it at two-thirds of the price, being ten *dirhems*, or to reject it altogether, and demand back his *deenars*. If, on the other hand, the weight is found to be fifty, and the fact be ascertained before or after the separation of the parties, the purchaser has an option of rejecting the sale and

---

the quantity mentioned, which is therefore said to be only a description.—See *Hamilton's Hedaya*, vol. ii. p. 368. Several rules have been given for distinguishing when the quantity mentioned is original, and when only descriptive. That which runs through the cases in the text, makes it depend on the articles sold; and when they are of such a nature as to be injured by division, "the more or less is description;" when of a nature not to be so injured, the "more or less is original." —*Kifayah*, vol. iii. p. 14.

reclaiming his ten *deenars*, or he may be content with the vessel and take back five *deenars* of the price. And the same rules would apply if the purchased vessel were of gold and the price in *dirhems*.

Or one of gold sold for silver.

If a person should sell a vessel for something of its own kind similar in weight, and the vessel is found to be in excess, the purchaser may either add to the price or reject the vessel, provided the fact of excess be ascertained before the separation of the parties; but if the fact be not ascertained till after their separation, the sale is void for want of possession to the extent of the excess. If, on the other hand, the vessel is found to be deficient in weight, the purchaser may either retain it, reclaiming a suitable return of price from the seller, or reject it altogether, whether a price were mentioned for each *dirhem's* weight or not.

A vessel sold for its similar.

With regard to articles of tale, the individuals of which are nearly alike, such as nuts and eggs, the rules are the same as those applicable to commodities of weight or capacity, and the contract depends on the quantity, whether one price be mentioned for the whole, or a separate price for each individual. When the articles of tale are different, such as goats, cows, and the like, as if one should say, "I have sold you this flock of *ghunum* on condition that it contains a hundred for a thousand *dirhems*," or "every sheep for ten *dirhems*," and the number is found to correspond with that bargained for, good and well; if it is found to exceed the number, the sale is invalid as to the whole, whether a specific price per head were mentioned or not; if the number is found to fall short of that stipulated for, and a price per head had not been mentioned, the sale is also invalid; but if a separate price per head were mentioned, the sale is lawful, and the purchaser has the option of taking what remains at the price mentioned, or of rejecting it. If a seller should say, "I have sold you this flock of *ghunum*, every two sheep for twenty *dirhems*," and should mention the whole as being a hundred, the sale would be invalid, though the number should be found to be the same as was specified.

Articles of tale similar.

Dissimilar.

The sale of a *koor* of wheat, when the quantity proves to be deficient, is invalid.

When a person purchases wheat on condition of its being a *koor* and finds the quality to be a *kufeez* less, the contract is invalid as to what remains, according to Aboo Huneefa, whose opinion is approved.* And in like manner, if a person should purchase a hundred nuts at the rate of a *fuls* the nut, and should find some of the nuts to be empty, or a hundred eggs at the rate of a *danik* the egg, and find some of them to be rotten, the contract is not lawful, on the same authority. In these cases the vice inherent in the contract, so far as relates to the empty nuts and rotten eggs, affects the remainder, according to Aboo Huneefa, and the whole contract is vitiated. And if a person were to purchase a package on condition of its containing ten pieces of cloth, and find that there were more or less, the contract is bad. If, however, a price were mentioned for each piece, and a deficiency were found, the contract would be good as to the existing quantity, the purchaser, however, having an option; but if there was found to be an excess the contract would be invalid. It has been said, that according to Aboo Huneefa, the contract would be bad in the former case also; but the correct opinion is, that in that case the sale is lawful.

Sale lawful by a special measure or weight.

Sale is lawful by means of a particular vessel the capacity of which is unknown, or of a particular stone the weight of which is unknown. It is implied, however, that the vessel is not of a nature to contract or expand; for otherwise sale by it is not lawful, with the exception, on a favourable construction, of a leathern bag for water, on account of its being generally used for that purpose. In like manner it is not lawful to make use of a stone which crumbles away, or any other weight that is liable to become light by drying, as a citrul or water-melon. And it is also a condition of the validity of the contract retaining its validity, that the vessel or stone shall be

* There is a distinction between this case and that of the hundred *kufeezes* on page 179, which I do not attempt to indicate on the margin. I think it is that the *koor* is considered as a whole, and that the quantity is therefore held to be descriptive, though the commodity is estimable by capacity.

preserved in its present condition, for if it should sustain any diminution before delivery, the contract would be rendered invalid.

A person having *dirhems* in his possession says to another, "I have purchased that piece of cloth," for instance, "for this," pointing to the *dirhems*, and they are found to be bad;* the sale is invalid. A person wishing to purchase a slave girl brings a purse, and says to the seller, "I have bought this slave girl for this purse," or "for what is in this purse," and the seller having agreed to the sale finds that what is contained in the purse is not the coin of the place; in such circumstances he may reject it and insist on having money of the place. If, on the other hand, the contents of the purse are coin of the place, the sale is lawful, and the seller has no option. The case would be different if the purchaser had said, "for what is in this jar;" for the seller would then have an option on seeing the *dirhems* contained in it. This is called the option of *kumiyut*,† not of inspection, for the option of inspection is not established with regard to money.

When the price is particularized, and proves to be bad.

When a person purchases a thing at its *rukm*,‡ being ignorant of the price indicated, the sale is invalid. If he should learn it at the meeting the sale is lawful; but if he should not learn it till after the separation of the parties the sale is void. So also if one should sell for the same price at which another sold, such price being known to the seller but unknown to the purchaser, and the purchaser should learn it at the meeting the sale is lawful, but otherwise it is void. A person sells a piece of cloth at its *rukm*, and then sells it to another before explaining the price to the first purchaser, the second sale is lawful; but if the seller had explained the price to the first purchaser, and before his approval had sold it to the other, the second sale would not be lawful. It is to be observed that by *rukm* is meant a mark indicative of the fixed price of anything.

When the price is referred to, but not known to the parties.

---

* Arab. *Sitook.*

† Literally, *quantity*, from *kum*, how many.

‡ Literally, *writing*.

Continued.

When a person says to another, "I have taken this from you for the price at which men sell it," the purchase is invalid; but when he says, "for the price at which it was taken by such a person," and seller and purchaser are cognizant at the time of contract of the price referred to, the sale is lawful; if not cognizant of it the sale is invalid. If, however, while still at the meeting, they should be made acquainted with the price referred to, the sale would become lawful; but the purchaser would in that case have an option, the price for which he is to be bound being then only made apparent to him. This option is called the *khiyar tukushoof-ool-hal.** And when the article sold for a price thus referred to is such that its price does not vary, as bread or flesh, it would seem that the sale is lawful.

Sale of a specified number of cubits of a mansion or bath.

The sale of ten cubits of a mansion or a bath is invalid, according to Aboo Huneefa, but lawful in the opinion of his disciples when the whole of the mansion or bath is a hundred cubits. And with the master it made no difference, according to the most authentic account, whether the seller should say, "ten out of a hundred" or not; but the learned differ as to the opinion of the disciples, in a case where the whole number of cubits is not mentioned. It is, however, correct to say that the sale is lawful in such circumstances. And it seems that both the master and his disciples were agreed that if the sale were on these terms, "one share out of ten shares of this mansion," it would be lawful.

Sale of a cubit from a log of timber.

A person purchases a cubit of a log of wood, or of a piece of cloth from a known end, the sale is not lawful; and even though the seller should cut off and deliver the cubit, the sale would still be unlawful, unless approved of by the purchaser. According to Aboo Yoosuf such a sale is lawful, and according to Moohummud it is invalid; but if the piece be cut off and delivered to the purchaser he is not at liberty to reject it.

A person says, "I have sold you my share in this man-

---

* Literally, option on the state being revealed.

sion for so much;" the sale is lawful if the purchaser know the share, otherwise it is not lawful.

Sale of a share in a mansion.

A person purchases from another a court-yard or piece of land, the boundaries of which are specified, but without any mention of the number of cubits in length or breadth, the sale is lawful; and it is sufficient for the legality of the sale if the purchaser be acquainted with the boundaries, though he should not know the names of the neighbours. And even though the boundaries should neither be mentioned nor known to the purchaser, yet if there be no dispute between the parties with regard to them, and the whole thing sold be sufficiently ascertained, the sale is lawful.

In the sale of land it is not necessary that the quantity be specified if the boundaries are known.

When a person says to another, "I have sold you a slave for so much," without naming him, and he is not in the purchaser's sight, the sale is void by reason of the double ground of uncertainty, as it may have reference to the slave of another person, or to another slave of the seller's. When a person says, "I have sold you my slave," and he is possessed of another, the sale is vitiated, but may be rendered lawful by the seller and purchaser agreeing that a particular slave is the one sold. Some, however, have said that it is not the first sale which is rendered lawful, but that a new sale is contracted by *taatee* or mutual delivery. And even where the seller has only one slave, some further description seems absolutely necessary. Thus, if one should say, "I have sold my slave for so much" (having only one slave), adding, "in such a place," the sale would be lawful; but if he should not say, "such a place," the sale would be unlawful.

Sale of a slave without naming him.

A person says to another, "I have sold you all that is in this mansion, of slaves, cattle, and clothes," the purchaser not knowing the contents of the mansion, the sale is invalid; but if instead of mansion he had said "apartment," the sale would be lawful; so, also, if he had said, "in this box or sack."

Sale of "everything in a mansion" is not lawful, unless the contents be known.

Section IX.

Of the Sale of things connected with other things, and of Sales with an exception.

Sale of milk in the udder, or a child in the womb, &c., unlawful.

The sale of milk in the udder, of a child in the womb, and of wool on the back of a sheep, are all unlawful, according to a well known tradition.* And though the milk or wool be delivered after the contract, the sale is still lawful, and does not become valid.

Sale of wheat in the ear.

The sale of wheat in the ear by measure or weight is lawful, even though the grains should not yet be confirmed or have acquired strength. It is not lawful to purchase the straw of such particular wheat; but after straw has been stacked or collected, and before it is strewed or spread out (for thrashing or treading out), the sale of it is lawful.

Moozâbunŭt, &c. unlawful.

The following sales are all unlawful:† 1. *Moozabŭnŭt*,‡ or the sale of dates growing on a tree for a similar measure by guess or conjecture of dates already plucked and gathered; 2. *Moohâkŭlŭt*,§ or the sale of wheat in the ear for a similar measure of wheat estimated by the eye; 3. *Moolâmŭsŭt*,‖ which is, when parties bargain about a thing, and agree that when the purchaser touches it the thing is to become sold; 4. Sale by *Ilka-ool-hŭjr*, or the

---

* See *Hamilton's Hedaya*, vol. ii. p. 433.

† Being expressly prohibited by the Prophet.—*Hamilton's Hedaya*, vol. ii. p. 434-5.

‡ Derivative, from the root *Zŭbŭn*, to the literal sense of which it bears no analogy, but is purely a technical term of law.—*Imameea Digest*, translated by Captain John Baillie, note, p. 122.

§ An infinitive of the fifth conjugation of increase, from the root *Hukl*, which literally signifies "corn putting forth tender blades;" also "the ground or soil in which such corn is growing."—*Ibid.*

‖ Derivative from *Lŭms*, touching.

cast of a stone, which is when a pebble is thrown at several pieces of cloth, and it is agreed that whichever is struck shall be sold; 5. *Moonâbŭzŭt*,* which is when each of the parties throws his cloth at the other, neither having seen the other's cloth, on the understanding that the throwing is to constitute a sale between them.

Sale of a stalk, without the wheat, &c.

The sale of a stalk without the wheat is lawful; and if one should purchase a shell without mention of its pearl, the sale is lawful, and the pearl belongs to the purchaser.

Of seeds in a melon or dates, or oil in seeds, &c.

When a person sells the seeds in a water melon to another, and is willing to cut it, the sale is void. So, also, with regard to seeds in a date, or the oil in seeds of sesame or in olives; and even though the seller should make delivery to the purchaser, the sale would not be lawful. And if one should sell the skin or tripe of an animal not yet slaughtered, the contract is unlawful; nor would it become lawful though the animal were subsequently slaughtered and the skin and tripe divested and delivered to the purchaser.

Of things attached to other things.

If a person should sell a beam in the roof of a house, or a cubit from one side of a piece of cloth, or from a piece of timber in a part distinctly specified, or the ornament of a sword which cannot be separated without injury, or half of any crop not yet ripe; or if the crop should belong to two parties and one of them should sell his share to another than his partner, in all these cases the sale is invalid. And if the seller should wish to take out the beam, or to cut the cubit from the cloth or timber, or to take off the ornament from the sword, or to reap the harvest when the whole of the crop belongs to himself, the purchaser is at liberty to cancel the sale before any of these things is actually done; but if once done by the seller before cancellation, the contract is imperative on the purchaser, who has no option. The sale of the stone in a ring is on the same footing; if it cannot be extracted without injury, the sale is unlawful, and the ring is a trust

---

* From *Nŭbz*, throwing.

in the hands of the purchaser, for which he is not responsible in case of loss; but if the stone can be extracted without injury, the sale is lawful, and the purchaser is liable for its price if it should happen to perish in his hands.

Right of property in the mean time is in abeyance.

In cases like the above, where the thing sold cannot be separated without injury from that with which it is connected, Moohummud being asked whether the right of property in the former vests in the purchaser, or is in abeyance, replied that it is in abeyance, and does not vest so long as the seller has an option to deliver it or not. He evidently alluded to the state of the thing before its separation; for if it be no longer in a state to justify the seller's refusal to deliver it, the right of property vests in the purchaser. If the purchaser should not dispute the matter till the seller has disposed of the ring or the apartment to a third party, and delivered it to him, the second sale would, according to Moohummud, dissolve the first.

General principle as to purchaser's responsibility.

It is a general principle in all cases of the above description, that with regard to everything which a seller can be compelled to deliver, a purchaser, when he takes possession of it under a sale, is responsible in the event of it being lost or damaged; but that with regard to things of which a seller cannot be compelled to make delivery, yet does deliver to a purchaser, the latter does not become possessed of them under the purchase, and is not responsible for them in the event of loss.

Case of things wrongfully acquired, being implicated, and sold with other property.

Ibn Sumaut relates of himself, that he said to Moohummud, "I wrongfully took possession of a beam, and inserted it into the ceiling of an apartment, and of a brick which I built into a mansion, and of a nail which I put into a door, and I afterwards sold the apartment, the door, and the mansion, is the sale lawful, and will the purchaser when he comes to a knowledge of these facts have an option of rejecting the apartment, the mansion, and the door?" and that Moohummud replied, "The sale is lawful, and the purchaser has no such option."

What improvements

Cultivators make improvements on the estate of their landlord: if the improvements are buildings or trees the sale of them is lawful, unless there be a stipulation for their remaining on the ground; but if the improvements be merely culture of the soil, as by ploughing and sowing of lands, or digging of channels for water, the sale of these by the cultivators is not lawful. by cultivators may be sold.

When the subject of sale is a mansion or land held by two persons jointly in undivided shares, and one of the partners before partition sells a specific apartment in the mansion, or a specific parcel of the land, the sale is not lawful even to the extent of his own share; but when he sells the whole of his share in the mansion or land, the sale is quite lawful. Sale by a partner in a house or land.

The sale or gift of a watercourse* is not lawful; but the sale or gift of a road is lawful. Sale or gift of a watercourse or road

If anything be excepted from the subject of sale which might lawfully stand by itself in a contract, the exception is lawful; as if one should sell a heap of anything with the exception of a *saa* of it, or a cask of vinegar or oil except ten *minas*. But if anything be excepted which could not lawfully stand by itself in a contract, the exception is not valid; as if a female slave be sold excepting the child of which she is pregnant, or a flock with the exception of one sheep, or an ornamented sword without the ornament. If one should sell a building or a mansion, and except from it the timber or bricks, or tiles, or ground, the sale is lawful when the purchase is made with a view to demo- General rule as to exceptions from a sale.

---

* Arab. *Musyul;* literally, place of flowing. The word is ambiguous, as it may mean either the enclosure (*rukbut*) of the channel, or the right of leading away water from it (*tusyeel*); and it would seem from the text that the sale is unlawful in all cases; and this appears to be confirmed by the *Hedaya*, vol. ii. p. 440. But, according to the authors of the *Kifayah* and the *Inayah*, when the situation and boundaries of the *rukbut* (which may either mean the body of water or the land upon which it is conveyed) are distinctly specified, the sale is lawful; when they are not specified, it is unlawful for uncertainty. When a *tusyeel* is meant, the sale is unlawful, according to both the commentators, because when the water is led away in a wooden trough, it rests on the air, and also for uncertainty, and for the latter reason when it is to be led through a channel in the earth. —*Kifayah*, vol. iii. p. 104; *Inayah*, vol. iii. p. 103.

lition. It is not lawful to sell fruit on a tree, and to except a known number of *rutls;* but when fruit is gathered, the sale of the whole of it with the exception of one *saa* is lawful.

Where the excepted part is unspecified.

If goats or a package of cloth be sold with the exception of one of them unspecified, the sale is invalid; but if the excepted individual be specified, the sale is lawful. So also with regard to everything estimated by tale, the individuals of which differ.

Sale of a female slave, with the exception of the child in her womb.

The sale of a female slave of whom the child in her womb has been emancipated is unlawful; and there are eleven other cases like this. In one, both the contract and exception are lawful; as when a person bequeaths a mother without the child of which she is pregnant, or bequeaths the child without the mother. In four, the contract and the exception are invalid; as when a person sells a female slave, or enters into an agreement of *kitabut* with her, or lets her to hire, or compounds a debt in exchange for her, and excepts in all the cases the child of which she is pregnant. And in the remaining six the contract is lawful, but the exception is void; as when the mother is given and delivered, either as a gift or in charity, or is made the subject of *muhr* in a marriage settlement, or of composition for intentional homicide, or of *khoola,* or is emancipated, with the exception in all the cases of the infant in the womb, the exception is void, but the contract is lawful and operative.

Sale of a road with reservation of a right of way.

A person sells the enclosed space of a road, reserving to himself a right of way or passage over it; the sale is lawful. So, also, if one should sell the lower part of a mansion, on condition that he is to have the right of erecting an upper story upon it.* It is reported among certain rare cases or opinions of Moohummud, that when a person says to another, "I sell you this mansion except a road in it from this place to the door of this mansion," and describes its length and breadth, and makes the stipulation

---

* See *ante*, page 51, where the *sale* of such a right is stated to be unlawful.

for himself or in favour of another, the sale is lawful, and the full price mentioned is the price of what remains of the mansion after deducting the road. But if the sale were "on condition that the seller shall have a road on it," the length and breadth of which are described, the sale would not be lawful.* So, also, if one should say, "I have sold you this my mansion for a thousand *dirhems*, on condition that I shall have this particular apartment," the sale is not valid; while if the terms were "except this apartment," the sale would be lawful. And if a person should say, "I have sold you this mansion except its buildings," the sale is lawful, and the buildings are excluded from it. Or, if he should say "this land, except a particular tree with its foundation," the sale would also be lawful, and the purchaser at liberty to prevent the extension of its branches over his property.

Exception in the form of a condition.

SECTION X.

Of the Sale of two things, one of which cannot be lawfully sold, and of the repurchase of a thing for less than it was sold for.

When a person combines a slave and a freeman, or meat duly slaughtered and carrion, and sells them together, the sale is void as to both, according to Aboo Huneefa, whether a price be specified for each or not; but in the opinion of the disciples, when a distinct price for each is specified, the sale is lawful as to the slave and the meat duly slaughtered. So, also, if one should purchase two sheep slaughtered and skinned, but one of them slaughtered by a *Mujoosee*,† or a *Mooslim* who wilfully neglected the *tusmeea*‡ over it; animals so slain being with us the same as carrion. When a person joins an absolute slave to a

Sale of two things, one of which is unlawful.

* Because there is here a condition for some advantage to the seller. See *post*, chapter x.

† Explained, *ante*, note *, p. 159.

‡ Ibid. note ‡.

Modubbur, or *Mookatib*, or *Oom-i-wulud*, or his own slave to that of another, and sells them together, the sale is valid with respect to the absolute slave, or the slave which is the seller's property for a share of the price. So, also, when a *wukf* * is sold together with property in general terms, the sale is valid as to the latter, according to the most authentic opinions. And when a person purchases two casks of vinegar and finds that one of them is wine, the contract is invalid as to the whole, according to Aboo Huneefa, even though the price were apportioned upon each; but when so apportioned, the contract is lawful as respects the vinegar, according to both his disciples. When a person purchases two slaves, and after taking possession of only one of them, sells them both together for a thousand *dirhems*, apportioning the price as five hundred for each; the sale is lawful with regard to the slave of which he obtained possession, but not lawful as to the other.† A person purchases a slave, and before possession sells him together with another slave of his own, the sale is lawful as to the latter, according to our three doctors. And when a person purchases a slave for a thousand *dirhems*, and getting possession of him without payment of the price, resells him, together with another of his own, to the seller for a thousand *dirhems*, each slave being priced at five hundred *dirhems*, the sale is lawful with regard to his own original slave, but not so as to the slave which he purchased.

Sale of a mansion with a public road, or a *Musjid*, private or public.

A person purchases a mansion together with a road or highway belonging to the general body of Moohummudans, the way being distinctly marked off by well-known boundaries, and after he has taken possession of both the mansion and way, a right is established to the latter. In these circumstances, the purchaser is at liberty to reject the mansion, or to retain it at a due proportion of the price; that is, when the road is confused or mixed with the mansion, but if distinguishable from it, he has no

---

* Explained, *ante*, note, p. 154.

† See *ante*, p. 21, as to the illegality of such a sale.

option, and is bound to take the mansion at its share of the price. And if the road be not marked off and bounded, so that the quantity of land contained in it cannot be ascertained, the sale is invalid. If for the road a private *Musjid* were substituted, the case would be the same as that of the road distinctly marked off and bounded; but if the *Musjid* were a *Jama* or general one, the sale would be invalid, because the sale of such a *Musjid* is unlawful. Nor would it make any difference though the general *Musjid* were in ruins, or only a vacant space remained where it had formerly stood.

When the illegal combination is in the price.

If a person should purchase a slave for five hundred *dirhems* in cash, and five hundred more due to him by a third party, the sale is invalid as to the whole.* When a person purchases a thing distinctly defined for ten *dirhems* in money, and a thousand *muns* of wheat, the quality of which is described, but the place of its delivery not indicated, which would invalidate the sale according to Aboo Huneefa, so far as relates to the proportion of the wheat, a question arises whether the taint would in his opinion affect the whole contract or not, and it seems proper that it should not affect it beyond the share of the wheat.

When repurchase by a seller, at a less price, is unlawful, and when lawful.

The repurchase by a seller, or by a person whose testimony is not available to him, of anything sold by him, or on his account (as for instance, by his agent), for less than the price for which it was sold, before the actual receipt of that price, whether such purchase be made for himself or another, and whether from the original purchaser or his heir (but not from his donee or legatee), the thing sold having sustained no diminution in substance, is unlawful, when both the prices are in things of the same kind;† and in this case *deenars* are considered one with *dirhems*. If the consideration be different in kind from the original price, or if the subject of sale have sustained

---

* As to the illegality of a sale, in consideration of a debt due by another. See *ante*, p. 6.

† A saying of *Ayesha*, one of the Prophet's widows; and other reasons are assigned for this.—See *Hamilton's Hedaya*, vol. ii. p. 442.

any blemish, the repurchase is lawful. And a repurchase for more than the original price, whether before or after its payment, is quite lawful. But a fall in the market price of the articles does not affect the case; for if the repurchase be for less than the original price, it is illegal, notwithstanding a fall in the market price, no regard whatever being had to the latter. And even though half the price were actually paid and received, and only half of the thing sold were repurchased at less than the remaining half of the price, still the transaction would be illegal; but if the purchaser should sell to a third party, and the original seller then purchase from the latter for less than the original price, the transaction would be lawful. If the thing purchased be returned by the second to the first purchaser for any reason that induces only a dissolution of contract as regards the world at large, it would not be lawful for the first seller to repurchase the thing for less than what he originally sold it for; but if the reason for its return makes it a dissolution as between the contracting parties, and a new contract, so far as third persons are concerned,* the first seller may lawfully repurchase it for less than the original price. And if the first purchaser should make a gift of the thing purchased, or sell it to a third party who reconveys it to him by gift or sale, in either of these cases he may lawfully resell it to the first seller for less than the original price. But if after a gift and delivery of the thing sold to a third party the first purchaser should retract his gift, and then sell back the thing to the original seller at less than the first cost, the sale would not be lawful.

Lawful after actual receipt of the price.

Receipt of the price, as implied in all the cases, legalizes a subsequent repurchase by the seller for less than was originally paid. And though he should find the money to be base (*zooyoof*) and should return it, still the legality of the repurchase would not be affected. In like manner, if the seller should accept as a composition for the price a piece of cloth, and then repurchase for less than the original price,

---

* See *post*, chap. xiii. of *Ikalut*.

the transaction would be lawful, and would not be invalidated by a subsequent return of the cloth on account of a defect; but if the coin should prove to be bad (*sitook*), the purchase would be invalidated.

Repurchase by an agent.

When an agent is appointed to sell a slave for a thousand *dirhems*, and does so, but afterwards wishes to buy him back, either on his own account or for another, for less than he sold him for, and before receipt of the price, he cannot do so lawfully.

Case of repurchase at the same price on credit.

It is stated in the Koodooree that one cannot lawfully sell merchandise for a price presently payable, and then repurchase it for the same price to be paid at a future time. And if one were to sell for a thousand *dirhems* payable in a year, and then repurchase for a thousand *dirhems* payable in two years, the transaction would not be lawful; but if a *dirhem* or more were added to the price, that would legalize the transaction, the increase in the price being opposed to the possible loss contingent on the extension of the period of credit.

CHAPTER X.

OF CONDITIONS THAT VITIATE, AND SUCH AS DO NOT VITIATE, A CONTRACT OF SALE.*

Conditions that cannot vitiate.

THE conditions of a sale may in the first place be such as are absolutely required by the contract, and would be implied in it without any stipulation. Conditions of this description cannot of course vitiate the contract; as for instance, a condition that the seller shall deliver the thing sold, or the purchaser make payment of the price.† Other conditions, again, though they are not actually required by the contract, may yet be in harmony with it, as tending to further or confirm its object. Of this nature is a condition that the purchaser shall give a surety or a pledge for payment of the price. Conditions of this description do not necessarily vitiate the contract, but may have that effect from some defect in the terms or form of the condition. Thus if the person proposed as surety for the price should be pointed out or named, and being present at the place of contract should consent to be surety, or being at first absent should subsequently

Conditions that may vitiate.

---

* The Prophet "has forbidden sale with a condition."—*Hidayah* (original, vol. iii. p. 111, *Translation*, vol. ii. p. 446); but the prohibition is not to be understood in such absolute terms as positively to require the invalidity of the sale (*Inayah*, vol. iii. p. 112), for he actually recommended an option by stipulation, as has been already stated in a note, on page 63. And the rules in the text have been apparently devised for the purpose of distinguishing the cases to which the prohibition is strictly applicable.

† The condition here is mere surplusage.—*Inayah*, ibid.

come and give his consent before the separation of the parties, the contract would be lawful on a favourable construction; but if the surety be not sufficiently indicated or named, the contract is vitiated by the condition. So, also, if the surety being present at the meeting should refuse his consent, or if his consent should not be positively given before the separation of the parties, or a dissolution of the meeting by one of them taking to some other occupation, the contract would be vitiated. In like manner when it is conditioned that the purchaser shall give a pledge for the price, and the pledge is known by being pointed out or named, the contract is lawful on a favourable construction. When the pledge is not produced and only indicated by name, it is said in the Moontuka that the contract is not lawful if the pledge so indicated be a specific chattel, whereas if it be a quantity of commodities estimated by weight or measure of capacity, and be properly described, the transaction is lawful. When the pledge is neither produced nor named, and it is merely stipulated that the purchaser shall give a pledge for the price, the contract is invalid unless the parties agree on the pledge, and it is delivered by the purchaser before their separation, or he at once pays down the price abandoning his right to credit; in all of which cases the transaction would be lawful on a favourable construction. If the condition should be that the purchaser shall pledge a *koor* of good wheat for the price, this is lawful, such a degree of uncertainty not being sufficient to vitiate the sale. And if a specific thing were mentioned as the pledge, and the purchaser should refuse to deliver it, he cannot be compelled, but may be directed either to deliver the pledge or its value, or to pay the price, or cancel the sale; and if he should refuse any of these alternatives, the seller may cancel the sale.

Conditions sanctioned by law or custom do not vitiate.

When conditions are not required by the contract, nor in strict accordance with it as tending to further its objects, but have been sanctioned by the law, such as a condition for option or credit, or though not expressly sanctioned by law are yet authorized by custom,* such as if a person should purchase one shoe on condition of another being made to match it; in these cases the contract is lawful on a favourable construction. So, also, if one should purchase a piece of thick leather on condition of the seller sewing or making it into a boot, or a high cap or turban on condition of his lining it; in these cases the contract is legal from regard to custom. And in like manner and for the same reason, the purchase of a boot having a rent in it on condition that it shall be stitched up, or of an old threadbare garment on condition that the rents in it shall be sown or darned, would be quite lawful. But the purchase of a piece of fine linen on condition that it shall be cut up and sewn would not be lawful, from the want of any known custom on the subject.

Conditions for some advantage to either of the parties, or to the subject of the contract, vitiate a sale.

If a condition has neither the sanction of express law nor of custom, and is of such a nature as to afford any particular advantage to one of the contracting parties, or to the subject of the contract when capable of claiming a right against another, the contract is invalid.† A person says to another, "I have sold you this my slave for a thousand *dirhems*, on condition that you will give me that slave of yours," the sale is invalid, there being here a condition of gift in the contract; but if he should say, "I have sold you this for a thousand *dirhems*, on condition that you will give me that slave of yours in addition," the sale would be lawful, the slave being merely an addition to the price. A condition in the sale of a slave, that if the purchaser should sell him the seller is to have a preference at the same price, would vitiate the contract. So, also, a condition that the purchaser shall make a gift to the seller, or bestow something on him

* It is only by analogy from the Prophet's prohibition that the contract could be considered unlawful; but analogy is over-ridden by positive law, and also by custom, since the intention is to avoid strife, which was also the motive for the prohibition.—*Inayah*, vol. iii. p. 112.

† This would lead directly to strife, and is clearly within the intention of the prohibition.

in alms, or sell or lend him something, would vitiate the contract; but a sale on condition of a loan by a stranger to such an one is lawful.

Qualification as to the subject of the contract.

When the condition is for any advantage to the subject of the contract, it is necessary to the vitiating quality of the condition, that the subject shall be a being capable of claiming or asserting a right against others. By this definition slaves are taken out of the category of animals in general, and if a person should purchase any animal other than a slave, a stipulation in its favour, as for instance, that the purchaser shall not sell or give it away, would not have the effect of vitiating the contract. But a stipulation of this kind with regard to a slave, whether male or female, would invalidate the sale. Sale of a slave with a condition that the purchaser shall feed him is lawful; but if the condition were that he shall be fed on sweetmeats or flesh, the sale would be invalid. And if a slave be sold on condition that the purchaser shall emancipate him, the sale is invalid according to the most probable reports of the opinions of our doctors. Hence, if the purchaser should emancipate the slave before taking possession, the emancipation would not take effect; but if he should first take possession and then emancipate, the contract would become lawful, according to Aboo Huneefa, on a favourable construction, and the purchaser be liable for the price; though according to the disciples, the contract would not become lawful, and the purchaser would be liable for the value. And they all agree in opinion that if the slave should perish in the purchaser's hands before emancipation, he would be liable for his value, and that the consequence would be the same if the purchasers should sell or give the slave away. A person purchases a slave girl on condition that he will dress her in silk, or not beat or afflict her; the sale is invalid.

Effect of condition for some advantage, involving a stranger.

If the condition be for some advantage between one of the contracting parties and a stranger, as if a person should purchase on condition that such an one, a stranger, shall lend the seller so much, or that the seller shall lend such an one so much, the contract is invalid according to one authority, but not so according to another; while in a third it is stated, as a saying of Moohummud, that everything which would vitiate a contract when stipulated to be done by the seller, is void when stipulated to be done by a stranger, and that anything which in the former circumstances would not vitiate the contract, is lawful when stipulated to be done by a stranger, the stranger being of course at liberty to sanction the condition or not at his pleasure.

Miscellaneous conditions.

When a person sells a piece of cloth on condition that the purchaser shall neither sell nor give it away; or a beast on the like condition, or provisions on condition that he shall neither eat nor sell them, the sale is lawful;* but if the condition were that he shall sell, or that he shall not sell, to a particular person, the sale would be invalid. So, also, if the condition were not to sell without the permission of such an one. And if a person should purchase a mansion on condition that he is not to pull it down or build it without the permission of such an one, the sale would be invalid; or if one should purchase a thing on condition of paying the price out of its sale, the contract would also be invalid. When a mansion is sold on condition that it shall be made into a *Musjid*, or bath, or cemetery, for the use of Moohummudans in general, or provisions are sold on condition that they shall be bestowed in alms on the poor, the sale is invalid; but if the condition were that a mansion be converted into a Christian church,† or that grape juice shall be made into wine, the sale would be lawful. And if one should say, "I sell this (slave) for three hundred *dirhems*, and on condition that he shall serve me for a year," or on condition, &c., without the connective "and," or on condition "that he shall serve thee for a year," the contract would be invalid, because all these expressions are tantamount to a lease in the sale. If a

* And the condition void, for there is no one to demand it, and it is treated as a mistake or surplusage.—*Inayah*, vol. iii. p. 113.

† The construction of a new church in a Mussulman territory is unlawful (though an old one may be rebuilt), and there is no person entitled to claim performance of the condition.

person should sell a piece of cloth on condition that the purchaser shall tear it, or a house on condition that he shall destroy it, the sale is lawful, and the condition void.

Sale in consideration of another's debt, without or with his consent.

When a person says to another, "I sell you this my slave for the thousand *dirhems* due to you by such an one as a payment from me to you on his account," the sale is lawful, and the seller a volunteer on part of the person referred to. But when a person sells his slave to another for a debt due to the purchaser by such a person, and the person is content, the sale is lawful, and the seller becomes entitled to the property, whatever it may be, which was due to the purchaser by the person referred to. Where, again, one sells a slave on condition that the purchaser shall pay his price to a creditor of the seller, the sale is invalid. So, also, if the condition be that the purchaser shall become responsible for him to a creditor for a thousand *dirhems*, the contract would be vitiated. And when a person is creditor to another in a *deenar*, and purchases from him a piece of cloth on condition that the debt shall not be accounted for in the price, the sale is bad.

Purchase of the produce of an orchard, with a condition.

A person purchases the whole produce of an orchard, on condition that the seller is to build up its walls, the sale is invalid. But if the seller were to say, "Buy, that I may build the walls," the sale would be lawful. If he should refuse to build he cannot be compelled to do so, but in that case the purchaser would have an option, and might either hold by or rescind the bargain.

Condition of delivery by instalments.

A person sells a thing on condition that he is to make delivery by instalments, the sale is not lawful; but if delivery in that manner is not made an actual condition of the sale, and is only stated after the sale, the seller* may take the whole. And if one should purchase on condition of delivery to him at his residence, and the residence as well as the purchaser are both within the city, the sale is lawful on a favourable construction, according to Aboo Huneefa and Aboo Yoosuf; but if the residence of the purchaser be without the city, or himself without and his residence within the city, the sale is not

* So in the original, vol. iii. p. 186.

lawful by general consent. So, also, if they were both out of the city, and the condition were that the thing sold should be carried to his residence, the sale would also be unlawful by general agreement.

Of payment in another city.

A person sells a slave on condition that the price shall be paid in another city, this vitiates the sale if the price be immediately payable. But if he were to sell for a thousand, payable in a month, and with such a condition, the sale would be lawful for the thousand in a month, but the condition void, because the sale is on credit for a fixed period, and the condition is intended only to specify or fix the place of payment, which is not valid with regard to a thing that does not require porterage or trouble for its conveyance. If, however, the price or consideration were of such a nature as to require porterage and trouble for its conveyance, the specification of a place of payment would be valid, and the sale be also lawful. A person sells on condition that so much of the price shall be in cash, and so much on credit, or that so much of it shall be on credit for one month, and so much for two months, the sale is not lawful.

Further miscellaneous conditions.

When a person sells a pack-horse on condition that he is tractable, the sale is lawful; but if one should purchase an ewe or a camel on condition of her being pregnant, the sale would not be lawful according to the Zahir Rewayut. Opinions differ as to the effect of such a condition in the purchase of a female slave, some being against its legality, as in the case of the same condition when applied to beasts; but the weight of authority seems to be in favour of the contract. According to one account, however, a distinction is to be made, and the sale is said to be lawful when the stipulation is on the part of the seller, but unlawful when the stipulation proceeds from the purchaser. Authorities also differ as to the legality of a stipulation in the purchase of a cow, that she shall be in milk, some considering the sale to be lawful, but others, apparently the majority, being of opinion that it is unlawful. There is also a difference of opinion with regard to a similar condition in the purchase of a female slave bought as a nurse; but the weight of authority and the *futwa* are in favour of its validity, the condition being considered necessary to her ability for the object in view, and to be like a qualification for a trade, in the same way as if a male slave were purchased on condition of his being a baker.

If a person should purchase a water-melon on condition of its being sweet, or olives, or sesame, on condition of their containing a certain quantity of oil, or undressed rice on condition that it will come white out of the water, and be so much in quantity, or a sheep, or bull, on condition of its containing a certain weight of flesh; in all these cases, the sale would be invalid, on account of the difficulty of determining the facts before trial. In like manner, if one should sell an ewe on condition of its giving so much milk, the sale would be invalid according to all reports; so, also, if the condition were that it should bring forth young in a month. A person purchases a female slave on condition that she sings such and such songs, but finds that she does not sing at all, the sale is lawful, and the purchaser has no option. But it has been said that this is true only when mention is made of this qualification to show that the slave is free from defect, and the distinction has been adopted. And in like manner, the sale of a butting ram, or a fighting cock, when these qualities are stipulated for as indications of a freedom from defects, is lawful. The sale of a dove on condition that it shall make certain sounds is invalid, because a dove cannot be forced to exhibit in this manner, and there are no means of ascertaining whether it possesses the qualifications or not. When a dog is sold on condition of his being a biter, or a pigeon on condition of its being a tumbler, the sale is not lawful unless these qualities are explained as defects. The purchase of a slave girl with a condition that she shall cook or write such things every day is not lawful. A person sells a crop of pot herbs on condition of cattle being sent by the purchaser to eat them off the ground, the sale, though contrary to analogy and the opinions of some, is lawful on a favourable construction, and the *futwa* is in accordance.

A person purchases land on condition that the seller shall pay the *Khiraj* or land-tax, the sale is invalid. **Purchase of land on**

Condition that the seller shall pay the *khiraj*.

And the result would be the same if the condition were that he shall pay a part of the *khiraj*, provided such part be of the original *khiraj* assessed upon the land; but if the part referred to be an addition to the original *khiraj*, the sale is lawful. A person purchases land on condition that the *khiraj* is three *dirhems* and finds it to be four, or four *dirhems* and finds that it is three, the sale is invalid if he were aware of the fact; but if he were not aware of it the sale would be lawful, the purchaser having an option to confirm the sale at the actual *khiraj*, or to reject it entirely. And if one should purchase *Khirajee* land as land not subject to *khiraj*, or land which is not subject to *khiraj* as if it were *Khirajee*, the seller having other *Khirajee* land the *khiraj* of which he ascribes to this land, and the purchaser be acquainted with these circumstances, the sale is invalid. If one should purchase on condition of paying what the neighbours are subject to, the sale would be invalid. So, also, if the condition were that no impost* should be exacted from the purchaser, the sale would also be invalid; but if one were to purchase on condition of not being liable for the first impost, the sale would be lawful.

Condition as to *khiraj* proving to be erroneous.

When land is sold without any mention of *khiraj* or condition regarding it, the sale is lawful; but if it should afterwards appear that the land is really subject to a heavy *khiraj*,—such as would in general be considered a defect,—the purchaser has an option by reason of the defect; but if the *khiraj* be not of that character he has no option. In like manner, when a person sells land stating the *khiraj* to be over an amount, and it subsequently appears to be so much more as would in general be accounted a defect, the purchaser is entitled to reject the sale. And if one should purchase a mansion on condition of its being free from casual exactions,† and such are subsequently demanded of him, he may return the mansion to the seller if alive, or to his heirs if he be

* Arab. *Jubayut*, Tributum.—*Freytag*.

† Arab. *Nuwaib*, pl. of *Naibut*. Incidens fortunæ casus.—*Freytag*.

dead. And if one should purchase a tavern or shop, on condition that its profit is twenty, but finds that in fact it is no more than fifteen, and it was meant by the condition to indicate the profit in past times, the contract would not be vitiated thereby; but if it were intended to insure that profit for the future, the contract would be bad. If the condition were in general terms, without any precise intention as to the past or the future, the contract would also be vitiated.

Other conditions proving erroneous.

When a person sells land with the condition of its containing such and such palm trees, or a mansion on condition of its containing such and such apartments, and the purchaser finds in either case a deficiency, the sale is lawful; but he has the option of taking the land or the mansion at the full price, or rejecting it altogether. A person purchases a sword on condition that it is ornamented with a hundred *dirhems* of silver, or a shoe on condition that it has a fellow to fit it, or a ring on condition that its stone is a *yakoot*,* or a stone on condition of its being set in a gold ring or hoop, and it is found that the thing stipulated for is either the property of a third party, or that, though it did once exist as stipulated for, it has subsequently perished; in these cases the purchaser has the option of taking what remains at the full price agreed upon, or rejecting it altogether; with exception, however, of the last case put, where if it should be found that there is in fact no gold ring or hoop, the sale would be invalid. The general principle in these cases is this. When two things are so connected that if one of them were sold the other would be included in the sale of it as an appendage without being mentioned, and a sale is made of the principal thing on an express condition that it is accompanied by the other, but it turns out that the principal only and not the secondary thing is forthcoming, then the purchaser has an option, and may either take the actual thing at the full price agreed upon, or reject

General principle.

* The *yakoot* comprehends, I think, the ruby, sapphire, and oriental topaz. See a little further on.

the bargain altogether. Where, again, there is no such original connection between the things, one of which is stipulated for as accompanying the other, and the thing so stipulated for is found not to exist, then the purchaser is entitled to take the existing thing at a fair proportion of the price.

Other conditions proving to be erroneous.

A person sells a garment on condition that it is dyed with yellow, when, lo! it is white, the sale is lawful, with an option to the purchaser. In the same way as when one sells a mansion on condition that there are buildings in it and there prove to be none, the sale is lawful with an option to the purchaser. On the contrary, if one should buy a garment on condition of its being white, when, lo! it is dyed with yellow, or a mansion on condition of its being free of buildings and buildings are found to be in it, the sale would be invalid. And if one should purchase fine linen on condition of its warp being a thousand and it proves to be fifteen hundred, the cloth is to be delivered to him.* And if the condition were that the cloth is a girdle of six yards and it proves to be only five, the purchaser may retain it at the full price, or if he please reject it. When a person says, "I have sold this cloth of *kuzz*†" or "*khuzz*,"‡ and it proves to be mixed, then if the warp be of the material stipulated for but the woof different, the sale is void; while if the woof be of the material stipulated for the sale is lawful, with an option to the purchaser in the case of the *kuzz*, but no such option in the case of the *khuzz* when the woof is of that material and the warp of something different. Aboo Yoosuf being asked with regard to a person who had purchased a garment on condition of its being linen, but a third of which proved to be cotton, answered "he is at liberty to return it, but if the greater part were cotton the sale would be invalid." A person purchases

* The fineness of linen or cotton manufactures is estimated by the number of threads in the warp, and the more there are the finer is the fabric.

† Raw silk; that is, reeled or thrown.

‡ Floss or spun silk.

fried barley on condition of its being mixed with a *mun* of butter, and mutual possession is taken, the purchaser looking on the while, it then proves that the butter is only half a *mun*, the sale notwithstanding is lawful, and the purchaser has no option. In the same way as if one should purchase soap on condition of its being composed of so many *joors* of oil, when it appears that the oil was less, but the purchaser was looking at the soap at the time of purchase, the sale is lawful and he has no option. So, also, if one should purchase a shirt on condition of its being made of ten cubits of cloth (looking on the while), when, lo! there are only nine cubits, the sale is lawful and he has no option.*

Subject continued.

If a person should purchase a book on condition of its being the book of marriage compiled by Mohummud, and find that it is a book on divorce, or physic, or marriage by another author, it has been said that the sale would be lawful, for a book is something black on a white ground, and there is but one *genus* with different species. And if one should purchase a camel on condition of its being Bactrian, and find that it is not so, he is at liberty to return it. When a person is sold as a slave girl and proves to be a lad, there is no sale; but this is a favourable construction of the law which has been adopted by our doctors. The general principle in this and similar cases is, that when a thing is distinctly pointed out as well as named in the contract, and is found to differ from the name, and the variance is in the *genus*, the sale is void. So that if one should sell the stone of a ring on condition of its being a *yakoot*, and find that it is glass, the sale is void. Where, on the other hand, the variance is only in quality or description, the contract is lawful, and the purchaser has an option on inspection, as if one should purchase the stone of a ring on condition of its being a red *yakoot* (ruby), and find it to be yellow.* A person pur-

General principle.

---

* The reader may compare this with what has been said with regard to manifest defects, *ante*, page 104.

† See *ante*, note, page 205.

chases a high cap on condition that its quilting is cotton, but on opening it finds it to be wool; opinions differ as to such a case, some saying that the sale is invalid, and that the purchaser should return the cap with compensation for the damage occasioned by ripping it up; but others, that the sale is lawful, and the purchaser entitled to damages for the variance; and the latter is the valid opinion. And if one should sell a *jubba*, or quilted waistcoat, on condition that the outside is of such a material, the lining of such another, and the quilting of such another, and it is found that the outside corresponds with the condition, but the other two differ from it, the sale is lawful with an option to the purchaser; but if the outside should differ from the condition, the sale would be void.

Further conditions.

A person purchases a camel on condition that it does not shriek or make a noise, and finds that it does, he may return it. And the result would be the same if he should purchase without such a condition, and the animal were found to shriek or make a noise to such a degree as would be generally considered a defect. A person purchases a female slave on condition that she has never borne a child, and it proves that she has, or on condition that she was born at Koofa, when in fact she was born at Busrah, in either case he may return her. But if a person should purchase a piece of cloth on condition that it is of Neishapoor, when in fact it is from Bookhara, or of Herat, when it is from Bulkh, or a turban on condition of its being of Shuhristan when it is from Samarkand, in all these cases the sale is invalid.

Stipulation of delay in delivery,

When delay is stipulated for in the delivery of the thing sold, and the thing is specific,* the contract is invalid;

* This restriction excludes the sale by *sulum*, the subject of which is an obligation; that is, something undeterminate. Mr. Hamilton says (vol. ii. p. 448), that "suspension in point of time is applicable only to a *debt*, in order that the debtor may have time to collect the sum within the prescribed time, and pay it accordingly." The word in the original Arabic is *dooyoon*, or obligations in the large sense which has been explained in the Introduction.

but when delay is stipulated for in payment of the price, and the price is an obligation, and the period of payment fixed, the sale is lawful, and where the period is left uncertain, the sale is invalid. Among unknown periods of payment, the *Neiroz** and *Mihrjan*† may be noticed; and with regard to these, when they are assigned generally, the contract is invalid; but if the *Majoosee Neiroz*, or *Sooltan Neiroz* be specified, and the date of occurrence is known to the parties, the sale is lawful. If the time fixed for payment be the arrival of the pilgrims, the reaping of the harvest, the treading out the corn, or the vintage, the sale is unlawful. If *fitr*‡ of the Christians be assigned, and they have already entered on the Fast, the sale is lawful, but otherwise it is unlawful. If a postponement to an unlawful date be cancelled before its arrival, the contract becomes lawful on a favourable construction, according to our doctors, who considered the contract to be in suspense, and that it became lawful on the removal of the impediment. Kurkhee has also cited an express decision of Aboo Huneefa on the case, and in this he is correct; but he has reported with regard to all invalid sales that our doctors considered that they became lawful by removal of the vitiating cause, but this opinion is incorrect. A person having purchased a slave for a thousand *dirhems* on condition of paying some part of the price every week, or the whole at the rate of five hundred a month, the contract was held to be bad.

unlawful as to goods, but lawful as to price.

---

* First day of the year; literally, new day.

† A festival observed by the ancient Persians in September.

‡ Literally, breaking a fast.

CHAPTER XI.

OF THE EFFECT OF UNLAWFUL SALES.

Distinction between null and invalid contracts.

SALE is of two kinds—Null and Invalid. When either of the things exchanged is not property, or the thing sold, though property, has no value in law,* the sale is null. Hence, if the price or the thing sold be blood, or carrion, or a free person, or if the thing sold be wine, a hog, or unlawful game, the sale is absolutely null, there being no contract. Where, again, both the things exchanged are property, and the thing sold has value in law, but the price wants that quality, as if one should purchase a commodity which has legal value for wine, a hog, unlawful game, or a *Modubbur*, *Mokatib*, or *oom-i-wulud*, or where a vitiating condition or the like enters into the contract, the sale is invalid.

Effect of an invalid sale on the right of property in the thing sold.

In the cases last mentioned, sale is contracted for the value of the thing sold, and the purchaser becomes proprietor of the latter on taking possession. Authorities differ, however, as to its being a trust in his hands, or at his risk and responsibility; some being of the one, and some of the other opinion.† It is a condition of possession having the effect referred to, that it should be taken with the seller's permission; for without his permission it is the same as if there were no possession. When a person takes possession without the permission of the seller being either given or refused, and possession is taken at the meeting, it is valid on a favourable construction; but if taken after the separation of the parties, it is neither

* Explained *ante*, note, page 3.

† In the remainder of the chapter it seems to be assumed that he is responsible.

valid by analogy nor on a favourable construction. Where, again, permission is given, the possession is equally valid, whether taken at the meeting or after the separation of the parties; and property in the thing sold passes to the purchaser both by analogy and on a favourable construction. The property, however, is of such a nature that it is subject to a right of dissolution; and it is abominable in a purchaser to make any disposal* of a thing which he has obtained by an unlawful sale, either by transferring his right to another or by using the thing himself. If, however, he should dispose of it, his act takes effect and cannot be dissolved, the seller's right to reverse the sale being annulled by it, whether the act be of a nature that admits of dissolution after it has once taken effect, as sale and the like, or does not admit of dissolution, as manumission and the like. From this, however, location and marriage are to be excepted, which do not invalidate the seller's right to reversal. If the purchaser should emancipate or sell a slave, or enter into an agreement of *tudbeer* with him, or if the slave being a female, she should conceive to the purchaser and become his *oom-i-wulud*, the seller's right to cancel the sale would be annulled, and the purchaser be liable to him for the value of the slave. So, also, he would be liable for the slave's value if he made a *Mookatib* of him. If the slave should pay his ransom and become free, the purchaser's liability for his value would be confirmed; but if the slave should be unable to fulfil the terms of his agreement, and should return in consequence to a state of slavery, and this should happen before any decree by the judge for his value to the seller, the latter would be entitled to restitution of the slave; while if the occurrence should not take place till after such decree by the judge, no means would be left to the seller of recovering the slave. If the purchaser by an illegal contract should bequeath the thing purchased, the bequest would be valid, and after the purchaser's death the seller would have no right to cancel the sale, a new right of property as it were being established in the

When voidable by the seller.

This right is barred by certain acts of the purchaser

* Arab. *Tusurroof:* free use and disposal at one's pleasure.

legatee. This is contrary to the case of an heir of the purchaser, from whom the seller would have a perfect right to recover the thing sold. And if the seller should die, his right to restitution would descend to his heirs.

By other acts of purchaser.

If the purchaser of a garment should cut it up and sew it, or line and quilt it, that would extinguish the seller's right to cancel the sale. And if the subject of sale were an open plain or field, and the purchaser should erect buildings or plant trees upon it, the seller's right to cancel would be extinguished according to Aboo Huneefa and Aboo Yoosuf, though it would remain good according to Mohummud.

Purchaser's responsibility in case of loss.

In an unlawful sale, what the purchaser is liable for is the value of the thing sold when it is of the class of things that are estimated by value, and a similar where it is of the class of similars; that is when the thing has perished in the hands of the purchaser, or has been destroyed by him, or given and delivered, or sold or pledged to a third party, and the seller's right to restitution is in consequence defeated. Where the pledge is redeemed, or the gift or sale cancelled, and the thing accordingly reverts to the purchaser's property, the seller's right to cancel the sale revives, provided that a decree has not already passed in his favour for the value of the thing sold. When the thing sold is still subsisting in the hands of the purchaser without any increase or diminution, it is to be restored to the seller and the sale cancelled.

When both or only one of the parties has a right to cancel the sale.

If the vice inherent in a contract of sale be radical, as entering into either of the things exchanged, each of the parties has a right to cancel the sale, but only in the presence of the other, according to Aboo Huneefa and Mohummud, though according to Aboo Yoosuf the right may be exercised in the presence or absence of the other party. Where, again, the vice in the contract is not of this essential character, as only arising from an improper condition, like a stipulation for some advantage to one of the parties, then both the parties have the right of cancellation before possession has taken place, but after possession it is only he in whose favour the stipulation was made that has the right of cancellation, and then only in the presence of the opposite party, who himself has no such right.

When the right to cancel is barred by an increase to the thing sold.

When any increase has taken place in the thing sold, and the increase is united to and has proceeded from the original, like beauty or improvement in condition, the seller's right to cancellation is not cut off by it; but where the increase though united to has not issued from the original, as a dye superadded to it, the seller's right to cancel the sale is cut off, and the purchaser is liable for the value or a similar quantity of the thing sold, according to the class of articles to which it may belong. And the result would be the same if the thing sold were cotton, and the purchaser should spin it into yarn, or yarn and he should weave it, or wheat and he should grind it. Where the increase is separated though it has issued from the original, as a child, fruit, or wool, the seller's right to cancellation is not affected, and the purchaser is bound to restore the original with its increase; but he is not liable for the loss of the increase if it should happen to perish in his hands, unless by his own act, when he would be liable. And if the original should perish, leaving the increase, the seller may reclaim the latter, with the value of the former as it stood at the time that possession was taken. Where the increase is separated from the original and had not issued from it, as gain, alms, or a gift received by it, the seller may reclaim the thing sold with the increase, but the purchaser is not liable for the loss of the latter if it should perish in his hands; and even if the loss were induced by his own act, Aboo Huneefa did not consider him liable, though the disciples were of a different opinion upon this point.

Effect of the thing sold sustaining damage in the hands of the purchaser.

When the thing sold sustains any damage in the hands of the purchaser, whether by accident or his own act, or that of the subject of sale itself, when an animate being, or the act of a stranger, the seller may recover the thing sold with compensation for the damage. And when the damage is occasioned by a stranger, the seller has the option of suing him direct for compensation, foregoing his claim against the purchaser, or he may proceed against the latter, who in that event would have a claim against the trespasser; but where the subject of sale is a slave, and he is slain by a stranger, the seller's remedy is against the purchaser only, and not against the stranger; to whose *akila*,* however, the purchaser may have recourse for the slave's value. When the seller himself is the aggressor and the subject of sale perishes in consequence, the sale is reversed, and the loss is the seller's, if nothing were done by the purchaser to prevent him from recovering possession; and even if something were so done by the purchaser, he would be in nowise liable on account of the loss, if it were obviously the effect of the seller's aggression; but if the loss were not the direct effect of the seller's aggression, though the sale would be cancelled, the purchaser would be held liable, subject to an abatement for the damage occasioned by the seller's aggression.

Profit on sale by purchaser should be bestowed in alms.

If a person should purchase a female slave by an invalid sale, and sell her at a profit, he ought to lay out the profit in alms; but if he lay out her price in the purchase of something else by which he makes a profit, he may lawfully enjoy the last profit. A person who purchases a female slave by an invalid sale cannot lawfully enjoy her; and if he should without her conceiving, the seller may still reclaim her from the purchaser, who is also liable to him for her *ikr* or ransom. If, however, she should conceive, the purchaser is liable for her full value, the seller's right to annul the sale being extinguished.

Property in a price, or consideration that is illegal, does not pass.

If a person purchase a slave in exchange for a *Mudubbur*, *Mokatib*, or *Oom-i-wulud*, and possession be mutually taken by the parties, property in the slave will pass to and be vested in his purchaser, but property in the others will not pass to nor be vested in the purchaser of them, though he should take possession with permission of the seller. So,

---

* "The *akilas* of a man are all those who are enrolled with him, provided he be an enrolled person." "The *akilas* of a person not enrolled or registered are, his tribe or family descended from one father."—*Hamilton's Hedaya*, vol. iv. pages 449-452.

also, if one should purchase a slave for property belonging to another without his permission, property in the slave would vest in the purchaser, but property in the thing given in exchange would not vest till sanctioned by its owner.

Purchaser's lien on the thing sold for repayment of the price.

A person purchases a slave by an invalid contract, takes possession of him with the permission of the seller, and pays down the price; the seller then wishes to take back the slave, but the purchaser may withhold him till he obtains repayment of the price. If the seller should die leaving no other property but the slave, the purchaser has a preferable right over the other creditors, and the slave is to be sold for payment of his right. Should the second price be equal to the first, the purchaser is entitled to the whole; if there be any excess over the first price it belongs to the creditors, while if there be any deficiency the purchaser is entitled to rank for it rateably with the other creditors on anything that there may appear to be of the inheritance. Should the slave happen to die in the purchaser's hands, he would be liable for his value. If the invalid purchase were in consideration of a debt previously due by the seller to the purchaser, and the purchaser having taken possession with permission of the seller, the latter should afterwards wish to avail himself of the flaw in the contract to cancel it, but the purchaser should desire to retain the slave on account of the old debt, he would have no right to do so. Or if the seller should die leaving much debt, and the slave in the hands of the purchaser, the latter would have no better right through the invalid contract than the other creditors.

Purchaser's liability in case of loss, how affected by a release.

A person sells a slave by an invalid contract, which after possession the parties agree to dissolve, the seller releasing the purchaser from the value. The slave then dies in the hands of the purchaser, who nevertheless is liable for his value; but if the seller had said, "I release you from the slave," and the slave had then died in the hands of the purchaser he would no longer be liable, because such a release would convert the purchaser's possession into a trust, for which he could not of course be held responsible in the event of loss.

Limited to the value at the time of contract.

A person purchases a slave by an invalid contract for five hundred *dirhems*, such being his value at the time, but he afterwards rises to the value of two thousand by a change in the market, the purchaser, however, is liable for no more than five hundred, which was his value at the time of sale. And if a person should usurp a slave whose value is a thousand, but afterwards rises to two thousand, and should then purchase the slave from his owner by an invalid contract, after which the slave dies; in these circumstances, if the usurper had reached the slave so as to renew his possession of him, he is liable for the two thousand; but if he had not reached the slave before his death his liability is limited to one thousand, because an increase during usurpation is a trust, and the usurper cannot become liable under the sale till possession, which in the supposed case would not have taken place.

When otherwise, in a case of usurpation.

Which is also the price to a claimant of pre-emption.

A person purchases a mansion by an invalid sale and takes possession, it subsequently falls into great disrepair, and the parties litigating the matter before the *Kazee*, he decrees in favour of the seller for its value on the day of seisin; it is at this value that a claimant for pre-emption is entitled to take it from the purchaser.

An invalid sale is cancelled by any return to the seller of the thing sold.

If a purchaser by an invalid sale should return the thing sold to the seller, the contract is cancelled, whether the return be made by reason of sale, or gift, or as alms, or a loan, or deposit, or any other cause. And in like manner, if he were to sell the thing to an agent for purchase appointed by the seller, and deliver the thing to him, he would be released from his responsibility on account of it.

Right to cancel not lost by mere conversion of land to a *musjid*.

If a person should sell by an invalid contract a piece of land which the purchaser converts into a *musjid*, the right of cancellation is not extinguished until the erection of the building; but if a building be erected the right to cancel is annulled, according to Aboo Huneefa; and the planting of trees upon land would have the same effect as erecting buildings.

Dispute regarding the validity of a sale.

When the parties to a contract of sale differ as to its legality, one of them maintaining that it was valid, and the other insisting that it was vitiated, then, if the vice insisted upon be a bad condition merely, or an illegal postponement of delivery, the word of the person maintaining the validity and the evidence of the other party are to be preferred, according to a general agreement of all reports. And even where the vice insisted upon enters into the essence of the contract, as if one should allege that he purchased for a thousand *dirhems* and a *rutl* of wine, and the other that he purchased for a thousand *dirhems* only, still the word of the party maintaining the validity of the contract and the evidence of the party insisting on the vice would be entitled to preference, according to the Zahir Rewayut.

CHAPTER XII.

OF THE EFFECT OF DEPENDENT SALES AND OF SALES BY ONE OF TWO CO-PARTNERS.

Conditions necessary to the validity of an owner's ratification.

WHEN a person sells the property of another, the sale is suspended, according to us, for the sanction or ratification of the proprietor; and the existence of both the parties to the contract, and of the subject of sale, is a necessary condition to the validity of his sanction. The existence of the price when it is money is not necessary; but when it is a specific thing other than money, the existence of the price is also essential to the validity of the sanction. When the sanction is valid, and the price is a thing capable of being rendered determinate by specification, and is still in existence, the seller and not the sanctioner is entitled to it; the sanctioner* having only a right of recourse against the seller for the value of his property if it were of the class of things estimated by value, or a similar if it were of the class of similars. And if the price should perish in the hands of the seller, whether before or after the sanction of the sale, it would perish as a trust; but if the thing sold should perish in the hands of the purchaser, the proprietor may make whichever he pleases of the purchaser and seller responsible for it. If the purchaser be made responsible, he may have recourse to the seller for a refund of the price if it had been paid; but if the seller be made responsible, and the thing sold were originally with him on his responsibility,

* Arab. *Mojeez*, "who permits or approves."—*Richardson*.

the sale becomes operative.* If the thing sold had been with him on trust, and he had first delivered and then sold, the sale would also become operative :† but if he had sold first and then delivered, the sale would not become operative, and the seller would in consequence be entitled to have recourse against the purchaser for what he had been made responsible for. If the owner should die before sanctioning the sale, sanction by his heir would not suffice to give it operation. Sanction by an owner himself renders a sale operative, even with regard to an increase of the thing sold which may have taken place after the sale, though previous to the sanction, of which increase the purchaser becomes in consequence the proprietor.

Contract is operative against the actual seller, unless he refer it to another.

If one should purchase to or for another the sale is operative against himself, unless he refer or ascribe it to the other, or be a youth, or otherwise inhibited. When a *fuzoolee*‡ refers or ascribes his purchase to another, as for instance, if he should say, "Sell this slave to such an one," and the seller should answer, "I have sold him to such an one," the sale is suspended; and it is enough in this case that one of the expressions should ascribe the sale to the other party. But if the seller should say to the *fuzoolee*, "I have sold this to you on account of such an one," and the *fuzoolee* answer, "I have accepted," or "have bought;" or if the *fuzoolee* should say in the first instance, "I have bought for such an one," and the seller answer, "I have sold," the contract would operate against the actual purchaser, and would not be suspended. The author observes, however, that he has seen it stated in another place, in a similar case, that the contract would not operate against the *fuzoolee*, but be suspended for the consent of the party referred to.

---

* As, for instance, if he had usurped it. See *ante*, page 3.

† The delivery would be a breach of trust, and make him responsible; because a trustee is not at liberty to commit a deposit to the charge of any other than a member of his family. See *Hamilton's Hedaya*, vol. iii. p. 260.

‡ One busying himself in things not belonging to him, or acting without authority.—*Richardson*.

What amounts to sanction by a proprietor.

A person sells the slave of another without his orders, and the other on receiving intelligence of the sale says to the seller, "I have given you the price," or "bestowed it on you in alms," this amounts to an approval of the sale if the slave be in existence. A person receives intelligence that a *fuzoolee* has sold his property, and remains silent, this is no sanction of the sale; but if, on receiving intelligence of the sale, he allows it before knowing the amount of the price, and afterwards on ascertaining it reverses the sale, the sanction and not the cancellation is good. A *fuzoolee*, or bailee, having sold without permission of the owner or depositor, the proprietor declares his allowance of the sale, while the subject of it is still in existence; he cannot, however, receive the price from the purchaser unless he be appointed by the actual seller his attorney for the purpose. A person sells the slave of another, without his permission, for a hundred *dirhems;* the purchaser then comes to the owner and tells him that such an one has sold his slave for so much, whereupon the owner answers, "If he has sold to you for a hundred *dirhems* I have already approved," the sale is lawful according to Moohummud, if the slave were sold for a hundred or more; but if he were sold for less it is not lawful. And in like manner it is not lawful if he were sold for a hundred *deenars*, because the approval is only of what was mentioned. So also if the owner should say, "If he sold to you for a hundred it is lawful," the sale would be lawful with the same distinction. But if the expressions were, "if he sell to you for a hundred *dirhems* I approve," it would not be lawful; for this is not an approval but a promise. And if the party should afterwards sell, the owner would still be at liberty to sanction the sale or not at his pleasure. A person sells the cloth of another without his permission, and the purchaser dyes it, after which the owner approves of the sale, which becomes lawful in consequence; but if the purchaser had cut up and sewn the cloth before the sale was approved, it would not become lawful, as that would be tantamount to an extinction of the thing sold.

When a *fuzoolee* sells a thing first to one person, and then to another, without the consent of the proprietor in both cases, it would seem that the second sale is a cancellation of the first, but some of our doctors have said that it is not a cancellation, and their opinion is correct. Hence, if the proprietor were to sanction both sales at the same time, each purchaser would be entitled to a half of the thing sold.

Effect of owner's sanction on two sales made by a *fuzoolee*.

Sale takes priority of marriage, location, or pledge, insomuch that if one *fuzoolee* were to sell a slave girl, and another *fuzoolee* were to give her in marriage, or let her to hire, or to pledge her, and her master should give his sanction at once to both the acts, the sale would be lawful and the other void.* Emancipation, *kitabut*, and *tudbeer* take precedence of everything else. Gift and location are preferred to pledge, and gift to location. Sale is preferred to gift in the case of a mansion, and is on an equal footing with it in the case of a slave.

Effect of sanction on different acts of different *fuzoolees*. Regulated by the nature of the Act.

A purchaser is entitled to cancel the sale at any time before approval by the true owner, and the *fuzoolee* seller has also the same power.

Sale may be cancelled at any time before sanction.

Among dependent sales is sale by an inhibited youth † who understands the nature of sale and purchase; and sales and purchases by him are suspended on the permission of his father, father's executor, grandfather, or the judge.‡ So, also, with regard to a lunatic, or an inhibited youth when he arrives at puberty but is imbecile, sale and purchase by either of these is suspended on the permission of his guardian or the judge. When an inhibited slave § sells any of his master's property, or property given to him, or purchases anything, the transaction is suspended on his master's sanction. And when a man sells a slave whom he has permitted to trade, and who has incurred debts without the permission of his creditors, the sale is suspended on their permission.

Sale by an inhibited person.

---

* See *ante*, page 142.

† That is, a youth not yet arrived at puberty.

‡ All these are included within the meaning of the term Guardian. —*Hamilton's Hedaya*, vol. iii. p. 520.

§ That is, one who is not *mazoon*, or permitted to trade.

Sale in a last illness.

Sale by a person in his death-sickness is another instance of suspended sale. If such person should sell a specific chattel to one of his heirs, the sale is lawful if he should recover; but if he die in that illness, and his other heirs refuse their sanction to the sale, it is not lawful.

Sale by an apostate.

Another instance of a suspended transaction is a sale or purchase by an apostate; if he be put to death for his apostacy, or die in it, or take refuge in an enemy's country, the sale or purchase is void; but if he return to the faith, it becomes operative.

Sale of land under *moozariut*.

When a person gives up his land under a contract of *moozariut* * for a fixed term, on condition that the seed is to be supplied by the labourer, and then sells the land, the sale is suspended on the consent of the cultivator, whether he has sown the land or not.

Sanction by purchaser to a second sale by seller not sufficient.

A person purchases from another a piece of cloth, but the seller notwithstanding disposes of it to a third party for ten *dirhems* more, and the first purchaser then sanctions the sale, it is not rendered lawful, however, by such sanction.

Sale by one of two partners of the whole of a joint property; of an undivided share; of a part of a commodity estimated by

A slave girl, the property of two persons, is sold by one of them without the consent of his partner, and the purchaser takes possession of and then emancipates her; the partner afterwards sanctions the sale, it is not lawful, however, as to his share. But it is stated in certain rare cases that if one of two partners in a mansion should sell a half of it undivided, the sale would have reference to his own share; and if a *fuzoolee* sell the half of a mansion held in partnership by two persons, the sale has reference to the shares of both; so that if one of the partners sanction the sale, it becomes valid as to the half of the sanctioner, according to Aboo Yoosuf, but Moohummud and Zoofr thought that it would be lawful only as to a fourth. Two men being joint proprietors of a heap of grain, one of them sells a *kufeez* from the heap, and measures it to the

* "In the language of the law it signifies a compact between two persons, one being a proprietor of land, and the other the cultivator, by which it is agreed that whatever is produced from the land shall belong to both in such proportions as may be therein determined."—*Hamilton's Hedaya*, vol. iv. p. 39.

purchaser after the sale; in such a case, whether the partner sanction it or not, the sale is lawful, and the whole price belongs to the seller. If one of the partners should sell a *kufeez* and the other sanction the sale, after which the seller measures it to the purchaser and the remainder then perishes, the other partner is entitled to half a *kufeez* as against the seller, but is without remedy against the purchaser; but if the partner had not sanctioned the sale up to the time when the remainder of the grain perished, he would be entitled to take back from the purchaser half the grain that was sold to him. If one of the partners should withdraw a *kufeez* from the heap, and sell that *kufeez*, and the other should then sanction the sale, the price of it would belong to them in equal shares; and if the other should not sanction the sale, but insist on taking back from the purchaser the half of what was sold to him, and the purchaser should then wish to have recourse against the seller for a whole *kufeez*, he is not entitled to do so, though he is at liberty to cancel the sale or reclaim from the seller half the price.

measure of capacity;

of his share in such a commodity, &c.

When wheat or any commodity estimated by weight is owned by two persons in common, and one of them sells his share to his partner or a stranger, then if the joint ownership originated in an intermixture of the properties of both, whether effected voluntarily or without their will, the sale by one of them of his share to his partner is lawful; but a sale to a stranger would not be lawful except with the partner's consent. And if the co-ownership arose from inheritance, purchase, or gift, the sale by one of them of his share to the other is lawful, and also to a stranger after the partner's permission; but one partner has no right of disposal over the share of his fellow.

Share in a wood without the land.

A person sells his share in a wood without the consent of his partner, and without the land; if the trees have arrived at a time fit for cutting, the sale is lawful, but otherwise it is invalid.

Of a share in a mansion.

When one person says to another, "I have sold you my share in this mansion for so much," and the purchaser knows the share though the seller himself does not, the sale is lawful after the seller has declared the share to be as stated by the purchaser; but where the purchaser does not know the share, Aboo Huneefa and Moohummud were of opinion that the sale was not lawful, whether the seller knew it or not. Aboo Yoosuf, on the contrary, thought it lawful in either alternative.

Of a well, &c.

A well and land being the joint property of two persons, one of them sells his share in the well and a road to it through the land, the sale is lawful as to the well, but not lawful as to the road without the sanction of the co-partner, on which it is suspended. If he allow the sale it is lawful as to the whole. If half the well were sold without the road it would be lawful. When a person sells the half of buildings with half the land on which they are erected, the sale is lawful whether it be to his partner or a stranger; but if he sell half the buildings without the land the sale is unlawful in both cases.

Dispute as to a sale having been authorised.

When a person sells the slave of another, and the purchaser wishes to return him, saying, "You sold him to me without the order of his owner," but the seller denies, saying, "Nay, but I sold him by the order of his owner," and the purchaser then adduces evidence of an acknowledgment by the owner of the slave that he did not authorize the sale, or an acknowledgment by the seller himself to the same effect, such evidence cannot be received; but if the seller should himself make a declaration before the judge that the owner never authorized the sale, it should be cancelled on the demand of the purchaser. If the owner of the slave should appear before the judge and deny his order for the sale, and the seller should then in his absence demand a cancellation of it, it would be the duty of the judge to cancel the sale, and to refuse a postponement of the case if desired by the purchaser, to allow of the owner's being sworn as to the want of authority from him. If the owner should then appear and swear, he would get back the slave; but if he refuse to swear, the sale would be restored *ab integro.* Should the owner appear before the judge in the absence of the purchaser, and deny the order for the sale, he would not be entitled to take the slave, and the seller might require his oath to this effect,—"By God, you did not order me to sell him." If he should refuse to swear, the authority would be proved; and if he took the oath, the seller would be responsible and the sale become operative.

CHAPTER XIII.

OF IKALUT,* OR THE DISSOLUTION OF SALES.

Definition. *Ikalut*, according to Aboo Huneefa, is a cancellation as regards the contracting parties, but a new sale with regard to other persons; and where cancellation is impracticable, as for instance, when the subject of sale is a female slave and she bears a child, the *Ikalut* is void.†

Valid at the original price. When a slave girl is sold for a thousand *dirhems*, and the parties agree to a dissolution of the contract for a thousand *dirhems*, it is valid; and if the agreement be for one thousand five hundred *dirhems*, the dissolution is valid at a thousand, the mention of the five hundred being treated as a mistake. When the dissolution is for five hundred, and the subject of sale is in the purchaser's hands, and in the same state as at the time of sale, without having sustained any injury, the dissolution is still valid at the thousand, the mention of five hundred being here also treated as an error. When valid at an abatement. But if it has sustained any injury the dissolution is valid at five hundred, the abatement in price being set off against the loss. Even when a dissolution is

---

* Ikalut has been sanctioned by the Prophet, in these words: "Whosoever makes an *akala* with one who has repented of his bargain, shall receive an *akala* of his sins from God, on the day of judgment."—*Hamilton's Hedaya*, vol. ii. p. 465.

† Aboo Yoosuf and Moohummud differed from their master, and also from each other, but no reference is made in the text to their opinions; probably, because that of Aboo Huneefa is held to be valid. The differences of opinion and the reasons for each, are given at length in Mr. Hamilton's *Translation*, vol. ii. p. 465.

in consideration of something of a different kind from the price, all the books agree that it is valid according to Aboo Huneefa at the original price, and that the statement of a different consideration should be treated as a mistake. Where an increase has taken place in the thing sold, and the parties dissolve the sale, the dissolution is valid according to Aboo Huneefa, if the increase had taken place before possession, whether the increase be united to or separated from the original; but if the increase take place after possession, and is separated from the original, the dissolution is void in his opinion; while if the increase be united with the orignal, the dissolution is good.

Dissolution must be made in words of the preterite tense.

According to the opinion of Moohummud, which has been approved and adopted as the *futwa,* dissolution of sale, like sale itself, cannot be effected except by expressions both of which are in the past tense. Thus, a man sells something, and then says to the purchaser, "Dissolve me the sale," to which the purchaser answers, "I have dissolved it to you;" this is no dissolution according to Aboo Huneefa and Moohummud, until the seller reply, "I have accepted." If the purchaser should say, "I have abandoned the sale," and the seller answer, "I am content," or, "I have approved," this amounts to a dissolution. If the seller should ask the purchaser to dissolve the sale, and he should answer, "Bring the money," and the seller should approve, the case would be the same as that already put,—"Dissolve me the sale," &c. A broker brings the price of a thing to the seller, having sold it under an absolute order, whereupon the seller says, "I will not give it for that price," and the broker then informs the purchaser, who says, "I also do not desire it," this, however, is no cancellation. A person purchases silk of which he takes possession; he then says to the seller, "It does not suit my purpose; take it and give me the price," but the seller refuses. The purchaser then says, "I have given up so much of the price, deliver to me the remainder," which he does; this is a dissolution, not a new sale.

May be effected by *taatee.*

Dissolution may also be effected by *Taatee,* or reciprocal delivery, even though the delivery be only by one of the parties. A person having taken possession of purchased grain and paid part of the price, says after a time to the seller, "There was an error in the price," whereupon the seller returns the part of it which he had received. Those who say that sale may be contracted by *Taatee,* though the delivery be on the side of only one of the parties, say that this is a dissolution, and they are right. A person purchases a piece of silk cloth, and having taken possession of it says to the seller, "It does not suit my purpose, take it back and restore me the price," but he refuses, and the purchaser then says, "I have abated so much from the price, give me the remainder," and the seller does so, this is a dissolution, not a new sale.

A seller requests a purchaser to cancel a sale, and the purchaser says, "Give me back the price," whereupon the seller writes him a bond for it and delivers it to him, and he takes the bond and restores the thing sold; this is a cancellation. A person sells a piece of cloth to another, and afterwards the purchaser says, "I have dissolved the sale of this cloth, cut it up into a shirt," and the seller does so before they separate, saying nothing; this also is *ikalut.*

Conditions necessary to the validity of *ikalut.*

It is essential to the validity of an *ikalut* that the contracting parties shall both be content; that the integrity of the meeting be preserved; that in the dissolution of a *surf* sale the parties shall mutually resume possession of the things exchanged before they separate; that the thing sold be in such a condition as to admit of the sale being cancelled for all the causes of cancellation, such as rejection under an option by stipulation, or of inspection, or for defect. If it be not in such a condition, as for instance by reason of an increase which would prevent cancellation for these causes, the dissolution would not be valid according to Aboo Huneefa. The existence of the thing sold at the time of dissolution is also a condition of its validity; for if it were defunct at that time, the dissolution would not be valid. But the existence of the price at the time of dissolution is not a condition of its validity. When a specific thing has been sold for an obligation,* and the parties afterwards dissolve the sale, the *ikalut* is valid if the specific thing be still existing in the hands of the purchaser, whether the price be in existence or not; but if the specific thing have perished before the dissolution takes place, the *ikalut* is not valid. So, also, though the specific thing were in existence at the time of the dissolution, yet if it should perish before being returned to the seller, the *ikalut* would be void. In like manner, if the subject of sale were two slaves, and possession being taken they should both die, and the parties then dissolve the sale, the *ikalut* would not be valid; and if one of them should be dead and the other living at the time of dissolution, then the *ikalut* would be valid, but if the living one should also die before his return, the *ikalut* would become void. If one specific thing be sold for another specific thing, and after reciprocal possession one of the things perishes in the hands of its purchaser, and the parties then dissolve the sale, the *ikalut* is valid, and the purchaser of the thing that perished is liable for its value, or its similar if it were of the class of similars, which he must accordingly deliver to the other party, reclaiming from him the other specific thing. So, also, if the parties should dissolve the sale while both the specific things are in existence, and one of the things should perish after the dissolution but before its return, the *ikalut* would not be rendered void; but if they should both perish before return, the *ikalut* would be void.

Consumption or destruction of an increase bars *ikalut*.

A person sells an orchard to another and makes delivery, the purchaser then eats of its produce for a year, after which the parties agree to a dissolution of the sale, but it is not valid. So, also, if the increase should perish, or be destroyed by a stranger, and whether it had been united to or separated from its original. But if one should make delivery of a slave in a sale or exchange for grain of any kind and take possession of the grain, and the slave should

* Arab. *deyn*; see *ante*, p. 7.

then die, after which the parties agree to a dissolution, the *ikalut* would be valid, and the purchaser be liable for the value of the slave.

Ikalut, with regard to moist things becoming dry.

A person purchases moist soap of which he takes possession, and it becomes dry, losing weight in consequence; the parties afterwards agree to a cancellation of the sale, which is valid, and the purchaser is not liable for any abatement from the price on account of the loss. A person purchases flesh or fish or anything else liable to become quickly bad, and goes to his house to fetch the price, his stay being protracted the seller becomes apprehensive that the article will get bad; in such circumstances he may on a favourable construction sell to a third party, who may lawfully purchase notwithstanding the previous sale; but if the second price be greater than the first it is incumbent on the seller to bestow the surplus in charity, while if the second price should fall short of the first he has no claim on the first purchaser on that account.

Miscellaneous cases.

A person purchases an ass and takes possession, but brings him back after four days and returns him to the seller, who does not expressly assent, but uses the ass, however, for some days, and then finally refuses to accept the dissolution and return the price, he is at liberty to do so.* A person sells a slave girl but the purchaser denies the purchase, it is not lawful for the seller carnally to enjoy her unless he resolve to give up any controversy about the matter, for the sale is not cancelled by the mere denial of the purchase; but if the seller determine to give up the point in dispute, he may then lawfully enjoy her. So, also, if the seller deny the sale while the purchaser insists for it, the seller cannot lawfully enjoy the slave; but if the purchaser should abandon his claim, and the seller hear that he has no intention of contesting the matter, he may then lawfully enjoy her.

Ikalut by an agent.

An agent for sale has power to enter into *ikalut* before receiving the price, according to Aboo Huneefa and Moo-

* Nothing having been done at the meeting to indicate consent.

hummud; but an agent for purchase does not appear to have such power. The principal may himself, in both cases, enter into an *ikalut* with either the seller or purchaser. And *ikalut* by an heir or executor is lawful; but *ikalut* by a legatee is not lawful.

Remeasure is not required after *ikalut*.

Conditional *ikalut* not valid.

Ikalut is lawful with regard to articles estimated by measurement of capacity without remeasure.* But it is not valid to suspend an *ikalut* on a condition; thus, if one should sell a piece of cloth, and the purchaser remarking, "I bought it cheap," the seller should then say, "If you find a purchaser for more sell it to him," and the purchaser finding such another purchaser does sell it, the second sale would be valid. But *ikalut*, according to Aboo Huneefa, is not rendered void by vitiating conditions because it is a cancellation.† When a person to whom a debt is due, but payable at a future time, purchases something from his debtor in exchange for the debt, and takes possession of the thing; but the parties then dissolve the sale, the debtor's right to credit does not revive. Whereas, if the thing be returned in consequence of defect under a judge's decree, the cancellation is complete in all respects, and the right to credit does revive. But if another person were surety for the debt, the suretyship would not revive in either case.

Trouble of re-transfer after *ikalut*.

A person purchases something which requires carriage and trouble in removing it, and transfers it to another place, after which the parties dissolve the sale, the trouble of re-transfer must be borne by the seller.

Consumption of an increase after *ikalut*.

A person purchases a cow, of which he takes possession, and the parties dissolve the sale; but while the cow is still in the purchaser's hands he milks her and drinks the milk, in these circumstances the seller is entitled to a similar quantity of milk. And if the cow should perish in the possession of the purchaser, though that would annul the *ikalut*, it would not release the purchaser from his responsibility on account of the milk, with respect to

* See note, page 30.

† And not a sale *de novo*, so far as the parties are concerned.

which the *ikalut* is good. And if one should purchase land with its crop which the purchaser reaps, and the parties then dissolve the sale, the dissolution is valid with regard to the land at a fair proportion of the price. But if a person should purchase land with trees upon it which he cuts down, and the parties then dissolve the sale, it is valid at the full price, the seller being entitled to no part of the value of the trees which must be delivered to the purchaser, that is, if the seller knew that they were cut down. If he were not aware of that fact at the time of the dissolution, he is at liberty to reject the land, or to take it at the full price.

Dissolution of a dissolution.

The dissolution of a dissolution is lawful, except in the case of a *sulum* sale. And if a person after *ikalut* should again sell to the purchaser, it is lawful; but if he sell to another party, it is not lawful. After a seller has dissolved a sale, he may enter into a dissolution of the previous sale to himself with the seller, and thus his resale to such seller is also lawful.

CHAPTER XIV.

OF A RIGHT IN A THIRD PARTY TO THE THING SOLD.*

Effect on a previous contract of a right in a third party to the thing sold.

WHEN a right to the thing sold is established against a purchaser, it occasions a suspension of the previous contract, on the permission of the person entitled to the right; but it does not dissolve nor cancel the contract. And there are different opinions as to the time when the sale is actually dissolved; but, according to that which is most valid, it is not dissolved till the purchaser has recourse to the seller for a refund of the price. So that if the claimant should sanction the sale after a decree by the judge in his favour, or even after he had resumed possession of the thing sold, at any time up to actual recourse by the purchaser to the seller, the sale would be valid.

When the right is to part only of the thing sold.

When the thing purchased is a single article, as one piece of cloth or one slave, and a right is established to part of it, whether before or after possession by the purchaser, he has an option with regard to the remainder,

---

* Arab. *Istihkak.* Infinitive, of an increased conjugation, from *hukk*, right. This form of conjugation very frequently signifies, *demand of the radical sense;* and the word has been translated by Mr. Hamilton, *Claim of Right* (title to chapter x. of "Sale"); but it more properly signifies *the having, or being entitled to, a right*, than the mere claim to it. In Moohummudan law, however, there is not much difference between a claim of right, supported by legal evidence, and its actual establishment in a court of justice; hence, a claim supported by evidence, has been said (page 112) to be tantamount to a defect, for which a purchase may be returned.

and may either take it for its proportion of the price, or reject it altogether. And if two things be purchased together, as two pieces of cloth, or two slaves, and possession of neither is taken till after a right is established to one of them, or possession of one is taken, and a right is then established in the other, the purchaser has an option with regard to the remaining article. But if a right to one of the things be established after possession has been taken by the purchaser, he has no option with regard to the other, though this be a splitting of the bargain as against him. Where the thing purchased is a commodity estimated by weight or measurement of capacity, and a right to part of it is established before possession by the purchaser, he has an option with regard to the remainder; but where the right to part does not transpire till after possession the point is in doubt, there being two reports of Aboo Huneefa's opinion on the subject.

Purchaser is entitled to a refund of the price. When, subsequent to the sale or usurpation of a thing, a right to it is established, the purchaser in the one case is entitled to have recourse to the seller for a refund of the price, and the usurper in the other is freed from responsibility. But if a person should purchase or usurp a piece of cloth and sew it up into a *kumees*, or wheat and grind it, or a sheep and roast it, and a right is then established to the article, the purchaser has no right of recourse to the seller for the price, nor is the usurper released from the consequences of his usurpation, on the contrary he is still liable to the owner * of the usurped article for its value.

Joint suit by seller and purchaser against claimant. When a third party proves to be entitled to a thing sold before possession by the purchaser, and the seller and purchaser concur in a suit against him, alleging that the seller purchased the thing from him, and after taking possession of it sold it to the purchaser, the evidence of which they may tender to that effect is to be received; but if they have no evidence at the time the judge is

* Arab. *Malik*.

to dissolve the sale between them, and the seller is to refund the price to the purchaser. Should the seller at a subsequent time obtain evidence of his assertion, the dissolution already awarded is not to be cancelled; but if the right had been established after possession by the purchaser, the dissolution ought to be cancelled and the cancellation would be binding on the purchaser, unless he had an option. If the parties themselves dissolve the sale without the decree of a judge, as, for instance, by the purchaser's demanding and the seller's refunding the price, the dissolution cannot be cancelled; and though the purchaser alone should dissolve the sale without the consent of the seller, the dissolution cannot be cancelled without the decree of a judge.

A gift of the price by the seller to the purchaser bars the latter's claim to a refund.

A person purchases a slave for a thousand *dirhems*, and the seller makes him a present of the price, either before or after possession of the slave, it subsequently appears that a third party is entitled to the slave, yet the purchaser has no claim against the seller. If the claimant give his sanction to the sale before a decree in his favour, the sale is lawful, and the gift also is lawful, according to Aboo Huneefa, if it were made before receipt of the price, the seller being in that case liable for a similar of the price to the slave's master; but if the gift were not made till after receipt of the price it is not lawful, and the purchaser is himself obliged to make good the price to the slave's master.*

A purchaser may have recourse to his seller, on eviction of his donee.

A person purchases a slave and gives him to another, who sells him to a third party, after which the slave is recovered from the hands of the last party under a claim of right; in such circumstances the first purchaser is not entitled to have recourse to the original seller for a refund of the price until the second purchaser has recourse to the donee; but when the second takes his recourse the first may do so also.† If there had been no sale by the

* See as to the different effect of a gift of the price before and after receipt, in barring a purchaser's right to reject for a defect—page 126.

† As a gift may be retracted (*Hamilton's Hedaya*, vol. iii. p. 300), the first purchaser may still be said to have an interest in the slave.

donee, the first purchaser might, immediately on the donee's dispossession, proceed against the original seller.

Case of a person purchased as a slave on his own assertion that he is so, and afterwards proving to be free.

When a person says to another, "Buy me for I am a slave," and he does so, but lo! the speaker is free; then if the seller be present, or absent at a known place, the purchaser has no remedy against the person who said, "Buy me, for I am a slave;" but if the seller be absent and the place of his residence unknown, the purchaser may revert to the speaker for the price which he was induced to pay to the seller, against whom the speaker may then have recourse for reimbursement.

Case of a slave girl asserting her right to freedom.

A person purchases a slave girl and takes possession of her, whereupon she claims to be free by origin, or the property of such an one, or his freed woman or *moodubburruh*,* or *oom-i-wulud*, and her assertion is verified by the person referred to, or an oath being tendered to the purchaser he refuses to swear; in either of these cases he has no recourse against the seller.† And though he should prove her to be the property of the person in question, his claim would not be admitted; but if he should prove a declaration by the seller to that effect, or prove that the woman was free by origin (such being her claim), or that she was the property of the person referred to, and that he had emancipated her, or made her a *moodubburruh* or *oom-i-wulud* before the purchase, in all these cases the claim would be admitted, and the purchaser entitled to a refund of the price.

How a purchaser may have recourse against a former seller, when the seller to himself is dead.

It is related of Sheikh ool-Islam Al Auzujundy, that being asked what should be done in the case of a person who had purchased a slave girl from another who was dead without leaving property or any heir or executors, but the seller to whom was present, he answered that the judge should appoint an executor to the deceased, against whom the purchaser might have recourse, and that such executor should then revert to the seller to the deceased.

A person purchases a thing, of which he is dispossessed

* Feminine of *Moodubbur*.

† The evidence is deficient in both.

under a claim of right, and then reverts to the seller for a refund of the price; but it afterwards happens that the thing came again into his hands under another title, he is not, however, required to surrender it to the seller. But if he had already declared the thing to be the property of the seller, and had then purchased it of him, he would, after the establishment of a right, and consequent refund to him of the price, be obliged to surrender the thing to the seller if it should afterwards come into his hands under another right. A person purchases a female slave, and having taken possession of her and paid down the price a right to her is established on evidence, whereupon the purchaser applies to the seller for a refund of the price; but the seller says to him, "You know well that the witnesses are liars, and that the slave was my property," to which the purchaser answers, "I testify that he was your property, and that the witnesses are liars;" still, however, this does not annul the purchaser's right to a refund of the price. But if the slave should ever come to him by any other means he would be bound to surrender her to the seller.

How a purchaser's right of recourse is affected by his declaration that the thing sold belonged to the seller.

A person purchases a female slave and takes possession of her, she is then purchased from him by alien enemies, from whom he again repurchases her, and after all this a claim to her is established against him on evidence, and the Kazee adjudges the slave to the claimant; the purchaser may, notwithstanding the intermediate transfers, revert to the original seller for a refund of the price.

It is not barred by an intermediate transfer to an alien.

A person purchases a slave girl on the security of another, who guarantees him against all contingencies; he then sells her, and the purchaser from him sells her to another, each party regularly taking possession of her; a right is subsequently established to her, but neither of the parties can have recourse to his seller until decree is first pronounced against himself by the judge; and, in like manner, the first purchaser cannot proceed against his surety until a decree is pronounced against himself. And if any of the parties should adduce evidence, after a decree had passed in favour of the claimant, that the slave

After repeated transfers, a purchaser cannot have recourse to his seller till recourse is first had to himself.

really belonged to the first seller, such evidence would not be received.* But if the slave, instead of proving to be the property of another, had set up a claim on evidence that she was free by origin, or that she was the slave of such a person who had emancipated her, or if another person had adduced evidence that the slave was his and he had made a *moodubburruh* of her, and the judge were to pass a decree to any of these effects, each party would then be at liberty to revert to the person who sold to him without waiting for a decree against himself, and the first purchaser would also be entitled to proceed against his surety without waiting till recourse was had to himself.

When evidence may be received in contravention of a previous decree.

A person purchases a slave girl, who is afterwards claimed from him as property absolutely, and is decreed by the judge to the claimant; the purchaser has thereupon recourse to the seller, when the seller adduces evidence that the slave was actually his property having been born in his house, that the decree of the judge in favour of the claimant was therefore void, and that the purchaser has no right of recourse for the price; in such circumstances the evidence should be received† if adduced in presence of the claimant; but some of our learned men are of opinion that the presence of the claimant is not a necessary condition. And so it has been directed in Farghana, (a city of Toorkistan).

Decree and the subject of it must be identified.

A claim to an ass having been established against a person in Bokhara he takes the decree of the judge, and the seller to him being in Samarkand, he produces the decree before the judge of that place, claiming restitution of the price; the decree being exhibited, the seller admits

---

* See note a little further on.

† The first claim was for the property *absolutely*, without reference to a specific title or ground of right, and the decree was therefore not on the issue subsequently raised. A decree is, I think, conclusive, according to the Moohummudan law, of the fact on which it is found, even against persons who were not parties to the suit in which it was pronounced. (See case marked above, and the next case.) And this maxim has been very generally adopted by the judges in all the courts of the East India Company.

the sale, but denies the claimant's right, and also denies that the decree exhibited is a decree of the judge of Bokhara. Whereupon the purchaser adduces evidence that it is in truth a decree of that judge. It is not lawful, however, for the judge of Samarkand to act upon it, and award restitution of the price in favour of the purchaser until witnesses testify that the judge of Bokhara decreed against the plaintiff for the identical ass which he purchased from this particular seller. If the seller should answer to the claim for restitution, that "the ass was born the property of the person who sold him to me, and you have no right of recourse to me," and should adduce proof of his allegation, the proof would be received if the claimant were present. The presence of the ass is also made a condition by some, but this is denied by the Imam Zuheer ood-deen. And in like manner when a slave has sued for his freedom, and the purchaser has in consequence reverted to the seller for restitution of the price, the presence of the slave is not a condition to the support of the claim.

CHAPTER XV.

OF ADDITION TO THE PRICE, AND ABATEMENT AND DISCHARGE FROM IT.

Increase issuing from the thing sold.

AN increase issuing out of the subject of sale, such as a child, fruit, milk, wool, and the like, is sold with it, and if the increase take place before possession, a share of the price is held to be opposed to the increase; but if it happen after possession it is then an accessory to the thing sold, and no part of the original price is opposed to it. Hence, if the seller should destroy an increase that had issued from the thing sold, previous to possession by the purchaser, a proportional abatement from the price would be the consequence, the price being apportioned between the original thing and the increase, according to the value of the former on the day of sale, and the value of the latter on the day of its destruction, without any option to the purchaser, according to Aboo Huneefa, though both his disciples were of opinion that the purchaser should have an option. And if a stranger were to destroy the increase he must make good its value, which, together with the original thing, would form the subject of sale.

Addition to the price—conditions of its legality.

An addition to the price, and to the thing priced or sold, is lawful while they are both subsisting, whether the addition be of the same kind as the price or not, and the addition is incorporated with the original contract. If the purchaser repent after making an addition to the price, and refuse to pay the addition, he may be compelled; and if the thing sold be returned for defect or any other cause, regard is to be had to the addition, in the same way as if it had been originally included in the sale. It is to be observed that when an addition is made to the price, it must be accepted by the other party at the meeting; for if it be not accepted till after the parties have separated, the addition is void.* It is also necessary that the thing sold should still be in a condition lawful for, or accommodated to, the contract; for though, if the purchaser should lease, or pledge, or slaughter, or sew up the thing sold, an addition to the price would still be valid, yet if he were to sell, or grind, or weave, or convert it into wine, an addition would no longer be lawful.

Natural and stipulated increase of the thing sold.

A natural increase issuing from the thing sold does not conflict with it, in relation to a stipulated increase, while the thing sold is still subsisting; so that the stipulated increase is an addition to the thing sold, apart from the natural increase, and the price is divided first between the thing sold and the stipulated increase, and the share apportioned to the former is then divided between it and the natural increase, the value of the original being taken as on the day of contract, the value of the stipulated increase as on the day when it was made, and the value of the natural increase as on the day of taking possession. A person purchases for a thousand *dirhems* a female slave valued at a thousand, and the slave before possession by the purchaser gives birth to a child also valued at a thousand; the seller then adds a male slave to the bargain, valued at another thousand, and the child improves in value until it rises to two thousand *dirhems;* finally, possession is taken by the purchaser of the whole, and the price of a thousand *dirhems* is paid down. Subsequently a defect is found in the child, and it is returned for a third of the thousand *dirhems.* And if the defect were found in the mother she would be returned for a sixth of the thousand, while if the defect were found in the male slave, he would be returnable for a half of the thousand.

---

* See *ante*, page 2.

Claim to the thing sold established after an addition to it.

A person sells a female slave, of whom the seller does not take possession, and the seller adds another female slave to the bargain; a claim is then established to the first slave, whereupon the purchaser is entitled to take the other at a fair proportion of the price.

Abatement from the price.

An abatement of part of the price is valid, and it is incorporated with the original contract like an increase, whether there remain anything to oppose to the abatement or not. A gift or discharge to the purchaser of part of the price before payment is an abatement. If the seller receive payment of the price, and then make a gift or abatement of part of it, by saying, "I have given or abated you a part of the price," the act is valid, and the seller is bound to restore accordingly; but if he should say to the purchaser, "I have discharged you from part of the price," after receiving payment, the discharge would not be valid. When an abatement, or gift, or discharge is made of the whole price, and this is done before receipt of payment, all the acts are valid, but they are not incorporated with the original contract; but when they are done after payment, though the abatement and gift are still valid, the discharge is no longer so. A discharge from the price after an *ikalut* is lawful, and the thing sold is an *amanut* or trust in the purchaser's hands after the *ikalut*.* A person sells a slave by an invalid contract, mutual possession follows, and the seller then discharges the purchaser from his value, after which the slave dies, the purchaser is, notwithstanding the discharge, still liable for his value; whereas, if the seller had said, "I discharge you from the slave," the discharge would have been effective.

Discharge.

* When there is no discharge of the price, and the thing sold perishes after *ikalut* in the hands of the purchaser, the *ikalut* is annulled. *Ante*, p. 231.

CHAPTER XVI.

OF SALE BY A FATHER, EXECUTOR, OR JUDGE OF A MINOR'S PROPERTY, AND PURCHASES BY THEM FOR HIM.

SALE by a father to his minor son, or purchase from him, on his own account, are both lawful on a favourable construction of law; but the rights of the contract revert to the minor himself, the father being only his representative. Hence it is that when the minor arrives at puberty he is entitled to demand the price from his father, though if the father sell to another, the son has no such right of demand in his own person when he arrives at puberty. Our learned men differ as to whether it be or be not a condition of the contract that there shall be both a proposal and an acceptance by the father; but the more valid opinion is, that it is not a condition of the contract; so that if the father should say, "I have sold this to my son such an one for so much," or "I have bought this from my son's property for so much," the contract is complete, and there is no necessity for his saying, "I have sold this to my son, and I have bought it."

Sale or purchase by a father to or from his minor son.

Form.

The sale by a father to his minor son is lawful when made for the value of the thing sold, with a slight allowance for mistakes in estimate; and where there is no father the paternal grandfather comes into his stead. A father sells a villa or other immoveable estate to his minor son for its fair value, the sale is lawful if the father be held in repute and respected among men as honest, but it is

Lawful at the value of the thing sold.

Exception.

not lawful if he be a profligate. And the sale by a profligate father of moveable property is not lawful, according to one report which is deemed valid, unless it be for the benefit of his son. Sale by a father to his son of mature age who has been long insane is also lawful, but it is not lawful if the madness be only temporary; by which is to be understood a continuance for any time short of a month, the madness, if it last for a month or more, being considered a long madness.

Approval by the judge. When a father or an executor sells the land of a minor, it has been said by one authority that the judge may cancel the sale if he think it for the advantage of the minor to do so; but when a sale by a father to his minor son is for a proper price, and is approved by the judge, there can be no doubt that it is perfectly legal.

Sale by a father from one minor son to another. When a person has two minor sons, and sells the property of one of them to the other, saying, "I have sold the slave of my son such an one to my son such an one," the transaction is lawful, and the children are bound respectively by the obligations of the contract.

How possession is effected when a father sells to his minor son. When a father sells his own property to his infant son, he does not become possessed of it for the son by the mere act of contract, so that if the property perish before he is in a condition to take actual possession of it, it perishes as against himself. Nor is a father released from the price for which he has rendered himself liable by the purchase of his son's property, till the judge appoint an agent to receive it from him; it is then to be restored to him, when it will remain in his hands as a deposit for his son. If a father sell to his minor son a house in which he is residing, he does not become seized on his son's behalf till he quit the house, and he ought to make delivery of it to an *ameen** appointed by the judge for that purpose. If the father should afterwards return to the house, or place his property or lodge his family there (being a wealthy person), he is to be accounted an usurper.

A person purchases a piece of cloth, or a slave, on

* A Trustee, from *amanut*.

account of his minor son, and pays down the price in cash out of his own money, he cannot, however, claim the price from his son unless he had called on persons to witness that the purchase was made on the son's account, and with the intention of reverting to him for the price. If the price were not paid down and the father should die, his estate is liable for it, and his other heirs have no right of recourse against the son, unless the father had called upon witnesses to testify that the sale was on his account. If, instead of paying down the price, the father becomes surety for it, though he should still, according to analogy, have a claim for a refund against his son, yet he has no such right on a favourable construction of the law. If a father purchase clothes or provisions for his son, it is not necessary that he should call upon witnesses to testify that the purchase is made for the son's behoof; but the case is different when the purchase is of a mansion or other immoveable property. When a father sells the property of his minor son, and delivers it without receiving payment of the price, he may resume possession of it, with a view to its retention till payment.

In making a purchase for his minor son, a father should have witnesses.

A woman purchases an estate for her minor son with her own property, on the understanding that she is not to revert to him for the price, the transaction is lawful on a favourable construction, the mother becoming first a purchaser on her own account, and the estate then becoming a vested gift from her to her son, and she cannot afterwards withhold it from him.

Purchase by a mother for her son.

A person is possessed of a mansion, and having a wife who has borne him a son, she says to him, "I have purchased this mansion from you for our own son out of his property," and the father answers, "I have sold it," the transaction is lawful.

A father having sold the property of his son, the latter says, "I was *major* at the time;" but the father says, "You were *minor*," in such circumstances the word of the *minor* is to be received.*

Dispute between a father and his son as to the latter's age at the time of sale.

* Majority, or puberty, depending on the physical condition of the

Sale to a father by his agent is lawful.

A father appoints an agent to sell a slave belonging to his son, and the agent sells him to the father himself, the sale is lawful.

Purchase or sale by an executor for himself is lawful when for the minor's advantage.

If an executor* purchase the property of an orphan for himself, the transaction is lawful when to the orphan's advantage. By an advantage is to be understood, when the property is not land, a sale by the executor for ten of property valued at fifteen, or a purchase by him for fifteen of property valued at ten. And when the property is land, double the value of the thing bought from the minor and half the value of the thing sold to him, are said to be fair *criteria* of what is for his advantage.

Form of the contract.

There is no report of Moohummud in any of the books as to the necessity or otherwise of an executor going through the double form of saying, "I have bought and I have sold," when he buys or sells for himself from or to the minor; but another writer reports that it is necessary, contrary to the case of a father, as already observed.

Sale to an executor by his agent is not lawful.

If an executor direct a person to purchase something from the minor's property, and he does so on account of his principal, the purchase is not lawful.

Miscellaneous sales by and to an executor of a minor's property.

When a youth permitted to trade sells property to the executor, it is the same thing as if the executor had sold to himself; but if the youth sell to a stranger, though much below value, the transaction is lawful according to Aboo Huneefa. An executor sells the land of a *minor* when it is expedient for the *minor;* though the executor sells with a view to expend the price on his own maintenance, it has been said that the sale is lawful, nevertheless the executor being liable to the *minor* when he makes such appropriation of the price. When an executor purchases from one of two *minors* for the other, the transaction is not lawful. So, also, if he permit them

---

son, is a fact more within his own knowledge than that of any person else.

* By an executor is to be understood the executor appointed by a father.—See page 248. It has been already observed (note on page 221) that he is included in the meaning of the term *Guardian.*

to trade in order that they may sell to each other, it is not lawful. And the rule is the same with regard to two slaves belonging to the *minors*, if he permit them to trade and one sells to the other, the transaction is not lawful. With regard to a father, he may lawfully authorize the youths themselves or their slaves to trade.

When one of two executors buys their ward's property from the other, it is not lawful, according to Aboo Huneefa. An executor purchases for his ward from a debtor of the ward, for twenty *deenars*, a mansion the value of which is thirty *deenars*, and when the debt is paid he agrees to a cancellation of the sale, this is not lawful. When an executor sells the property of his ward on credit for a longer period than is usual in such cases, the sale is unlawful; or though the period should not be unusually long, yet if there be any reason to apprehend that the purchaser will refuse payment on its expiration, or that the price may otherwise be lost, the sale is also unlawful; but if there be no reason for such apprehension it is lawful.

Powers of sale by an executor over his testator's property—when the heirs are *minor*;

When an executor sells an inheritance to another than himself, and the heirs are minors, the sale is lawful as to the whole, whether it be villas or other immoveable estate or chattels, and whether the heirs be present or absent, or the deceased have left debts or not; but the sale must be for the value of the property, with the ordinary allowance for error in valuation. And, according to modern decisions, the sale of immoveable estate by an executor is lawful only in one of the three cases following; that is, where there is a purchaser willing to give double its value, or the sale is necessary to meet the minor's emergencies, or there are debts of the deceased, and no other means of paying them.

when they are *major* and present.

If all the heirs be of full age and present, and there are no debts of the deceased, the executor has no power of disposal over the inheritance; while if there be debts covering the whole property, all authorities are agreed that the executor may sell the whole, and that if the property be not entirely swallowed up by the debts he may sell enough of it for their liquidation. With regard to the surplus, after payment of the debts, Aboo Huneefa considered that the executor has power to sell that also, but both his disciples thought that he had no such power. If there be no debts of the deceased, but he has left legacies, these are lawful to the extent of a clear third of his estate, and the executor has the same power of selling the estate for their liquidation, and with the same difference of opinion as to the surplus as in the case of debts. What has been said with regard to the executor's power of selling the estate for payment of debts and legacies, when all the heirs are of full age and present, is subject to this qualification, that if the heirs prefer to defray them out of other property the executor is deprived of all power of selling the estate.

When *major* and absent;

If the heirs be of full age and absent (by which is to be understood, according to Moohummud, an absence of three days), and there are neither debts nor legacies, the executor has power to sell the moveable property of the deceased, but not his immoveable property, even though there should be reason to apprehend its destruction.

when some are *major* and some *minor*.

If some of the heirs be of full age and some *minors*, and the former are absent, and the estate free from debts and legacies, the executor may sell the moveable property and also the *minors'* share in the immoveable property, but not the share of the others in the latter. If there be debts or legacies, the executor has the same power of selling for their liquidation, and with the same difference of opinion as to the surplus of the estate as before mentioned. If the heirs who have arrived at maturity be present, and the estate is free, the executor has power of sale over the *minors'* shares in the immoveable as well as the moveable property, but no such power over the shares of the others; while if there be debts or legacies the executor has the same power over the estate, with the same difference of opinion as to the surplus as has been already specified.

Executor's executor, &c.

All that has been said with regard to the executor of a father is equally applicable to the executor of such executor, or to the executor of a paternal grandfather, or the executor of such executor, or to an executor appointed by the judge, or the executor of such executor. An executor appointed by the judge is like an executor appointed by a father, except in one particular, which is, that when the judge appoints an executor for a purpose he is executor for that purpose alone; but when the father appoints an executor for a purpose, he is executor for all purposes.

Sale by a woman, supposing herself to be her husband's executrix.

A woman after the death of her husband sells property that belonged to him, supposing herself to be his executrix, and her husband having left *minor* children; she after some time declares that she was not the executrix, her assertion, however, is not to be credited as against the purchaser, but the sale remains in suspense till her children arrive at puberty. If they should admit that she was the executrix the sale by her is lawful; but if they deny the fact the sale is void; and though the purchaser should have manured the purchased land, he has no recourse for reimbursement against the woman. What has been said is on the supposition that the woman sues for a cancellation of the sale, on the ground that she was not the executrix; but if the *minor* sue on that ground his claim is to be heard, when he has permission to trade or litigate from the judge, or other person having power to give him the permission, and if he fail to recover his estate the woman is answerable to him for the value of what she sold.

Suit by the *minor* to reverse the sale.

Permission to sue granted by a judge.

When a youth or a weak-minded person has a father, or his executor, or a paternal grandfather, or his executor, and the judge permits the party to sue, but the father, &c., objects, the permission is valid, though the power of the judge is in general postponed to that of the father or executor.

Sale or purchase by or to a judge of a minor's property.

When the *kazee* sells his own property to a *minor*, or buys the *minor's* property from him, the transaction is not lawful; but the *kazee* may lawfully purchase the *minor's* property from an executor, though the executor were appointed by himself.

CHAPTER XVII.

OF MORABUHUT, TOWLEEUT,* AND WUZEEUT† SALES.

Definition. *MORABUHUT* is the resale of a thing for a similar to its first price, with some addition for profit; *Towleeŭt* is a resale for an exact similar to the first price without any addition; and *Wŭzeeŭt* is a resale for a similar to the first price with a known abatement, and they are all lawful.

Qualification of a *Morâbŭhŭt* sale when the prime cost was not in similars. When a person sells a thing for a profit, and its original price was of the class of similars, the sale is lawful, provided that the profit be known, whether it be in things of the same or a different kind to the original price. If the price were not of the class of similars, as a personal chattel for instance, and the sale for a profit be to any other person than one who has become possessed of that identical chattel, the sale is not lawful; but if the sale be to the person who has become possessed of it, and be in exchange for that particular chattel now in his hands, with a profit say of ten *dirhems*, the sale is lawful. And

* "*Morâbŭhŭt* is an infinitive of the fifth increased conjugation from the radical word *Rebhŭ*, signifying profit or gain, and therefore obviously implies a transaction in which profit is obtained. *Mowâzaŭt*, again, is an infinitive of the same conjugation, from the root *wŭzâ*, to abate or deduct, and literally as well as technically signifies deduction from the original price. *Towleeŭt*, of the second conjugation, has a variety of literal significations corresponding to those of its primitive or root *wela*. One of these, viz., friendship, or equality, is by no means remote from the technical sense, viz., a resale at prime cost."—Translation of *Imameea Digest*. Note, page 83.

† *Wŭzeeŭt* is an infinitive of the second conjugation from the root *wŭzâ*, and has the same signification as *mowazaŭt*.

where a thing is sold at a relative profit, as eleven for ten,* the sale is not lawful unless the prime cost be known at the meeting, whereupon it becomes lawful, and the purchaser has an option, and if he decide in favour of the sale it is obligatory on him at the rate mentioned, on a favourable construction. And the rule is the same if a thing be sold by *Towleeŭt*, and the purchaser does not know in how much it stands him, the sale being in such a case unlawful; but if the price be known to him at the meeting the sale becomes lawful with an option, as in the other case.

Addition to the prime cost, and payment in a strange coinage.

If a person purchase a piece of cloth for ten *dirhems*, and give a *deenar* or a piece of cloth in addition to the price, the prime cost is only ten *dirhems*, and it is to be so taken as against the purchaser in a subsequent sale by *Morâbŭhŭt*. And if the *dirhems* were of a coinage different from that of the town, and the sale be for a profit of a *dirhem*, the new purchaser is liable for ten similar to those originally paid, and one of profit in the coin of the place. But if base *dirhems* were given in payment of the first transaction, and the seller allowed them, the purchaser may resell the article for a profit on the prime cost, as if it had been paid in good coin.

Resale after gift or sale and return of the thing sold.

If the purchaser of an article make a gift of it which he afterwards retracts, or if he sell it, and it is subsequently returned to him for a defect, or under an option, or by *ikalut*, he may lawfully dispose of the article for a profit on the original price; but if the sale had been completed, and the thing had returned to his possession by right of inheritance or gift, he could not lawfully sell it by *morâbŭhŭt*.

Resale of a part of commodities previously purchased.

When the thing sold is an aggregate of commodities that are estimable by measurement of capacity or weight, or are similars of tale, the purchaser may sell a part

---

* Literally, "*for a profit of ten eleven;*" but explained by the author of the *Kifayah* (vol. iii. p. 144) to signify a profit of one in ten, two in twenty, three in thirty, &c. The expression implies that the profit is in parts of the prime cost, and as that is unknown when the price is a specific chattel, resale in *that* case at a relative profit is unlawful.—*Hamilton's Hedaya*, vol. ii. p. 471.

of the aggregate by *morâbŭhŭt.* If the aggregate be composed of things that are entirely different, or are dissimilars of tale, and a distributive part of it is resold by *morábŭhŭt,* the sale is also lawful; but if the part be specific, and the original price was one sum, the resale is not lawful; while, if the original price had been apportioned to each of the articles, the resale of any of them at an advance on the price would be lawful, according to Aboo Huneefa and Aboo Yoosuf. If a person purchase a piece of cloth, and half of it happen to be burnt, he cannot lawfully sell the remaining half for a profit on half the price, though what remains be by measurement in cubits a full half of the original. And if a person purchase two pieces of cloth without mention of a particular price to each of them, he cannot lawfully sell one of them by *morâbŭhŭt;* but if a particular price had been assigned to each, he may lawfully do so according to Aboo Huneefa and Aboo Yoosuf, but not so in the opinion of Moohummud.

Resale of a slave usurped, or unlawfully purchased.

The usurper of a slave, when adjudged to be responsible for his value, at a time when the slave had absconded, may, on the return of the slave, lawfully sell him for a profit on the value at which he was made responsible; but in reselling him he should say, "He stood me in so much." So, also, if one should purchase a slave for wine, and take possession, after which the slave absconds, and decree is passed against the purchaser for his value, the purchaser may lawfully resell him at a profit on such value.

Resale by one of two purchasers after partition.

Two persons having purchased commodities that are estimable by measurement of capacity or weight, or are similars of tale, and having made partition of them, each may lawfully sell his share by *morâbŭhŭt;* but if they had purchased cloth or the like and made partition, it would not be lawful to either of them to sell his share by *morâbŭhŭt.*

Sale of *deenars* by *morâbŭhŭt.*

If a person purchase *deenars* for *dirhems,* he cannot lawfully sell the *deenars* by *morâbŭhŭt.*

Resale for a profit on

A person purchases merchandise and marks it for more than the prime cost, he afterwards sells it at an advance on the price so marked, without saying it stood me in so much, this is lawful; but it is implied that the purchaser is aware that the mark is not intended to indicate the prime cost of the goods; for if he imagine the mark and the prime cost to be identical, the mark is a deception on the part of the seller, and the purchaser is at liberty to retract if he please.

a marked price.

The wages of the fuller, dyer, and embroiderer may be lawfully added to the prime cost; so, also, the expense of spinning, or twisting, of porterage, or of driving cattle to market. The principle in all *morâbŭhŭt* sales is, that regard is to be had to the custom of merchants, and anything may be lawfully added to the prime cost, the addition of which is sanctioned by such custom; but that nothing can be added which wants such sanction. Neither what has been expended in provisions by the way, nor rent, nor allowances for trouble, can be lawfully added, there being no custom to authorize their addition; nor the wages of a shepherd, nor the expense of instructing a slave in a trade, or the Kooran, or any branch of learning, nor the rent of a house for keeping him in. In like manner, the wages of a slave-driver or keeper cannot be added, nor the expense of storing provisions, nor the fees of a physician, horsebreaker, or horse-doctor, or the wages of domestic servants, or the ransom paid for offences, or what is taken by violence in the way, unless there be some custom for adding it. The wages of a broker may be added, but not the price of housings or coverings or the like for cattle; but the clothes of slaves and the expense of their maintenance, unless excessive, may be lawfully added. So, also, the food of cattle, unless there be some return issuing from them, as milk, wool, or butter, in which case the value of this return must be deducted, and only the surplus added to the original price.

Expenses that may be added to the prime cost;

such as may not be added.

If the purchaser should clean the cloth himself, or do any other of the works above specified, he is not at liberty to make any addition to the prime cost on that account, nor if the acts had been done by another gratuitously, or

A charge for acts done by the purchaser cannot be added to

the prime cost.

by a person to whom the things on which these acts were performed had been lent.

Effect of a deception in stating the prime cost.

If the seller by *morâbŭhŭt* is guilty of any deception the purchaser is at liberty to reject the thing or to take it at the full price stipulated; and if there be any deception in a case of *towleeŭt* he may deduct the amount from the price. If the article perish before it is returned by the purchaser, or anything happens to it which would prevent cancellation of the sale on discovery of the deception, the purchaser is liable for the full price mentioned, and is without any option.

When a blemish must be disclosed.

When a thing sold sustains a blemish in the hands of the seller or the purchaser, by an act of Providence, or by the deed of the purchaser himself or of the subject of sale, it may be lawfully resold by *morâbŭhŭt*, without any mention of the circumstance. But if the blemish be occasioned by an act of the seller or a stranger, it must be disclosed before the thing can be resold by *morâbŭhŭt*. And in like manner if an increase take place in the thing sold, such as fruit, a child, or wool, and it be still subsisting in the hands of the seller, or have perished by his act or that of a stranger, he cannot lawfully resell the original thing by *morâbŭhŭt* without mentioning the circumstance; but if the loss have happened by an act of Providence there is no necessity for mentioning it. And if a person purchase a female slave who is already a woman,* and have intercourse with her, he is not obliged to mention the fact when reselling her by *morâbŭhŭt*; but if she were a virgin when he purchased her, he could not lawfully sell her by *morâbŭhŭt*, without mentioning the fact of his having carnally enjoyed her.

When a credit allowed on the first sale must be disclosed.

When a person purchases a thing on credit, he cannot lawfully sell it by *morâbŭhŭt* without mentioning the fact, that is, if the credit were stipulated for by the contract; but if it merely arose from the custom of merchants, as if, for instance, the thing purchased were one for which sellers are not in the habit of requiring prompt payment, but of receiving the price by instalments per month, or

* As distinguished from a virgin.

every ten days, most of our learned men are of opinion, that it is not necessary to mention the credit. Where again the credit was by stipulation, and the fact is not mentioned to the purchaser, he has, on becoming acquainted with it, an option of either retaining or rejecting the article. But an intermediate loss or destruction of it, before he became cognizant of the credit, would render the sale obligatory upon him. And in every case in which mention of any circumstance is incumbent on the seller, and it is not disclosed, the purchaser has an option, on becoming acquainted with it, of keeping the thing at the full price agreed upon, or rejecting it. But if the thing sold be not in existence in his hands, the sale becomes imperative, and he has no choice.

General rule as to concealments.

An abatement from the price must be deducted when selling by *morâbŭhŭt;* and if an abatement be made to a purchaser after he has actually resold the thing for a profit, he must give the purchaser from him the benefit of the abatement, with a suitable deduction also from the profit. But this does not apply to a credit; for if a thing were purchased without payment of the price, it may be lawfully sold by *morâbŭhŭt,* and though a delay of a month were subsequently granted for payment of the price on the first transaction, the purchaser would not be under any obligation to grant a similar delay for its payment on the second.

An abatement from the prime cost must be deducted.

When a person purchases a thing from his partner in trade, he need be under no apprehension in reselling it by *morâbŭhŭt,* if it were the private property of the partner; and if the thing were joint property he may resell the partner's share for a profit on the price at which the article was purchased from the joint stock, and his own share for a profit on the price at which it was originally acquired by the partnership. When one person purchases a piece of cloth for five *dirhems,* and another purchases another piece for six *dirhems,* and they sell the two pieces together in one bargain by *morâbŭhŭt* or *mowazaŭt,* the price is to be divided between them according to their relative shares in the prime cost of the articles.

Resale of property purchased from a partner.

Effect of ignorance of the prime cost at the time of contract, obviated by mention during the meeting.

When a person disposes of a thing to another at what it stood him, and the other does not know in how much it stood him, the sale is invalid; but if the seller inform the purchaser during the meeting, the sale becomes valid, and the purchaser has the option of taking or rejecting the thing at the price indicated. And if a person sell a thing for a profit of eleven for ten, or the like, the purchaser on being made acquainted with the price, may take or reject the thing at his pleasure; but if he knew the price before the contract, he has no power of rejection.

Sale at a rateable reduction on the prime cost.

If a person purchase a piece of cloth for ten *dirhems,* and then sell it at a reduction* of ten for eleven, each *dirhem* is to be divided into eleven parts, which will make one hundred and ten in the whole, and in every eleven of these one part is to be abated, making in all ten parts. In like manner, if he sell at a reduction of ten for twelve, each *dirhem* is to be divided into twelve parts, which will make one hundred and twenty in all, and out of these, twenty are to be abated. And the same way in other cases.

---

* Arab. *Wŭzeeŭt.* This and the other case above mentioned, are the only examples of *Wŭzeeŭt* that I have met with. But what has been said of *Morâbŭhŭt* must be generally applicable, *mutatis mutandis,* to *Wŭzeeŭt* also. It may be observed that *Wŭzeeŭt* is not mentioned in the *Hidayah,* though in both its commentaries, the *Kifayah* and *Inayah,* it is enumerated among the different kinds of sale.

CHAPTER XVIII.

OF SULUM.*

SECTION I.

Definition, Constitution, Conditions, and Legal Effect of Sulum.

SULUM is a contract by which a right of property is promptly established in the price, but the establishment of it in the thing sold is deferred.† It is constituted when one person says to another, "I have advanced to you ten *dirhems* for a *koor* of wheat," and the other answers, "I have accepted." But it may also be constituted by the word "sale." **Definition.** **How constituted.**

The conditions of *sulum* are of two kinds; one of which has relation to the contract itself, and the other to the things exchanged. Of the former kind there is only one condition, which is, that the contract shall be free from any stipulation of option to both or either of the contracting parties, as distinguished from an option of a third party having a right, which therefore does not vitiate a *sulum*. Hence, if a person should prove to be entitled **Conditions.**

---

* This kind of sale is contrary to analogy, as being of a thing which may not be in existence at the time of contract, but it has been authorized by the *Kooran* and a saying of the Prophet. See *Hamilton's Hedaya*, vol. ii. p. 516.

† This is rather a description of its legal effect than a definition. It may be defined to be "an immediate advance of a price (in money or goods) for commodities to be delivered at a future fixed period." And as the commodities are undeterminate, and the price is produced, *Sulum* is "the sale of an obligation for a thing," as stated in page 7.

to the capital stock,* after possession of it has been taken, and the parties to the contract have separated, and the person so entitled should then allow the *sulum*, the contract is valid. And if a person to whom an option has been reserved should annul his option before the actual or bodily separation of the parties, and while the capital stock is still subsisting in the hands of the seller, the contract would, according to us, become lawful. But all are agreed that it would not become lawful if the capital stock had perished, or been destroyed.

That relate to the things exchanged; to the capital stock. The conditions that relate to the things exchanged are sixteen in number, whereof six have relation to the capital stock and ten to the goods for which the advance is made.† Of the conditions that relate to the capital stock, four are applicable to its genus, species, quality, and quantity, all of which must in general be distinctly explained. The genus, as *dirhems* or *deenars* in the case of money, or wheat and barley in the case of commodities estimated by measurement of capacity. The species, as Ghutreefee and Adawlee *dirhems*, and Muhmoodee or Hurwee *deenars*. This condition, however, is required only when different coins of the same denomination are current in the city; for if there be but one currency it is sufficient to mention the general name of the coin. The quality, as good, bad,‡ or medium. The mention of the quantity of the capital stock is a condition only when it consists of commodities of the class of similars; and even with regard to these when distinctly pointed out, it is not necessary according to Aboo Yoosuf and Moohummud, though their master was of opinion that in that case also it is a condition that the amount of the capital stock shall be known. Thus if a person say to another, "I have advanced you these *dirhems*" (not knowing their

* Arab. *ras-ool-mal*; literally, *head of the property*. The price is so termed.

† Arab. *Al mooslum feehi*; literally, *the advanced for*.

‡ Arab. *jeyyed, rudee*. The translator of the *Hidayah* has substituted the superlatives *best* or *worst* (vol. ii. page 523) for the positives *good* and *bad*, which appear in the original Arabic.

weight) "for a koor of wheat," or "this wheat" (not knowing its measure) "for so many *minas* of safflower," the contract is not valid according to Aboo Huneefa, but valid according to his disciples. If an advance be made for two different things, and the capital stock is an article estimable by measurement of capacity or by weight, the transaction is not lawful according to Aboo Huneefa, unless the proportion of it applicable to each of the things be explained; but this he did not consider necessary when the capital stock is anything else than an article estimable by measurement of capacity or by weight. According to the disciples, the explanation is unnecessary in both cases; but when the capital stock consists of two things, as *dirhems* and *deenars*, for instance, advanced for a known quantity of wheat, and the amount of one of them only is mentioned, the transaction is invalid in their opinion also. Where, again, the capital stock consists of articles of longitudinal measure, or of dissimilar articles of tale, mention of the quantity is not a necessary condition, and it is quite sufficient if they be pointed out, according to all our doctors. The fifth condition is, that when the capital stock is in *dirhems* or *deenars* they shall be paid down in cash.* And the next condition is, that whatever it may consist of, whether things undeterminate or specific, possession of it must be taken at the meeting before the actual separation of the parties; but whether at the beginning or end of the meeting is of no consequence, for the whole meeting is for this purpose considered as but one instant. And if possession be taken after the parties have risen together walking, still, if before their bodily separation, it is sufficient; and though one of the parties should fall asleep, or if both should sleep sitting, the meeting would still

* In that case, both the things exchanged being obligations, possession of one of them (which by the nature of the contract cannot be the thing sold) before the separation of the parties is absolutely necessary. See *ante*, p. 135. It may be observed that this necessity is founded on a saying of the Prophet, who prohibited the opposing of one debt to another.—*Hamilton's Hedaya*, vol. ii. p. 528.

continue; but if they both should go to sleep, laid down or reposing, that would be a separation. A case is put in the *Nuwazil* of a person who advanced ten *dirhems* by way of *sulum* for ten *kufeezees* of wheat, and not having the money with him he went into his house to fetch it; and it was held that if he entered so as to be within sight of the other party to whom the advance was made, the *sulum* was not void, but that it would be void if he disappeared from the other party's sight. If the person to whom the advance is made should refuse to accept it during the meeting, he may be compelled to do so by the judge.

Conditions that relate to the goods advanced for.

Of the conditions that relate to the goods for which the advance is made, the four first are applicable to their genus, species, quality, and quantity, all of which must be mentioned. Genus; as wheat or barley. Species; as wheat of irrigated lands, wheat of land that has not been irrigated, wheat of the hills, or wheat of the plains. Quality; as good, bad, or medium. Quantity; as by measurement of capacity, weight, tale, or longitudinal measure. It is necessary that the quantity be known by a standard which may not be lost from among men. And if a particular measure be adopted, as for instance one should say, "By this vessel," or "this basket," or "the weight of this stone," the transaction would not be lawful unless the capacity of the vessel or weight of the stone be known. So, also, with regard to longitudinal measure, it is required that the quantity be fixed by a cubit which may not be lost from among men; and if a particular stick be assumed the length of which is not known, or the forearm of the party, or of any particular person, the transaction would not be lawful. Nor would it be lawful if the measure adopted were one belonging to a particular person, when it differs from the measures in general use. If the measure should correspond with those in general use, the reference to it would be surplusage and the transaction lawful. And it is also necessary that the instrument of measure adopted shall not be one liable to contract or expand; hence a leathern bag is not lawful except in the case of the *koorb* for water, the use of which is sanctioned by general usage.

The fifth condition* is, that the goods advanced for shall be deliverable at a future known period; and if presently deliverable the *sulum* is not lawful. Opinions differ as to the shortest period within which a *sulum* is not lawful. According to Moohummud it is a month, and the *futwa* is in conformity with his opinion. The period is not cancelled by the death of the purchaser;† but it is cancelled by the death of the seller,‡ so that the amount of the *sulum*, or goods deliverable, may be immediately taken from his estate.

The sixth condition is, that the goods advanced for shall be in existence from the conclusion of the contract until the stipulated period of its delivery.§ Hence, if they were non-existent at the former period, but in existence at the latter, or *vice versâ;* or if they were existent at both periods, but non-existent at any intervening point of time, the contract would be unlawful. By existence is to be understood that the goods are to be found in open market; and by non-existence, that they are not to be had there, though they may be found in people's houses. If the goods be in existence at the stipulated period of delivery, but are not taken possession of till they are no longer to be had, the *sulum* contract still retains its validity; but the purchaser has the option of cancelling it, or waiting till the goods are again to be had.

The seventh condition is, that the goods advanced for be of a nature to be determined by specification. Hence a *sulum* of *dirhems* or *deenars* is not lawful.

---

* This condition is founded on the saying of the Prophet before referred to: "Whosoever of you enters into a *sulum*, let him do so for a known measure, known weight, and to a known period."—*Hidayah*, vol. iii. p. 199. See *Translation*, vol. ii. p. 516.

† Arab. *Rub oos sulum;* literally, *master of the sulum.*

‡ Arab. *Al mooslum ilehi;* literally, *the advanced to.*

§ This condition is also founded on a scrupulous regard to a saying of the Prophet, viz.,—"Do not advance for fruit till its goodness have commenced."—*Hidayah* (original), p. 202. For the meaning of this expression, which Mr. Hamilton here translates, "until their ripeness be apparent" (vol. ii. p. 520), see *ante*, note, page 141.

The eighth condition is, that the goods advanced for be of one or other of the four following descriptions, viz., goods estimable by measurement of capacity, goods estimable by weight, similars of tale, and goods of longitudinal measure.* Hence *sulum* is not lawful of animals or any parts of them from the head to the extremities, nor of slaves whether male or female, on account of their difference in understanding and dispositions.

The ninth condition is, that the place of delivery shall be mentioned of all articles that require porterage and trouble, such as wheat and barley. This, though it appears to be only the opinion of Aboo Huneefa, is correct. Aboo Yoosuf and Moohummud have said that this is not an absolute condition, but that when made a condition it is valid; and that when there is no such condition the place of contract is the place of delivery. When the purchaser has imposed on the seller the condition of delivery in a particular city, delivery in any part of the city is a sufficient compliance with the condition, unless the city be large, that is a *fursukh*† or more between its borders, in which case the *sulum* would not be lawful, unless the quarter of the city in which delivery is to be made be also mentioned, as ignorance of this particular circumstance has a tendency to engender disputes between the parties. Where the commodity is one that does not require porterage and trouble in its transference, as musk or camphor,

---

* The authority for the first two is inferred from the saying of the Prophet, mentioned, note, p. 261, and *sulum* of the two others is said to be lawful "because it is possible to define them exactly."—*Hamilton's Hedaya*, vol. ii. page 517. The impossibility of defining exactly any other commodities than the four specified, is no doubt the reason for restricting *sulum* to them. But the difficulty seems to be felt of including the two last within the sanction of the Prophet's saying; for, after a good deal of reasoning on the subject, the author of the *Kifayah* admits that it is only by a favourable construction that cloth is included; but, being manufactured by man with the aid of implements, and the manufacturer and implements being alike, there can only be a small degree of difference in the productions, which may in worldly matters be disregarded.—*Kifayah*, vol. iii. p. 200.

† A parasang, a league, about 18,000 feet in length.—*Richardson*.

all are agreed that mention of the place of delivery is not necessary, and that in such circumstances it is to be understood that delivery is to be made at the place of contract. It should be observed, that when the contract is made on the sea, or a high mountain, delivery is to be made at the nearest convenient place when the commodity is one that requires porterage and trouble.

The tenth and last condition is, that the things exchanged shall not be comprehended under one of the two causes or occasions of *keba*, or usury, which are quantity and kind.* This rule is of universal application except in the case of prices, which may be lawfully advanced for other things estimated by weight, from a regard to the necessities of mankind.

Legal effect of *sulum*. The legal effect of *sulum* is a deferred establishment of a right of property in the purchaser or master of the *sulum* to the thing advanced for, as opposed to an immediate establishment of such right in the seller to the price or capital stock.

Purchaser's option on the goods being delivered. When the *sulum* is valid, and the seller produces the goods, the purchaser has no option with regard to them, unless they are found to be different to what was stipulated for, and in that case the seller may be compelled to deliver others in correspondence with the contract.

SECTION II.

Of things with regard to which Sulum is or is not lawful.

Things estimated by capacity may be advanced for things estimated by weight, and *vice versa*. When a piece of Herat cloth is advanced for another piece of Herat cloth, or a *kufeez* of wheat is sold for a *kufeez* of barley, the *sulum* is not lawful. A thing that is measured by capacity may be advanced for a thing that is weighed, when the latter is a proper subject for *sulum*, that is, when it can be the *mabeea* or thing sold in a con-

* That is, that they shall not both be weighable, or both estimable by measure of capacity, or both of the same kind; for postponement of delivery in such cases would be unlawful. See *ante*, p. 165.

tract of sale,* and is capable by description; so that an advance of wheat for gold and silver is not lawful according to us, and the transaction is void.† What is estimated by weight may also be lawfully advanced for what is estimated by capacity. But a thing estimated by weight cannot be advanced for another thing estimated by weight, when both are articles that can be rendered specific in a contract, as iron for saffron. When *dirhems* or *deenars* are advanced for articles estimated by weight, the *sulum* is lawful; so, also, according to Aboo Yoosuf, when an ingot of silver, or fragments or particles of gold, or a manufactured vessel of silver, is advanced for saffron, the transaction is lawful. *Fooloos* may be lawfully advanced for articles of weight except their own kind, and if copper vessels be advanced for articles of weight, the transaction is lawful when the vessels are not estimated or reckoned by weight, but by the piece; but in the last case also it is unlawful if the vessels be advanced for *fooloos*. It is not lawful to advance one thing estimated by measure of capacity for another thing so estimated.

Of things that are not similars, one may be advanced for the other when the latter can be fixed by description.

When two things, neither of which is estimated by capacity or weight, differ in kind, one of one kind may without fear or objection be exchanged for two of the other from hand to hand, or even with a postponement of delivery, if that for which the advance is made be capable of being bound down or defined by description, with the same accuracy that similars can be defined.‡ As

* This excludes *dirhems* and *deenars*, which are always price. See *ante*, p. 19.

† If the capital stock or price were in money, the transaction would be a *surf*, and any delay in the delivery of either of the things exchanged would be unlawful. See *post*, towards the end of Book ii. chapter 1. But if the capital stock were anything else than money, the reason for excluding gold and silver from the articles which may be the subject of *sulum* is not so apparent; and the restriction is limited to *dirhems* and *deenars* by the *Hidayah*. See *Translation*, vol. ii. p. 516. See also *post*, page 269.

‡ This implies that they are similars of tale or goods of longitudinal measure.

this is not the case with jewels, pearls, or animals, the advance of a piece of Herat cloth for any of them is not lawful. Where, again, the things are of the same kind, and neither of them estimable by weight or measurement of capacity, though there is no objection to the exchange of two for one from hand to hand, it cannot be lawfully done with a postponement of delivery according to our learned men, so that if one were to advance two pieces of cloth of Herat for one piece of the same kind, the transaction would not be lawful.

Rule when the commodities advanced for are partly of the same and partly of a different kind to the advance.

When a thing of capacity is advanced for two things, one of which is also of capacity, and the other is of weight, or anything is advanced for two others, one being of its own kind and the other of a different kind, the contract is void as to the whole according to Aboo Huneefa, but according to both his disciples it is lawful in the former case in proportion to the article estimated by weight, and in the latter in proportion to the thing of different kind. And there is no objection to an advance for articles of the same kind, whether of capacity or of weight, with a condition that part of them shall be deliverable at one time and part at another time; nor is there any necessity that the share of the advance applicable to each part should be mentioned.

Things in their nature measurable may be advanced for, to be delivered by weight, and *vice versa*.

When an advance is made for goods in their nature estimable by measure of capacity, to be delivered by weight, as, for instance, wheat or barley by the balance, there are two reports, and according to that which is most relied upon, the transaction is lawful. And the same may be said with regard to things estimable by weight which are to be delivered by measure of capacity.

A *sulum* sale of butter is lawful either by measure or weight (though there is a report of Moohummud's against its legality by weight). And the rule is the same with regard to every commodity usually measured by the *rutl*, the *sulum* sale of which is lawful either by measure or weight.

Advance for things not in season.

If an advance be made for milk in its season to be delivered by a known measure or weight at a fixed period, the transaction is lawful. And the same may be said of vinegar and grape juice. It is to be observed, however, with regard to milk, that its restriction to a season has reference to countries where milk is not procurable at certain times of the year; but that in our country, where it is always procurable, its *sulum* sale at all seasons is lawful. With regard to vinegar also, which is always procurable, there is no restriction of seasons; but this not being the case with grape juice, its sale by *sulum* is lawful only in the proper season.

An advance for new wheat before its appearance is not valid, because it is a *sulum* sale of a thing not procurable. Upon the authority of this case, it is held that when an advance is made for the wheat of a particular place of which the supplies of grain are not likely to fail or be cut off, as, for instance, wheat of the countries of Khorassan, Irak, and Furghana; or of great cities, as Samarkand, Bokhara, and Cashan, the sale is lawful; but that if the place be such that its supply of grain may probably fail, as, for instance, the wheat of a particular piece of land, or particular village, the sale would not be lawful. If a reference to the village be made only as descriptive of the quality of the article, the sale is valid. Hence, though an advance for wheat of Herat is not lawful, an advance for cloth of Herat is lawful, as it falls within all the conditions of a *sulum* sale.

Sulum not lawful of dissimilars of tale.

With regard to all articles of tale, the unities of which materially differ, as melons and pomegranates, a *sulum* sale of them by tale is not lawful. Where, again, the unities of such articles do not materially differ, as walnuts and eggs, a *sulum* sale of them is lawful, whether by tale, measure, or weight. According to Aboo Yoosuf, the rule for distinguishing these two classes from each other is that when the unities differ in value, the articles of tale belong to the first class, and that where the unities do not differ in value, the articles belong to the second class; and according to the same authority, when goose eggs or ostrich eggs are advanced for eggs of the common hen, the *sulum* sale is lawful without any restriction as to season;

but that when eggs of the common hen are advanced for goose eggs or eggs of the ostrich, it is only when the contract is made at a time that these are procurable that it is lawful.

Miscellaneous articles.

A *sulum* sale of paper is lawful by tale or weight; of *fooloos* by tale; so, also, of love-apples, pears, and apricots by tale; and of onions and garlic by measure or by tale. A *sulum* of glass is not lawful unless it be broken, when it may be stipulated for by a known weight; nor is it lawful with regard to vessels made of glass, the individuals of which differ; but it is lawful of vessels made of earthenware. And there is no objection to such a sale of bricks or tiles when the mould is known; and a mould is sufficiently known when its length, breadth, and depth are ascertained by a generally received cubit or measure of length; and if only one mould is in use in the city, particular mention of the mould is not necessary. So, also, *sulum* is lawful with regard to cloth, after explanation of its length and breadth, according to some known cubit or standard of measure, whether the cloth be fine linen or silk; and in the case of linen, the mention of weight is not a condition of legality; whether it be so in the case of silk, opinions differ; but, according to that which is considered most authentic, the weight of silk should be mentioned in a sale of it by *sulum*. If the weight alone were mentioned without the number of cubits, the sale would not be lawful, unless the price per cubit were distinctly specified. And a *sulum* of cloth made of *Khuz*,* if its length, breadth, and fineness be explained, though without mention of its weight, is lawful; but the mention of its weight alone, without its length, breadth, and fineness is not sufficient. So, also, a *sulum* sale of carpets, sitting mats, and mats made of reeds, is lawful when the number of cubits, quality, and manufacture are known; and in like manner of sacks, sackcloth, and robes of known quality, length, breadth, and fineness.

* Floss silk.

Heads or extremities of animals. Flesh generally.

Sulum is not lawful with regard to the heads or extremities of animals; nor is it valid as to flesh, according to Aboo Huneefa. But according to the disciples it is lawful when the genus, species, age, part, quality and quantity of the flesh are explained; as, for instance, a sheep, a wedder two years' old, the flank or thigh, fat, a hundred *rutls*. With regard to flesh taken off the bones, that is meat without bones, there are two reports, the most authentic of which is against the sale; but as to fat generally, or the fat tail of a sheep, all are agreed that its sale by *sulum* is quite lawful. Fish is either fresh or salt, and a *sulum* sale of both by tale is unlawful; but if the sale be by weight it is lawful as to salt fish, and also as to fresh fish if the contract take place in its season, and the time of delivery is likewise within its season, and it be procurable during the whole intermediate period; without these qualifications the *sulum* sale of fresh fish is not lawful. For small fish an advance may be validly made for their sale by measure or weight; with regard to large fish, there are two reports of Aboo Huneefa's opinion; according to one of which, and it is that which coincides with the opinion of the disciples, the sale of them also is lawful in the same way. There can be no *sulum* sale of any kind of birds, not even of such as do not materially differ, as sparrows. Nor is it lawful with regard to the flesh of birds; but it has been said that this is to be understood only of such birds as have not been acquired, and are not kept in confinement for the purpose of propagation; and that with regard to birds acquired and so confined, the sale of their flesh by *sulum* is lawful in the opinion of our three doctors, according to the most authentic report, though there is one report of Aboo Huneefa's opinion being against its legality.

Fat. Fish. Birds.

Bread and flour.

A *sulum* sale of bread is not lawful, according to Aboo Huneefa and Moohummud, neither by weight nor by tale; but according to Aboo Yoosuf it is lawful, and his opinion has been preferred and adopted for the *futwa*. Bread may be advanced for wheat and flour, according to the opinion of both the disciples, which is also adopted for the *futwa,* though contrary to that of their master; and a *sulum* sale of flour is lawful both by measure and weight.

Jewels or pearls. No jewels or pearls can be the subject of a *sulum* sale, except small rubies, which are sold by weight, and used as medicine, the *sulum* of which by weight is lawful. There is no objection to such a sale by measure of plaster and quick lime, for they are known to be estimated by measure of capacity and deliverable at all times; nor to such a sale of oil when the species is known, nor of wool by weight; but if such and such heaps of wool be stipulated for without weight, the *sulum* is not lawful; and an advance cannot be lawfully made for the wool of a particular sheep or goat, nor for its milk or butter, nor for new butter, nor new olive oil, nor new wheat. Nor can wool be lawfully advanced for hair, both being articles estimated by weight; but this objection applies only to hair that is usually sold by weight, for if it be sold by measure of capacity, delay in its delivery is lawful.

Plaster.

Oil and wool.

Among *Zimmees, sulum* is lawful with regard to wine, but not with regard to a hog; and if one of them embrace the faith, the *sulum* becomes void. In everything except wine, the rules of *sulum* are applicable alike to Mooslims and Christians.

Cotton, flax, silk, and metals. There is no objection to a *sulum* sale of cotton, flax, silk, brass, or native gold or silver,* iron, lead, copper, and orichalc,† all of which substances are of the class of similars.

Leaves of plants. And henna, and the leaves of the indigo plant, or wood, and dry odoriferous herbs that are estimated by measure follow the same rule; but with regard to odoriferous herbs, when moist or fresh, and pot-herbs and fire-wood, none of which are of the class of similars, a *sulum* sale of them is not lawful.

---

* Arab. *Tibr,* properly, gold or fragments of gold before it has been submitted to the hammer or fire, but also applied by some of the Arabs to silver.—*Freytag.* See *ante,* page 264.

† Arab. *Shibih.* "A metallic substance, resembling gold in colour, but very inferior in value. It was well known to the Romans."—*Encyclopædia Britannica.*

Trunks of palm trees.

When an advance is made for a known quantity of the trunks of palm trees, and their length, thickness, period, and place of delivery are all specified, the transaction is lawful. So, also, with regard to different kinds of wood, timbers, and reeds; and by the thickness of reeds is meant the size of the bundle of them that can be bound by a cord of a certain length, as a span, cubit, or the like. Thread also is of the class of similars, and it is said that everything that is weighed is so in like manner.

When an advance is made for water to be delivered by weight, and the places from whence it is to be drawn* are explained, the transaction is lawful; and since a *sulum* of water is lawful, it is so also of ice.

Section III.

Of Possession of the Capital Stock and the Goods advanced for.

The capital stock cannot be released nor anything of a different kind substituted for it.

The seller cannot lawfully release the purchaser from the capital stock, and if he do so and the purchaser accepts the release, the *sulum* is rendered void. And it is not lawful for the seller to receive instead of the capital stock anything else of a different kind; but if a better or worse quality of the same kind of thing be offered to him, and he consent to receive it, the transaction is lawful. It has even been said, that if a better quality of the same kind be offered to him he may be compelled to receive it; but according to Zoofr, whose opinion seems to be approved, he cannot be compelled to accept even a thing of better quality against his will.

A change of the things advanced for is also unlawful.

A change in the articles advanced for is also unlawful. But if the receiver of an advance render good articles instead of inferior the advancer may be compelled to take them, though not so of course when inferior articles are offered instead of good.

Difference in quantity or quality

When the receiver of an advance brings articles differing in quantity or quality from those for which the advance

* Arab. *Musharia*: places for watering animals.—*Richardson.*

was made, and wishes to adjust the difference by some modification of the price, there are eight different cases, four of which are applicable to articles of long measure, and four to articles estimated by measurement of capacity or weight. With regard to the former, when the article advanced for is cloth for instance, and the receiver of the advanced brings cloth better in quality or in greater quantity than was agreed for, and says, "Take this, and add to me a *dirhem* for it," the transaction is lawful, the additional *dirhem* being set off to the better quality, or the increased length; but when he brings cloth of inferior quality, or less in length than what was agreed for, and says, "Take this, and I will restore you a *dirhem*," and this is done, the transaction is not lawful; while if, in bringing the articles of inferior quantity, he had merely said, "Take this," without any offer of restitution, and the advancers were content, the transaction would be lawful, this being no more than a discharge from the quality of the article. Again, with regard to articles of capacity or weight, where an advance of ten *dirhems* has been made for ten *kufeezes* of wheat, and the receiver of the advance brings fine wheat, saying, "Take this, and add to me a *dirhem*," the transaction is not lawful. But if he bring eleven *kufeezes*, saying, "Take this, and add to me a *dirhem*," or nine *kufeezes*, saying, "Take this, and I will restore you a *dirhem*," and the advancer give his consent, the transaction is lawful; while if he bring ten *kufeezes* of inferior quantity, and say, "Take this, and I will restore you a *dirhem*," the transaction would not be lawful. But, according to Aboo Yoosuf, the transaction is lawful in all the cases without any distinction.

of the commodities adjusted by a modification of the price.

*Huwalut** and the taking of security, or a pledge for the capital stock, are all valid; but still, if the parties separate before possession of it is taken, the *sulum* is void.

Huwalut, pledge or security for the capital stock.

* *Huwalut* is the transfer of a debt from the liability of one person to that of another, with, of course, the consent of the creditor and the transferee. See Translation of *Hedaya*, vol. ii. p. 606.

When a pledge is taken and the parties separate, the pledge being still in existence, the *sulum* contract is dissolved; but if the pledge perish at the meeting the contract is valid.

Pledge or security for the commodities advanced for.

When a pledge is taken as security for the subject of the *sulum*, and the pledge happens to perish, its loss is tantamount to payment or delivery. And where the receiver of the advance happens to die involved in debt, and the pledge is subsisting, the advancer has a preference over it to other creditors, but he cannot appropriate the pledge in lieu of his debt; on the contrary, he must sell it for articles of the same kind as he is entitled to, in order that there may be no change or commutation of the subject of the *sulum* previous to delivery. *Huwalut* and a surety may also be lawfully taken for the subject of the *sulum;* with this difference, that in the former case the receiver of the advance is released from further liability, while in the latter he is equally liable with the surety, the advancer being at liberty to make his demand on whichever of them he pleases.

Surrender and possession.

When the receiver of an advance brings the goods and vacates them for the advancer, the latter becomes possessed in the same way as with other commodities that are undeterminate. But if the advancer should say, "Measure what is due to me by you in your own sacks," or "Measure it and place it in your house," and he does so, this is not a sufficient delivery. And when an advance has been made for a *koor* of grain, and the advancer desires the person who receives the advance to measure it in the sacks of the former, and this is done in the advancer's absence, here also the delivery is insufficient; and if the articles should happen to perish, they perish as the property of the receiver of the advance; but if the advancer were himself present, the delivery would be sufficient according to general agreement, whether the sacks were his own or those of the other party. Where the advancer delivers sacks containing some grain of his own, and says, "Measure what you owe me in the sacks," and it is done in the advancer's absence, there is some difference of opinion among the learned, but the valid opinion is that in such a case the delivery is sufficient; but if the receiver of an advance for corn should grind it by desire of the advancer, the latter does not become possessed, and if he take the flour it is unlawful. When possession is taken by a servant or son of the person who receives an advance, by the order of the advancer, this is lawful, and the latter becomes possessed.

Case of a receiver purchasing goods and delivering them to the advancer.

A person makes an advance of *dirhems* for a *koor* of wheat, and the receiver of the advance makes a purchase from a third party of wheat, on condition that it is a *koor*, and delivers it in payment of his debt to the advancer. Two measurements are necessary to justify the free disposal of the *koor* on his part, either by consuming it himself, or by selling it to another, or the like, viz., one measurement by the receiver of the advance, and another measurement by the advancer; and the second measurement cannot be dispensed with, though the advancer were present at the first measurement. So, also, if the receiver of the advance should desire the advancer to take possession of the purchased wheat, and he should do so, still a double measurement by him would be necessary, one on account of the receiver as his representative, and the other for himself; and in this case also a single measurement would not suffice.* In like manner, if the receiver of the advance should deliver money to the advancer in order that he may purchase wheat, and on condition of his measuring and taking possession, and he should measure and then take possession in payment of his right, still a

---

* Because there are two contracts, in which case the Prophet's prohibition, referred to in the note on page 30, is applicable. See *Hamilton's Hedaya*, vol. ii. pages 483-531. But, suppose that after the advancer has taken possession, the wheat perishes in his hands before measurement, does the loss fall on him or on the receiver of the advance? In Mr. Hamilton's *Translation*, it is positively stated that the loss falls on the latter; but this is probably an inference of the Persian translators, for it does not appear in the printed edition of the Arabic text.

second measurement on his own account would be necessary. But if the receiver of an advance should purchase wheat by conjecture, or obtain it from his own land, or by inheritance, gift, or will, and deliver it to the advancer, and then measure it in his presence, the single measurement would be sufficient; and in like manner, if he should borrow grain by measure, and deliver it to the advancer, a repetition of the measurement would not be necessary. All that has been said with regard to articles of capacity is equally applicable to articles of weight.

Effect on a *sulum* of a right in a third party to the capital stock, or of a defect in it when it is specific.

When the capital stock is something specific, and it is found that another party is entitled to it, or that it is defective, and the claimant does not allow the sale, or the receiver of the advance is not content with the defect, the contract is null, whether the discovery of the right or of the defect be made before or after the separation of the parties. But if the claimant allow the sale, or the receiver of the advance acquiesce in the defect, the *sulum* is lawful in either alternative.

When it is undeterminate.

When the capital stock is undeterminate, and after possession of it has been taken it is found at the meeting that another party is entitled to it, who thereupon assents to the transaction while the capital stock is still in existence; in such circumstances the *sulum* is lawful; but if the claimant withhold his assent, the effect of possession is dissolved to the extent of his right, and the transaction becomes so far the same as if possession had never been taken. Still, if the deficiency be supplied by delivery of a similar, of which possession is taken at the meeting, the *sulum* is lawful, but not otherwise. If the capital stock be paid in coin which is found at the meeting to be bad,* and the receiver of the advance is willing to take it, still the *sulum* is not lawful; but if he return the bad coin and receive others instead at the meeting, the *sulum* is lawful. Where again the coin is only base,† and the receiver of the advance allows it at the meeting that legalizes the *sulum* in the same way as if he were to return the bad coin and

* *Sitook.* † *Zooyoof.*

receive good instead at the meeting; but if the parties separate before such commutation of the coin, the *sulum* is void.

When the objection applies to only a part of the capital stock, as if it be found after the separation of the parties that a person is entitled to part of it, then, though the discovery should not be made till after the separation of the parties, if the claimant allow the transaction, and the capital stock is still in existence, the *sulum* is lawful, while if he reject it, the *sulum* is void to the extent of his right. Where the capital stock was paid in coin, part of which is found to be bad, and the discovery is not made till after the separation of the parties, the *sulum* is so far void, be the amount small or great, or be it accepted or rejected by the receiver of the advance, and whether changed or not on the spot; and in no case can it be made lawful by possession after the meeting. But where a portion of the coin is only base, then, though the discovery should not be made till after the separation, yet if the receiver of the advance acquiesce, the *sulum* is lawful; while if he should reject the coin, and it is not changed on the spot, all are agreed that the *sulum* is void to the extent of the rejected portion; but if it be exchanged on the spot, and the amount of the rejected coin is small, the *sulum* is generally allowed to be good on a favourable construction; and even where it is considerable, though Aboo Huneefa was of opinion that the *sulum* is void, both his disciples considered that it would not be void.

When the objection applies to a part only of the capital stock.

When the person who is to receive an advance is indebted in something similar to the capital stock, a question arises whether the latter can be set off against the debt or not, and two cases present themselves for consideration; one where the debt is due on an actual contract, and the other where it arises merely by implication from the fact of possession. In the former case, and when the contract was prior to the contract of *sulum*, as, for instance, if the advancer had previously sold to the person who is to receive the advance, a piece of cloth for ten *dirhems*, and had neglected to take the price till being about to make an

Set off of a previous debt to the capital stock.

advance of ten *dirhems* on account of wheat, he sets off the two debts against each other; in such circumstances, if both the parties be content with the set off, it is valid; but if one of them should refuse his consent, the set off would not be good. When, on the other hand, the contract upon which the debt is due is posterior to the contract of *sulum*, the set off is not valid, though both the parties should concur in making it. Where, again, the debt has arisen by implication from the fact of possession, as in a case of usurpation or loan, the set off takes place whether the parties concur in making it so or not. In this it is implied, however, that the debts to be set off are equal in amount; for if one should exceed the other, and one only of the parties assent to the deficiency while the other refuses, it is only when the party who refuses is entitled to the smaller debt that the set off is valid; since if the refusing party were the one entitled to the larger debt, the set off would not be valid.*

Set off of a debt to the commodities for which the advance has been made.

When the master of the *sulum*† is liable for a debt arising out of a responsible possession, as, for instance, if he should usurp or borrow something from the other party after entering into the contract, a set off takes place; and if he had usurped a *koor* of grain before the contract, and it is still subsisting in his hands at the expiration of the term of the *sulum*, and he makes it a set off, the set off is good, whether the grain be in the presence of the parties at the time or not. Where, again, the *koor* was a deposit with the advancer whether before or after the contract, and the person who received the advance makes the debt a set off, it is not valid unless the *koor* be in the presence of the parties at the time. If the

---

* A case is stated in the *Hidayah* (Translation, vol. ii. page 529), of the set-off of a debt to *part* of the capital stock and the contract is said to be invalid *pro tanto* of the debt, and the reason would seem to apply equally to a set-off to the *whole* of the capital stock. But the author has not made any distinction between a debt by actual contract, and one implied from possession, and it is probable that in the case referred to the debt to be set off was of the former description.

† That is, the advancer or purchaser.

koor were usurped after the contract but before arrival of the period of delivery, it would become a set off on the arrival of the period; whereas, if it had occurred previous to the contract, it would be necessary that it should be expressly made a set off in order to become legally so. In all these cases, it is implied that the thing usurped is similar to that to which the party is entitled; for if the usurpation were of an article superior in quality, the set off would not be good without the assent of the receiver of the advance, while if it were of an article inferior in quality to the *sulum*, the set off would not be good without the consent of the advancer.

Section IV.

Of Disputes between the contracting Parties as to matters of fact.

Dispute as to the kind of goods advanced for.

If a dispute take place with regard to the kind of articles for which an advance has been made, the advancer insisting that he had advanced ten *dirhems* for a *koor* of wheat, and the receiver alleging that it was for a *koor* of barley, both parties are to be put on oath if they have no evidence, on a favourable construction of the law, commencing with the oath of the receiver according to the first opinion of Aboo Yoosuf, but with the oath of the advancer according to his last opinion. When both parties have sworn, the judge is then to ask them what they desire to be done; and if both or only one of them should answer, "Let it be cancelled," the judge is to cancel it; but if both should answer, "We will not cancel," he is to leave them to themselves, in the hope that one of them will at length credit or acknowledge the truth of the other's assertion. If either party should refuse to swear, the judge is to decide against him according to the claim of his adversary. And if either should offer evidence, it is to be received. If both should adduce evidence, and the parties are still at the meeting of the contract, the judge, according to Moohummud, is to determine the case as if there were two contracts, decreeing against the master of the *sulum* for twenty *dirhems*, and against the receiver for a *koor* of wheat and a *koor* of barley; but if the parties have separated from the meeting, and the master of the *sulum* had paid ten *dirhems* and no more, the case is to be treated as a single contract, and determined according to the evidence of the master. According to Aboo Huneefa and Aboo Yoosuf, however, the matter is to be disposed of in both cases as one contract, and upon the evidence of the master of the *sulum*.

As to the quantity of the goods. When the dispute has relation to the quantity of the goods for which the advance has been made, it is to be determined in the same way as above laid down.

As to their quality. Where the quality of the goods is in dispute, and neither of the parties has evidence, analogy would require that both should be put on oath, and it seems to prevail; while if only one of them should adduce evidence, the judge is to decree according to it, whether he be plaintiff or defendant. If both should adduce evidence together, then, according to Aboo Huneefa and Aboo Yoosuf, there is no doubt that the judge should determine as in one contract on the evidence of the master of the *sulum*, while according to the opinion of Moohummud, as stated in several places, he ought to determine for two contracts; and the author adds, this is agreeable to analogy, and we adopt it. A person having made an advance of ten *dirhems* for a *koor* of wheat to another person, the latter insists that there was a condition for inferior wheat, while the master of the *sulum* denies that there was any condition at all; in such circumstances, the word of the former is to be preferred; but in the converse case it is said that preference should be given to the word of the latter according to Aboo Huneefa, though in the opinion of his disciples the word of the former is here also to be preferred.

Dispute regarding the capital stock—as to its kind. When the parties differ as to the capital stock, and it is a thing that does not admit of being particularized by specification, and the difference is with regard to its kind, the master of the *sulum* saying he advanced ten *dirhems* for a *koor* of wheat, while the receiver insists that it was a *deenar* for a *koor* of wheat, and neither of them has any evidence, both should not be sworn according to analogy, but the word of the master be preferred. On a favourable construction, however, they are both put on oath. If both should adduce evidence, the judge, according to Moohummud, is to decree for two contracts, that is against the master of the *sulum* for a *deenar* and for ten *dirhems*, and against the receiver of the advance for two *koors* of wheat. There is no distinct report in the books as to what was the opinion of Aboo Huneefa and Aboo Yoosuf in this particular case; but, according to Kurkhee, they considered that the judge ought to decree for only one contract and on the evidence of the receiver of the advance, and this is held to be valid. When the dispute between the parties is as to the amount or quality of the capital stock, it is to be determined in the same way as already laid down for disputes with regard to the amount or quality of the goods for which it may be advanced.

As to its amount or quality.

The principle of the differences of opinion between Aboo Huneefa and Aboo Yoosuf on the one hand and Moohummud on the other, when the contracting parties are at variance with regard to the kind, quantity, or quality of the capital stock, or of the goods advanced for, and both adduce evidence, is this, that, according to the two elders, the judge is to determine as far as possible for one contract, and for two only when it cannot be helped, while, according to Moohummud, he is to determine for two contracts when possible, and for one only in the other alternative.

Reason of the difference between the two elders on the one hand, and Moohummud on the other.

When the parties dispute as to the place of delivery, the word of the receiver of the advance is to be preferred according to Aboo Huneefa, and both parties are not to be sworn; but, according to his two companions, they ought to be sworn. This, however, is only when neither of them adduces evidence; for if either of them should adduce evidence the judge is to decree according to it, whether the party be plaintiff or defendant. But if they should both produce evidence together, it is reported that

Dispute as to the place of delivery.

the judge is to decree according to the evidence of the plaintiff, and on one contract.

As to the term. When the parties dispute as to the term, this dispute does not induce a mutual oath; but there are conflicting opinions among our three doctors. If the dispute be as to the fact of a term, and the party insisting for the term is the advancer, his word is to be preferred; but if the party claiming the term be the receiver and the advancer denies it, the word of the former is to be preferred, and the contract held to be valid on a favourable construction according to Aboo Huneefa, while in the opinion of the disciples preference is to be given to the word of the advancer, and the contract is invalid. This, however, only when neither of the parties adduces evidence; for if either adduce evidence, it is to be received; and if both should adduce evidence, that of the party insisting for the term is to be preferred. If the parties agree as to the condition of a term, but differ as to its period, the word of the advancer with his oath are to be preferred, that is when neither of them adduces evidence; for if either do so, decree is to be given in conformity with his evidence; and if both adduce evidence together that of the defendant is to be preferred, and there should be no decree for two contracts, according to all our doctors. If the parties differ as to the expiration of the period, after agreeing that it was a month for instance, the word of the defendant is preferred. While if they differ both as to the length and the expiration of the period, the word of the advancer is to be preferred as to the former, and the word of the receiver as to the latter; and if both adduce evidence together, that of the receiver is to be received in proof of the more extended period.

As to the receipt of the capital stock at the meeting. When the dispute between the parties has reference to the receipt of the capital stock at the meeting, and the advancer adduces evidence that the parties separated before receipt, while the receiver adduces evidence of possession before the separation, the capital stock being also in his hands, the evidence of the latter is to be preferred, and the *sulum* held to be lawful; and though *dirhems* were actually in the hands of the advancer, yet if the receiver should say, "I deposited them with him," or "he forcibly took them back from me after possession," and should adduce evidence of the possession, his word would be preferred.

Mode of deciding when the dispute relates to the quality of cloth.

When in a *sulum* of cloth it was conditioned that the cloth should be of good quality, and the receiver of the advance brings cloth which he insists answers the condition, while the advancer denies that it does, the judge should submit it to the inspection of two persons experienced in such matters (one would be sufficient, but two more cautious), and if they should declare the cloth to be good, the advancer may be compelled to receive it.

Condition as to place of delivery.

If it were a condition of the contract that delivery should be made at a particular place, but the receiver of the advance says to the advancer, "Take it in another place, and take from me the hire of carrying it to that place," and the advancer takes possession accordingly, it is lawful, but he cannot lawfully take the hire. And he must restore what he may have received on that account, but he may in that case either retain or return the goods, and insist on delivery being made at the place originally stipulated for; but if the goods should perish in his hands he has no redress.

Demand of delivery at another place.

The master of the *sulum* meets the receiver of the advance after the arrival of the period, in a city different from that in which it was stipulated that delivery should be made, and demands the goods, it is lawful for him to do so if the value of the goods in the city where they meet be equal to or less than their value in the other city. But this doctrine is disputed by some judges in our times, and it is proper to receive it with a restriction of its application to a case of necessity, as, for instance, where the receiver has taken up his abode in another place, and the advancer is in consequence disabled from obtaining his strict right.

SECTION V.

Of Ikalut, Composition, and the Option of Defect in Sulum Sales.

Ikalut as to the whole of the goods advanced for.

Ikalut in *sulum* is lawful. When the parties agree to a dissolution with regard to the whole of the things for which the advance has been made, the *ikalut* is lawful, whether it take place before or after the arrival of the term, or whether the capital stock be still subsisting in the hands of the receiver, or have perished. When the *ikalut* is lawful, and the capital stock, being something determinable by specification, is still in subsistence, the thing itself must be restored by the receiver to the advancer. If it have perished, and was of the class of similars, the receiver of the advance must make restitution of a similar, or if it were not of that class then he must restore its value. When the capital stock is something not determinable by specification he must restore a similar, whether it be still in existence or have perished. And in like manner when the master of the *sulum* has taken possession of it, and the parties agree to a dissolution while it is still in his hand, the dissolution is lawful, and the master is bound to restore the actual thing of which he took possession. When the parties agree to a dissolution as to part only of the goods advanced for, and it takes place after the arrival of the term, the *ikalut* is lawful if the remainder be a known part of the whole, such as a half or third for instance, the remainder being still referred to the arrival of the original term. And if the dissolution take place before the arrival of the term, and no stipulation is made for the prompt delivery of the remainder, it is lawful in that case also, the remainder being still referred to the arrival of the term. And even though there were a stipulation for prompt delivery of the remainder the dissolution would be valid, but the condition invalid, according to Aboo Huneefa and Moohummud, who considered *ikalut* a cancellation of sale as already explained.

As to part of the goods.

If the advancer desired to take something else in lieu

of the capital stock after a dissolution, it is not lawful for him to do so according to the opinion of our three sages. And they were also all agreed that possession of the capital stock at the actual meeting where the dissolution takes place is not a condition of its validity.

A substitute for the capital stock not lawful.

A person makes an advance of a slave girl for a *koor* of wheat, and the person to receive the advance takes possession, the parties then agree to a dissolution, after which the slave girl dies, the dissolution is nevertheless valid, and the receiver is bound to restore her value, as of the day when he took possession.* And if the dissolution should take place after the death of the slave, it would still be lawful, and the receiver answerable for her value.

Case of loss of the capital stock after dissolution.

Ben Ahmud, being asked with regard to a person who made an advance and then purchased the goods for which the advance was made from the receiver of the advance at a price greater than the capital stock, or at the capital stock, whether this was a dissolution of the *sulum* contract, replied that it was not, and that the purchase was not valid. In like manner, if the advancer should sell the goods to the receiver of the advance for more than the capital stock, or for the capital stock, there would be no valid sale, nor a dissolution of the *sulum*. But when the advancer makes a gift of the goods to the person who received the advance, this amounts to a dissolution of the *sulum*, and the latter is bound to restore the capital stock.

Case of purchase or sale of the goods by the advancer from or to the receiver.

When the subject of *sulum* is wheat and the capital stock a hundred *dirhems*, and the parties enter into a composition on the condition that two hundred or one hundred and fifty *dirhems* are to be returned, the transaction is void. But if the advancer should say to the receiver, "I have compounded with you for a hundred *dirhems*," or "for fifty *dirhems*," of the capital stock, the composition would be lawful; for a composition for the capital stock in a case of *sulum* is an *ikalut* or dissolution. The learned differ, however, as to the construction to be put on the

Composition.

* The dissolution of an ordinary sale is annulled by the subsequent loss of the thing sold in the hands of the purchaser. See *ante*, p. 231.

terms, "I have compounded for fifty *dirhems* of the capital stock," whether they become a dissolution of the whole or only half of the contract. And if the terms were, "I have compounded with you for two hundred *dirhems* of the capital stock, while one authority says that the *ikalut* would be valid at the capital stock, the excess being considered surplusage, another declares that it would be actually void.

Advance by two parties, and composition by one of them for his part of the capital stock.

When two parties make an advance for grain, and one of them enters into a composition with the receiver for his capital stock, the composition is in suspense according to Aboo Huneefa and Moohummud, and is lawful if approved of by the other party, but otherwise it is unlawful. There is no doubt of this when the advance is made out of copartnership property; but where the funds are not copartnership property, as if, for instance, the advance were ten *dirhems*, and each of the advancers were to pay down separately five *dirhems*, Moohummud has not left any recorded opinion on the case; and while some of the learned have stated that the composition is good as to the share of the person who makes it, according to general agreement, others maintain that this opinion is not correct.

Composition by a surety.

When a person has made an advance and taken a surety for the goods, and the surety enters into a composition with the advancer for the capital stock, the composition is in suspense for the confirmation of the receiver of the advance, whether the surety were a volunteer or gave his security at the desire of the receiver. If the receiver confirm the composition it is lawful, but otherwise it is void, and the *sulum* contract remains as before, according to Aboo Huneefa and Moohummud. And it is only where the capital stock is money that Aboo Yoosuf entertained a different opinion; for if it were a specific thing, as a piece of cloth or a slave, then all were agreed as to the composition being in suspense on the confirmation of the receiver.

Discovery of previous

Wheat for which an advance was made is taken possession of by the advancer, and it sustains some damage in his hands, he then finds a defect which existed in it previously; in such circumstances, according to Aboo Huneefa, if the person who received the advance is willing to take back the wheat with its new defect, the subject of the *sulum* may be returned; but he may refuse to do so if he please. In the event of his refusal the advancer should, according to Aboo Yoosuf, return a similar to what he took possession of, and then proceed against the receiver of the advance for the goods agreed upon, while according to Moohummud he can only have recourse against the receiver for so much of the capital stock as may correspond to the original defect. Husham relates that he put a question to Aboo Yoosuf regarding a man who had advanced ten *dirhems* for a piece of cloth, of which he took possession and cut it up, and afterwards found a defect, and that Aboo Yoosuf answered, the person had no right to recourse for such defect.

defect in the goods after a supervenient damage.

SECTION VI.

Of Agency in Sulum.

When a person appoints an agent to make an advance of *dirhems* for him for a *koor* of wheat, and the agent does so, observing the proper conditions of *sulum*, the transaction is lawful. It is the agent who is entitled to demand the goods advanced for, and it is he also who is to deliver the capital stock. If the agent advance money belonging to his constituent, he is to receive the goods and deliver them to the constituent. If he advance money of his own, having received nothing from the constituent, he may have recourse to the latter for the money which he advanced; and for that reason when he has received the goods he is entitled to retain them until he receive repayment of his advance. If they should perish in his hands before he has asserted his right of retention, they perish as an *amanut*, or trust; and if they perish after assertion of his lien, they perish, according to Aboo Yoosuf, as a pledge, while in that case, according to Moohummud, the

Appointment of agent by the advancer.

Advance by agent of his own money.

debt abates whether the value of the pledge be small or great, and this was also the opinion of Aboo Huneefa, according to a report of Shums ool Aimut Al Surukhsee.*

Advance out of constituent's property.

If the capital stock be advanced from property of the constituent, and the agent take a surety or a pledge for the *sulum*, it is lawful. And if on arrival of the term the agent should give further time, or release the debtor from the grain for which he is liable, or make a gift of it to him, these acts are also lawful, but the agent is answerable for them to his principal. So, also, if he receive payment in grain of a quality inferior to the condition, or abandon the *sulum*, or agree to a dissolution of the contract, his acts in these cases are lawful, but he is responsible to his principal for a similar of what he contracted for.

The person who makes the contract must remain at the meeting till payment of the capital stock.

When an agent has made a contract of *sulum*, and directs his principal to pay the capital stock, but retires himself from the meeting, the *sulum* is void. So, also, if a person who is to receive an advance should, after entering into the contract, appoint an agent to take possession of the capital stock, and should himself retire from the meeting before possession is taken by the agent, the *sulum* would be void.

Case of agent departing from his instructions

When an agent departs from his instructions, and makes an advance for something different from what his principal directed him, the principal may make either the agent or the receiver of the advance responsible for his money. If he adopt the former course, the *sulum* remains valid against the agent; and if he adopt the latter course, while the agent and receiver of the advance are still at the meeting, and the agent then pays down other money, the *sulum* is lawful; but if he do so after the separation from the meeting, the *sulum* is void.

Appointment of agent to

When a person appoints an agent to receive an advance for him of money on account of grain, and the agent does

---

* In a case of pledge, if the pledge perish and its value be *less* than the debt, the pawnee forfeits that part of his claim only which is equal to the value of the pledge, and the balance or excess must be paid to him by the pawner.—*Hamilton's Hedaya*, vol. iv. p. 193.

so and then pays over the money to his principal, the agent is liable for the grain, and has a claim against his principal for the *dirhems* as a loan. And if one's agent make an advance for grain, and the principal himself takes delivery of it, or cancels the contract with the receiver of the advance, these acts are lawful on a favourable construction, but the receiver is at liberty to refuse delivery to him.

receive an advance.

When two agents are appointed, one cannot act separately.

If two persons be appointed agents for the purpose of making an advance, one of them cannot lawfully do so; and if both make the advance, one of them cannot lawfully discharge the receiver.

When an agent is appointed to make an advance for corn,* flour and wheat are comprehended under the term on a favourable construction, but if the advance be made for barley, it is a variance, and the agent is responsible for the money to his principal; but the latter may, if he please, take it from the receiver.

Sub-agent.

When an agent for *sulum* appoints another to receive the goods advanced for from the person who is liable to make delivery, the latter is released on making delivery to the person so appointed. And if the agent's agent be his slave, or his son, being in his family, or a person hired for the purpose, the act is lawful as against the principal; but if an entire stranger be appointed, the first agent is responsible for the loss of grain in his hands; while if the grain reach the agent himself, he and the sub-agent are alike relieved from all responsibility.

Substitute.

It is not in the power of an agent for *sulum* to appoint another agent to act in his stead, unless the principal authorized him to act according to his discretion.

Advance by the agent to himself or one of his family.

An agent for *sulum* cannot lawfully make an advance to himself or his slave, or, according to Aboo Huneefa, to his son, wife, or either of his parents; but both his companions differed from him in this respect.

If a person say to another, "Advance what you owe me for a *koor* of wheat," and specify the person to whom

* Arab. *Tuâm* ; literally, *food.*

Authority by a creditor to his debtor to advance the amount of his debt.

the advance is to be made, the agency is valid according to all our doctors; and even though no particular individual be indicated, the agency is still valid according to the disciples, though Aboo Huneefa considered it to be invalid in that case.

Appointment of a *Zimmee* as agent.

The appointment of a *Zimmee* as an agent for *sulum* is lawful, but abominable.*

* Arab. *Mukrooh.* See *post*, Chapter XX. of "Abominable Sales."

CHAPTER XIX.

OF *KURZ* OR LENDING AND BORROWING FOR CONSUMPTION,* AND ISTISNAA OR MAKING TO ORDER.

Of what things *kurz* is lawful, and of what unlawful.

KURZ or loan for consumption is lawful with regard to all things that belong to the class of similars, such as articles of capacity or weight, or similars of tale, as eggs. And it is not lawful with regard to things which do not belong to the class of similars, such as animals, cloth, and dissimilars of tale. Property, however, is acquired in a thing of which possession has been taken under an invalid loan,† for invalid loans are transfers of property for an unknown consideration, and though, therefore, unlawful, they induce a right of property when followed by possession, in the same way as unlawful sales induce such right when followed by possession. It is also to be observed, that a thing of which possession has been taken under an invalid loan is specific for the purpose of restitution, while a thing possessed in virtue

* "The Arabic and Latin languages both express by distinct technical terms this contract, and a deed of *areeut*, which, though in their nature essentially different, are confounded in our language under the general and vague application of loan. The *mutuum* and *commodatum* of the Roman law appear to correspond exactly with the *kurz* and *areeut* of Moohummud."—Note to page 171 of the *Imameea Digest*. The *mutuum* "exists when things *quæ pondere numero mensurave constant*, as coined money, wine, oil, corn, *aes*, silver, gold, are given by one man to another, so as to become his, but on the condition that other things of a like kind shall be returned."—*Smith's Dictionary*. As the identical thing lent is not returned, but another in its stead, there is an exchange of property for property, and hence the introduction of *kurz* among sales in the Moohummudan law.

† The loan for consumption or *kurz* is always implied, unless otherwise explained.

of a lawful loan is not specific for that purpose, even though it be still subsisting in the hands of the borrower. It is optional with him, however, to make restitution of the actual thing, or a similar to it at his pleasure.

Any use of an unlawful loan is unlawful.

In every case where a loan is unlawful, it is also unlawful to make any use or advantage of the thing lent. The sale of it, however, is lawful.

How bread, wheat, and flour may be borrowed.

Bread may be lawfully borrowed by weight, but not by the piece, according to Aboo Yoosuf, and the *futwa* is in accordance with his opinion; but he saw no necessity, and gave no sanction, according to one authority, for a loan of wheat and flour by weight, or of dates in that way, even in a place where they are usually weighed. According to another report, however, he considered that flour may, on a favourable construction of law, be lawfully borrowed by weight where agreeable to the practice of men, and the *futwa* is in accordance with this view.

Firewood, timber, &c.

It is not lawful to borrow firewood, or timber, or reeds, or fresh odoriferous herbs or vegetables; but henna, and indigo, and odoriferous herbs in a dried state, which are estimated by measure of capacity, may be borrowed without any apprehension. And the borrowing of paper by the piece is lawful, and of nuts by measure, and love-apples by tale; of bricks and tiles also by tale, when the individuals do not materially differ; of flesh by weight; of saffron also by weight, but not by measure, and of ice by weight.

Gold and silver may be borrowed by weight only.

It is lawful to borrow gold and silver by weight, but not by tale. With regard to *dirhems*, of which one-third only is silver and two-thirds are copper,* a man need be under no apprehension in borrowing them by tale when they pass current among men; but when they are not currently received except by weight, then they can be borrowed only by weight, while if two-third parts of the *dirhems* are silver and one part only is copper, they cannot be lawfully borrowed except by weight, though commonly received by mankind in sales by tale. And the rule is the same with regard to *dirhems* which are half silver and

* For the different kinds of *dirhems*, see *ante*, p. 138.

half copper, which cannot therefore be lawfully borrowed except by weight.

Stipulation to suspend the repayment of a loan is void.

If a person lend on credit, or after a loan enter into a stipulation for deferring its payment, the original credit and the stipulation are void, and repayment may be demanded immediately.* When, however, a person directs by his will that a loan shall be made to a particular individual for a month, for instance, the postponement of the payment is lawful. There is no difference between a credit given before, and one given after the destruction of the thing lent. There is a device, however, by which credit may be lawfully allowed for the repayment of a loan: it consists in the borrower transferring the obligation of his debt to a third party to whom the lender may lawfully give credit, and the credit so given is obligatory on him.†

Stipulation of any kind of advantage to the lender is abominable.

Moohummud says, in his book of *surf*, that Aboo Huneefa abhorred every loan from which any advantage is derived to the lender.‡ Al Kurkhee, however, considered that the objection is applicable only to cases where the advantage is made an express stipulation of the loan; and that in all others, as, for instance, a case where the borrower makes a return of better things than he was liable for, there need be no apprehension in availing oneself of the proffered advantage. But Khussaf says that he liked not this distinction, and Al Hulwaee, that it is positively unlawful; while Moohummud has recorded that it was abhorred by the ancients; but he has also stated in another place, that there is no objection to the lender accepting a present from the borrower when it is not made a condition of the loan, which shows that he himself departed from the opinion of the ancients. But the Sheikh ool Islam, Khwahir Zaduh suggests that the opinion of

* As *Kurz* is an exchange of property for property, and the articles lent are of the class of similars, a stipulation for suspending repayment would amount to the *reba* of delay. See *ante*, page 165.

† See *ante*, note on p. 271, as to *huwalut*.

‡ It is stated in the *Hidayah*, that the Prophet prohibited loans productive of any advantage. Vol. iv. p. 1085. Translation, vol. iv. p. 119.

the ancients may be reconciled with that of Moohummud, by supposing that the former had reference to a case where the advantage to the lender is made an express condition of the contract which is allowed to be abominable, without any difference of opinion. And there seems to be no doubt that a present may be lawfully accepted from a borrower when it is known that he does not give it from any view to the forbearance of the loan, but from a regard to propinquity or friendship subsisting between the parties, particularly when the borrower is distinguished for the liberality of his disposition. Where, on the other hand, there is any apprehension that the present may be given with a view to forbearance on the part of the lender in demanding repayment of the loan, the acceptance of the present ought to be carefully avoided. And when there are none of the reasons abovementioned for the present, the situation is one of difficulty, and avoidance of the present is proper until the borrower give an express assurance that he has no view to any forbearance in the matter.

Repayment in articles of a better quality than those borrowed is lawful, but not with any excess in quantity, unless it be very trifling.

When a debtor repays his debt in things better than he received, the creditor is not obliged to receive the repayment; though if he accept, the payment is lawful. And when there is a term for payment, and the debtor pays within the term, the creditor may be compelled to receive it. A trifling excess by weight in repayment, as a *danik** in the hundred, is lawful; but an excess amounting to one or two *dirhems* in that number would not be lawful; and there is a difference of opinion with regard to an excess of half a *dirhem*, which according to one authority ought to be returned.

***Sooftujah*, or bills of exchange.**

Sooftujah† is abominable, unless the money be borrowed in absolute terms, and payment is made in the other city without any stipulation to that effect.

---

* A small silver coin, the sixth part of a *dirhem*.

† Stated in the *Kamoos* to be "the lending of money to a person who has assets in the country where the lender's family resides, on condition of its being repaid there, and thus guarding against the dangers of the road."—Note to p. 180 of the *Imameea Digest*. See also *Hamilton's Hedaya*, vol. iii. p. 244.

A person says to another, "Lend me a thousand *dirhems*, on condition of my lending you this my land, that you may cultivate it while the *dirhems* remain in my hands," and he cultivates the land; in such circumstances he is not actually bound to distribute the produce in alms, but the transaction is abominable.* **Surrender of land to a lender, to receive its profits till repayment of a loan is abominable.**

When a person has borrowed *fooloos* or Adawlee *dirhems*, and they cease to be current, he is bound, according to Aboo Huneefa, to make repayment of similars though non-current; while, according to Aboo Yoosuf, he is liable for their value on the day that he received the loan, and, according to Moohummud (whose opinion has been adopted), for their value on the last day that they were current. Some of the learned, however, of our time have given the preference to the opinion of Aboo Yoosuf, which appears to be most proper in our times. **Loan of *fooloos* or *dirhems* that lose their currency.**

A person having lent Bokhara *dirhems* in Bokhara, meets the borrower in another city where they are not to be obtained; in such circumstances the lender ought, according to Aboo Huneefa and Aboo Yoosuf, either to allow the borrower time to go and return, trusting him in the mean while and taking a surety, or to receive the value of the *dirhems*. A person borrows arti- **Miscellaneous cases.**

---

* A loan of this kind was sometimes superadded to a pledge, and was a recognised device for securing to the pawnee some advantage from the pledge. It is thus explained in the book on *heela* or devices, in the *Futawa Alumgeeree*, vol. vi. p. 606 :—"A person wishes to take a pledge from another, and to derive some advantage from it, as, for instance, the pledge being land, he wishes to sow it; or a house, to occupy it. The device in this case is to take a pledge, obtain possession, and then take an *areeut* of the same thing from the pledger. When this is done, and permission is granted to the pawnee to make use of the thing, he may lawfully avail himself of this advantage; and the *areeut* does not cancel the pledge, which, however, is in abeyance during the subsistence of the *areeut*, so that, though the pledge should perish, the debt would not be extinguished, and after the desired advantage has been obtained, the pledge revives as before. This is contrary to the case of a lease, which would extinguish the pledge." With regard to the last point, see *ante*, p. 221.

cles of weight or of capacity, and when redemanded they are not procurable; the lender must wait for the return of the proper season, according to Aboo Huneefa, whose opinion has been approved. A person borrows grain in a city where it is cheap, and meeting the lender in a city where it is dear, is seized by the latter who demands his right; the borrower cannot, however, be detained and the lender should be directed to trust him till he has an opportunity of rendering the grain in the city in which it was borrowed. One Christian lends wine to another, and afterwards embraces the faith of *Islam*, his right in consequence falls to the ground; but if the borrower become *Mooslim* he must restore the value, according to Moohummud, and one report of Aboo Huneefa's opinion also.

Composition by the borrower for less than the amount of the loan.

A person to whom a thousand *dirhems* is due by another on loan, enters into a composition with him for a hundred, payable at a fixed term; the abatement is valid, but the hundred is presently payable unless the borrower deny the loan, in which case the hundred would not be due till the expiration of the term.

Purchase by him of the thing borrowed.

A person lends another a *koor* of wheat, and the borrower then purchases it from the lender for money; the transaction is lawful, whether the wheat be still subsisting in the hands of the borrower or not. And when the money is paid at the meeting, the purchase retains its validity; but if the money be not paid at the meeting, the purchase becomes void. The case would be different if a *koor* of wheat were also due to the borrower by the lender, and both the parties should sell to each other what was due to him for what was due by him; for here the transaction would be lawful, though they should separate.* When the purchaser pays his money at the meeting and afterward finds a defect in the *koor*, he is not at liberty to return it for the defect, but having been liable only for a similar to the article borrowed, he is entitled to compensation for the defect out of the price. And if the

* Because possession is implied, see *ante*, page 136.

purchase be for a *koor* similar to what is obligatory on the borrower, the transaction is lawful when the *koor* is specific; but not lawful when it is undeterminate, unless possession take place at the meeting. But if the purchase be of the identical *koor* borrowed, the transaction is void, and being so does not effect any dissolution of the loan; while, if the borrower sell back to the lender the identical *koor*, the sale is lawful.

Disposal before possession. In a valid loan free use and disposal of the subject of loan before possession of it is lawful.*

By whom loans are unlawful. Loans by the following persons are unlawful, viz. a slave engaged in trade, a *Mookatib*, a youth under age, and an insane person. When loans are made to these persons and the thing lent is destroyed, opinions differ as to the responsibility of the parties; but if the lender find the specific thing which he lent to any of them still subsisting in his hands, there is no doubt that he has the best right to it.

Appointment of an agent to borrow is unlawful, but a messenger may be employed for the purpose. A person says to another, "Borrow for me from such an one ten *dirhems*," and he does so, takes possession, and declares, "I delivered them to my principal," he is personally liable for the property, and is not to be believed as against his principal. And if a person send a letter to another with a messenger requesting him to send so many *dirhems* "as a loan from you against me," and he sends them by the person who delivers the letter, they do not become the property of the writer until they actually reach him, according to one report of an opinion of Aboo Yoosuf. But if one should send a messenger to another, saying, "Send me ten *dirhems* in loan," and he should answer "Yes," and send them accordingly, the sender of the messenger becomes liable if he admit the receipt by the messenger. And if one send a person to borrow a thousand *dirhems*, and they are lent to him and perish in his hands, the sender is liable if the messenger had said, "Lend to such an one (the sender);" but if the messenger had said, "Lend to me for such an one," the messen-

---

* See *ante*, page 23.

ger himself would alone be answerable. The reason is, that while an agent may be lawfully appointed to lend he cannot be lawfully appointed to borrow; but if a messenger be employed for the latter purpose it is lawful. If, then, a person appointed to borrow employ language that indicates that he is acting as a messenger, the loan to him is binding on his principal; but if he employ language that indicates he is acting as an agent, as when he refers the act to himself, he becomes a borrower for himself, and is entitled to the money which he has received, and may therefore refuse to render it to his principal. A person having borrowed ten *dirhems* sends his slave to receive them from the lender, who insists that he gave them to the slave, and is supported in his assertion by the acknowledgment of the slave, who further alleges that he paid them to his master; the master, however, denies the receipt, and his word is entitled to preference, so that he is in no wise liable, and the lender cannot even have recourse against the slave.

Case of lender being directed by the borrower to apply the thing lent to borrower's use.

A person borrows a *koor* of wheat from another, and directs him to sow it on the borrower's land, the loan is valid, and the borrower becomes possessed of it as soon as it is applied to his property. But if one should borrow money and desire the lender to throw it into the water, which he does, the borrower is in nowise liable, according to Moohummud.

Areeut.

An *areeut** or loan for use of everything of which *kurz* or loan for consumption is lawful, is in fact a *kurz*, and an *areeut* of anything of which *kurz* is not lawful remains an *areeut*.

---

* *Areeut* signifies *an investiture with the use of a thing without a return* (*Hamilton's Hedaya*, vol. iii. page 277). It is the loan of a thing to be identically returned, as a book after perusal (*Ibid.* page 283, note), and corresponds exactly with the *commodatum* of the Roman law, which was "distinguished from *mutuum* in this, that the thing lent is not one of those things *quæ pondere, numero measurave constant*, as wine, corn, &c., and does not become the property of the receiver, who is therefore bound to restore the same thing."—*Smith's Dictionary.*

A person by whom a thousand *dirhems* are due gives to the creditor some *deenars*, which he desires him to change and take his right out of them, he receives the *deenars* and they perish in his hands before the change is effected; in such circumstances they perish as the property of the person who delivered them. And the result is the same when the receiver of the *deenars* has actually made the change and received *dirhems* for them, but if the *dirhems* happen to perish in his hands before he has taken payment of his right out of them. But if he first take his right and they then perish, they are his property and the loss is his own. And if the debtor in delivering *deenars* to his creditor, say, "Take them in payment of your right," and he takes them, the responsibility for loss is with the creditor, or if the debtor say, "Sell them for your right," and he sells them for *dirhems* equal to his demand, and takes possession, he becomes seized of his right by the possession after the sale.

Case of a debt in *dirhems* being paid by delivery of *deenars*.

If a lender should desire to take back the actual *koor* that he lent, he has no right to it, and the borrower may insist on giving another.

Lender cannot resume the identical thing lent.

Twenty men come and borrow from a person, desiring him to pay the money to one of their number, which he does; he cannot, however, demand from that person more than his share, From this case another point may be inferred, viz. that the appointment of an agent to take possession of a loan is valid, though the appointment of one to borrow is not so.

Case of a number of persons borrowing and desiring that payment may be made to one of them.

Istisnaa,* or making to order, is lawful with regard to everything in which it is customary, such as the making of turbans, boots, and vessels of copper or brass, and the like. This is on a favourable construction of the law.† When there is general usage with regard to the article ordered, and it is accurately described, so that it may be known, *istisnaa* is lawful. But with regard to articles for

Istisnaa.

* Literally, *requiring work*. Infinitive of an increased conjugation, from *sunaa*, making.

† It should be unlawful by analogy, because it is the sale of a thing not in existence, which was expressly prohibited by the Prophet. The

which there is no usage, such as cloth—as, for instance, if one should employ a weaver to manufacture cloth from thread to be supplied by himself — the transaction would not be lawful. The form or manner of the order is as follows: as, for example, if one should say, "Make me a boot of your own leather to fit my foot for so much," shewing him his foot; or one should say to a silversmith, "Make me a ring of your own silver," and should explain the weight and describe the kind of ring required: in these cases, the transaction would be lawful. So also if one should say to a water-carrier, "Give me to drink for a *fuls*," though the quantity of water that may be drunk is unknown.

Nature of the contract.

Istisnaa is in its inception a contract of hiring; but it terminates by becoming a sale for an instant, as it were, before the surrender or delivery. The workman has no option, and may be compelled to do the work; but the person who gives the order has an option, and may either take or reject the article as he thinks proper.* According to the most correct view of the matter, the subject of the contract is the thing required to be made; for which reason if the contractor bring an article manufactured by another person, or by himself at a time previous to the contract, it is lawful, and a sufficient compliance with the contract. The manufactured article also does not become specific to the contract until it has been actually approved, so that if the manufacturer should sell the article to another party before inspection by the person who gave the order, the sale would be lawful.

---

reasons for a more favourable construction are the example of the Prophet himself, who gave an order for a ring and a pulpit, and the usage of mankind since then to the present times."—*Kifayah*, vol. iii. page 225.

* This is in accordance with the nature of the contract, which is not a promise but a sale, the workman being the seller, and the person who bespeaks the work the purchaser. The latter, therefore, has an option on seeing the article, which the former has not, as a seller is not entitled to the option of inspection. — *Ante*, page 86; and see *Hamilton's Hedaya*, vol. ii. page 540.

If a term be fixed for the completion of the work the transaction becomes a *sulum*, according to Aboo Huneefa, and is lawful only on the conditions of *sulum*, without option. But according to both the disciples the transaction retains its original character, and the assignment of the term is considered as only a means for securing despatch. If the article be one, the ordering of which is not sanctioned by usage, and a term is assigned for the completion of the work, the transaction is a *sulum*, according to all their opinions, unless there be something in the manner of the assignment to indicate that despatch only was the object of the party, as if he should say, "On condition that you finish it to-morrow, or the day after."

Effect of a term being assigned for completion of the work.

A person gives an order to another for something to be made, and the parties dispute as to the work, the employer saying, "You have not done what I directed you," and the manufacturer answering, "I have done it," in such circumstances neither of the parties has a right to an oath against the other. And if a workman bring a claim against a person, on the ground that he ordered him to execute a certain piece of work which the other denies, he is not to be put on his oath.

Dispute as to the work being properly done.

CHAPTER XX.

OF ABOMINABLE* SALES AND UNLAWFUL GAINS.

Ariyyut. *ARIYYUT*, which is permitted, is in reality a gift, not a sale. The transaction is this:—a person makes a gift to another of the dates of a palm tree in his garden; but having afterwards some doubt of the propriety of the person coming daily into his garden where his family usually are, and being at the same time unwilling to depart from his promise, or retract his gift, he gives him some dates that have been already pulled, in lieu of those upon the tree. This is lawful according to us.†

Aynut. There is some difference of opinion among the learned as to the meaning of *aynut* which has been prohibited.‡ Some have explained it in this way:—a person in need comes to another, wishing to borrow from him ten *dirhems*, but the other being unwilling to accommodate him gratuitously, says, "You cannot have a loan, but I will sell

---

* Arab. *Mukrooh*, passive participle, signifying disliked or abominated. According to Aboo Huneefa and Aboo Yoosuf, it approaches near to what is forbidden, without being actually unlawful.—*Hamilton's Hedaya*, vol. iv. p. 86.

† It is termed in the *Hidayah*, Araya, which is the plural form, but is not classed among abominations in that work; and it seems to have been permitted by the Prophet in the sense explained in the text.—*Translation*, vol. ii. page 434. If considered in the light of a sale, it would approach very near to *Mozabunut*, which has been prohibited (see *ante*, p. 186), and would therefore be abominable.

‡ In the *Hidayah* it is stated to be *abominable*; but it is introduced only incidentally in the chapter on "Bail."—See *Translation*, vol. ii. page 589.

you this piece of cloth, if you like, for twelve *dirhems*, and its value is ten *dirhems* for which you can sell it in the market." The borrower is content, and purchasing the cloth for twelve *dirhems* resells it in the market for ten *dirhems*, by which means he obtains the accommodation he requires, and the proprietor of the cloth realizes a gain of two *dirhems* by the transaction. Others describe the matter as requiring the intervention of a third party. Thus, the lender sells the cloth for twelve *dirhems* to the borrower, and delivers it to him; the borrower then sells and delivers it for ten *dirhems* to the third party, who resells and delivers it for ten *dirhems* to the lender, and the latter consequently derives a profit of two *dirhems*, while the borrower has the accommodation which he required. According to Aboo Yoosuf, *aynut* is lawful when it does not pass the limits of what is usual in such matters.

Bye-al-wufa, or mortgage.

*The sale which is in use among men in our times as a contrivance for *reba*, and to which they have given the name of *Bye-al-wufa*,† is in fact a pledge, and the thing sold is in the hands of the purchaser as a pledge in the hands of the pawnee; he is not its proprietor, nor is he free to make use of it without the permission of its owner; he is responsible if he eat or destroy the fruit of a tree so sold to him, and his debt, when the *wufa* is for a debt, is extinguished if the thing should perish in his hands; but he is not responsible for the loss of an increase if it should perish without his act; and the seller may reclaim the thing sold when he pays his debt. According to us, there is no difference between this transaction and a pledge in any of its effects or consequences.‡ *Thus in the Fusool-al-Amadeeah.* To this

---

* As there are different opinions with regard to the legality of the *Bye-al-wufa*, I think it proper to give all that occurs on the subject in the *Futawa Alumgeerce*, with the names of the original works from which the extracts have been taken. This sale is the common form of mortgage in use in India, where it is usually styled *Bye-bil-wuffa*.

† *Wufa* means the performance of a promise, and the *Bye-al-wufa* is a sale with a promise to be performed. The nature of the promise is explained a little further on.

‡ This is the opinion of one section of the learned, who think that

effect, decisions have been given by the Siyyid Aboo Shoojaa of Samarcand, and the Kazee Alee As Soghdee in Bokhara, and many other learned men. *So in the Moheet.* And the form of the transaction is this: the seller says to the purchaser, "I have sold you this thing for the debt due to you by me, on condition that when I pay the debt the thing is mine;" or thus—"I have sold you this for so much, on condition that when I give up to you the price, you will give up to me the thing." *So in the Buhr-oor-Raik.* And what is valid is, that the contract which passes between them, if it be in words of sale, is not a pledge.* It is then to be considered if the two parties have mentioned a condition of cancellation in the sale, and if so, the sale is invalid. And even if they should not have mentioned this in the sale, but have both, in expressing themselves, used the word sale with a condition of *wufa*, or have expressed themselves as in the case of a lawful sale, but with the meaning that the sale is not to be binding or obligatory, the result is the same. Where, again, sale is mentioned without any condition, and the stipulation is then mentioned after the manner of a mutual promise,† the sale is lawful, and the *wufa* binding as a promise. *Thus in the Futawa* of Kazee Khan.

A case is given in the *Nasfeeut* of a person who sold a

---

the transaction is to be regarded in all respects as a pledge, according to the intention of the parties, who, though they say sale, mean pledge. —*Kifayah*, vol. iii. p. 820.

* This is the opinion of another section of the learned, who consider that the transaction should be treated as a sale in some respects; that is, to the extent of conferring on the purchaser the right of using the property, but not that of selling or giving it away.—*Hidayah*, as explained by the *Inayah*, vol. iv. p. 152.

† Arab. *Muwaidut.* In an authority cited in the *Kifayah* (vol. iii. page 820), in nearly the same terms, instead of this word the word *meead* is used, which is an inflection from the same root, and is commonly employed in India to signify the time or fixed period for the performance of a promise. And after the words "the sale is lawful," the passage proceeds thus,—"and the *wufa* is binding at its fixed period, for periods in engagements are binding; and this period is so, from regard to the necessities of men."

mansion for a fixed price by *Bye-al-wufa,* and mutual possession having been taken, then let the mansion to the purchaser on the conditions of a valid *ijaruh* or lease, under which possession was taken. In such circumstances, it being asked if the purchaser was liable for rent, the answer was in the negative.* *So in the Tatar Khaneeut.* A person sells an orchard to another by *Bye-al-wufa,* and mutual possession having been taken, the purchaser makes an absolute sale of it to a third party to whom he gives delivery, and then withdraws; in such circumstances, the original seller may litigate the matter with the third party, and reclaim the orchard from him. And in like manner, if all the parties should die leaving heirs, the heirs of the original proprietor may require a release of the property from the hands of the heirs of the second purchaser, who may then have recourse to the heirs of the first purchaser for the price paid to him to the extent of the assets in their hands, and the heirs of the first purchaser may then reclaim the restoration of the property and retain it on account of the debt to their ancestor until that be paid. *So in the Juwahir al Akhlatee.* In the *futawa* of Aboo 'l Fuzl, a case is mentioned of an orchard which was in the hands of a man and a woman, and the latter having sold her share to the former on condition that he should restore it to her on repayment of the price, and the man having subsequently sold his own share, it was asked if the woman had a right of pre-emption, and the answer was, that if the sale was a *maamilut*† sale, she had such a right, whether her share of the orchard were in her own hands or in the hands of the man. *Thus in the Moheet.* And in the *Atabeeah* it is said that a *Bye-al-wufa* and a *maamilut* sale are one.‡ *So in the Tatar Khaneeut.*

* See *ante*, note, page 293.

† From *Umul*, practice.

‡ The *Bye-al-wufa* is called in the *Hidayah*, *Mooutad*, which means practised or accustomed, viz., in Samarcand and neighbourhood, as explained in the *Kifayah*, vol. iii. page 820. There are four different opinions regarding the *Bye-al-wufa*. The first treats it as a pledge, as already mentioned; the second treats it as a lawful sale; of this opinion was the author of the *Hidayah*, as inferred by the commen-

Tuljeea.

Tuljeea is a contract to which a man is sometimes forced by the necessity of his affairs, when he becomes in a manner driven to it. It is of three kinds; one of these goes to the substance of the contract, as if a person should say to another, "I declare that I have sold my mansion to you," when in fact there is no sale, though he testifies and declares to one, and sells in appearance; such a sale is void. Second, when the *tuljeea* is in the consideration of the sale, as if two parties agree in private that the price of a thing shall be a thousand, but state openly that it is two thousand. The true price in this case is that which is privately agreed upon, and the public statement is treated as if made in jest. The third case is when they agree in private that the price shall be a thousand *dirhems* and sell openly for a hundred *deenars.* According to Moohummud, the sale ought to be void by analogy; but it is valid on a favourable construction for a hundred *deenars.* A *tuljeea* sale, according to Aboo Huneefa, is in suspense: if subsequently approved of by both the parties, it becomes lawful; and if rejected by them it is void. And when the parties agree to declare a sale, when in fact there is none, the sale is void, and cannot be rendered lawful by subsequent approval.* When one of the parties alleges a *tuljeea,* and

---

tator in the *Inayah*, from his referring to the *Moontad* as a lawful sale. It may be observed in passing, that the translation of the *Hidayah* (vol. iii. page 455) gives but an imperfect rendering of the Arabic text. According to the third opinion, the *Bye-al-wufa* is an invalid sale; and according to the fourth, it is entirely void.—*Inayah,* vol. iv. pages 153-154. The *Bye-al-wufa*, as now in use in the British territories in India, and sanctioned by the regulations of the British Government, contains a stipulation, that if the sum borrowed be not repaid (with or without interest) by a fixed period, the sale shall become absolute;" and it is stated in the preamble to Regulation 1 of 1798, that it had long been a prevalent practice to lend money on the mortgage of landed property with such a stipulation. And it is probable that it was the prospect of forfeiture, in the event of non-payment at the fixed period, that originally led to its adoption as a device for evading the prohibition against *Reba.*

* This applies to the first kind of *tuljeea*, which has been already stated to be void.

the other denies it, the burden of proof is on the former, and of the oath on the latter.

Sale of a *Zoonnar*, &c.

The sale of a *Zoonnar** to a Christian, or a *Kulunsuwwut* † to a Majoosee is not held to be abominable; but the sale of a beardless youth to a profligate is abominable.

Is it incumbent to inquire as to the legality of a thing one is purchasing?

A question arises, is a man who purchases a thing from a merchant obliged to inquire if it be lawful or unlawful. When, from the character of the times and the city, it is probable that the things which are brought to its markets are lawful, the question may be answered in the negative; but when it is more probable that the thing is unlawful, or the vendor is known to be a person who sells indiscriminately things that are lawful and unlawful, caution should be observed, and the inquiry made, whether the thing be lawful or unlawful.

It is incumbent on a seller to make known a blemish in what he sells.

A person wishes to dispose of property which he knows to be blemished, it is incumbent on him to make known the blemish, and if he fail to do so, he is, in the opinion of some of our learned men, a profligate and infamous person, whose testimony ought to be rejected. Others, however, think that this is going too far.

Sale of grape juice.

It is not abominable, according to Aboo Huneefa, to sell grape juice to a manufacturer of wine; but it is abominable according to the disciples, though the sale is lawful; and there is the same difference of opinion with regard to the sale of grapes to a maker of wine. There is no objection to the sale of a sheep to an infidel who will kill it by strangulation, or beating it on the head till it die.

Interfering with a bargain without intending to purchase.

A person makes a bid or offer for a thing at a fair price, and another makes a higher offer without any intention of purchasing himself, and merely to allure on the purchaser to raise his bid; this is abominable;‡ but if the first offer had been below the actual value of the thing there would be no objection in another bidding over

* A girdle or cord, worn round the waist by Christian monks.

† A high mitre or turban.

‡ This seems to have been prohibited by the Prophet, under the name of *nujish.*—*Hamilton's Hedayah*, vol. ii. p. 460.

the first bidder to excite him to bid up to the full value; on the contrary, to do so would be laudable instead of being worthy of blame.

Moozaidut.

There is no objection in selling to one who offers a higher price, or advances on the offer of another;* but

Istiswam.

istiswam, or bidding against the bid of another, is abominable.† The difference between that and *moozaidut* is this: when a proprietor of goods has proclaimed them, and a person asks for them at such a price, whereupon the proprietor ceases proclaiming them, and is considering the demand, it is not proper for another person at this time to make any larger offer, and this is what is called *istiswam*, or bidding against the bid of another. But if the proprietor does not stop in proclaiming his goods, there is no objection to another person making a higher offer; and this is what is called *moozaidut*. If the sale be by a broker, and after the bid of one person the broker were to say, "Come, I will ask the proprietor," there would be no objection in another increasing the offer in these circumstances; but if the broker had actually referred to the proprietor who had told him to sell and take the price offered, it is not proper for another person to interpose and increase the offer, and his doing so is *istiswam*.

Sale by a citizen on account of a countryman.

It is abominable for a citizen to sell on account of a countryman or peasant;‡ that is, when there is a scarcity in the city, and the sale is at an enhanced price; for in other circumstances there is no objection to his doing so.

Sale at the *Azan* on Friday.

It is abominable to sell at the *Azan*, or call to prayers on Friday; by which is meant, the *Azan* after the sun has begun to decline from the meridian.

Profit arising from unlawful sales, how to be applied.

A person sells a slave girl by an invalid sale, and reciprocal possession is taken, whereupon the purchaser sells her to a third party at a profit; this profit, however, it is incumbent upon him to bestow in alms; but if the seller purchase something with the price obtained for the slave

---

* In other words, selling to the highest bidder.

† Also prohibited by the Prophet.—*Hamilton's Hedaya*, vol. ii, page 460.

‡ It was prohibited by the Prophet.—*Ibid.* page 461.

girl, and make a profit by the transaction, he may lawfully appropriate it to his own use. The reason for this distinction is that money being incapable of specification in contracts, the taint does not attach to the profit made by it, while the slave girl being a specific individual on which the contract actually depends, the taint of the first invalid sale attaches to the gain or profit which is made by her resale. This distinction, however, is applicable only to a case where the taint arises from some defect in the right of property, and is not applicable to cases where there is in fact no right of property at all, as where a thing usurped or in trust is fraudulently disposed of; for there the taint comprehends or affects as well things which are specific as things which are not specific, according to Aboo Huneefa and Moohummud. A person usurps a slave and sells him for another slave, whom he sells for some chattel, and then sells the chattel for money; according to the *Imam*,* he ought to bestow in charity any surplus he may have received above the value of the usurped slave for which he was responsible. So, also, if one usurp a thousand *dirhems*, buy a slave with them, sell him for two thousand, buy with the two thousand some chattel, and sell that for more; but the *Kazee*† says, that in both cases the surplus may be lawfully appropriated to the usurper's own use. And if one purchase a slave girl by an invalid sale, and then sell her for another slave, he may lawfully enjoy the second, though he cannot the first; but if he sell the second slave girl, the *Kazee* says that any profit he may make by the transaction should be disposed of in alms. He agrees with the *Imam* as to the case of an invalid sale, saying that if one resell a thing sold to him by an invalid sale for a chattel, and then sell this chattel for more than the amount for which he was made liable

---

* This term is commonly applied to Aboo Huneefa, who seems to be here intended.

† Aboo Yoosuf was first the *Kazee*, or judge, and afterwards the *Kazee-ool Koozzat*, or chief justice of Baghdad; and is here apparently intended, as Moohummud only is above stated to have concurred in the distinction taken by Aboo Huneefa.

under the invalid sale, he must bestow the surplus in charity. It thus appears that he makes an invalid sale something worse than an usurpation. A person purchases a slave girl by an invalid sale, takes possession of her, and then sells her; a decree is afterwards given against him by the judge for her value in favour of the first seller; this he pays, and discharges the first seller from the price which he is entitled to receive back from him; by the second sale, however, he had received something more than he paid to the first seller for the slave's value, and was, according to Aboo Huneefa and Aboo Yoosuf, obliged to bestow the surplus in alms.

SECTION.

Ihtikar; or, Hoarding up Grain.

Ihtikar described.

Ihtikar is abominable. It is when a person purchases up grain in a city, which he refuses to sell, and the people are distressed in consequence. But there is no objection to the purchasing and withholding from sale when this can be done without injury to the people. When grain is purchased at a short distance from the city, and brought in and withheld from sale to the injury of the inhabitants, this is abominable; but if drawn from a considerable distance and hoarded, the party is not to be prevented.* And if grain be purchased in one city, and drawn or brought to another where it is hoarded, there is nothing abominable in the transaction. So, also, if one should sow his own ground and withhold its produce from sale, he cannot be termed a hoarder; though it is better that he should dispose of the surplus over what is required for himself, when the necessities of the people are great.

---

* The ground of this distinction, as well as of the objection to hoarding, is the saying of the Prophet—"The drawer (*jalib*) is provided for, and the hoarder (*moohtukir*) is accursed." This last expression may either mean "outcast from the mercy of God," which can be said only of infidels; or "remote from the rank and abode of the pure and good." It is in the last sense it is to be understood in this place.—*Hidayah* and *Kifayah*, vol. iv. p. 1081.

To withhold grain for a short time is not hoarding; but to withhold it for a long time is hoarding; a month is considered a long time by our doctors, while anything under that is accounted a short time. There is a difference in hoarding when a person waits only for an advance in prices, and when he awaits for an actual dearth; for in the latter case, the sin is greater than in the former. On the whole, trafficking in grain is not laudable. According to Aboo Yoosuf, the objection to *ihtikar* extends to everything by which men can be injured; but according to Moohummud, it is limited to what is food for man or beast.*

According to Moohummud, the *Imam* † may compel hoarders to sell, when he is apprehensive that the inhabitants of the city may perish; and he is to say to the hoarder, "Sell for what men are selling, or at such advance as may be usual in such matters." But he is not to fix prices according to general agreement, except in cases of great emergency, when the possessors of grain are raising its price to an exorbitant rate, and the *kazee* is unable to protect the rights of *mooslims* unless a price be fixed. In such circumstances there is no objection to its being done, with the counsel of persons of discretion and experience.

When the case of a hoarder is first brought before the *kazee*, he is to direct him to sell any surplus he may have over and above the food of himself and family, and to forbid his hoarding. If he attend to the prohibition, good and well: if not, and the matter is brought a second time before the judge, and it appear that the hoarder still adheres to his practice, the judge is to admonish and reprove him severely. If he persist, and the matter is again brought to the notice of the judge, he ought to imprison and keep him in custody. The Koodooree has stated in his commentary, that if the *Imam* be apprehensive of the

---

* It is stated in the *Kifayah*, that this is also the opinion of Aboo Huneefa as well as Moohummud, and that the *futwa* is in accordance with it.—Vol. iv. p. 1081.

† The Ruler.

people of a city perishing, he may seize grain from the hoarders and divide it among the necessitous, who are to return a similar quantity when they can. And according to another authority, it seems to be incumbent on the *kazee* to sell the grain of hoarders without their authority and against their will; and that, if he be apprehensive of loss of life to the people of the city, he may adopt the same course with persons who have brought grain to the city from other places.

Tulkee.

Tulkee, or forestalling, is abominable when injurious to the people of the city;* but otherwise it is not abominable, unless some deception be practised on the people of the caravan with regard to the price of grain in the city. If they be deceived as to the price in the city, the forestalling is abominable.

Implied usury.

It is abominable for one to place *dirhems* with a baker or butcher, or the like, in order that he may take bread or meat from time to time according to his occasions. Let him rather deposit his money with the tradesman, and then take from him as occasion may require for a specified part of the deposit; for, if he leave the money with the tradesman in the manner of a sale, the latter would be responsible.†

Separation of slaves who are related within the prohibited degrees—when abominable.

When two slaves are related to each other within the prohibited degrees of consanguinity, and one of them is an infant and the other an adult, or both of them are infants, it is abominable to separate them by sale, gift, or the like;‡ but the sale is lawful in its effect. And if the slaves belong to different owners, one of them being the

---

* It was also prohibited by the Prophet.—*Hamilton's Hedaya*, vol. ii. p. 461.

† That is, he would be liable either for repayment of the money or its value in goods. And this makes the transaction tantamount to a *kurz*, on which the lender, being saved from all risk in keeping it, derives an advantage. But the Prophet has forbidden *any* advantage to be derived from a *kurz*. *Hidayah*, vol. iv. p. 1085; *Translation*, vol. iv. p. 119.

‡ It was prohibited on three several occasions by the Prophet, in very strong terms, which shew that he had an amiable and tender disposition.—*Hamilton's Hedaya*, vol. ii. p. 462.

property of the vendor, and the other of his minor son, or slave, or *mookatib*, it is not abominable to separate them. But where both belong to one person, it is abominable for him to sell one of them, even to his minor son. The separation is not abominable when the slaves are not within the prohibited degrees of propinquity,* as, for instance, where one is the child of the uncle of the other; nor when the prohibition arises from fosterage† or from affinity.‡ Nor is it abominable to separate married persons, one of whom may therefore be rejected for a defect, or on account of an offence, or a debt. When one of two slaves belongs to a person, and the other to his wife or his *mookatib*, they may be separated without any objection.

When the owner of both the slaves is an infidel, it is not abominable to separate them, whether the owner be free or a *mookatib*, or a *mazoon* slave in debt or out of debt, a minor or adult, and whether both the slaves be *mooslims* or infidels, or one only of them be a *mooslim*. And if an alien enemy enter the *mooslim* territory under protection, having two slaves in his possession, both of whom are infants, or one an infant and the other adult, or if he should purchase the slaves in the *mooslim* territory from one of his countrymen living there under protection, and should wish

---

* They are the same in the Moohummudan as in the English law.

† Arab. *Riza*. This relationship exists between a child and the woman, other than its natural mother, by whom it has been nursed, and all the lineal ascendants and descendants by blood or fosterage of that woman; also her husband, or rather the author of the particular milk on which the child was nursed, and his lineal ascendants or descendants, by blood or fosterage.—*Futawa Alumgeree*, vol. i. pages 483-484. The prohibitions of marriage between relations by fosterage, are the same as in the case of relationship by consanguinity.—*Ibid.* page 390.

‡ Arab. *Sihreeut*. The prohibition by affinity is limited to the ascendants and descendants of the married pair, and marriage between one of the latter and the ascendant or descendant of the other is prohibited for ever. But it is also prohibited to a man to cohabit at the same time with two women so nearly related to each other that, if either were a man, marriage between them would be prohibited, as, for instance, two sisters, or an aunt and niece.—*Ibid*. p. 391.

to sell one of the slaves, a *mooslim* may lawfully purchase the slave from him. But if he had purchased the slaves in the *mooslim* territory from a *mooslim*, or from another alien enemy of a different country, residing there under protection, it would be abominable for a *mooslim* to purchase one of the slaves.

When a man is possessed of three slaves, one of whom is an infant and the other two adults, one of the latter may be lawfully sold without any objection. But if both the adults be equally near in degree to the infant, though differently related to him, as, for instance, his parents, or paternal uncle or aunt, they are not to be sold except together, whether they be infidels or *mooslims*; but if they are equally near to him and in the same relationship, as when they are all uterine brothers or sisters, either of the two elders may be sold on a favourable construction of the law. And if the adults be in different degrees of propinquity to the infant, the more remote of them may be sold separately without any objection.

A woman declares that a young girl with her is her child; it is abominable to separate them, though the parentage of the girl should not be established. Any separation which it is abominable for a free person to make, is equally abominable when made by a *moohatib* or a slave who is a merchant.

BOOK II.

SURF SALES.

CHAPTER I.

DEFINITION, CONSTITUTION, EFFECT, AND CONDITIONS OF SURF.

Surf is a sale of something that is price in its own nature for something else of that description,* and it is constituted in the same way as other sales. Its legal effect also is to establish a right of property in each of the parties to the thing which he has purchased from the other. **Definition.** **Constitution.**

With regard to its conditions, it is necessary, in the first place, that both the things exchanged shall be taken possession of before the separation of the parties.† By possession is to be understood not merely a surrender or vacating on the part of the seller, but manual and corporal seizure by the purchaser. And by separation meant bodily separation from the meeting, that is, by each of the parties moving in a different direction, or one of them going away while the other remains at the place of meeting; and how long soever the meeting may last, **Conditions.**

---

* That is, one of the precious metals, silver and gold, which are supposed to have been created to perform the function of price. The definition given in page 7 is therefore not sufficiently comprehensive, as it does not include silver and gold when specific, as, for instance, in the form of manufactured vessels.

† For the reason of this, which is the leading condition of *Surf*. See *ante*, note, p. 164, and *Hamilton's Hedaya*, vol. ii. pages 552-553.

though the parties should fall asleep, or faint, or get up, or walk together a mile or more, till they actually and bodily part from each other, there is no legal separation. And if two persons be indebted to each other in a thousand *dirhems* and a hundred *deenars* respectively, and one of them should call to the other from beyond a wall or from a distance, saying, "I have sold what you owe me for what I owe you," there would be no sale. So, also, if they should make an exchange by means of a messenger, because in these cases there is an actual and bodily separation at the time of the contract.

It is a second condition of this contract that an option cannot be stipulated for to either of the parties, and a third condition that there can be no credit or postponement of delivery. When a credit is stipulated for, but possession is taken before separation, that neutralizes the effect of the credit, and the contract is valid. And when an option or a credit is stipulated for, but cancelled before separation, the contract is lawful on a favourable construction. There is this difference between a stipulation for an option or credit on the one hand, and the absence of possession on the other, that the two former vitiate the contract from its inception, because they are inherent in its constitution, while the latter vitiates it after it has once been valid; for possession, according to the best opinions, is only a condition of its continuance in a state of validity. The effect of this distinction may be illustrated by Aboo Huneefa's opinion in the following case:—A person purchases for silver a female slave having a silver collar round her neck, and the parties separate before possession, the contract is in consequence annulled so far as relates to the *surf* for want of possession, but it is not vitiated as regards the slave. While if there had been a stipulation for option or credit, the sale would be vitiated altogether according to Aboo Huneefa, though it is true that according to the disciples, the *surf* only, and not the ordinary sale, would here also be vitiated.*

* Because, in their opinion, the *taint*, though affecting the *surf*

When a *surf* is vitiated by separation of the parties from the meeting before possession, the purchaser is not divested of his right of property in the thing purchased, till actual restitution to the seller.

A fourth condition is requisite to the contract of *surf* when both the things exchanged are of the same kind, for then equality of weight is also necessary; but where the things exchanged are of different kinds, as when gold is sold for silver, reciprocal possession only,* and not equality of weight, is required.

---

part of the contract from its inception, does not vitiate the rest of it, while the *vice* in a part taints the whole, according to their master.

* For reciprocal possession, being a necessary condition in this case, there is an express saying of the Prophet.—See *Translation of Hedaya*, vol. ii. p. 553.

CHAPTER II.

OF THE RULES OF THE CONTRACT WITH REFERENCE TO THE THINGS CONTRACTED FOR.

SECTION I.

Of the Sale of Gold and Silver.

***Dirhems* and *deenars* are never specific in exchange.**

DIRHEMS and *deenars* are never specific, according to us, in contracts of exchange, and the sale of gold for gold, or silver for silver, is not lawful except like for like, whether the metals be in their native state, or be manufactured, or coined. If either of these articles be sold for its kind, and the weight of both or one of the things exchanged be unknown to both or one of the parties, and they separate in ignorance, the contract is vitiated, though the things should after the separation be weighed and found to be equal. But if the things be weighed at the meeting before separation, and found to be equal, the sale is lawful on a favourable construction. And the sale of silver for silver, or gold for gold, is lawful when they balance each other in the scales, though the actual weights be unknown. The sale of one for the other as gold for silver, by conjecture, or even with an actual excess of one over the other is perfectly lawful.

Base and bad coins how exchanged for good.

Base* coins cannot be lawfully exchanged for good, except with equality of weight; while the sale of bad† coins for good is not lawful unless the latter be more in

---

* Arab. *Nubuhruj* and *Zooyoof*.

† Arab. *Sitook*. For an explanation of these terms, see *ante*, note, page 140.

weight than the silver contained in the former. When black or red silver is sold for white, equality is a requisite condition. When the silver in *dirhems* preponderates over the alloy, they are to be treated as silver; and when the gold preponderates in *deenars*, they are to be accounted as gold. When the alloy preponderates in either, the coin loses its character, and becomes a mere chattel.

A *deenar* and two *dirhems* for two *dirhems* and two *deenars*.

If a *deenar* and two *dirhems* be sold for two *dirhems* and two *deenars*, the transaction is lawful; the *deenar* on that side being opposed to the two *dirhems* on this, and the two *deenars* on this to the two *dirhems* on that. And even if eleven *dirhems* be sold for ten *dirhems* and a *deenar*, the sale is lawful; because the ten *dirhems* on one side are opposed to the same number on the other, and the *deenar* to the remaining *dirhem*.

Iron for iron, or copper for copper.

*The sale of iron for iron, or copper for copper, or other things exposed to the objection of *reba* or usury, is like gold and silver so far as regards the equality of the things exchanged for each other, but not so in respect of mutual possession. All iron is of one kind, whether it be good or bad, and its sale is unlawful except equal weight for weight; but though the parties should separate before reciprocal possession the sale retains its ability, provided, however, that the things opposed to each other are specific. And this condition applies to all articles estimated by weight.† There is no objection to the sale of red brass for orichalc,‡ though the latter be in the proportion of one to two of the former, if from hand to hand; because there is more work in the orichalc,§ and the excess of quantity on one side is opposed to the excess of work on the other. But superiority of work does not alter the nature of the substance, and as both the articles are comprehended under the same category of

---

* The remainder of this section is thrown into a sub-section in the original, as, properly, it does not form a part of the subject of *surf*.

† See *ante*, page 20. ‡ See *ante*, note †, page 269.

§ That is, I suppose, because it is a composition which requires more labour and skill to make.

quantity, that is weight, credit in the transaction is unlawful. So, also, there is no objection, with the like exception, to the sale of orichalc for white copper, or white copper for red brass, in the proportion of one to two, from hand to hand. And if a person purchase two *mithkals* of silver and a *mithkal* of brass for one *mithkal* of silver and three *mithkals* of iron the sale is lawful, one of the two *mithkals* of silver on one side being opposed to the single *mithkal* on the other, and the remaining *mithkal* of silver, and the brass being opposed to the iron.

Iron or copper vessels. Vessels made of copper and iron may, by custom, become articles of tale, and may then be sold for each other in any way; but where they are still usually sold by weight, equality of weight is necessary in the sale of them for anything of the same kind. When a person purchases a vessel of brass for a *rutl* of iron, without specification of the latter, and without fixing a term for its delivery, and takes possession of the vessel, the sale is lawful if the iron be delivered before the separation of the parties. If they separate before delivery of the iron, and the vessel be not one which is usually sold by weight, there is still no objection to the sale; but if the vessel be usually weighed, the parties have no choice. If possession of the iron be taken at the meeting, but not of the vessel until the parties separate, the sale is not vitiated. And in like manner, if one purchase a specific *rutl* of iron for two *rutls* of good tin unspecified, and possession is taken of the iron at the meeting, but the parties separate before possession of the tin, the sale is vitiated; while if both of the things be unspecified, the contract is invalid, whether possession be taken at the meeting or not.*

---

* See *ante*, page 21.

Section II.

Of the Sale of Ornamented Swords, and similar articles, in which Gold or Silver is connected with other substances; and of the Sale of things, the Weight of which is found to be more or less than was stipulated for.

Sale of a sword ornamented with silver.

If a person purchase a sword ornamented with silver, or a bridle plated with silver* for pure silver, heavier than the ornament, the sale is lawful; but if the pure silver be lighter than, or only equal to, the ornament, or if their relative weights be unknown, the sale is not lawful. When the quantity of the *dirhems* is unknown at the time of sale, but is afterwards ascertained at the meeting to be more than the silver in the ornament, the sale is lawful; but if this fact be not ascertained till after the separation of the parties, the sale is unlawful. And in like manner, according to Koodooree, when people of knowledge in such matters differ as to the fact, some saying that the silver in the *dirhems* is more than the ornament, but others that it is only equal to it, the sale is also unlawful. When the *dirhems* are more than the ornament, but the parties separate before mutual possession, the sale is dissolved as to the whole, if the ornament cannot be separated from the sword without damage; while, if the ornament be separable without damage, the sale, though void as to the *surf*, that is the exchange of the precious metals, is lawful with regard to the sword. And if the ornament be gold and the price *dirhems*, the sale is lawful, whatever may be the relative quantities of the precious metals; though here also a stipulation for delay in payment of the price would invalidate the sale as to the whole, whether the ornament be of the same metal with the price or not, or can or cannot be separated from the sword without injury. But notwithstanding such stipu-

---

* Arab. *Moofuzzuz;* literally, *silvered*

lation, if the price were actually paid down before the separation of the parties, the sale would be lawful on a favourable construction.

Of gold ornaments set with pearls or jewels.

When a person sells to another an ornament of gold set with pearls and jewels for a price in *deenars*, and the purchaser takes possession of the ornament at the meeting, then, if the *deenars* be only equal in weight to the gold in the ornament, or their relative quantities be unknown, the sale is unlawful both as to the gold in the ornament and the jewels, whether the latter can be detached without injury or not; while if the *deenars* in the price be heavier than the gold in the ornament, the sale is lawful as to both gold and jewels. If the whole price be then paid down before the separation of the parties, the contract remains valid, and the result is the same if only so much of the price be paid down as is equal to the gold in the ornament. But if no part of the price be paid down before the separation of the parties, the contract is vitiated so far as relates to the gold in the ornament; and it is vitiated also with regard to the pearls and jewels when they cannot be detached without injury from the setting. When the sale is for *deenars* on credit, it is unlawful, because as regards the setting it is a *surf* which is vitiated by the credit, and the contract being vitiated in part is vitiated as to the whole. This implies that the pearls and jewels cannot be separated from the setting without injury; for if they can be so separated, though the sale is still unlawful as to the pearls and jewels, according to Aboo Huneefa, it is not vitiated as to them in the opinion of his disciples.

When a person purchases a sword ornamented with silver for a price greater then the ornament, and pays down so much of the price as is equal in weight to the ornament, the sale is lawful as to the whole, though he should not explain that so much of the price as is paid down is for the ornament.

Of a sword detached from its ornament.

Husham relates that it was said by Aboo Yoosuf on an occasion, that when a person sells a sword without its ornament, the sale is lawful only under an express condition that the ornament shall be taken off; and if the parties separate before this is done, the sale is void, though the purchaser should take actual possession of the sword; for he observed that there is no proper possession of the latter till detached from the ornament.

A slave girl with a silver collar.

A person purchases for two thousand *mithkals* of silver a slave girl valued at one thousand, and having on her neck a collar of a thousand *mithkals*, and he pays down one thousand of the price, after which the parties separate; in these circumstances, the part paid down is held to be for the collar; and the result would be the same if both the slave and collar were purchased together for two thousand *mithkals*, one thousand on credit and the other cash, the payment in cash being considered as the price of the collar.

An ornamented sword purchased without payment of the price, and resold.

A person purchases an ornamented sword for *deenars*, and taking possession of it without payment of the *deenars*, sells it to another, who also takes possession of the sword, but without payment of the price until the parties separate; both the sales are void, and the sword reverts to the original seller. But if possession of the sword and its price were taken on the second sale, that would be valid, notwithstanding the invalidity of the first, and the first purchaser would be liable for the value of the sword to the original seller. And if two parties be entitled to an ornamented sword, and one of them sells his share for a *deenar*, whether to his copartner or a stranger, and reciprocal possession takes place, the sale is lawful; but if the sword be in the house when one of them sells his share to his partner and pays down the *deenar*, and the parties then separate before actual possession of the sword is taken, the sale is dissolved.

A sword ornamented with silver, or a vessel or ingot of silver, sold for silver, and found to weigh more or less than what was stipulated for.

When a person purchases a sword ornamented with silver to the extent, as supposed, of a hundred *dirhems* for two hundred *dirhems*, and it is afterwards found that the ornament is in reality of the weight of two hundred *dirhems*, the case presents two views for consideration. If the fact be not ascertained till after reciprocal possession and the separation of the parties, the contract is void as to the whole; but if it be ascertained before the separation, the purchaser has an option, and may either add another hundred to the price or cancel the entire contract. And if the parties were both aware from the beginning that the ornament weighed two hundred *dirhems*, and they, nevertheless, entered into the bargain for two hundred, it would be unlawful, though the purchaser should desire to add another hundred to the price before the separation of the parties. When a bracelet of silver is sold for a hundred *dirhems* on condition of it weighing a hundred, and it is weighed before the separation of the parties, and found to weigh more, the purchaser has an option, and may either add to the price, taking the bracelet for a similar to its weight, or, if he please, reject it: and there is the like result if the bracelet be found to weigh less than the weight stipulated for. And if the parties separate, and then find the bracelet to weigh a hundred and fifty, the purchaser has an option, and may either reject it, or take two-thirds of it, for a hundred; and in like manner, if there be a deficiency, he may take the bracelet for a similar to its weight, or reject it at his pleasure. When an ingot of silver is purchased for a hundred *dirhems* on condition of its weighing a hundred, and after reciprocal possession it is found to weigh two hundred, the purchaser is entitled to no more than a half, and has no option.

Same, when sold for gold.

In the above cases, the purchase is for something of the same kind as the thing sold; but when this is not the case, as if the sword ornamented with silver, or an ewer, or ingot of silver, were purchased for *deenars*, and in each case the weight were to exceed what was stipulated for, the sale would be lawful under all the circumstances mentioned. With this difference between the case of the ingot and that of the ewer, that while the excess over the stipulated weight in both would belong to the purchaser, he would have to pay for it in the former case, while in the latter he would obtain it for nothing. When the price of a silver vessel is in *deenars*, and the vessel is found to be deficient of the weight stipulated for, the purchaser may either reject the whole, or take it at the full price.

A pearl purchased on condition of it

When a pearl is purchased for *dirhems* on condition of it weighing a *mithkal*, and is found to be more, the purchaser is entitled to the whole; but if it be sold "every *mithkal* for so much," and the actual weight is found to exceed the stipulated weight, the purchaser must either reject the bargain or pay in proportion to the weight. being a certain weight.

Of things gilt, or washed with gold or silver.

If a sword be gilded, or washed* over with gold or silver, and be purchased for something the same in kind as the gilding or washing, the sale is lawful in all cases, no regard being had to the gilding or washing, as the gold or silver is consumed. And if a bridle washed with silver be purchased for *dirhems* less or more than the silver contained in the washing, the sale is also lawful. So, also, if a gilded mansion be purchased on credit, the contract is lawful, though the gold used in gilding the ceilings be more than the price.

SECTION III.

Of the Sale of Fooloos.

Fooloos may be made a medium of price.

Fooloos take the place of *dirhems* when adopted as a medium of price. They do not become specific in a contract, even though actually particularized by the parties; and the contract, therefore, is not cancelled by their loss.†

Purchase of *fooloos* for *dirhems* or for *fooloos*.

When a person purchases *fooloos* for *dirhems*, and pays down the price, the sale is lawful, though the seller should not have the *fooloos* at the time. And if he should borrow them from another party and deliver them to the purchaser, either before or after separation, the transaction would be lawful; provided that possession of the *dirhems* had been already taken at the meeting. And in like manner the sale is lawful, though the parties should separate after possession of the *fooloos*, and without possession of the *dirhems*.‡ If *fooloos* be sold for *fooloos*, and the parties

---

* Arab. *Moomuwwuh*, from *Ma* water, as distinguished from *Moofuzzuz*. See *ante*, page 319.

† This may seem inconsistent with what has been said on page 137, with regard to specific *fooloos*; but I think it is there implied that they are not employed as money.

‡ The sale is not a *surf*, and possession of both, therefore, is not necessary, but the articles being undeterminate or obligations, actual possession of one of them is requisite.—See *ante*, page 135.

separate before reciprocal possession, the sale is void; but if possession be taken by one of the parties and not by the other, or if, after possession by both and their subsequent separation, a right be established to the *fooloos* in the hands of one of the parties, the contract retains its validity. And when a person purchases a gold or silver ring, whether it contain a stone or not, for so many *fooloos*, having no *fooloos* at the time, the sale is lawful, whether reciprocal possession take place before separation or not; for this is an ordinary sale, and not a *surf.* When a person delivers a *dirhem* to another, saying, "Give me half of it in *fooloos* and the other half in a little *dirhem*," this is also lawful; but if the parties separate before possession is taken of the latter, the contract is dissolved as to it, though good with regard to the *fooloos;* while, if the large *dirhem* be not delivered till the separation of the parties, the sale is void as to the whole.

Fooloos ceasing to be current after sale, but before delivery.

If a person purchase a hundred *fooloos* for a *dirhem*, and possession is taken of the latter, but not of the former till they cease to be current, though the sale should not be void according to analogy, but the purchaser entitled to take or reject the whole, it is void on a favourable construction of law. But if possession be taken of fifty *fooloos* before they cease to be current, the sale is void only as to half, and half the *dirhem* must be returned. If, instead of ceasing to be current, they become cheap or dear, the sale is not at all vitiated, and the purchaser is entitled to the remainder.

SECTION IV.

Of Surf with regard to Mines and Goldsmiths' Dust, and of hiring Persons to extract Gold and Silver from the Ore of Mines.

Sale of gold or silver ore.

If a person purchase gold ore* for gold, or silver ore for silver, the transaction is not lawful, unless it be known that the precious metal contained in the ore is equal to that which is given for it. So, also, if the purchase be

* Arab. *Turáb;* literally, ground earth, dust.

made for gold and silver, it is unlawful. But if gold ore be purchased for silver alone, or silver ore for gold alone, and the transaction be from hand to hand, it is lawful, and the purchaser has an option on the article being submitted to his inspection. If, however, no gold or silver can be extracted from the ore, the sale is unlawful, and the price must be restored. And if one should purchase a *kufeez* of the ore without specification for a chattel, or for gold, or a chattel for a *kufeez* of the ore without specification, the sale would not be lawful, by reason of the uncertainty attaching to the subject of the contract. But the purchase of a half or a fourth of it is lawful; and the seller and purchaser are co-partners in what may be extracted from the ore according to their relative shares. When the ore is a mixed ore of gold and silver, its sale for either gold or silver is unlawful, but if it be sold for gold and silver, the transaction is lawful, each metal being in that case opposed to the kind different from itself in the ore. If the existence in the ore of both or one of the metals be unknown to the parties, the sale is unlawful. The sale of either gold or silver ore, for an ore similar to itself, is unlawful; but either may be lawfully sold for ore of a different kind, and the transaction is a *surf*. If, however, none of the precious metal can be extracted from the ores or either of them, the sale is void. While, if the ore be purchased for a piece of cloth or any other chattel, the sale is lawful, and there is no occasion for observing any of the conditions of *surf*.

Sale of goldsmiths' dust.

The sale of goldsmiths' dust* is regulated by the same general rules. Ibn Sumaut has stated on the authority of Aboo Yoosuf, that when goldsmiths' dust is purchased for a chattel, and neither gold nor silver is found in the dust, the sale is invalid; because it is obvious that the purchaser intended not the dust, but what he supposed to be contained in it; but when gold or silver is found in the dust, the sale is lawful. It is not proper, however, for the goldsmith to appropriate the price to himself, unless he had

* Viz., sweepings; Arab. *Turâb.*

made some allowance to the parties for whom he worked, at the time he settled with them, for any of their property that might have fallen down into the dust. And it is abominable for a person to purchase the dust from a goldsmith, until informed by him that he has made such compensation, as it is obvious that the dust must contain something belonging to other parties.

Partition of gold or silver ore.

When two persons are jointly possessed of ore from a mine of gold or silver, they cannot lawfully make partition of it by conjecture, because partition is like sale, and it cannot be known whether there be equality or not in the transaction until the metal is extracted. When the metal is extracted and divided by weight, the partition is lawful.

Loan of gold or silver ore.

When a person borrows from another gold or silver ore, he is bound to make restitution of an equal quantity of what may be extracted from the ore; and, with regard to the quantity, the borrower's word is entitled to preference. If one should borrow gold or silver ore, on condition of returning a similar quantity of the like ore, the transaction would be unlawful.

Property is not acquired in an opening made into a mine.

If a person should dig into a mine, and then sell the hole or opening, the sale is unlawful, because he sells what is not his property; for he dug, not with a view to acquire any right of property in the hole, but rather with a view to the acquisition of such right in what might be taken out of the hole. The hole, therefore, does not become his property; contrary to the case of a person digging a hole in waste land, in which property is acquired by the digging, such being the view with which a digging of this kind is made.

Hire of a person for ore distinctly specified.

It is lawful to hire a person for ore distinctly specified; but the hireling has an option on becoming acquainted with what is in the ore, and if he choose to return it, he may then have recourse to the hirer for the wages of a workman like himself. If the wages agreed upon be a certain weight of the ore without specification, the contract is unlawful. And if a person be hired to dig in a mine for half the produce, the contract is unlawful, and he is entitled to the wages of workmen like

Hire of a person to dig in a mine;

himself. A person may be hired to extract the metal from gold or silver ore or from goldsmiths' dust, in three different ways. The hirer may say, "I have hired you to extract for me a thousand *dirhems* out of this silver ore," or "a thousand *mithkals* out of this gold ore," when it is unknown whether such a quantity can or cannot be extracted from the ore particularized; in such a case the hiring is unlawful. Or he may say, "I have hired you for so much, to extract the gold or silver for me out of this ore;" in this case the hiring is lawful. Or he may say, "I have hired you to extract a thousand *dirhems* of silver from the ore without pointing it out;" and in this case the hiring is also unlawful, in the same way as if one should hire another to sew a *kumees* for a *dirhem* without pointing out the linen from which it is to be made.

to smelt ores.

When a person delivers a bridle to another to be washed over with silver of a known weight, such silver to be considered a loan to the first party, who is also to pay a known or fixed hire for the work, the transaction is lawful; and both the loan and the hire are obligatory upon him; but if the silver and the hire be agreed for in one sum, as if a person should say, "Wash this with a hundred *dirhems* of silver, on condition that I am to give you for price and hire ten *deenars* of gold in the whole," and the parties separate thereupon, the transaction is invalid.

A person employed to wash a thing with silver.

SECTION V.

Of the Destruction before Possession of the thing purchased under a Surf Contract.

A person purchases a silver bracelet for a *deenar*, and before he takes possession of it another person breaks it; the purchaser, however, is content to take the bracelet and to proceed against the aggressor for compensation; he may lawfully do so. And if a person purchase a silver bracelet for a *deenar*, and deliver the *deenar*, and another person then burns or totally destroys the bracelet at the meeting, the purchaser is still at liberty to allow the con-

Case of damage to the subject of sale.

Case of its total destruction.

tract, and follow the burner for its value in gold: if he obtain it while yet in company with the seller, the *surf* is lawful, but any excess of the value over a *deenar* must be bestowed in charity; while if the parties to the contract had separated before the purchaser obtained the value from the aggressor, the *surf* would be void, and the seller be obliged to return the *deenar* and take his recourse against the aggressor for the value of the bracelet, according to Moohummud and the first opinion of Aboo Yoosuf; the latter, however, afterwards departed from this opinion, and coincided with Aboo Huneefa, who considered that the *surf* would not be void in that case if the separation had taken place after the purchaser had made his choice to make the aggressor responsible.

CHAPTER III.

RULES WITH REGARD TO DISPOSING* OF THE THINGS EXCHANGED, AFTER THE CONTRACT OF SURF.

SECTION I.

Of Disposals before Possession, and of what is, and is not, a set-off to the things exchanged.

Any disposal of the consideration before possession is unlawful.

A PERSON before taking possession of the consideration† in a *surf* sale purchases something else for it from the seller, or from a third party, or takes something in exchange for it before possession from the seller, in these cases the transaction is not lawful, and the *surf* remains as before, and may be completed by possession of the original consideration.

Substitution of black for white *dirhems*, or one coinage for another.

In a *surf* sale of a thousand white *dirhems*, distinctly specified for a hundred *deenars*, black *dirhems* may be lawfully substituted for the white ones, with consent of the parties. By black *dirhems* are to be understood *dirhems* coined of black silver, not *dirhems* of Bokhara, which cannot be lawfully substituted for white *dirhems* in such a sale. And in like manner, *deenars* of a different coinage from what was specified, may be lawfully substituted with consent of the opposite party; but the transaction is accounted payment, not an exchange. And it has been said that if the substituted coinage be superior to what was specified, there is

---

* Arab. *Tusurroofat;* plural of *Tusurroof.*—See *ante*, note, p. 211.

† Arab. *Budl;* literally, a substitute or equivalent. The term applies to both the things exchanged.

no occasion for the purchaser's consent, because he gets more than he was entitled to.

Release or gift before possession.

When one of the parties to a *surf* releases the other, or makes a present to him of the consideration, it is said that the *surf* is dissolved; but if the other refuse to accept, there is no dissolution; and if the donor refuse to take back the gift, he may be compelled to do so. A person sells a silver bracelet weighing ten *dirhems* to another for ten *dirhems*, and delivers the bracelet, but before taking possession of the price the purchaser gives him back the bracelet as a gift; in these circumstances, if the price of the bracelet be paid to him before the separation of the parties, the sale is valid and the gift lawful; but if they separate without payment of the price, the sale is dissolved and the gift is void, the bracelet reverting to its seller as his original property.

Set-off of previous debt is lawful.

A person purchases a *deenar*, and ten *dirhems* being due to him by the seller, the parties agree to make them a set-off* to the *deenar*, and this is lawful on a favourable construction. And if the debt occur after the *surf*, though it does not become a set-off unless made so by the parties, and even when agreed to by them, is not lawful according to one report, yet there is another report in favour of its legality, which is held to be valid.† A person to whom a thousand *dirhems* were due by another, bought from him a hundred *deenars* for a thousand *dirhems*, and the parties then agreed that the former thousand *dirhems* should go as a set-off to the latter; Aboo Yoosuf's opinion being asked on the case, he said if the set-off were made before separation it was lawful, but if not made till after separation, it was unlawful, and such was the opinion of Aboo Huneefa. When the seller of a *deenar* borrows ten *dirhems* from the purchaser, or usurps them from him, they become a set-off to the *deenar* without any neces-

* Arab. *Kissas;* retaliating, making equal.

† This appears to be inconsistent with what has been stated in page 187, where the other report is said to be valid. A different authority is cited; and, practically, the point is not of much importance.

sity for mutual consent, for possession has already taken place.

A person has a deposit with another party, and is indebted to him for something of the same kind with the deposit; the deposit, however, does not became a set-off to the debt till the parties come to a mutual agreement to that effect; nor even after such agreement until the bailie or keeper of the deposit return to his house and take possession of it anew. But if the thing happened to be in his hand at the time that they agreed to the set-off, nothing further is required. The rule is the same with regard to a thing which has been usurped, and is subsisting in the hands of a creditor of the proprietor. And with regard to two debts, the rule is that when both are deferred, or one is deferred, and the other presently due, or one is perfectly valid and the other exposed to objection on account of some error, that there can be no set-off of one against the other unless expressly agreed to by the parties.

Rule as to a previous deposit or usurpation.

Deferred debts.

Section II.

Of Morâbŭhŭt in Surf.

When a person purchases gold for ten *dirhems* and sells it at a profit of a *dirhem*, the transaction is lawful. And when a silver bracelet weighing ten *dirhems* is sold for a *deenar*, and after reciprocal possession the purchaser sells it at a profit of one *dirhem* or a profit of half a *deenar*, the transaction is also lawful, because in the latter case, when he resells the bracelet for a *deenar* and a half, the things opposed to each other are different in kind, and in the former when the resale is for a *deenar* and one *dirhem*, the *dirhem* is opposed to its similar contained in the bracelet, and the remainder of the bracelet is opposed to the *deenar*.

Gold purchased for silver, or silver for gold, may be sold by way of *Morâbŭhŭt*.

When a person purchases gold for gold, or silver for silver, a resale by *morâbŭhŭt* is unlawful. When a person purchases a slave girl having a silver collar of a hundred *dirhems* for a thousand *dirhems*, and after reciprocal posses-

But not so, gold purchased for gold, or silver for silver.

sion by seller and purchaser, the latter sells her at a profit of ten or eleven *dirhems*, the resale is invalid according to Aboo Huneefa, but lawful according to the disciples with respect to the slave without the collar; according to Kurkhee, however, Aboo Yoosuf came over to the opinion of Aboo Huneefa. And if one purchase for a hundred *dirhems* an ornamented sword, the ornament of which is fifty *dirhems*, and after reciprocal possession resell it at a profit of twenty *dirhems*, or of eleven for every ten, or of a specific piece of cloth or the like, the sale is unlawful; but if the sword be resold at a profit of one *dirhem* on the blade, as distinguished from the ornament, the sale is lawful. And there is no objection to the resale by *morâbŭhŭt* of a bridle washed over with silver.

Section III.*

Of Addition, and Abatement, and Composition, in Surf.

Abatement. When a person purchases for ten *dirhems* a silver bracelet weighing ten, and after reciprocal possession an abatement is made to him of one *dirhem* which he accepts and resumes possession of, whether before or after the parties have withdrawn from the place of sale, the whole sale is vitiated according to Aboo Huneefa, but according to Aboo Yoosuf the abatement is void, and the *dirhem* must be restored, and the sale remains valid; while according to Moohummud the first contract is valid, and the abatement is to be viewed in the light of a gift which the purchaser may refuse until delivery. Addition. When, on the other hand, the purchaser makes an addition of a *dirhem* to the price, and delivers the *dirhem* to the seller, the contract is vitiated according to Aboo Huneefa; but in the opinion of both the disciples the addition is void, and the first contract is valid.

Addition or abatement When things of different kinds are sold for each other, as for instance, a *deenar* for ten *dirhems*, and an addition or

* This section contains selections from sections 3 and 4 of the original.

abatement is made by one of the parties to the other, the addition or abatement is lawful according to general agreement. It is, however, a condition in the case of the addition that possession shall be taken before the separation of the parties; but as to the abatement it is equally lawful, whether before or after separation, and the return of the portion abated is obligatory. If the purchaser of the *deenar* make an abatement from it of a *kerat*, the seller becomes his partner in the *deenar*.

when the things are different in kind.

Composition.

A person purchases a silver ewer weighing a thousand *dirhems* for a hundred *deenars*, and after reciprocal possession a defect is found in the ewer of such a nature as to entitle the purchaser to return it, the seller, however, compounds with him for the defect for a sum in *deenars*, such a composition is complete,* whether the sum agreed upon be taken possession of before the separation of the parties or not; because the subject of the composition, or the thing compounded for, is a share of the price corresponding to the defect, and such share being *deenars*, and the consideration of the composition *deenars* also, the composition is of the same kind as the right compounded for, and the transaction therefore is not a *surf*. If the composition be for ten *dirhems*, though it is still lawful when possession is taken before the separation of the parties, yet if they separate before possession, the composition is void, because the consideration being of a different kind from the right compounded for, the transaction is regarded as a *surf*.† And though the *dirhems* given in consideration be more than the value of the defect, the composition is still lawful according to all our doctors; because it is a composition for a share of the price corresponding to the defect, and such share being *deenars*, the purchase of them for *dirhems* more than their value is lawful.

---

* Arab. *Mazee;* literally, past.

† In the former case, the composition is a mere extinction of right; but in the latter, being of a different kind, it cannot be an extinction, and must be regarded as a sale; and, being a *surf* sale, reciprocal possession is necessary before separation.

Composition of a claim.

When a person claims a hundred *dirhems* from another, and the latter (it matters not whether he deny or admit the claim) compounds it for ten *dirhems*, payable immediately, or at a future time, and the parties separate before possession, the composition is lawful. So, also, though there be a stipulation of option to one of the parties, and they separate before possession, the composition is not rendered void. But if the composition be for five *deenars*, and the parties separate before mutual possession, the composition is void; and when they do not separate till after possession, it is valid.

For a share in an inheritance.

A woman dies leaving an inheritance consisting of slaves, cloth, gold and silver, and ornaments set with jewels and rubies, and the like, and being survived by her husband and father. The latter being in possession of the whole property enters into a composition with the husband for a hundred *deenars*. This composition may be made in two ways; first, the husband's share in the gold may be ascertained, and may be either more than the consideration for the composition, or less than, or only equal to it; in the former case the composition is lawful, but in the latter cases it is unlawful; secondly, the husband's share in the gold may not be ascertained, and in this case the composition is unlawful. If the composition be for five hundred *dirhems*, it is to be viewed in the same manner; but if the composition be for a hundred *dirhems* and fifty *deenars*, it is valid in any way. Then, if reciprocal possession take place before separation, the composition retains its validity, but if there be no such possession, the composition becomes void to the extent of the *surf* and the share of the rubies and jewels that cannot be detached from their setting without injury; while, as to the remainder of the things, it retains its validity. If the husband take possession of the *dirhems* and *deenars* which are the consideration of the *surf*, and the inheritance, or the things composing it, are in the house of the father, but not present at the meeting where the composition takes place, the composition is void so far as relates to the gold and silver, that is, when the father admits to the husband that he has the property, for such an admission makes the husband's share an *amanut* or trust in his hands, and as possession of a trust cannot become a substitute for possession under a purchase, there is a separation of the parties without reciprocal possession, which invalidates the transaction to the extent of the *surf* and the other things that cannot be detached without injury, as jewels and pearls set in ornaments. But when the father denies to the husband that the property is in his possession, he is an usurper of the husband's share, and his possession being capable of conversion into a possession under the purchase, reciprocal possession takes place as soon as the father receives the consideration, and the composition is therefore not invalidated as to the *surf*.* The result is the same when the father admits the possession of the property, and it is actually in the presence of the parties at the meeting where they agree to the composition, the composition being then also valid as to the whole.

---

* See *ante*, pages 38, 39.

CHAPTER IV.

OF DIFFERENT KINDS OF OPTION IN SURF.

Option by stipulation. WHEN a person purchases from another a thousand *dirhems* for a hundred *deenars,* stipulating for an option for a day, but cancels the option before separation, the sale is lawful; and if the parties separate before cancellation, but having first reciprocally taken possession, the sale is invalid.* The effect is the same if the option be to the seller, or to both the parties, and whether the period be long or short; and also when the thing sold is a manufactured vessel or an ornamented sword, or a golden collar set with pearls and jewels, which cannot be detached from it without breaking the collar. But with regard to a bridle washed over with gold or silver, and the like, the reservation of an option in its sale is valid. When a person purchases a slave girl with a golden collar, weighing fifty *deenars* for a thousand *dirhems,* and stipulates for an option for a day, with regard to them both, the sale is invalid as to the whole, according to Aboo Huneefa; but according to Aboo Yoosuf and Moohummud the sale is valid as to the slave for a proportionate share of the price; and the result would be the same if the purchase were for a hundred *deenars.* If the slave and collar are purchased for a hundred *deenars,* with a condition for credit, the effect is the same as if the stipulation were for an option. But if the purchase be for wheat, or any other chattel, the reservation of an option for a day or more is quite lawful; or if a *rutl* of brass be purchased for a *dirhem,*

* Without the reciprocal possession it would be actually void.

with a condition for option, the contract is lawful, for it is not a *surf*.

There is no option of inspection with regard to *dirhems* and *deenars*, or anything that is indeterminate;* but there is an option of inspection with regard to everything that is specific, such as native gold or silver, and things mounted or ornamented with the precious metals. **Option of inspection.**

Where a contract has relation to *dirhems* and *deenars*, as if a *deenar* be purchased for ten *dirhems*, and it appears that a third party is entitled to half the *deenar*, the purchaser may reclaim half the *dirhems*, and is entitled to half the *deenar*, without any option. If it be the *dirhems* that are affected by the right, and they are attached in consequence by the claimant, the possession is rendered nugatory, but the contract is not void, and the purchaser of the *dirhems* may have recourse to the seller for similars. When the claimant assents to the sale, it is to be considered whether his assent be given after possession or before it. In the former case the possession becomes lawful, and the claimant is barred from any interference with the thing of which possession has been taken, though he may proceed against the person who paid it; while in the latter case his assent and dissent are alike; for he may resume the *dirhems*, or take similars of them, and the contract is not rendered void in either case, provided this be done before a separation of the parties. But if they have actually and bodily separated, and it then appears that the *dirhems*, in whole or in part, belong to a third party, it is only when that party gives his sanction to the sale, and the *dirhems* are still subsisting in the hands of their purchaser, that the contract is lawful; and if the claimant refuse his sanction, the *surf* becomes void to the extent of the right, be it much or little. When the contract is for something specific, as, for instance, a bracelet, and a right arises to a part of it, the purchaser has an option, and may reject the remainder, or take it at a proportion of the price. If a claim be made, but **Option in consequence of a right.**

* See *ante*, page 85.

before any order is given with respect to it, the claimant sanctions the sale, it is lawful, and the claimant is entitled to the price, which the seller is first to receive and then to deliver to him.

Option of defect when a *deenar* or golden vessel is sold for *dirhems*.

The option of defect is applicable to *surf* contracts. When a person sells a *deenar*, or a vessel of gold, for *dirhems*, and finds, after reciprocal possession, that the *dirhems* are base (*zooyoof*) he may return them, and if he do so the *surf* is void, according to Aboo Huneefa and Zoofr; but according to Aboo Yoosuf and Moohummud, if the purchaser change the base *dirhems* at the meeting where the return takes place, the *surf* is lawful. If he change them before the separation of the parties at the original contract, the *surf* is lawful in all their opinions. If only a small part of the coin be found to be base, the contract is not invalidated on a favourable construction of law. If the *dirhems* are bad (*sitook*), and the discovery is made at the meeting of the contract, the purchaser of them cannot legalize the contract by taking the *dirhems;* but if he reject them, and receive good ones at the meeting, the case is the same as if possession were postponed till the end of the meeting, and the contract is lawful. And even if he knew them to be bad at the time of taking possession, and took them notwithstanding, still the sale is not lawful, and he may reject the *dirhems* and insist for good ones, unless his knowledge were founded on actual explanation by the other party, and his naming them as *sitook*. In that case the contract would be lawful, as depending on the specific *dirhems*. But if the *dirhems* are only pointed out, as if one should say, "I have purchased those *deenars* for these *dirhems*," it is necessary that both the parties should be aware that the *dirhems* are bad, and also that each should be conscious that the other is aware of the fact; for without both these elements the contract cannot be brought to depend on the specific *dirhems*, and must be held to have reference to good ones. If the *dirhems*, or some of them, be found to be bad after the separation of the parties, the *surf* is rendered void to the extent that they are so, whether it be sanctioned or not sanctioned, and whether the bad *dirhems* be exchanged for good ones or not. When the thing exchanged for the *deenar* is specific, as a bracelet, or vessel, or piece of native silver,* and after mutual possession, it is found to be blemished, but the purchaser is content to take it, the sale is lawful; while if he reject it, whether before or after separation, the contract is void, and the possessor of the *deenar* may return either that specific one or its similar. When the vice in the contract is essential, as if the thing sold is the property of another, or different in *genus* from what it was described to be, and the contract is invalidated in consequence, the specific *deenar* must be restored if in existence, and its similar only when it has perished.

When sold for a specific thing in silver.

A person purchases an ornamented sword, and finds a blemish in part of it, he may return the whole but not the part, for the whole is one thing and a blemish in part affects the whole. If he return the whole without a judicial decree, and the parties separate before possession, the return is void; for a return with mutual consent is a new sale as regards third parties, and possession in *surf* being required as a right of the law, the law is a third party, and the parties to the contract have separated without taking possession. But where the return is under a judicial decree it is not void, for it is then a cancellation as to the world at large. A person purchases a silver bracelet for gold, and finds it to be blemished, he may return it; and if it perish in his hands or sustain another blemish, he may have recourse to the seller for compensation on account of the original blemish; but if the price were in silver, he has no recourse for compensation.

When the thing sold is an ornamented sword.

If the seller of *dirhems* say to the purchaser, "I am free from every defect," and they are found to be bad, he is not released; but if they are only base, the release is good.

Release from defects.

---

* Arab. *Tibr;* here applied to silver. See *ante*, note *, page 269.

CHAPTER V.

OF THE CONTRACT, AS IT IS AFFECTED BY THE CONDITION OF THE CONTRACTING PARTIES.

SECTION I.

Of Surf in a last illness.

Sale to one among several heirs.

WHEN a person in his last illness sells a *deenar* to one of his heirs for a thousand *dirhems*, and reciprocal possession takes place, the transaction is a specific legacy to an heir, according to Aboo Huneefa, and is unlawful without the sanction of the other heirs. And the result is the same if the sale be for the value of the *deenar*, or less than its value. But according to the disciples, if the *deenar* be sold for its value, or more than its value, the sale is lawful without the consent of the heirs. And if the sick person purchase from his son a thousand *dirhems* for two hundred *deenars*, and mutual possession takes place, and there are other heirs of mature age, the sale is not lawful, according to Aboo Huneefa, without their consent, whether the value of the *deenars* be a thousand *dirhems*, or more or less. But according to the disciples, when the value of the *deenars* is a thousand *dirhems* or less, the transaction is lawful without the sanction of the other heirs. And when a sick person sells to a stranger a thousand *dirhems* for a *deenar*, and reciprocal possession is taken, after which the sick man dies leaving the *deenars* and no other property, the heirs may reject the contract in all that exceeds a third of his estate;* and if they should do so the purchaser may take back his *deenar* and return the thousand,

* It is only to that extent that a Moohummudan has power to bequeath his property; and the restraint extends to gratuitous acts in a last illness.

or he may deduct from the thousand the value of the *deenar*, and deduct also a third of the full thousand. And if the sick person had destroyed the *deenar*, the purchaser may deduct its value from the thousand, with a third of what may remain of the thousand.

SECTION II.

Of Surf with one's Slave, Relation, or Partner; and Surf by a Judge, or his Ameen or Agent, or by an Executor.

Between a master and his slave;

There is no *reba* or usury between a slave and his master.* And if the slave be in debt, still there is no *reba* between them, but it is incumbent on the master to return to the slave what he may have received from him, whether he had purchased from him one *dirhem* for two *dirhems*, or two *dirhems* for one *dirhem*.† The rule is the same with an *oom-i-wulud*, or a *moodubbur*. And if one sell to his *mookatib* one *dirhem* for two *dirhems*, or two *dirhems* for one *dirhem*, the case is one of *reba* or usury, and the sale is unlawful. A person partially emancipated is, according to Aboo Huneefa, in the same predicament as a *mookatib*; but, according to the disciples, he is like a freeman who is in debt.

or parents married persons, relations, or partners;

Parents, and married persons, and relations, and partners in trade (in matters not appertaining to the trade), are, with regard to *reba* or usury, in the same predicament as strangers. With regard to partners by reciprocity,‡ when one of them purchases from the other one

---

* "Because whatever is in the possession of the slave is the property of the master, so that no sale can possibly take place between them; and hence the impossibility of usury."—*Hamilton's Hedaya*, vol. ii. p. 500. It is implied that the slave is *mazoon*, or permitted to trade, and free from debt.

† It is probably debt to a moderate extent that is here alluded to; for when the slave is deeply involved, *reba* between his master and him is positively unlawful. See *ante*, page 172.

‡ Arab. *Mootufawizan*. "This species of partnership is an universal partnership in all transactions where each partner reciprocally commits the business of the partnership to the other, without limitation or restriction."—*Hamilton's Hedaya*, vol. ii. p. 297.

dirhem for two *dirhems*, this is not a sale, and the things remain their joint property as before the transaction.

or a judge, a father, or an executor, and a minor. No transaction in *surf* by a judge or his *ameen* with an orphan, or of a father with his minor son, or of an executor and his ward, is lawful which would not be lawful between strangers. In like manner, when a father purchases property from his minor son for himself, or a *moozarib** sells to the proprietor of the capital stock, nothing is lawful in these cases except what is lawful between strangers. When an executor exchanges *dirhems* belonging to an orphan for *deenars* of his own at the market rate, or sells a silver vessel belonging to the orphan to himself for its weight, the transaction in either case is unlawful, or if two orphans be under the protection of one guardian, and one being possessed of *dirhems* and the other of *deenars*, the guardian exchanges the one for the other, the transaction is not lawful.

The same rules are to be observed by a judge as by other parties. The same rules are applicable in *surf* to the judge, his agent, and his ameen, as apply to the rest of mankind, that is, reciprocal possession at the meeting is a necessary condition; and when a judge acts with regard to the property of an absent person, or an orphan, reciprocal possession has reference to the judge; and if he sell the property of the orphan to himself, or exchange his *dirhems* for *deenars* of his own, the transaction is not lawful.

Section III.

Of Agency in Surf.

Reciprocal possession by agents is necessary. When two agents enter into a *surf*, they cannot separate before reciprocal possession, but the absence of their principals is of no consequence. Two persons having entered into a *surf* sale appoint agents for possession; if the agents take possession before the separation of the

* The managing partner in a *Mozaribut*, or contract, in which the capital is contributed by one party, and the labour and skill by the other, with an agreement for mutual participation in the profit.

principals, the possession is lawful, but it is not lawful if taken after their separation.

If two agents be appointed by a person to enter into a *surf*, one of them cannot act alone without the other; and if both enter into a contract, and one of them retire before reciprocal possession, the contract is void as to his proportion, that is a half, but valid as to the proportion of the other; and even if they concur in appointing the principal himself to take possession or to make payment, and then retire, the *surf* is void. When a person appoints an agent to purchase a particular silver ewer for *dirhems*, and he does as directed, with the intention of purchasing for himself, the thing purchased is his principal's, but if he buy it for *deenars*, or a chattel, the ewer is his own. If the agent be appointed to purchase a particular ewer without any mention of the price, and he buys it for *dirhems* or *deenars*, the ewer is the principal's; but if he purchase it for a chattel or a quantity of anything weighable or measureable, the thing purchased is the agent's own.

Case of a collar sold by an agent as gold, and returned to him as copper gilt.

When a person commissions an agent to sell a golden collar for him, and he does so, making delivery and receiving the price, and the purchaser comes afterwards and says, "I found the collar to be copper, merely washed over with gold," and the principal denies that it was so, the case may present itself in two ways. In the first place, the agent may also deny the fact, but it being established against him by evidence, or his refusal to be sworn, the thing may be returned to him by decree of the judge; in these cases the principal is bound to take back the collar. In the second place, the agent may acknowledge the fact, and the thing be returned to him, either by his voluntarily taking it back, or by decree of a judge. In the former case the agent is liable, and has no right of recourse against his principal, but in the latter, though the agent be also liable, he may contest the matter with his principal.

Appointment of a *Zimmee*, or

It is abominable for a Mooslim to commission a *Zimmee*, or an alien enemy, to change *dirhems* or *deenars* for him.

alien, as an agent, is abominable. Case of an agent for *surf* selling to the slave of his principal.

When an agent is appointed to exchange *dirhems*, and he does so with a slave of his principal, the transaction is to be considered under two aspects. If the slave is not in debt, the *surf* entered to by the agent is unlawful in the same way as if it had been done by the principal himself;* but the agent does not incur any responsibility. And if the slave be in debt the *surf* is lawful, as it would be in the same circumstances if entered into by the principal himself; the agent, however, ought not to make delivery to the slave until he receive payment of the price.

An agency to exchange coin has reference to the coin of the time and country.

When an agent is appointed to change *dirhems* for *deenars*, and principal and agent are both in Koofa, and the agent makes the *surf* for cut *deenars* of that place, it is lawful according to Aboo Huneefa, but according to the two disciples it is not lawful except for Syrian *deenars*. In truth, the agency has relation to the coin of the country, and it is proper to observe that in the time of Aboo Huneefa, the cut *deenar* of Koofa and the *deenar* of Syria were both current, and Aboo Huneefa decided with regard to the current coin of his time; while in the times of Aboo Yoosuf and Moohummud, the only gold currency was the Syrian *deenar*, and they too decided according to the currency of their time. The difference between them and their master was therefore a difference of times rather than of opinions.

Section IV.

Of Pledge, Huwalut,† and Kufalut‡ in Surf.

Pledge.

According to Moohummud, when a person purchases ten *dirhems* for a *deenar*, and pays down the *deenar*, taking a pledge for the *dirhems*, the transaction is lawful. And if the pledge perish while the parties are at the meeting, it perishes for the debt, which is therefore held to be paid,

* See *ante*, note †, page 241.

† Explained *ante*, note, page 271.

‡ Suretyship, which may be either for a person's appearance, or for his performance of an engagement.—*Hamilton's Hedaya*, vol. ii. page 567.

and the contract is lawful; but if the pledge perish after separation, the contract is void, and there is no payment. The pledge, however, if the parties separate while it is still subsisting, remains at the risk of the pawnee, and he is responsible, in the event of its loss, for whichever, of its own value or the debt for which it was pledged, may be least in amount.

Huwalut and *kufalut* are also lawful for the price in a *surf* contract. And if the surety or the transferee make delivery at the meeting before the separation of the contracting parties, the contract is valid, but if both or either of them withdraw from the meeting, though the surety or transferee should remain, the *surf* is void. **Huwalut and Kufalut.**

Section V.

Of Surf with regard to things usurped or deposited.

When a man usurps a bracelet of silver or gold belonging to another, and destroys it, he is liable for its full value as a manufactured article, to be rendered in something of a different kind; the word and oath of the usurper being entitled to preference with regard to its weight and value. When the judge has awarded satisfaction against the usurper for the value of the bracelet, it becomes his property in exchange for the recompense; but it remains to be seen if the original proprietor take possession of the recompense before the separation of the parties, and if he do so it is universally agreed that the effect of the satisfaction remains unimpaired; and even though he should not take possession before the separation, still the satisfaction would not be rendered void according to our three doctors. And in like manner, if the parties should settle the value of the bracelet by mutual agreement, but payment is postponed for a month, the transaction would be quite lawful in their opinion.* **The usurper of a gold or silver vessel is liable for its full value.**

* There is some obscurity in the text; but I have endeavoured to give what appears to me to be the author's meaning, which may be further explained thus:—The decree of the judge, or the private set-

So, also, one who breaks it.

In like manner, when a person breaks a vessel of silver or gold, he is liable for its value in something of a different kind, whether the damage by the breaking be great or small.

Purchase by an usurper.

When a person usurps a thousand *dirhems* from another, and then purchases them for a hundred *deenars* of which he takes possession before separation, the transaction is lawful, though the *dirhems* be not in his hand at the time of purchase; and the result is the same if he compound for the *dirhems* with a hundred *deenars*, of which he takes possession at the meeting. And it matters not whether the *dirhems* be still subsisting in the house of the usurper, or have perished, the purchase being alike valid in both cases if possession of the *deenars* be taken at the meeting. The result would be still the same if the usurped article were a silver vessel, and the usurper should purchase or compound for its value in something of the same or a different kind, and the lawful owner take possession of the recompense before separation; but if he should fail to take possession before separation, while the purchase would be unlawful on any construction of law, whether the usurped article were in existence or not, the composition in the event of the article having perished, either actually, as by being burned, or impliedly, by being blemished, though it ought still to be void by analogy, would be lawful on a favourable construction, though the parties should separate before possession were taken of the recompense.

By a *Bailee*.

When a person with whom a thing is in deposit purchases it for something of a different kind, and the parties

---

tlement of the parties for the value of the bracelet, seems to have the same effect as a sale in transferring the right of property from the lawful owner to the usurper But when the value is to be paid (as appears to be implied) in money, though of a different kind to the metal contained in the bracelet, the transaction is a *surf;* and, by the ordinary rule, possession of the value should be taken before the separation of the parties; and if not taken, a sale would be rendered void in such circumstances. The effect is different with regard to the decree or settlement, which, on the contrary, seem to retain their efficacy, though the parties should separate, down to the moment of actual payment.

separate before he has renewed his possession of it, the *surf* is void. If a person deposit an ornamented sword with another, and having placed it in his house, the parties afterwards meet in the market, and the bailee purchases the sword for a piece of cloth and ten *dirhems*, both of which he delivers, and the parties then separate, the sale is dissolved in whole. So, also, if the consideration of the purchase be another ornamented sword, which is delivered, but without repossession of the first sword by the bailee, the sale is void; but if reciprocal possession be taken before separation, the sale is lawful; the silver ornament in the one sword being opposed to the silver of the other, and the shoulder-belt and blade of the one being opposed to the shoulder-belt and blade of the other; and if there be any excess in the ornament of the one, it is set against the shoulder-belt and blade of the other.

SECTION VI.

*Of Surf in an Enemy's Country.**

Between a *Mooslim* or *Zimmee* and an alien.

A *mooslim*, or a *zimmee*, enters into a foreign country, with or without protection, and makes an usurious contract with an alien,† as, for instance, by purchasing one *dirhem* for two *dirhems*, or one *dirhem* for a *deenar*, payable at a fixed term of credit, or he sells to an alien wine, or pork, or carrion, or blood, for something that is property; in all these cases the contract is lawful in the opinion of two of our three doctors; but, according to the *Kazee*,‡ nothing is lawful between a *mooslim* and an alien enemy except what is lawful between two *mooslims*. The opinion of the two others, however, is held to be valid. But if an alien come into our country under protection, and a *mooslim* sells to him in this manner, the transaction is not lawful.

---

* Arab. *Dar-ool-Hurb*. The expression does not necessarily imply that there is actual war between the country and the *Mooslims*.

† Arab. *Hurbee;* literally, enemy.

‡ See *ante*, note †, page 307.

Between two *Mooslims.*

And if a *mooslim,* who has entered into a foreign country under protection, contract with a person of the place who has embraced the faith there, though without taking refuge with us, as, for instance, if he sell him one *dirhem* for two *dirhems,* the contract is not lawful. And when two *mooslim* merchants enter into a foreign country, nothing is lawful between them that is not lawful in a *mooslim* country. Or when two foreigners in their own country adopt the *mooslim* faith, and interchange with *reba* or usury, or one sells to the other wine, or pork, or the like, though the contract is lawful, and only abominable according to Aboo Huneefa, it is positively unlawful according to his disciples. And if it be a *surf,* and the parties come out to a *mooslim* country before reciprocal possession, the contract is void, or valid only in so far as possession may have been taken. If foreign merchants came to us under protection, and one of them purchases from the other one *dirhem* for two *dirhems,* we do not sanction between them anything that is not lawful among *mooslims.* And the rule is the same as to *zimmees;* and also as to *mooslim* captives in a foreign country. If one foreigner sell to another a *dirhem* for two *dirhems,* and both the parties then come out into the *mooslim* territory, either as *mooslims* having embraced the faith, or as *zimmees,* and the matter is contested before the judge, after reciprocal possession has already taken place, the judge is not to object to the contract nor cancel it; but if the dispute take place before possession, he ought to cancel the contract. In like manner, if an usurious contract be made by them in the foreign country, and the parties enter the *mooslim* territory before possession, but reciprocal possession takes place after their entry, and the matter is then brought before the judge, he is to cancel the contract in this case also. And if a *mooslim* and foreigner enter into such a contract in the foreign territory, and the foreigner then comes out to our territory before reciprocal possession, and the matter is litigated before the judge, he is to cancel the contract; but if the possession had taken place in the foreign territory, he is not to interfere with the case.

INDEX

OF

NAMES AND ARABIC TERMS.